QUEEN
OF THE LAKES

QUEEN OF THE LAKES

Mark L. Thompson

Wayne State University Press
Detroit

GREAT LAKES BOOKS

A complete listing of the books in this series can be found at the back of this volume.

99 98 97 96 95 94 5 4 3 2 1

Library of Congress Cataloging-in-Publication Data

Thompson, Mark L., 1945-
Queen of the Lakes / Mark L. Thompson.
p. cm. — (Great Lakes books)
Includes bibliographical references (p.) and index.
ISBN 0-8143-2393-6 (alk. paper)
1. Bulk carriers—Great Lakes—History. 2. Shipping—Great Lakes—History. I. Title. II. Series.
VM393.B7T49 1994
387.2′45′0977—dc20 93-34403

Designer: Mary Primeau

For my mother, Marian K. Thompson,
whose love has been unconditional and
whose support has been inspiring

Contents

Ships are the nearest things to dreams that hands have ever made.
—Robert N. Rose
"My Ship o' Dreams"

Preface

My paternal great-great-great-great-great-grandfather came to the Great Lakes region from France in 1730. A cousin to King Louis XV, Robert Navarre had been appointed sub-intendant and royal notary at Detroit, then known as Fort Pontchartrain. After crossing the Atlantic aboard a sailing ship, the twenty-one-year-old Bourbon noble travelled from Quebec to Montreal in a bateau, then shifted to a canoe for the arduous trip to Georgian Bay on northern Lake Huron by way of the historic river route. Navarre and his retinue then paddled down the eastern shore of Lake Huron to the St. Clair River, Lake St. Clair, and the Detroit River, arriving after a voyage of two months' duration at the fledgling frontier settlement on the banks of the Detroit River.

From that time, Robert Navarre and his descendants, my ancestors and I, have lived along the shores of the Great Lakes, mainly at Detroit, Toledo, and, more recently, Rogers City, a small community on the northwest shore of Lake Huron. In 1870, Navarre's descendants were joined by the family of my maternal great-grandfather, Carl Tosch, who came to the U.S. from Prussia. Carl Tosch, his wife Amalie, and infant son Fritz sailed from Hamburg to New York aboard the sailing ship *Friedeburg*. After an overland trip by rail to Buffalo, they boarded a passenger steamer, like tens of thousands of other immigrants, for the trip across Lake Erie to Detroit. After five years in Detroit, the Tosch family boarded another passenger steamer for the trip north to Rogers City and the homestead that awaited them.

Since the arrival here of Robert Navarre and the Tosches, the history of my family has been integrally joined with that of the Great Lakes region. Over successive generations we have served as government officials under French, British, and U.S. flags, and we have toiled as farmers, timbermen, miners, railroadmen, autoworkers . . . and sailors.

The ships have always been there, virtually a part of our everyday lives for nine generations, more than 260 years. For most of that period, they were the primary mode of transportation in the region. Before the railroads and, more recently, the highways, ships moved people and goods to and from hundreds of port cities that had developed along the shores of the majestic inland seas of North America. For Robert Navarre and Carl Tosch, and right up until my father's generation, the passenger and package ships that plied the lakes linked the residents along the northern lakes with the world beyond.

While most of the passenger and package freighters had succumbed to competition from the railroads by the time my father reached manhood, around 1930, ships were still the dominant form of transportation for grain, iron ore, coal, and limestone. The unique Great Lakes bulk freighters that had evolved in the 1870s and 1880s proved to be so efficient that they staved off all competition from other modes of transportation. The long ships were vital to the economies of many cities around the lakes through which the bulk cargoes moved.

At Rogers City, where my father grew up, a large limestone mining operation had developed, and the small community became home port for a fleet of self-unloading bulk freighters, the first fleet on the Great Lakes to be made up entirely of self-unloaders. Like so many young men from port cities around the lakes who were attracted by the good pay and the chance to avoid the comparatively mundane employment on a farm or in a mine or quarry, my father was drawn inexorably to the ships. While his career as a merchant seaman was a fairly brief one—which is often the case—he never lost his love for the ships, and he never strayed far from them. He lived in Rogers City, and for twenty years worked as a dock foreman at the nearby port of Stoneport; the ships were part of the fabric of his daily life.

It is not unusual, then, that my sister, brother, and I grew to share our father's fascination with the ships, or that my mother would encourage that interest. The freighters have been a constant in our lives. While we developed other interests and pursued careers in other fields, I don't think we have ever had a family get-together where we didn't at some point talk about ships, and the library at our family home in Rogers City has always been well-stocked with books about the shipping industry on the Great Lakes.

My brother Gary sailed summers to support himself while studying chemistry in college, then gave up his studies to opt for a career as a merchant seaman. My route to the boats was a bit more circuitous, with forays into politics and education, but the outcome was the same. Some who know me well undoubtedly realize that it was inevitable, others will be greatly disappointed that I would "settle" for a blue-collar job aboard a freighter. I would merely assure the latter group that I am happy doing what I do, extremely happy. I recall an incident that took place during the summer of 1989 when I first went back to work full-time on the boats. It was a beautiful, warm July morning and the 1,000-foot *Columbia Star* was upbound on northern Lake Michigan. I got off duty at about 9:30 a.m. and decided to sit out on deck for awhile to enjoy the fresh air and scenery. During the next hour the *Star* passed under the majestic expanse of the Mackinac Bridge and threaded its way through the narrow channel separating Mackinac and Round islands. The view was breathtaking and tranquil at the same time, and I remember repeating over and over to myself, "I'm really here, I'm really working aboard a freighter again. Thank you, God!"

Not every day aboard a freighter is cause for such rejoicing, but it is preferable to anything else I've tried during my otherwise white-collar career. I enjoy the work, the pay, the travel, the camaraderie of my shipmates, the opportunity it gives me to write . . . and the time off, though not necessarily in that order. This book probably wouldn't have been written if I hadn't gone back to work on the boats. It has required considerable research that I wouldn't have had time to do if I didn't have the winters off.

I've been fascinated by the ships that bore the "Queen of the Lakes" title since I first heard my father use the phrase to describe the *Carl D. Bradley*, which was the longest ship on the lakes from 1927 until 1949. I was probably only four or five years old at the time, but I still remember that moment and how excited I was to learn that one of our freighters from Rogers City was the "Queen," the longest ship on the lakes.

While writing my first book on the Great Lakes shipping industry—*Steamboats and Sailors of the Great Lakes*—I began compiling a list of ships that were Queen of the Lakes, based largely on references made in other works. That first list of mine was dramatically different than the list of ships that appears in this book. Another researcher and writer once wrote that "great caution should be exerted when estimating the reliability of translated, diluted, and resurrected data on any subject, especially ships."[1] That point was driven home forcefully in the months I spent researching this book.

The first list I began working with was extracted from one of Dana Thomas Bowen's highly respected books about the lakes. It spanned the period 1887-1942 and listed twenty-three vessels that were "the longest ships on the lakes."[2] In the ensuing months, I was dismayed to find that the list was filled with errors. In fact, only thirteen of the twenty-three ships listed ever had any claim to the Queen of the Lakes title. The other ten were "also-rans"; big ships, to be sure, but never the longest on the lakes.

Bowen was not the only writer who led me astray, however. Norman Beasley sent me on a wild goose chase when he claimed in his *Freighters of Fortune* that the *Australasia* was the longest ship on the lakes,[3] as did Fred Landon in *Lake Huron* when he wrote that "the *Chamberlain* with a capacity of 1,000 tons and the *Marine*, of 1,200 tons, were the largest vessels on the lakes in 1874."[4] The *Australasia* was never the largest ship on the lakes, and I can find no record whatsoever of either the *Chamberlain* or *Marine*.

Even J. B. Mansfield in his seminal *History of the Great Lakes*, published in 1899, caused me considerable wasted effort with his assertion that "The largest boat ever constructed for the lake service is the Moose."[5] A bit of detective work on my part revealed that it was the freighter *Morse*, not *Moose*, that Mansfield was referring to—an instance where a simple typographical error caused me a few more gray hairs.

While some of these lapses can be attributed to sloppy research or typographical errors, many are undoubtedly the result of disparate definitions of "largest" as it applies to ships on the lakes and different means of measuring the lengths of ships. In varying usage within the maritime community, the term "largest" can be used to refer to a ship's length, its tonnage, or its carrying capacity. The longest ship does not necessarily have the greatest tonnage or carrying capacity, and vice versa. I have reserved usage of the Queen of the Lakes title for ships that have been the longest on the lakes, based on their overall length. Others have accorded the title to ships that had the greatest length between perpendiculars or the greatest carrying capacity. In fact, during the mid-1800s, when the magnificent "palace steamers" dominated shipping on the lakes, the Queen of the Lakes title often went to a particularly luxurious passenger steamer.[6] While the focus of this book is on the longest ships that have sailed the lakes, I endeavor to alert readers when other ships had larger carrying capacities or higher tonnages than a vessel I've identified as Queen of the Lakes.

It should be noted that three different length measurements are commonly used to describe ships. I have reserved the Queen of the Lakes label for ships of the longest length overall (LOA). Other researchers and writers have opted for one of the other measuring schemes in their works, particularly length between perpendiculars (LBP).[7] While LOA delineates the length of a vessel between its extreme fore and aft extensions, LBP measures the length from the fore side of the stem to the after side of the rudder post along its summer loadline.[8] LBP thus ignores any rake to the stem or overhang of the stern that lies fore or aft of the vessel's waterline when loaded to its summer marks. For most contemporary ships on the lakes, the LOA is about twenty feet longer than the LBP, but the difference would be even more extreme for a sailing ship or saltwater ship with a dramatically raked bow. Using LBP instead of LOA is somewhat similar to measuring a building's height without taking into consideration its roof. I understand why naval architects place so much store in the LBP measurement, but for purposes of identifying the longest ships on the lakes, the overall length of a vessel seems a much more valid criteria and is used throughout this book.[9]

Much of my research was conducted at Bowling Green State University's Institute for Great Lakes Research, located just outside Toledo, Ohio. Founded by the late Dr. Richard Wright, who devoted most of his life to the study of ships on the Great Lakes, the Institute is a vital resource for anyone seriously interested in doing research on the Great Lakes shipping industry.

I have also extracted considerable information from *Telescope* and *Inland Seas*, the excellent publications, respectively, of the Great Lakes Maritime Institute of Detroit and the Great Lakes Historical Society of Vermilion, Ohio. Both groups are to be commended for the quality of their publications and their commitment to documenting and preserving the rich heritage of the Great Lakes shipping industry.

My home in Traverse City, Michigan, is far distant from Detroit, Toledo, or Vermilion, and my research efforts have been facilitated by the public libraries in nearby communities, including those in Traverse City, Petoskey, and Charlevoix. The friendly assistance of the local library staffs and the splendid interlibrary loan program have made it possible for me to do a great deal of research without ever leaving my beloved northern Michigan.

When I have needed the resources of a larger library, I have most often used the resources of the Detroit Public Library, a truly outstanding facility. In particular, its Burton Historical Collection contains many valuable works on the early history of the Great Lakes region and the maritime industry on the lakes.

I also owe a deep debt of gratitude to a long list of writers and researchers who have published works on the Great Lakes shipping industry, most of whom I've never met. That list has to be headed by the likes of Mansfield, Boyer, Bowen, Barry, Dewar, Rattigan, Rev. Van der Linden, Glick, Greenwood, Benford, Father Dowling, Clary, Hatcher, and LesStrang. I have enjoyed, learned from, and used their works extensively, as have thousands of others who share our common interest.

This book is dedicated to my mother, but everyone in the Thompson family has played a role in writing it. My children are sensational kids who make me very proud to be their father. Meredith and Scott have paid the greatest price for my love affair with ships, for working on the boats takes me away from them for over half the year. I hope they know that every day I'm away from them they are constantly in my thoughts and prayers.

My sister Lizabeth and her husband Gordon Dickson have been supportive in ways too numerous to enumerate here; their hospitality, thoughtfulness, and generosity are unbounded. Suffice it to say that they would make great shipmates.

My brother Gary has sailed on the Great Lakes, Pacific Ocean, Gulf of Mexico, and Atlantic Ocean and shared with me many wonderful sea stories and valuable insights into the maritime industry. We don't get to spend much time together, but I always look forward to seeing Gary and his daughter Jenny.

Invaluable assistance in writing and publishing this book was also provided by Canada Steamship Lines, N. M. Paterson and Sons, Bethlehem Steel Corporation's Great Lakes Steamship Division, Dossin Great Lakes Museum, Great

Lakes Maritime Museum, Lake Superior Maritime Museum, Cleveland-Cliffs Iron Company, Oglebay-Norton's Columbia Transportation Division, Michigan Bureau of History, American Steamship Company, Bay Shipbuilding Corporation, the St. Lawrence Seaway Development Corporation, Interlake Steamship Company, and Arthur Evans and the very professional staff at Wayne State University Press.

While I was writing *Queen of the Lakes*, I was also working aboard various ships in the Interlake Steamship fleet. Needless to say, crewmembers I sailed with during that three-year period had a major impact on my life, and on this book. They know who they are: the crews on the *Elton Hoyt, 2d, Herbert C. "Action" Jackson, Mesabi Miner, Kaye E. Barker, George A. Stinson, Paul R. Tregurtha* and *James R. Barker*. No sailor could ask for better shipmates. A lot of them share my keen interest in the history of our industry, and many long hours on the run were passed swapping sea stories.

Three of the ships I sailed on, the *George A. Stinson, James R. Barker* and *Mesabi Miner*, once shared honors as Queen of the Lakes. A fourth, the *Paul R. Tregurtha*, has been the longest ship on the lakes since its launching in 1981. I particularly appreciated the opportunity to serve on those thousand-footers while working on this book. There was a time when I held nothing but disdain for the "footers" and other ships built in the new stern-ender design. My experiences on the *Barker, Miner, Stinson*, and *Tregurtha* gave me a new appreciation for the latest generation of ships on the lakes, and I hope that is conveyed to readers.

Most likely, this book will not be a bestseller, but that doesn't detract one iota from my pride in having written it. It is a worthy story, this saga of ships that have been Queen of the Lakes, and I am pleased that I can share it with you.

Notes

1. Louden G. Wilson, "How Now David Dows," *Telescope* 10 no. 6 (June 1961): 103.
2. Dana Thomas Bowen, *Memories of the Lakes* (Cleveland: Freshwater Press, 1969), 19.
3. Norman Beasley, *Freighters of Fortune* (New York: Harper and Brothers, 1930), 87.
4. Fred Landon, *Lake Huron* (New York: Bobbs-Merrill Company, 1944), 355.
5. J. B. Mansfield, *History of the Great Lakes*, vol. I (Chicago: J. H. Beers and Co., 1899; reprint, Cleveland: Freshwater Press, 1972), 414.
6. James P. Barry, *Ships of the Great Lakes* (Berkeley: Howell-North Books, 1973), 81.
7. See, for example, the discussion given in the "Explanation" section of Rev. Peter J. Van der Linden, ed., *Great Lakes Ships We Remember* (Cleveland: Freshwater Press, 1979).
8. It should be noted that a ship's assigned loadline can change over time, even though no change has been made to the dimensions of the vessel's hull. The loadline is assigned based on standards for safe levels of reserve buoyancy and can be altered by such things as the installation of watertight doors, watertight subdivision of the cargo hold, or even replacement of telescoping hatch covers with single-piece covers. Any raising of a ship's loadline would increase its LBP, but not its LOA, which will remain constant throughout its life unless the vessel is lengthened.
9. LOA measurements used throughout the book have been drawn from a variety of sources: naval architectural drawings, newspaper reports, government documents, various vessel directories, and information supplied by vessel owners. In no instance was a single source used to determine a ship's LOA.

Introduction

It is the way of man to change things. He is ever seeking to improve and better his lot. So it is that his ships have changed. The ship that was launched yesterday and proudly acclaimed as the super ship is only a stepping stone to one that is launched today. Into tomorrow's ships will be built all the experiences of the ships that have gone before.

—Dana Thomas Bowen
***Lore of the Lakes*, 1940**

Days of Wooden Ships, 1678 to 1882

Ships had been evolving for several thousand years before the first one sailed on the waters of the Great Lakes. While Native Americans had travelled these waters for thousands of years in their canoes, the first true ship known to have seen service on the lakes was the *Frontenac*, launched at Fort Frontenac on Lake Ontario in 1678. It was a small, two-masted vessel of only about ten tons and probably no more than forty or forty-five feet long.[1] Presumably its launching was not viewed with much significance by the small group of Frenchmen who were present for the event. By Old World standards, she was indeed a puny, crude craft.

Bas-relief carvings in the tomb of Queen Hatsheput of Egypt show that there were oared vessels on the Red Sea in about 1500 B.C. that were seventy feet long. Columbus's *Santa Maria*, which sailed across the Atlantic more than two centuries before the launch of the *Frontenac* had been rated at about 150 tons. The English warship *Sovereign of the Seas*, launched four decades before the *Frontenac*, had a gun deck that was more than 172 feet long. In comparison, the diminutive *Frontenac* seemed to be a throwback to an earlier era of shipbuilding.

If there was any celebration at the launching of the *Frontenac*, it was not because of her size or the quality of shipbuilding exhibited in her construction. Only if those early French explorers and settlers fathomed the significance of placing that first European-style sailing ship upon the waters of North America's inland seas would they have had just cause for celebration.

That singular act, which may have seemed relatively insignificant at the time, set in motion an evolutionary process that has continued for more than three hundred years and still shows no signs of abating. The tiny *Frontenac* is the direct ancestor of all the ships that have ever operated on the Great Lakes, including today's massive thousand-foot ore carriers.

The construction of the *Frontenac* had been ordered by Robert Cavalier, Sieur de la Salle, who in 1674 had bought the land at the foot of Lake Ontario upon which Fort Frontenac had been built a few years earlier. In 1677, La Salle, as he is better known today, was granted a royal charter to build vessels and trade on the Great Lakes and Mississippi River. The *Frontenac* and three similar ships built in 1678 were used to ferry men and building materials across the lake to the mouth of the Niagara River in the fall of that year. The material was then hauled overland to what is now the New York bank of the river, about four miles above the spectacular falls at Niagara that prevented vessels from moving between Lake Ontario and Lake Erie.

During the ensuing winter, the shipbuilders La Salle had recruited in Europe constructed a brigantine of about sixty tons and seventy feet in length from green timber cut in the area.

The new ship was considerably larger and more ornate than the *Frontenac.* While information about her is scanty, she seems to have followed the design of the two-masted Dutch galleots that had been used for many years on the Zuyder Zee and in the shallow waters along the coasts of the low countries.

Launched in late spring or early summer of 1679 and christened *Griffon,* the tubby-hulled ship with its high poop deck at the stern departed the Niagara River in August to explore the upper lakes. Under the command of La Salle and his Danish pilot, Lucas, and with a motley international crew of Flemings, Italians, and Normans, *Griffon* became the first ship to sail on Lake Erie, Lake Huron, Lake Michigan, and their connecting waterways. It also has the dubious distinction of being the first ship lost on the lakes.

La Salle left the *Griffon* at Washington Island in Green Bay on Lake Michigan to explore the Mississippi River to its mouth on the Gulf of Mexico and claim the heartland of North America for the king of France. The ship, heavily laden with furs to pay off La Salle's anxious creditors in Montreal and Quebec, departed for Niagara under Lucas's command on September 18, 1679, and was never seen again. *Griffon* and its small crew disappeared, probably as a result of a fierce four-day storm that descended on the lakes shortly after she set sail.

For the next one hundred years, virtually every ship built for service on the lakes was owned by the governments of either New France or Britain. In fact, after the British took control of Canada at the close of the Seven Years War in 1760, all goods were required to be shipped aboard government vessels, a cause of much chagrin for the growing numbers of merchants and traders in the region. Government-controlled shipbuilding facilities were not able to keep pace with the rapid rate of development in the region. By 1780, for example, there were only fourteen British ships on the lakes, operating primarily on Lake Ontario and Lake Erie.

So much cargo was consigned to Detroit in 1784 that only about half of it could be moved by the available ships operated by the British government. (While the Americans had won their freedom in the Revolutionary War, which ended in 1783, the British continued to control most of the area around the Great Lakes until 1796.) Detroit merchants petitioned the British Lords of Trade and received permission to build and operate commercial ships on the lakes. The merchants were required, however, to crew the ships with British officers and men.

The first privately-owned ship built on the lakes was probably the forty-five-ton, sloop-rigged *Beaver.* Built at Detroit in 1785 with materials brought in from Montreal and New York, the *Beaver* was thirty-five feet long, with a beam of thirteen feet and a draft of about four feet. Intended initially for use on Lake Superior, the small vessel could not be towed up the rapids of the St. Marys River at Sault Ste. Marie, so she operated only on Lakes Erie, Huron, and Michigan.

Even in 1785, the violent chute of the St. Marys created a bottleneck for commerce on the lakes. Formed as a result of the difference in elevation between Lake Superior and the lower lakes, the waters of the St. Marys drop more than twenty feet in a distance of only several hundred yards. Even craft as small as the canoes used in the growing fur trade generally had to be unloaded and their cargoes portaged around the rapids, a backbreaking and time-consuming labor.

In 1797, the North West Company, competitor to the famous Hudson Bay Company and John Jacob Astor's American Fur Company, built the first canal and lock at Sault Ste. Marie in an effort to expedite the movement of the heavily laden canoes moving to and from the fur-rich Lake Superior region. The rudimentary wooden lock was thirty-eight feet long and just under nine feet wide; it raised or lowered small craft nine feet. Vessels going upstream still had to overcome severe rapids, so oxen were used to tow canoes to the head of the canal.

Commerce in the region was dominated by the flourishing fur trade that reached its peak around 1800. The sparse population on the northern lakes was made up primarily of Native Americans, itinerant fur trappers—the colorful voyageurs—fur traders, Jesuit missionaries, soldiers, and a few government officials. Those who were of European stock operated mainly out of the small settlements and trading posts at Mackinac Island on northern Lake Huron, Green Bay on northern Lake Michigan, and at Sault Ste. Marie.

With the exception of the Native Americans, who had probably inhabited the area continuously for more than four thousand years, the early residents of the northern lakes area cannot accurately be called "settlers." Most of them were involved in the fur trade, and, as stocks of fur-bearing animals in the region were depleted, traders and trappers moved farther to the west and north.

Communities along the lower lakes began primarily as military forts and trading centers, but very early on an effort was made to attract permanent settlers, mainly farmers. In addition to the growing cities of Quebec and Montreal on the St. Lawrence River, Detroit had evolved into a significant settlement by 1800, and promising villages had been established at Port Huron on the St. Clair River, at Toledo, Cleveland, and Erie on Lake Erie, at Niagara Falls, and at Oswego on Lake Ontario.

The big influx of settlers into the Great Lakes region didn't begin until after the War of 1812, but when it began immigrants from the East Coast and Europe literally poured into the area in a frenzy of colonization that lasted for more than a century. Lake navigation played an important role in that unparalleled movement of people and goods. Until at least 1850, water was the cheapest, if not the only, form of transportation available in the region, and the demand created by the influx of settlers had a profound impact on shipping on the lakes.

Early in 1815, a group of businessmen in Kingston, Ontario, contracted with two shipwrights to build the first steamboat on the lakes. Launched on September 7, 1816, and given the historic name *Frontenac*, the steamboat was 170 feet long, with a 32-foot beam inside her paddlewheel guards and a hold depth of 11 feet. Her paddlewheels, each 40 feet in circumference, were mounted amidships and driven by a rudimentary steam engine built in Birmingham, England, and rated at fifty horsepower. Like virtually all steamboats built prior to 1900, the *Frontenac* was also rigged as a three-masted schooner; sails provided auxiliary power should her engines fail. In fact, except for the paddleboxes that jutted out from the sides of her hull to enclose her paddlewheels and the tall black smokestack that rose from her deck amidships, the *Frontenac* looked like the schooners that were her contemporaries.

While the *Frontenac* was under construction along the Canadian shore, a group of businessmen in New York state signed an agreement with Robert Fulton, inventor of America's first successful steamboat, authorizing them to build and operate a steamboat on Lake Ontario. Modelled after the *Sea Horse* that was then running on Long Island Sound, the vessel was built at the Sackets Harbour Navy Yard, near the east end of Lake Ontario. Christened *Ontario*, the first U.S. steamboat built on the lakes was launched in March of 1817. Rated at 237 tons and only 110 feet long, with a beam of 24 feet and a depth of 8 feet, she was considerably smaller than the Canadian *Frontenac*. The *Ontario* carried only two masts.

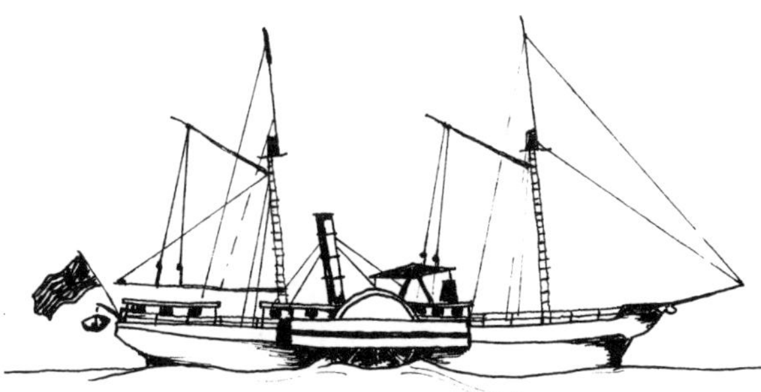

A drawing of the *Str. Ontario* copied from a sketch in the logbook of Captain James Van Cleve. The pioneer steamer's engine and paddlewheels were located amidships. Because her crude steam engine wasn't always reliable, the *Ontario* was also outfitted as a gaff-rigged, two-masted schooner. (Author's collection)

A drawing of the passenger steamer *Walk-in-the-Water* by Samuel Ward Stanton, a noted marine artist at the turn of the century. The first passenger steamer on the upper lakes—those lying above Niagara Falls—the *Walk-in-the-Water* operated mainly between Buffalo and Detroit, with occasional forays as far north as Mackinac Island at the head of Lake Huron. (Author's collection)

Interestingly, while the *Ontario* was put into service in April of 1817, the *Frontenac* did not make her first voyage until June of 1817, even though she had been launched in September of the previous year. The *Ontario* mainly carried passengers and cargo between Oswego and Niagara in New York and York (now Toronto) in Canada, operating at a maximum speed of about seven miles an hour. The *Frontenac* was on a similar run, but also called at Prescott and Kingston in Ontario.

A year after the two pioneering steamboats went into operation on Lake Ontario, the first steamboat intended for use on the upper lakes was launched at Black Rock, near Buffalo. The *Walk-in-the-Water*, supposedly named after a Wyandot chief who lived on the Detroit River, was slightly larger than the *Ontario*, being 135 feet long, 32 feet wide, and with a depth of just under 9 feet. Rated at 338 gross tons, she, like the *Ontario*, was rigged as a two-masted schooner.[2] One historian has noted that "It is something of a question whether the sails were to augment the steam engine, or whether the steam was auxiliary to the sails."[3] Put into service in August of 1818, the *Walk-in-the-Water* ran between Buffalo and Detroit, with stops at Cleveland and Erie. Occasionally, she also ran up Lake Huron as far as Mackinac Island. On her maiden voyage *Walk-in-the-Water* carried twenty- nine passengers, while on later trips she carried up to a hundred. The fare from Buffalo to Detroit at that time was $18.[4]

The first steamboats plodded along at speeds that could often be matched by the schooners of the day, yet they became immediately popular with travellers and were greeted with much fanfare at every port they called at. Some of that popular-

During the first half of the nineteenth century, the busiest trade route on the lakes was between Buffalo and Detroit. Fleets of steamers carried tens of thousands of immigrants and tons of merchandise across Lake Erie each year. In addition to Detroit, other busy ports included Erie, Cleveland, Chicago, and Milwaukee. (Author's collection)

ity can undoubtedly be attributed to the increased reliability of the steamboats: they could still make six or seven miles an hour even when there was no wind and sailing vessels were becalmed. For many travellers, however, the appeal of the early steamboats was based largely on the novelty of their propulsion system and their comparatively luxurious appointments. One early traveller on the *Frontenac* called her "a delightful mode of conveyance," and went on to say that "it required some recollections to perceive I was not in the Kingston [Ontario] Hotel."[5] Luxury accommodations soon became a hallmark of passenger steamers on the Great Lakes.

With great fanfare, the 363-mile Erie Canal was opened in 1825, connecting Troy, New York, on the Hudson River with Buffalo, New York, at the east end of Lake Erie. The impact on transportation between the populous East Coast of the U.S. and the Great Lakes region was immediate and dramatic. Once the canal was functional, the cost of moving freight from New York City to Lake Erie dropped from a staggering $120 a ton to only $4 a ton.[6] Within a decade there were three thousand canal boats in operation, and one left Albany almost every hour. The cost of passage, including meals, ranged from $9.07 to $14.52, depending upon the type of boat in use.[7] Almost overnight, Buffalo became a thriving port city, a funnel through which all passengers and cargo flowed in or out of the lakes.

Another improvement in passenger travel came in 1833 with the launching at Detroit of the *Steamer (Str.) Michigan* for service on the Buffalo to Detroit run. Owned by Newberry and Dole, Detroit merchants involved in shipping furs and fish to markets on the East Coast and carrying westbound passengers on return voyages, the *Michigan* was 156 feet long, 53 feet wide, had a depth of 11 feet, and differed in many respects from the steamboats that had preceded her. She was, according to most, the prototype for a style of steamship that remained distinctly American. The most unique aspect of the *Michigan* was a tier of upper deck cabins the builders had added atop her main deck. All previous steamboats and sailboats had their cabins within the hull, below the main deck. Adding the tier of cabins on the main deck greatly increased the number of passengers the *Michigan* could carry, and it became the accepted style on the lakes until the *Great Western* was launched in 1839 with yet a second rank of cabins atop the main deck.

The *Michigan*'s unique hull design accommodated the placement of the row of cabins on deck. Instead of paddlewheels and paddleboxes jutting out from the sides of her hull, the *Great Western* had a main deck extending out over her paddlewheels, forming a buoyant side sponson over the entire length of her hull and adding considerable extra deck space. This design innovation, too, was soon adopted for virtually all steamboats built in the U.S.

The *Michigan*'s pilothouse was at the forward end of the row of cabins, instead of being located amidships or at the stern, as was the tradition in steamboats preceding her. Subsequently, other steamboats with cabins on their decks adopted the design, as did the unique Great Lakes bulk freighters that made their debut on the lakes in 1869. Sailboats didn't have pilothouses, but were steered from a cockpit area at the stern, where crewmembers could keep an eye on the set of the sails.

The *Michigan*'s eighty-horsepower steam engines, one for each of the two paddlewheels, comprised her fourth innovative feature. While the extra engine greatly increased her power and made her one of the fastest steamboats on the lakes, capable of making twelve to fifteen miles an hour in calm weather, the design caused some problems. When heavy seas caused the *Michigan* to roll from side to side, one paddle would lift clear of the water and race, while the other dug deep and labored. This made the ship very difficult to steer, and it would jerk noticeably from side to side.[8] Because of the problem, steamboats launched after the *Michigan* reverted to the practice of using one steam engine to drive both paddlewheels.

While the jerky motion of the *Michigan* may have been annoying to her passengers and crew, they probably worried more about the possibility of a boiler explosion. In 1830, the *Str. Peacock* won the tragic distinction of having the first boiler explosion on the Great Lakes. While she was tied up at the wharf in Buffalo, the water ran low in her boiler, and an inexperienced crewmember in the engine room let in a full flow of

An 1836 painting of the Detroit waterfront by William James Bennett shows the steamer *Michigan*, on the left, with flags flying and her decks crowded with passengers. The *Michigan* is generally accepted as having been the first Great Lakes passenger steamer with cabins on the main deck. Until the launching of this landmark steamer by Detroit merchants Newberry and Dole in 1833, passenger accommodations were always located below deck. (State Archives of Michigan)

cold lake water. The resulting explosion blew the top off the boiler and killed fifteen persons.[9] Before tin safety plugs and hollow boiler tubes were invented, the accident toll from exploding boilers reached alarming proportions. When popular British author Charles Dickens made a trip on Lake Erie in 1842 aboard the *Str. Constellation*, he wrote that her high-pressure engine "conveyed that kind of feeling to me, which I should be likely to experience, I think, if I had lodgings on the first floor of a powder mill."[10] While many persons were vehemently opposed to the steamboats because of the potential for boiler explosions, ships like the *Michigan* actually lost little business as a result.

By 1833, it was clear that steamboats were destined to dominate the dynamic and highly profitable passenger trade, while sailing vessels would be relegated to handling freight. In that year, the steamboats carried 61,485 passengers, two-thirds of whom were westbound from Buffalo.[11] For shipowners, the steamboats were more expensive to build than sailboats, but they were proving to be a lucrative investment, returning as much as seventy to eighty percent of their cost in a single year of operation.[12] In fact, Oliver Newberry, the progressive merchant and shipping pioneer who was the driving force behind construction of the *Michigan*, was soon hailed as Detroit's first millionaire.[13]

The *Michigan* was part of a small, but growing, fleet of steamboats in service on the lakes. In 1833 there were already eleven steamboats operating on Lakes Erie, Huron, and Michigan; fifty-six more would be added in the next decade. To people living around the lakes, it must have seemed as if the fleet was suddenly growing exponentially. Many would remember that there had been only ten ships on the lakes in 1810, just fifty in 1820, and about one hundred in 1830. In the three seasons between 1830 and the launching of the *Michigan* in 1833, the size of the Great Lakes fleet had almost doubled.

Outside observers might have been less impressed with the progress of the shipping industry on the lakes. If we trace the history of shipping on the Great Lakes back to the 1678 launching of the first *Frontenac* on Lake Ontario, or even the 1679 launching of *Griffon* on Lake Erie, the industry was already more than 150 years old in 1830, yet it comprised only about two hundred vessels. And they were not large ships, either. In 1810, the average ship on the lakes was rated at only 60 tons, no larger than the *Griffon* that had been launched in 1679. Nearly a quarter-century later, in 1833, the average vessel was still rated at less than 90 tons, but the launching of ships like the *Michigan*, at 472 tons, was heralding a new era. While the predominance of older, smaller ships kept fleet averages down, one-fourth of the total ships operating on the lakes in 1834—forty-eight vessels—were in the 150-750 ton range.[14] The largest of the new ships were also approaching the 200-foot mark, respectable by any standard. In fact, in 1837 the largest ship in the world was the 210-foot *U.S.S. Pennsylvania.*[15]

One of the best-known and most highly respected captains on the lakes at the time was James Van Cleve, who began his maritime career in 1826 as a clerk aboard the *Ontario.* By 1838, Van Cleve had risen through the ranks, or, in nautical terminology, "up the hawsepipe," to command of the steamboat *United States* that operated on Lake Ontario and the upper St. Lawrence. During a visit to New York City at the close of the shipping season of 1840, Captain Van Cleve met John Ericsson, a Swedish engineer and inventor who had recently invented the screw propeller. The propeller had been successfully demonstrated on the tug *Francis B. Ogden* on London's Thames River, but Ericsson had been unable to generate any commercial interest in his invention.

Van Cleve was immediately interested, convinced that the device would revolutionize ship propulsion. He returned to Oswego, New York, where he put together a group of investors interested in funding construction of a steamboat fitted with one of Ericsson's propellers. Launched in the summer of 1841, the 91-foot, 138-ton *Vandalia* was the world's first commercial propeller-driven ship. She made her maiden voyage in November of that year and was an immediate success.[16] The propeller proved to be a much more efficient means of driving steamboats than paddlewheels. The *Vandalia*, for example, could run all day at seven miles an hour on only ten cords of wood, far less fuel than would have been required on paddlewheelers of comparable size. In addition, a propeller cost much less to build and took up far less space than the cumbersome paddlewheels.

In designing the *Vandalia*, Van Cleve, Ericsson, and Sylvester Doolittle, the shipbuilder, placed the boat's engine and boilers all the way aft, minimizing the length of the propeller shaft. This arrangement would eventually become standard on virtually all Great Lakes steamboats. The stern location of *Vandalia*'s machinery gave her a comparatively large cargo hold and carrying capacity for a ship of her size, but created problems in the construction of her hull. Placing the heavy machinery all the way aft, with no compensating redesign of the ship, would have caused the hull to sag at the stern, particularly when the vessel was empty.[17] To counter this condition, builders of the *Vandalia* are reported to have installed longitudinal arched braces along each side of her hull that acted like trusses and provided the necessary rigidity. The bracing is not shown, however, in two extant drawings of the *Vandalia*, including one made by Captain Van Cleve. The two artists may have merely left the heavy bracing out of their drawings because it reportedly made *Vandalia's* hull appear "decidedly ugly."[18]

Nonetheless, the system of arched trusses was clearly adopted about the time of the *Vandalia* and was used to strengthen the hulls of virtually all subsequent wooden steamboats.

The early propeller-driven ships also had serious problems with tailshaft bearings wearing out and water leaking into the hull at the stern tube, where the propeller shaft penetrated the hull. These problems were largely eliminated in 1854 when John Penn invented stern bearings made of lignum vitae, an extremely hard tropical wood.[19]

To provide auxiliary power for the *Vandalia*, she was outfitted as a single-masted sloop. Other steamboats of her era carried much more elaborate sailplans, including the *Michigan*, which was fully rigged as a three-masted schooner.

From the launching in 1830 of the *Sheldon Thompson*, the first three-masted schooner, that rigging had rapidly become the most popular on the lakes. In 1835, the *Wellington* was launched at Windsor as one of the last of the Great Lakes square-rigged ships; by 1870 square-riggers had almost disappeared.[20] The fore-and-aft arrangement of the schooner's sails had proven particularly effective on the Great Lakes—which have prevailing westerly winds. It was common, however, for schooners to also be fitted with square-rigged topsails, because they were useful when running before the wind while crossing Lakes Superior, Erie, or Ontario. About this time, all sailing vessels with three or more masts, regardless of their sailplan, began to be referred to as "ships" instead of "boats."[21] Regardless of their size, however, steam-powered vessels continued to be referred to as "boats," although "propellers" were differentiated from "steamers," the name used for paddlewheelers.

The *Vandalia* was so successful that before she completed her first season of operations, plans had already been made for construction of three more propeller-driven vessels at Oswego. However, most shipowners and shipbuilders continued to rely on the paddlewheel technology that had proven itself over the previous two decades. D. N. Barney of Cleveland was clearly of that mind when he contracted for the construction of a new passenger steamer in 1844. The ship's keel was laid early in 1844 at G. W. Jones Shipbuilding on the Cuyahoga River at Cleveland, and she was launched that fall. Described as a "mammoth steamer," the *Empire* was 265 feet long, the longest

A Stanton drawing of D. N. Barney's passenger steamer *Empire*. When it was launched in 1844, the 265-foot ship was the longest vessel on the lakes. The *Empire* had two decks of cabins atop its main deck, a design innovation that had been pioneered in 1839 by the builders of the *Great Western*. While ships like the *Ontario*, *Walk-in-the-Water*, and *Michigan* were navigated and steered from a position at their sterns, in the fashion of sailing vessels, the *Empire* sported a pilothouse atop the second tier of cabins at its bow. The forward pilothouse would eventually become a distinctive trademark of ships on the lakes. (Author's collection)

Passenger trade on the Great Lakes was already in decline in 1854 when the Michigan Central Railroad launched the *Western World*. The elaborate 337-foot steamer was likened to a floating palace. Shown here in a Stanton drawing, the *Western World* operated for only three seasons on the lakes and ended her career as a drydock at Bay City, Michigan. (Author's collection)

ship on the lakes at that time. At 1,136 tons, the *Empire* was also the first Great Lakes vessel to exceed 1,000 tons. She had two upper decks of cabins and massive paddlewheels that were 30 feet in diameter and 12 feet wide. Her paddlewheels were driven by a powerful 500-horsepower engine. Put into operation the following season, the *Empire* carried mainly passengers, bagged flour, and package freight.[22]

The *Empire* was eclipsed in 1849 by the *Mayflower*, built at Detroit for the Michigan Central Railroad. The new steamer was intended to serve as a link between Buffalo, still the major port of debarkation for settlers coming from the East, and the Michigan Central Railroad's trackage running west out of Detroit. The *Mayflower* was twenty feet longer than the *Empire* and rated at 1,300 tons. Steamboat services operated by the Michigan Central and other railroads in the Great Lakes area, connected rail lines at the east end of Lake Erie with those that had been developed west of the lake.

By 1852, Lake Erie was paralleled along its southern shore by tracks of the Lake Shore Railroad running between Buffalo and Toledo. In 1854, the Great Western Railroad was completed along the Canadian shore of the lake, and "in a very few years traffic arrangements were so perfected on these new rail lines that the current of commerce was diverted from water to land."[23] Passenger traffic on Lake Erie was the first to be affected. The trains offered travellers faster passages than the steamboats. They were also the only means of travel available during the winter months when navigation was brought to a halt on the lakes.

In 1854, the Michigan Central Railroad attempted to recapture the passenger trade between Buffalo and Detroit by launching the sister ships *Western World* and *Plymouth Rock* at Buffalo on July 7 and July 10, respectively. The 2,002-ton *Western World* was 337 feet long at her waterline, with a beam of 42 feet and a width of 72 feet over her paddlewheel guards. The *Plymouth Rock* was just shy of 336 feet in length and rated at 1,991 tons. Both were driven by robust 1,500-horsepower steam engines, three times as powerful as the engine installed on the *Empire* only a decade earlier.

Acclaimed as the largest steamers afloat anywhere at the time they were launched, they were typical of the luxurious, even ostentatious, steamboats that operated on the Great Lakes in the mid-1850s. This was the period of the "palace steamers," and both of the new ships were quite literally floating palaces, outfitted with copious quantities of stained glass, panelling and trim of rare woods, moldings decorated with gold leaf, the finest carpets, crystal chandeliers, silk and damask curtains, and elaborate murals, mirrors, and statuary. Their impressive selection of cabin accommodations, rivalling those that could be found anywhere in the world, even included bridal suites.[24]

The exteriors of the ships were just as gaudy and must have delighted spectators who gathered at ports to welcome their arrival. A drawing of the *Western World* by artist-historian Samuel Ward Stanton shows a massive pennant bearing the ship's name flying from the single mast just aft of her pilothouse. Four flagstaffs atop her cabins bore slightly smaller pennants with the names of her primary ports of Detroit and Buffalo and the names of the two railroads she linked, the Michigan Central and New York Central. Another pennant flew from her bowsprit, or steering pole, and a gigantic American flag flew from her stern. *WESTERN WORLD* was spelled out in huge block letters on the side of her hull, just below her massive paddlewheel boxes, which were decorated with a beautiful starburst design. Her two smokestacks towered high above the cabins and the walking beam of her engine, while her superstructure was further cluttered by the longitudinal arches that spanned most of her length. Atop the forward end of her cabins, just back from the bow, was a fittingly elaborate wheelhouse, looking much like an oversized Victorian birdcage. The domed roof of the wheelhouse was adorned with a man-sized eagle with swept-back wings, conveying the impression that the boat was flying through the water, even when it was tied securely to a dock.[25]

Built at a cost of $250,000 each, the two Michigan Central ships operated on Lake Erie for only three seasons before declining business forced their disappointed owners to lay them up in 1857. A number of factors were converging that would unalterably affect passenger trade on the Great Lakes. During the boom years of immigration prior to 1857, when it seemed that the twin spirals of demand and profits would continue ever upward, shipowners had clearly overbuilt. The excessive number of vessels operating on the lakes, combined with growing competition from the railroads and an ebbing in the tide of immigration, left fleets like the Michigan Central with ships that were no longer economically viable.

After lying idle at their dock in Detroit from the fall of 1857 until 1862, the valuable engines of the *Western World* and *Plymouth Rock* were removed for use in newer ships being built on the Atlantic Coast, and their hulls were converted to drydocks. The stripped hull of the *Western World*, once the grandest ship on the lakes, ended her days ignominiously as a drydock at Bay City, Michigan, while the *Plymouth Rock* met a similar fate at a shipyard in Port Huron, Michigan.[26]

The passing of the two ships did not mark the end of the passenger trade on the lakes, however. Smaller, more versatile vessels were able to eke out a living, even during the period of economic difficulties that descended upon the country in 1859 as the result of overspeculation in railroads and real estate. Passenger steamers and excursion boats would continue to be popular on the lakes until the 1960s, when private ownership of automobiles became almost universal in the U.S. and people preferred motoring to travel by boat.

By 1859, however, a chain of events had already been set in motion that would forever change the nature of the shipping industry on the lakes, ensuring that the passenger trade would never again achieve the dominance it had prior to that time. The opening of the first large lock at Sault Ste. Marie, Michigan, in 1855 connected the mineral-rich Lake Superior region with the growing urban centers along the lower lakes and signalled the beginning of what one historian termed "the modern era of the Great Lakes."[27]

Rich deposits of iron ore had been discovered near Marquette in Michigan's Upper Peninsula in 1844. Within two years, the first mining operation was underway there. While modest quantities of iron ore were shipped to furnaces in southern Ohio and Pennsylvania between 1846 and 1855, the impassable rapids of the St. Marys River at Sault Ste. Marie made it necessary to offload the ore there, portage it around the rapids, then load it aboard another vessel for shipment down the lakes. The process was both time-consuming and expensive, and it soon became obvious to government officials and businessmen interested in development of the Lake Superior region that the bottleneck at "the Soo," as it was commonly called, had to be eliminated.

In April of 1853, the state of Michigan contracted with the St. Marys Falls Ship Canal Company to construct a canal and locks around the violent rapids at the Soo. Construction began in June of 1853. Two years later, on June 18, 1855, the *Str. Illinois* locked through upbound, opening commerce by way of what was to become the busiest shipping canal in the world.

In a monumental feat of engineering, using what would now be considered almost primitive equipment, a canal more than a mile long, 100 feet wide, and 12 feet deep had been dug around the rapids. To overcome the difference between the level of Lake Superior and that of the St. Marys River and the lower lakes, two locks, each 350 feet long and 70 feet wide, lifted or lowered vessels a total of 18 feet.[28]

A month after the opening of the locks, the two-masted brigantine *Columbia* transitted downbound with the first shipment of iron ore to move down the lake without having to be portaged, part of a total of 1,400 tons shipped that year. Demand for the rich ore from the mines on Lake Superior increased rapidly, with 11,500 tons moving through the locks in 1856, followed by 35,000 tons in 1857.

In November of 1860, Abraham Lincoln was elected president of the United States, but before he took office in March of the following year, seven southern states had seceded from the Union over the issue of slavery. Lincoln barely had time to move into the White House before the first cannonades were fired at Fort Sumter, South Carolina, marking the beginning of the bloody war that would ravage the nation for four long years. The demand for iron ore to feed the Union war machine dramatically increased shipments through the Soo locks. By 1865, the final year of the conflagration, more than 236,000 tons moved down the lakes.

While some of the ore was shipped in the holds of passenger steamers, the construction of the first ore docks at Marquette in 1859 gave sailing vessels a distinct advantage in the trade. The ore dock consisted of a twenty-five-foot-high trestle built along the face of the slip where the boats would moor. A ramp at one end allowed railroad cars full of ore to be pushed to the top of the dock and positioned over hoppers contained within the structure of the dock. The contents of the railroad cars were dumped into the hoppers. Steel chutes attached to the bottom of the hoppers could then be lowered and positioned over the cargo hatches of a ship tied up at the dock. When a trap door at the bottom of the hopper was opened, the ore would slide down the chute and into the waiting vessel's hold.

In the days when the ore had been laboriously loaded aboard ship by men pushing wheelbarrows, it didn't make any difference whether it was dumped into the hold of a steamboat or a sailing vessel. The cargo holds of steamboats could only be accessed through gangways in the sides of their hulls, however, since their decks were covered by cabins. Thus they were totally unsuited to loading at the new docks. Sailing vessels, on the other hand, were generally loaded through hatches that lined their open decks. It was these ships, in fact, that the inventors had in mind when they designed the innovative ore dock at Marquette.

The development in the mid-1860's of the first system to unload bulk cargoes from ships further solidified the position of the sailing vessels in the bulk cargo trades. That system, first used by Bothwell and Ferris in Cleveland, involved using horses to lift iron tubs out of the ship's hold with the aid of ropes running through snatch blocks attached to the vessel's rigging. The tubs, which still had to be loaded by hand, were then dumped into wheelbarrows situated on planking erected over the holds and pushed ashore where they could be dumped. Today, the system seems very crude, but its development cut unloading time about in half, allowing as much as two hundred tons to be unloaded in a day. In 1867, Bothwell improved on the system by replacing the horses with a steam engine that could handle three ropes and tubs simultaneously. Unloading time was again cut in half, and a vessel of four hundred tons' capacity could be unloaded in a single day.

Like the loading docks, these unloading systems could not be used on steamboats, whose cargo holds were inaccessible from above. Because of the substantial economies these systems afforded to shippers, their use rapidly spread to ports throughout the Great Lakes system. After years of playing second fiddle to the big steamers, the sailing vessels suddenly found a profitable niche for themselves in the growing iron ore trade. Indeed, sailing vessels reached their peak on the Great Lakes in 1868, partially as a result of their adaptability to the bulk trade. A record total of 1,855 sailing vessels were registered that year, compared to only 624 steamboats, and they had twice the carrying capacity.

While sailing vessels could be loaded and unloaded more efficiently than the steamboats, they still suffered from the same disadvantage that had previously cost them the passenger trade: they were totally dependent on the wind for propulsion. If there was no wind, and that was often the case, the ships couldn't move. If winds were light or if they were sailing into headwinds—other common situations—sailing vessels would make very slow passages. At the same time, sailing up or down the narrow channels of the winding river systems connecting the lakes was particularly difficult. To keep wind in their sails and maintain headway, schooners and barks often had to tack back and forth across the rivers, greatly increasing the actual distances they travelled and the time it took for passages. Much of the benefit of their ability to load and unload cargo faster than steamboats was lost by their dependence on the vagaries of the winds.

Beginning in 1845, owners of sailing vessels attempted to at least partially sever their reliance on the wind by having their ships towed through the rivers by steam tugs. Powerful sidewheel and propeller tugs could often be seen towing as many as eight sailing vessels at a time through the rivers. By 1868, there were thirty-two tugs providing towing services to sailing vessels on the busy Detroit and St. Clair rivers.[29]

The entrepreneurial spirit of Elihu M. Peck, a Cleveland shipbuilder, seems to have been challenged by the discord that existed between the growing importance of the bulk trade on the lakes and the inherent limitations of the steamboats and sailing vessels of the day. Born in Otsego County, New York, in 1822, Peck had come to Cleveland at the age of sixteen and apprenticed himself as a shipbuilder in the yard of Philo Moses.

He opened his own shipyard in 1847, near what is now West 58 Street. He entered into a partnership with Irvine U. Masters in 1855 to form the firm of Peck & Masters.[30]

From the scanty biographical information available on Peck, it appears that he was brusque and not easily approachable, but a fair man, nonetheless, and clearly loyal to his partner and employees. For example, when Masters died in 1864, Peck retained his name on the firm and, during slack periods, built boats on speculation to keep his employees working. The *Cleveland Plain Dealer* noted that "providentially, these speculations were always successful."[31] Peck was obviously a progressive man. He is reported to have been active in the formation of the People's Gas Light Company in Cleveland and later became its president. He was also a director of the Savings and Loan Association, and undoubtedly highly thought of in his community.

By 1869, the forty-seven-year-old Peck had been a shipbuilder for twenty-two years and ran a yard that was among the most successful on the lakes. Peck & Masters had launched more than fifty vessels, and a newspaper of the time reported that "It will be seen that nearly all the vessels, whether sail or steam, built by Mr. Peck were of the first class, being mainly barques and large propellers. They will be recognized by those familiar with lakes commerce as models in size, beauty, and strength, whilst several have made unusually quick trips."[32] The fifty ships totalled 27,000 tons, or an average of 540 tons each.[33] Among them was the package freighter *Nebraska*, launched in 1867 and the longest and largest ship on the lakes at 280 feet in length and 1,483 gross tons.

Some of the ships built by Peck, however, would seem to suggest that he was not always willing to conform to the accepted ship design practices of the period. His first ship, the 200-ton schooner *Jenny Lind*, is described as having been "slightly ugly."[34] At a time when conventional schooners had severely raked stems, flared bows, and rounded sides, Peck's ungainly creation had a blunt, scowlike bow and an almost square cross-section. While she was not pretty to the eye, the utilitarian design allowed the *Jenny Lind* to carry more cargo than other ships of her size.[35] It was as if Eli Peck had discovered, and applied to the *Jenny Lind*, what was to become the basic precept of the Great Lakes bulk shipping industry: the key criterion for evaluating a bulk vessel is how much cargo it can efficiently carry.

It is generally agreed that "all naval architects and marine engineers are historians, at least to the extent that they base their design decisions on experiences learned in the past. The history of ships is one of evolution and the design lineage of every ship afloat can be traced back for countless generations."[36] The idea for the boxy hull of the *Jenny Lind*, resulting in a higher carrying capacity than other ships her size, may not have been original with Peck. From the opening of the Erie Canal in 1825 and the Welland Canal in 1829, a class of vessels with a unique hull form had evolved. The small dimensions of the locks in the two systems severely limited the size of vessels passing through them. Shipowners, always eager to achieve the highest possible return on their investments, sought a hull design that would allow vessels to carry the maximum amount of cargo within the size limitations imposed by the canal systems. What evolved was the "canaler," built to the maximum length, beam, and depth allowed by the locks. A little extra carrying capacity was achieved by building the canalers with blunt bows, a stem that was almost vertical, and a flat stern with little cutaway.[37] It is entirely possible that these homely, but utilitarian, canalers were the prototypes for Peck's *Jenny Lind.*

While most of the ships that Peck built after the *Jenny Lind* were much more conventional in design, in 1869 he again deviated from the mainstream of ship construction on the lakes when he built the *R. J. Hackett.* It would have been impossible for Eli Peck to envision the unparalleled impact the *Hackett* would have on the Great Lakes shipping industry for the next century. For the unpretentious, odd-looking wooden ship that came off the ways at Peck and Masters on November 16, 1869, was the first "Great Lakes bulk freighter."

Onlookers who witnessed the launching of the *Hackett* were probably disappointed by her appearance. They were used to sleek schooners and luxurious passenger steamers and propellers, but the *Hackett* looked a great deal like that homely little schooner, the *Jenny Lind*, that Peck had built twenty-two years earlier at the start of his career. Like the *Jenny Lind*, the *Hackett* had a very boxy hull, as if she were nothing more than an oversized version of the undistinctive canalers operating on the Welland and Erie canals. She was just an inch over 208 feet long at the waterline, and because of her straight stem and blunt stern, her overall dimensions were almost the same as the canalers. She had a beam of 32 feet, 5 inches, a depth of 12 feet, 6 inches, and a gross tonnage of 749. Altogether, she was much smaller than the *Nebraska*, then the Queen of the Lakes.

While her hull was much like that of the *Jenny Lind*, the *Hackett* was powered by a 390-horsepower, steeple compound engine that Peck had placed all the way aft so that her propeller shaft would not have to run through the cargo hold. On the main deck, above her engine room, was a deckhouse with the galley and accommodations for crewmembers. The deckhouse was topped by a tall black smokestack, and the *Hackett's* two lifeboats were suspended from davits situated on each side of the after cabin.

In the manner of passenger steamers and package freighters, Peck installed the *Hackett*'s wheelhouse just back from the

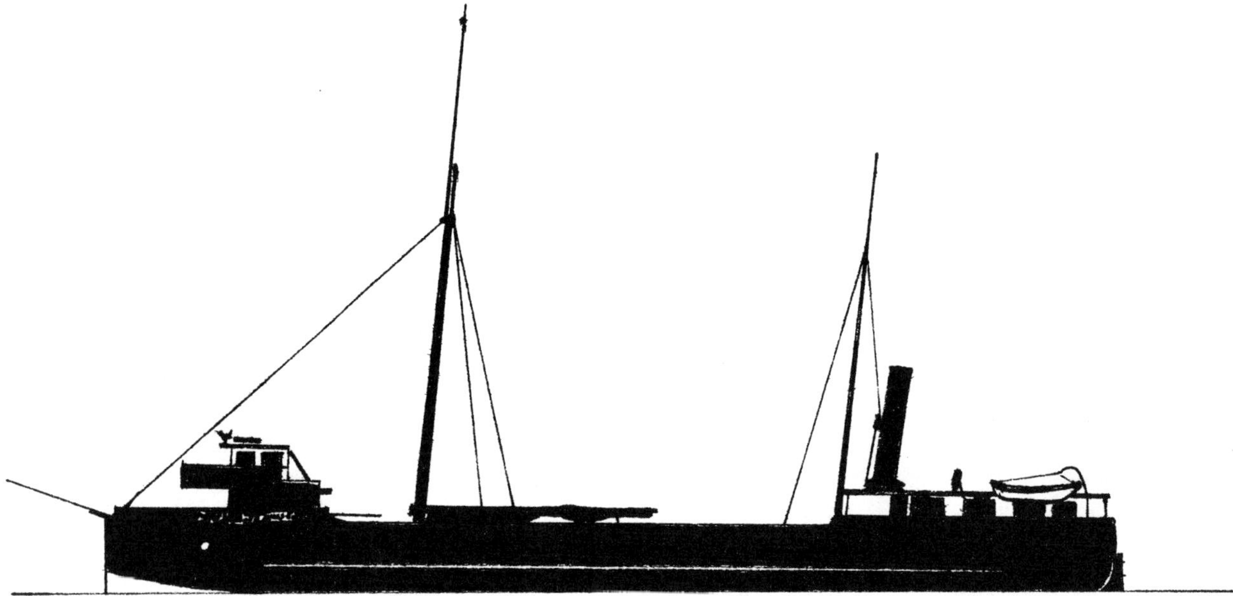

A drawing of Captain Eli Peck's *R. J. Hackett*, made from one of the few surviving photos of the small bulk freighter. Built at Peck's shipyard in Cleveland in 1869, the pioneering design of the *Hackett*—pilothouse forward and engine room aft—became the model for hundreds of bulk freighters built on the lakes over the next century. Initially referred to as a "steam barge," and dismissed by many in the maritime community, the *Hackett* is arguably the most important ship ever launched on the Great Lakes. (Author's collection)

ship's bow, atop a deckhouse containing the captain's cabin. The wheelhouse was surrounded by a small promenade deck on the front and two sides. Other deck crewmembers were housed in cabins within the hull, below the main deck. In addition to her steam engine, the *Hackett* had three masts; sails could be set from two of the masts to provide auxiliary power or stabilize the vessel in a blow. The masts were also rigged with blocks and tackle to be used when unloading. The *Hackett*'s deck looked much like those on sailing vessels of the time. A series of hatches ran down the center of her deck, spaced on twenty-four-foot centers so they would line up with the chutes on the ore dock at Marquette. The hatches were closed with wooden covers, and they could be covered with tarps in foul weather to keep water out of the cargo hold.

Peck's creation looked like the odd offspring of an illicit union between a propeller steamer and a schooner. People weren't sure how to describe the strange new vessel, though most seem to have referred to it, in less than flattering terms, as a "barge" or "steam barge."

Peck and an investor, Captain Robert J. Hackett—after whom the boat was named—had built the new bulk freighter on speculation, but after her launching they were unable to find a buyer. Rather than let the *Hackett* sit idle, they formed the Northwestern Transportation Company and managed to sell a minor interest in the company to Harvey Brown, agent for the Jackson Iron Company and several other firms that operated mines in the Marquette area. Captain Hackett agreed to run the new company, and he set up offices in Detroit, which was to become the ship's home port.

When the *Hackett* was put into operation in the spring of 1870, under the command of Captain David Trotter, she proved to be an able carrier. She ran at a very respectable twelve miles an hour, much faster than any sailing vessel in the bulk trade, and could carry a prodigious 1,100 tons of iron ore, 45,000 bushels of grain, or 700,000 board feet of lumber.[38] She may not have been pleasing to the eye, but she did the job she was designed for. In fact, the early success of the *Hackett* inspired Peck to build the tow barge *Forest City* in 1870. While almost identical to the *Hackett*, the *Forest City* was unpowered, designed to be towed as a consort. After completing the 1870 season in tow of the *Hackett*, the *Forest City* was given her own engines the following year so that she could operate independently.

If imitation is indeed the sincerest form of flattery, the staid Peck, who undoubtedly chafed at the uncomplimentary comments that greeted the launching of the *Hackett*, must have taken great solace in the fact that her unusual design was almost immediately copied by other shipbuilders and shipowners. It must have been with mixed emotions, however, that he watched as freighters modelled after the *Hackett* began to drive the beautiful sailing vessels out of the bulk trade market, and eventually out of existence. The numbers of sailing craft on the lakes began to decline in 1869, almost as if in direct response to the launching of the *Hackett*. By 1886, there were more steam

The *Str. Forest City*, virtually a twin to the *Hackett*, shown entering a lock at the Soo towing its barge consort. The ship's captain can be seen on the open-air bridge on top of the wheelhouse. Built in 1870 by Captain Peck as a barge consort to be towed by the *Hackett*, the *Forest City* was given its own steam engine the following year. (Dossin Great Lakes Museum, Detroit)

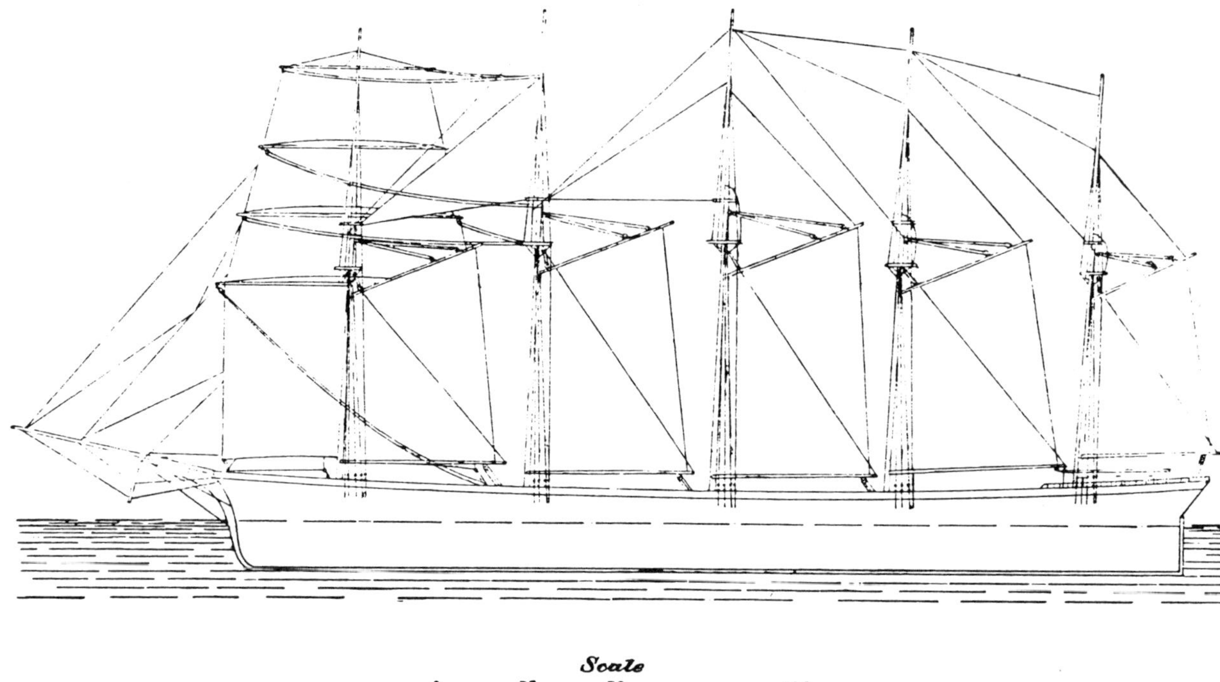

A drawing of the *David Dows* that was used to illustrate an 1882 magazine article about the unique five-masted sailing ship. While classified as a schooner, the ship's foremast carried square sails like those on a bark, in addition to a gaff-rigged fore-and-aft sail. The five masts were each more than 150 feet tall. Fully outfitted the *Dows* sported over 5,000 square yards of canvas. (Author's collection)

freighters than sailing vessels. And before his death from pneumonia on May 8, 1896, Captain Peck saw freighters based on the design of the *Hackett* become the most common style of ship on the Great Lakes.

By 1896, the latest generation of the *Hackett*'s progeny were massive, steel-hulled leviathans. Ships like the *W. D. Rees* and *Coralia* were over four hundred feet long and had gross tonnages more than four times that of the *Hackett*, which was then still in operation. Despite their increased size, it was clear to all that they were her descendants and heirs to the bulk trade that would forevermore dominate shipping on the lakes. The Great Lakes bulk freighter—with its boxy hull, pilothouse forward, engine aft, and long hatch-lined deck—was a unique class of vessel and the most efficient bulk carrier in the world.

The little *Hackett* was a familiar sight on the lakes until November 12, 1905, when she caught fire and burned at Whaleback Shoal in Green Bay while en route to Marinette, Wisconsin, with a load of coal. No reverential ceremonies marked the passing of the vessel that had launched the modern era of shipping on the lakes. The *Hackett*'s enduring tribute lay in the fact that for more than one hundred years her pioneering design would serve as the basic pattern for virtually every bulk freighter launched on the inland seas of North America.

Adherents of the white-winged sailing vessels did not simply fold up their sails and disappear into oblivion when the *Hackett* was launched, however. The 1870's and 1880's were, in fact, what some have referred to as the age of the "lake clippers": first-class sailing vessels averaging about six hundred tons that operated primarily in the grain and ore trades.[39] Indeed, the largest and most majestic of all sailing ships to operate on the lakes was floated in 1881, amidst much greater fanfare than had attended the launching of the *Hackett*.

The *David Dows* was the largest schooner in the world and the longest ship on the Great Lakes when she was launched at the Bailey Brothers shipyard in Toledo, Ohio, on April 21, 1881, for M. D. Carrington of the prominent shipping firm of

Carrington and Casey. At 278 feet overall and 1,418 gross tons, she represented the response of the sailing fleets to the growing popularity of steam vessels.

Designed for the coal and grain trade between Buffalo and Chicago, the *Dows* is generally referred to as the world's first five-masted schooner.[40] Her sailplan was somewhat of an oddity, however. Her foremast sported square sails, like a bark, but it also carried a fore-and-aft sail, like a schooner. Her other four masts had only fore-and-aft sails. With her full inventory of sails set, the *Dows* must have been an awe-inspiring sight to behold. The masts towered more than 150 feet above her deck and carried between 5,000 and 6,000 square yards of the finest duck canvas.[41] A *Toledo Blade* article about her launching noted that was enough fabric, "to furnish clean shirts for a large portion of the Democratic Party in Ohio."[42]

The jet black hull of the *Dows* was built of oak and strengthened with iron straps that were one inch thick and eight inches wide. At the turn of her bilge the planking was a full six inches thick. A bowsprit thrust forward an impressive thirty-seven feet from her gracefully flared bow. The bowsprit is reported to have been decorated with a carved dragon figurehead that was twenty-four feet long from nostrils to tail. The dragon was vividly described in the *Chicago Interocean* newspaper as "natural enough to be about as repulsive as anything can be."[43] It is curious to note that the figurehead is not obvious in the few photos that exist of the *Dows*. It may have been removed at some time, perhaps after her collision with the schooner *Charles K. Nims* on September 10, 1881, when the bow of the *Dows* was damaged.

The *Dows* had a large and roomy forecastle cabin, located on her main deck just back from the bow. It housed a dayroom and berths for eight crewmen, complete with marble-topped wash basins. Such spaciousness and luxurious appointments for deckhands were virtually unheard of at the time. One veteran Great Lakes sailor later noted that in the forecastles of most of the sailing ships of the 1870's, "the air was so bad a lamp would scarcely burn, and there was not a single room sufficiently tight to keep water out in a head sea or when it rained, and when you encountered heavy seas or it rained you went to bed with your oil skins to keep dry."[44]

The captain and the two mates had private rooms in another deckhouse near the *Dow*'s stern, which also contained the galley. Her dining room, like her cabins, was large and airy and had rich wood-grained doors and carved ceiling panels. The crew itself was rather small for a ship the size of the *Dows*, twelve in all. In addition to the captain and two mates, there were nine unlicensed crewmembers, including a cook, cook's helper, and seven deckhands.

A steam donkey engine was mounted on the deck and aided the deckhands in weighing anchors, pumping bilges, and raising sail. Even then, it took the crew a full eight hours of steady work to make sail. On short trips, her captain often chose to dispense with the arduous and time-consuming task of setting sails, opting instead to have his ship towed by steam tug to its next port.

While the *Dows* had been designed to carry 150,000 bushels of wheat at her maximum draft, because of the shallowness of the harbor at Toledo she could take on only 87,000 bushels when she loaded for the first time at the Wabash Grain Elevator. There is no record that she was ever able to carry more than 119,000 bushels, meaning that three to six feet of her designed draft went unused throughout her career because harbors were not dredged to the depths anticipated by her builders. In fact, another Carrington and Casey schooner, the *George W. Adams*, while shorter than the *Dows*, managed to carry 125,000 bushels because of her wider beam.[45]

The *Dows* carried her first load of grain to Buffalo, arriving amidst great fanfare. After unloading what the Buffalo newspaper referred to as "her ten boatloads of wheat,"[46] she was taken in tow by the steam tug *Mollie Spencer* for the short trip to Erie, Pennsylvania. There she loaded 3,000 tons of coal for delivery to Chicago. When the *Dows* attempted to leave Erie, however, she ran hard aground and was stranded for two days. The massive *Dows* would experience many similar mishaps throughout her tenure on the lakes.

In addition to being susceptible to grounding because of the extreme depth of her hull, the *Dows* was always a hard ship to maneuver. During the season of 1883, her masts were removed, and she was used as a tow barge. When she was subsequently rerigged, her topmasts were left off to simplify the sailplan and reduce the amount of time it took to set and tend her sails. Even then, she spent most of the balance of her checkered career travelling at the end of a towline behind a steam tug.

On Thanksgiving Day of 1889, while being towed down Lake Michigan with a load of coal for Chicago, the *Dows* began taking on water. Worsening weather conditions forced the tug *Aurora* to drop her tow, and the *Dows* went to anchor about ten miles south-southeast of Chicago and six miles east of Calumet Harbor. With water flooding her cargo hold and ice rapidly building up on her decks, the overworked donkey engine that drove her bilge pumps gave out and the decks were soon awash. Fearing that the ship would sink at any minute, the crew of the *Dows* climbed up into her rigging. They were rescued several hours later by the tug *Chicago*, but their ship was by then beyond saving.

On the morning of November 29, 1889, the once-

The five-masted schooner *David Dows* locking through at Sault Ste. Marie on a trip to Lake Superior. When the 278-foot, wood-hulled ship was launched at Toledo for Carrington & Casey in 1881 it was not only the longest ship on the lakes, but the longest schooner in the world and the first five-masted schooner ever built. It represented an attempt by adherents of sailing vessels to show that schooners could compete with the steamboats that were rapidly dominating trade on the lakes. (State Archives of Michigan)

magnificent *Dows* shuddered one last time and with a lurch to port sank in thirty to thirty-six feet of water. As if struggling to the end to escape her fate, she settled on the bottom in an upright position with all five of her masts visible above the water. Subsequent salvage efforts were unsuccessful.[47]

For devotees of sailing ships, the trouble-plagued career and tragic demise of the *Dows* must have seemed to seal the fate of the gull-winged vessels they loved so much. Their hopes for a permanent role in shipping on the lakes died on the cold waters of Lake Michigan along with the ship they had once pointed to with so much pride. After dominating the shipping lanes for centuries, the sailing ships died a lingering death. Around 1900, there were still more than eight hundred sailing vessels on the lakes, most of which were small schooners involved in the lumber trade. No longer part of the mainstream of shipping on the lakes, their numbers were steadily dwindling.

On September 26, 1930, the aging 182-foot schooner *Our Son* floundered in a gale off Sheboygan, Wisconsin, while bound for Muskegon, Michigan, with a load of pulpwood. Launched at Lorain, Ohio, in 1874, she was owned by the House of David religious sect from St. Joseph, Michigan, and was used to haul freight between their colony at St. Joseph and High Island in northern Lake Michigan, which they also owned.[48] *Our Son*'s seven crewmembers were rescued by the passing *Str. William Nelson.* As the seven huddled on the cold, steel deck of the *Nelson* and saw their little ship slip beneath the storm-tossed waters of Lake Michigan, they were acutely aware that they were witnesses to the end of an era. For *Our Son* was the last sailing vessel to operate in the bulk trades on the Great Lakes.[49]

It was noted previously that the opening of the Soo Locks in 1855 set in motion a chain of events that were to forever change the nature of the shipping industry on the lakes. The locks opened commerce between Lake Superior and the lower lakes and set the stage for exploitation of the rich iron ore deposits that had been found in the region. The second major event in that chain was the launching in 1869 of the wood-hulled *Str. R. J. Hackett*, the prototype for the Great Lakes bulk freighter. The *Hackett* and the steam-powered ships modelled after her proved to represent the most efficient way to ship bulk cargoes. Their advent led ultimately to the demise of sailing vessels and allowed bulk cargoes, particularly iron ore, to displace the passenger trade as the most important commerce on the lakes. On a cold, blustery day in February of 1882, the third—and, arguably, the final—event in the chain took place on the banks of the Cuyahoga River at Cleveland. On that day the *Str. Onoko*, the first iron-hulled bulk freighter on the Great Lakes, slid down the ways at the Globe Shipbuilding Company.

The art and science of wooden shipbuilding had been stretched to its technical limits in ships like the 278-foot *Dows*. While a few did break the 300-foot barrier, it was virtually impossible to join planks and timbers securely enough to build wooden hulls much longer than that and still achieve the necessary longitudinal strength. In fact, problems of hogging and sagging had been encountered when wooden ships approached 200 feet in length. That had led to the use of timber trusses, sometimes called "hogframes" or "Bishop's arches," to make the hulls more rigid, like those reportedly used on the *Vandalia*. As ships got longer, the trusses got larger. In order to provide sufficient stiffening to the otherwise limber hulls, the twin arches often stretched almost the entire length of the hull and towered high above the deck. Some were even further strengthened through the use of masts and guy rods.[50] Even elaborate systems of hogframes could not provide sufficient longitudinal strengthening for wooden hulls much longer than 300 feet, however.[51] For all intents and purposes, as long as shipbuilders were limited to the use of wood in construction, ships were not going to get any bigger than they were at the time the *Dows* was launched in 1881.

All that changed with the construction of the 302-foot *Onoko*. The shift to the use of iron, instead of wood, marked the beginning of a new age in vessel construction, one that would eventually see ships surpass 1,000 feet in length on the Great Lakes. It was with the launching of the *Onoko* that the modern era of shipping truly began . . . and it is justly fitting that as she departed Cleveland on her first trip she was hailed as Queen of the Lakes.

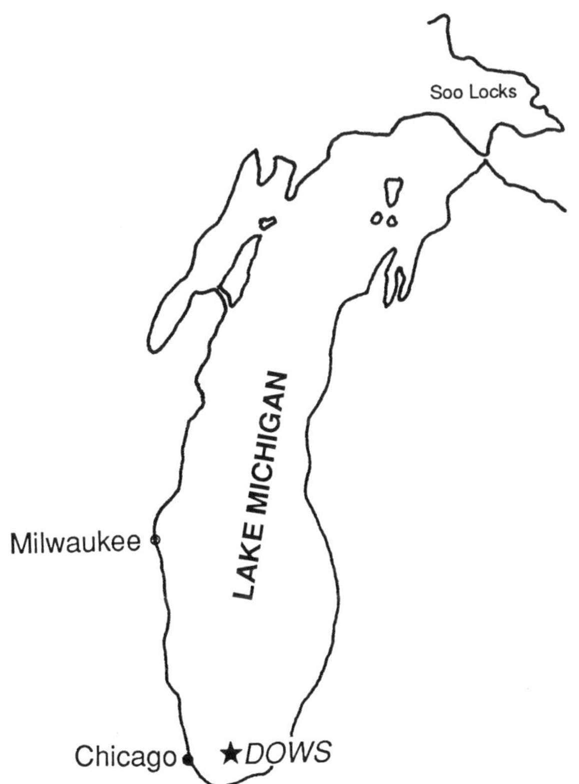

The trouble-plagued career of the *David Dows* came to an end in a November storm on Lake Michigan in 1889, after only nine seasons on the lakes. The massive schooner, loaded with coal, sank ten miles south-southeast of Chicago, near the present site of Gary, Indiana. (Author's collection)

Notes

1. Richard F. Palmer, "First Steamboat on the Great Lakes," *Telescope* (Mar.–Apr. 1984): 37–38.
2. Ibid.
3. Harlan Hatcher, *Lake Erie* (New York: Bobbs-Merrill Company, 1945), 107.
4. J. B. Mansfield, ed., *History of the Great Lakes*, vol. I (Chicago: J. H. Beers and Co., 1899; reprint, Cleveland: Freshwater Press, 1972), 186.

5. James P. Barry, *Ships of the Great Lakes* (Berkeley: Howell-North Books, 1973), 39.
6. Harlan Hatcher and Erich A. Walter, *A Pictorial History of the Great Lakes* (New York: Bonanza Books, 1963), 252.
7. Mansfield, 184.
8. Ibid., 397.
9. Hatcher, *Lake Erie*, 126.
10. Ibid., 129.
11. Mansfield, 185.
12. Ibid., 184.
13. Barry, 45.
14. Mansfield, 185.
15. Robina Farbrother, ed., *Ships* (London: Paul Hamlyn Ltd., 1963), 13.
16. Barry, 52–53.
17. The correct term is actually "hogging," a condition in which the center portion of the hull rides higher than the ends. In "sagging," the bow and stern have greater buoyancy than the middle of the hull and ride higher. Either condition results in unacceptable and dangerous stresses on the hull.
18. George A. Cuthbertson, *Freshwater* (New York: Macmillan, 1931), 72.
19. Farbrother, 15.
20. Ivan H. Walton, "Developments on the Great Lakes, 1815–1943," *Michigan History Magazine* 27 (1943), 91.
21. "Models of Great Lakes Vessels," *Telescope* 7 no. 1 (January 1958): 6.
22. Walton, 83.
23. Mansfield, 191.
24. Barry, 79.
25. Wheelhouse designs based on German Gothic architecture, with domed or onion-shaped roofs and often trimmed with delicately-carved gingerbread decorations, were popular on the lakes from 1850–90, but caught on nowhere else, according to Francis J. Skyker in "The Gothic Age on the Great Lakes," *Telescope* 8 no. 5 (May 1959): 8.
26. Walton, 87.
27. Mansfield, 191.
28. Stanley Newton, *The Story of Sault Ste. Marie* (Sault Ste. Marie, MI: The Sault Evening News Printing Company, 1923; reprint, Grand Rapids, MI: Black Letter Press, 1975), 151–53.
29. Mansfield, 509.
30. Masters is described as being a "financial partner" in the firm, rather than a seafaring man, although he had worked as a carpenter in the shipyard of Luther Moses. In 1863, he was elected mayor of Cleveland. He died the following year.
31. William Donahue Ellis, *The Cuyahoga* (New York: Holt, Rinehart and Winston, 1966), 113.
32. Ellis, 147.
33. *Inland Seas* VI (1950): 114–16.
34. Ellis, 127.
35. Ellis, 178.
36. Harry Benford, "Sixty Years of Shipbuilding," paper presented at the meeting of the Great Lakes Section, Society of Naval Architects and Marine Engineers, October 5, 1956, 1.
37. Fred Landon, *Lake Huron* (New York: Bobbs-Merrill Company, 1944), 349.
38. Ellis, 68.
39. Walton, 92.
40. By comparison, the largest wooden sailing ship ever built was Donald McKay's *Great Republic*, launched in 1853. She was 335 feet long and rated at 4,555 tons. Unfortunately, the ship burned before it ever put to sea; it was salvaged and rerigged, but not on the scale of her original plans. In a vain effort to forestall the demise of sailing ships on the oceans, massive five-, six-, and even seven-masted schooners were built on the East Coast during the early part of the twentieth century. Like the *Dows*, the seven-masted *Thomas W. Lawson* was a flop. Built of steel at Quincy, Massachusetts, in 1902, she was a little over 375 feet long, with a tonnage of 5,218. The ship was wrecked in 1907.
41. Kenneth R. Dickson, "The Largest Schooner (1881) in the World Revisited," *Inland Seas*, 42, no. 1 (Spring 1986): 4. Others, including both Barry and Clary, refer to the *Dows* as carrying 70,000 yards of canvas, which is unlikely. Barry attributes his figure to an April 21, 1881, article in the *Toledo Blade*.
42. James Clary, *Ladies of the Lakes* (Lansing, MI: Woolly Bear Productions, 1981), 86.
43. Harlan Hatcher, *A Century of Iron and Men* (New York: Bobbs-Merrill Company, 1950), 86.
44. Dickson, 4.
45. Ibid., 5.
46. Barry, 130.
47. Clary, 93–94.
48. Charles M. Anderson, *Memo's of Betsie Bay* (Manistee, MI: J. B. Publications, 1988), 14.
49. At least one two-masted schooner, the *Helen MacLeod*, is known to have been operated by commercial fishermen on Lake Huron through the end of World War II, but such vessels were not engaged in the carriage of bulk cargoes.
50. Francis J. Skyker, "Reinforced Wooden Vessels on the Great Lakes, *Telescope* 7, no. 4 (April 1958): 3.
51. One of the longest wooden ships ever built on the lakes was the *Chieftain*, launched at Bay City, Michigan, by James Davidson in 1902. The three-masted schooner was 342 feet long at her waterline and registered at 2,704 gross tons. She did not operate after 1928, though her hull survived at Bay City until destroyed by fire in 1953.

1

An Iron Queen

February is usually a harsh, unfriendly month in Cleveland. Most who have endured even one of the long winters there will tell you that by February their minds begin to play tricks on them. After months of lifeless grey skies, interminable snow, biting winds, and frigid temperatures, it seems to many that through some ghastly quirk of nature winter has become a permanent condition. It's no wonder that residents tend to be reclusive in February, limiting their excursions out-of-doors to the bare minimum.

It was relatively unusual, then, to find a large crowd of Cleveland citizens gathered along the old river bed at the foot of Taylor Street on the morning of February 16, 1882. Bundled against the frigid winds that rushed up the Cuyahoga River off Lake Erie, they had crowded into the new Globe Shipbuilding yard to witness the launching of the *Str. Onoko*. The first iron-hulled bulk freighter ever built at Cleveland, the *Onoko* would on that day also become the longest and largest ship on the Great Lakes.

Prominent among the throngs of specatators was shipyard superintendent John Smith, who had personally overseen construction of the remarkable new vessel. Smith, a native of Wales who had developed a reputation for working with iron while employed by the Grand Trunk Railroad, was almost oblivious to the cold as he basked in the many gestures of praise from attending officials of Globe Iron Works, the shipyard's parent corporation. Globe had gambled both its reputation and financial solvency to build the new freighter, investing heavily in the new shipyard and convincing one of the leading shipowners on the lakes that an iron-hulled ship would be superior to those built of wood.

Construction had gone remarkably smoothly, but as the huge ship sat poised on her ways Globe officials remained uncertain as to how she would actually perform. Iron had been used in ship construction since 1822 when the little *Aaron Manby* had been built at the Surrey Commercial Docks on the Thames in England for service on France's River Seine. The U.S. Navy had pioneered iron shipbuilding on the lakes in 1843, when the steamer *Michigan* was launched at Erie, Pennsylvania. She was the first iron vessel built by the Navy, as well as the first iron ship on the lakes.[1]

The 163-foot *Michigan* was still operating almost forty years later, which had to be reassuring to the people from Globe, but some of them were no doubt aware of the embarrassing circumstances of the naval ship's send off. If so, it's likely that they were praying silently that those events would not be repeated that day. The launching of the *Michigan* had attracted an equally large crowd, many certain that the unusual iron ship would never float. The atmosphere was tense as the timbers that held the ship were removed and she began to slide slowly down her ways toward the water. Then, in an instant that would forever be frozen in the memories of shipyard officials, she ground to a halt. The repeated, strenuous efforts of the yard's workers failed to dislodge the ship from her perch. After awhile, the throngs of disappointed onlookers disbanded. Even the frustrated shipyard staff went home, and the *Michigan* sat abandoned on her ways. How surprised and delighted the workers must have been the next morning, when upon their arrival at the shipyard they found the *Michigan* floating buoyantly alongside her now-vacant ways. During the night the stalwart little ship had launched herself and was even then proving all her skeptics wrong. Not only did the iron ship float, but over the years she proved to be an able and seaworthy vessel.[2]

The first iron-hulled commercial vessel built on the lakes was the *Merchant*. She was launched in 1861, twenty years before the *Onoko*, for the Erie and Western Transit Company's Anchor Line. A propeller-driven steamer of 200 feet in length and 700 tons,[3] she operated on the fleet's passenger and freight routes between Buffalo and Chicago.[4]

Despite the success of the *Michigan* and *Merchant*, in the third quarter of the nineteenth century wood remained the building material of choice on the lakes. It was plentiful, it was inexpensive, and, even more importantly, it was a material that shipbuilders and shipowners were familiar with. The fabrication of iron ships required shipbuilders to abandon their comfortably familiar and time-tested construction techniques. To build with iron, they needed to develop new procedures and tools and retrain their workers, who were already masters at building with wood.

A Stanton drawing of the iron-hulled *Merchant* with its auxiliary sails set. The first commercial vessel on the Great Lakes built with an iron hull, the *Merchant* was launched in 1861 for the famed Anchor Line of the Erie & Western Transit Company. Despite the success of the *Merchant*, wood remained the preferred building material on the lakes until the 1880s. (Author's collection)

For shipowners contemplating the purchase of iron vessels, the shift to iron represented not just an acceptance of the obvious problems arising from the use of a new building material, but the assumption of certain risks as well. They knew that the iron ships would cost far more to build than wooden vessels, but they had no body of statistical evidence to insure that the iron ships would be sufficiently more durable to justify the increased outlay. In fact, shipowners were aware that insurance underwriters felt that after five years of service an iron hull was a poor insurance risk.

Despite the inherent uncertainties, the Detroit Dry Dock Company had begun building commercial iron vessels at their shipyard at Wyandotte, Michigan, in 1873. They turned out a number of iron sidewheel passenger steamers,[5] an iron tug, two iron car ferries, two iron package freighters, and even an iron-hulled steam yacht, all before 1880. In 1877, attempting to placate the skeptical insurance underwriters, they built the passenger steamer *City of Detroit* with a composite iron and wood hull. Marine insurers thought the iron hull plates were brittle and would shatter and break if a ship built with them ever grounded—a common occurence on the lakes at that time. An acceptable compromise was reached with composite hulls, which had a layer of oak planking to protect the iron plates below the waterline. Detroit Dry Dock continued to build composite hulls through at least 1890, although shipyard officials felt that the oak sheathing was unnecessary.

In 1881, Detroit Dry Dock turned out the first iron-hulled bulk freighter on the Great Lakes, the *Brunswick*. She was 235 feet long at her waterline, with a beam of 35 feet, 6 inches, a depth of 15 feet, 6 inches, and measured at 1,120 gross tons. Just slightly larger than the 1869-built, wood-hulled *R. J. Hackett*, after which she was modelled, the landmark vessel had a short life on the lakes and is today virtually forgotten by historians. Launched on May 21, 1881, for Charles Bewick of Detroit, the *Brunswick* was involved in a collision with the schooner *Carlingsford* off Dunkirk, New York, on November 12 of that same year, while westbound with a load of coal from Buffalo. After less than a season on the lakes, she sank to the bottom of Lake Erie, and into obscurity, taking four of her crewmembers with her.[6] Many pointed to the loss of the *Brunswick* as irrefutable evidence that iron ships were inherently unsafe.

By the time news reached Cleveland of the sinking of the *Brunswick*, the iron freighter that had been ordered by Philip Minch was already nearing completion at the Globe shipyard. While the investors who had helped finance the new ship were alarmed by the news, Minch assuaged their fears by assuring them that the *Onoko* would generate handsome profits for them. On that cold February morning when the new vessel was finally prepared for launching, however, even Minch probably had some doubts as to whether it would live up to his expectations.

STR. ONOKO

302'x38'8"x20'7"
Queen of the Lakes
February 16, 1882 to September 4, 1886[7]

Any reservations he had were undoubtedly forgotten when the mammoth freighter finally slid from its ways into the cold waters of the Cuyahoga amidst an appropriately boistrous roar from the crowd of onlookers. Christened *Onoko* after an Iroquois chieftain, the new ship had looked slightly ungainly when it had been cradled on the ways, but once in the water it took on a totally new appearance, and one that pleased Minch's trained eye.

Onoko was dramatically larger than the wooden bulk freighters that yards had turned out in recent years. Her deck stretched longer than a football field—302 feet, 6 inches—and with a beam of 38 feet, 8 inches and a depth of 20 feet, 7 inches, she measured at a whopping 2,164 gross tons. Her 900-horsepower, fore-and-aft compound engine also made her one of the most powerful ships on the lakes. To provide auxiliary power, she was fully rigged as a three-masted schooner.

Looking on proudly as the *Onoko* bobbed on the waters of thc Cuyahoga, Minch knew intuitively that the iron ship would be a good carrier. It was clearly descended from the design pioneered by Eli Peck when he built the *R. J. Hackett*, although many people would later point to Minch's ship as "the true prototype of the modern lake vessels."[8] With her pilothouse forward, her engine aft, and a long, uncluttered deck in between, Minch was confident the *Onoko*'s boxy hull would soon carry record cargoes of iron ore. To him, she represented the perfection of the shipbuilding art and was fully deserving of the title Queen of the Lakes.

The iron-hulled *Onoko* in the latter part of her career. Two of the ship's four original masts have been removed and two "doghouse" cabins built on deck to house added crewmembers. (Institute for Great Lakes Research, Bowling Green State University)

Minch must have been devastated in succeeding days when he heard his marvelous new ship referred to disparagingly as "a monstrosity,"[9] a "floating boot box,"[10] and a "monster floating warehouse."[11] On each visit he made to Globe during the balance of the winter, the former shoemaker studied the *Onoko* critically as she lay inert at her fitout dock. Regardless of what others were saying, she looked beautiful to him. Her iron hull was painted black, not a particularly pretty color, but it had been capped with an attractive white band that ran from bow to stern. At her bow, the *Onoko* had a raised forecastle deck containing quarters for the deck crew. Atop the forecastle deck was a cabin for the captain and deck officers, set back as far as possible from the bow. On top of the cabin was the wheelhouse. It was smaller than the cabin below it, so a walkway was formed all the way around the wheelhouse for use by the captain and mates who navigated the ship. An even better vantage point could be had by climbing to the top of the wheelhouse, where a railing enclosed the ship's "flying bridge." It was from the flying bridge that the deck officers would most often navigate the ship, calling their instructions down to the wheelsman in the wheelhouse below them.

The forward superstructure was painted white, as was the large cabin at the stern containing the galley and quarters for engine room personnel. The long deck in between was broken only by the eight hatches through which the ship would load cargo and the four tall masts that were spaced evenly down the deck. The masts and the tall black smokestack that towered above the after cabin were all slightly raked backward: Minch thought they created an illusion of speed even when the ship was tied to its dock.

With little need for auxiliary sail power, the *Onoko*'s two center masts were eventually eliminated and her remaining fore and aft masts were reduced in height. When the traditional two-watch system was replaced by a three-watch system, an additional small, rectangular cabin, or "doghouse," was constructed on her deck amidships to accommodate the additional crewmembers.

Although many other shipowners ridiculed Minch for building an iron ship, he was clearly vindicated by the record established by the *Onoko* over the next three decades. By 1899, she was being referred to as "one of the most remarkable steamers on the lakes."[12] In ten of her first sixteen years of service, she carried the largest cargoes of any boat on freshwater "and [had] earned money enough to load her down."[13] Before the end of the century, the *Onoko* set records for iron ore, wheat, and corn, then broke her own records on subsequent trips. She could carry 3,073 tons of ore, or about 110,000 bushels or wheat or corn, and her powerful engine made it possible for her to tow a barge consort that added to her per-trip carrying capacity. At $3 a ton for ore and 14-cents a bushel for grains, Minch and his investors could afford to smile at those who still found fault with the *Onoko's* appearance. Convinced of the future of iron freighters, Minch's group contracted with Globe in 1884 for the construction of the *William Chisholm*, and in 1885 for the *J. H. Deveraux*, both of which were slightly smaller than the *Onoko*.

Some industry insiders, including officials at Globe Ship Building, predicted that ships would stay the size of the *Onoko*, arguing that vessels larger than her would be too costly to load and unload.[14] In fact, for a period of more than five years, the *Onoko* remained the largest ship built at the Globe yard. It is hard to explain that conservative thinking. At several of the ports on the upper lakes, chute-type ore loading docks already existed that were capable of rapidly loading vessels the size of the *Onoko*. In November of 1870, for example, the *R. J. Hackett* had loaded 1,065 tons of ore at Escanaba in only one hour and forty-five minutes. At that rate, the larger *Onoko* could have been loaded in something in the neighborhood of six hours, certainly not an excessive period of time for that era.

Unloading would have taken considerably longer, but there, too, major strides had been made prior to the launching of the *Onoko*. In 1880, the first steam-powered Brown Hoist unloader had been installed at Erie, Pennsylvania. Developed by Alexander Brown, the Brown Hoist still depended on laborers to hand-fill the buckets, or barrels, that were lowered into the hold of a ship. Once filled, however, the barrels were lifted from the hold and dumped into waiting rail cars or storage piles by cables controlled from a central point. The system could be set up so that cargo could be unloaded simultaneously from each hatch of a ship.

The year after the *Onoko* was launched, a similar unloading system went into operation at the South Chicago docks of the Illinois Steel Company. Developed by Robert Aspin, the Champion Ore Hoist consisted of several derrick-type hoists lined up side-by-side on the dock and spaced so they would match up with the hatches of ships unloading there. Tubs lowered through the hatches were filled by hand, but then a steam engine hoisted the tubs and emptied them into a trough that straddled the railroad tracks paralleling the dock. The ore could then be loaded directly into rail cars passing below the troughs.

Both the Brown and Champion hoists were significant improvements over previous unloading systems, which depended almost totally on manual labor, but unloading was still a painfully slow and laborious process. It often took longer to unload a ship than it did to move the ore from ports on the northern lakes to Erie, Cleveland, or Chicago. Shipowners were undoubtedly deeply troubled by the amount of time their valuable vessels spent tied up at the unloading docks.

At the same time, the *rate* at which cargo was loaded or

unloaded was unchanged, regardless of the size of the ship. Those who believed large vessels would be less efficient to load or unload than smaller ships failed to recognize that fact. If it took three days to unload 3,000 tons of iron ore from a ship the size of the *Onoko*, it would also take three days to unload three smaller ships each carrying 1,000 tons of ore. On a per-ton basis, the larger ship would spend the same amount of time at the dock as a smaller one. The larger ship would still be more efficient, because it could move the 3,000 tons of cargo down the lakes in a single trip, with a single crew. While that fact may not have been clear to people in 1882, it is a principle that guides the industry today: the greatest efficiency is achieved through the use of the largest vessel possible, taking into consideration the amount of cargo to be moved and the size restrictions imposed by the trade route. The *Onoko* was more efficient than the smaller ships she was in competition with, but less efficient than the larger ships that would eventually displace her as Queen of the Lakes.

Philip Minch died in 1887, and his son and heir, Captain Peter G. Minch, died in 1892. Their prosperous shipping company was taken over by the elder Minch's son-in-law, Henry Steinbrenner, and Henry's son, George M. Steinbrenner. In 1905, the Steinbrenners reorganized the fleet as Kinsman Marine Transit, the name denoting the family operation of the firm. At that time the plain, black stacks of the *Onoko* and other ships in the Kinsman fleet were adorned with a large letter "K." The "K" was subsequently replaced by an "S," reflecting the pivotal role of the Steinbrenner family in the development and operation of the fleet.

In 1915, the *Onoko* was in her thirty-fourth season of operations on the lakes, having outlived both Minches and most of the critics who had claimed that her iron hull would not be durable. Though she had been the largest ship on the lakes when launched, her Queen of the Lakes title had long since passed successively to the line of freighters following in her wake. She was one of the oldest bulk freighters in service and less than half the size of the ships that were in the forefront of the industry.

With one exception, her career on the lakes had been without incident. On May 16, 1896, the *Onoko* had been involved in a tragic accident off Racine, Wisconsin, on Lake Michigan. While operating in heavy fog, she collided with and sank the schooner *Mary D. Ayer*. Five of the *Ayer*'s crewmen died as a result of the collision. The iron hull of the *Onoko* was virtually undamaged.

Then, on September 14, 1915, the aging workhorse was downbound on Lake Superior after loading 109,600 bushels of wheat at Duluth for delivery to Toledo, Ohio. When only seventeen miles out of the Duluth harbor, engineering personnel were startled to discover water coming up through the deck grates in the *Onoko*'s engine room. The engineer on watch immediately notified the captain and started the pumps in an effort to control the flooding. In short order it was obvious that the pumps could not keep up with the deluge coming through the hull. With water rising ever higher in the engine room, the captain had no recourse but to give the signal to abandon ship. As the stern of the *Onoko* sank ever lower into the calm waters of Lake Superior, the ship's lifeboats were launched and the sixteen crewmembers and one passenger rowed slowly away from the disabled vessel.

After 1905, the stack of the *Onoko* bore the "K" that identified her as part of the Kinsman fleet operated by Henry and George Steinbrenner, heirs to the shipping line begun by Philip Minch. Later, the Steinbrenners replaced the "K" with an "S," to emphasize the role they played in the continued operations of the former Minch fleet. (Author's collection)

The *Str. Renown*, a tanker operated by Standard Oil, was nearby at the time and picked up the occupants of the two lifeboats. When the flooding in the engine room reached the blistering hot boilers of the *Onoko*, the boilers exploded with a loud roar, emitting billowy clouds of steam. On the deck of the *Renown*, the stunned survivors of the *Onoko* and their rescuers watched in hushed silence as the once-proud ship shuddered slightly and plunged stern-first to the bottom of the lake. In a matter of seconds, she was gone.

Word of the loss of the *Onoko* was flashed around the lakes. At Cleveland, Henry and George Steinbrenner and the employees of Kinsman Transit were staggered by the news. With only sketchy details to go on, the Steinbrenners at first concluded that the ship may have sunk as the result of sabotage. War had broken out in Europe several months earlier, and while the U.S. remained neutral in the spreading conflict, the wheat the *Onoko* carried on her final voyage was consigned to the British and their allies.[15] The Steinbrenners feared that extremists who violently opposed any U.S. aid to the warring factions, or Americans of German or Austrian extraction—and there were many of them in the Duluth area—had somehow sabotaged their ship.

During the ensuing investigation, however, sabotage was ruled out as the cause of sinking. It was generally agreed that one of the *Onoko*'s hull plates had rusted through or that engine vibration had caused a plate to drop off. With the hulk lying in 340 feet of water, no firm conclusion could be reached. As the *Onoko* was stricken from the roll of ships in the U.S.

Stanton's drawing of the ill-fated *Western Reserve*. The steel-hulled Minch freighter broke in half and sank during a freak August storm on Lake Superior in 1892. Captain Peter Minch, his wife, and two children were aboard the ship at the time for a summer holiday trip up the lakes. They were among the thirty-one victims of the sinking of the big freighter. With the death of Captain Minch, the Minch shipping interests were taken over by Henry Steinbrenner, who had married Captain Minch's sister. (Author's collection)

Great Lakes fleet, the only consolation for the Steinbrenners was that no lives had been lost in the mishap.

The kinsmen of the Steinbrenner-Minch clan had not always been so fortunate. When Captain Peter Minch was still at the helm of the company, he had contracted for the construction of the fleet's first steel-hulled freighter, the steamer *Western Reserve.* Launched at Cleveland Ship Building in 1890, she was slightly larger than the *Onoko* and one of the most modern ships on the lakes, certainly the pride of the Minch fleet. On August 28, 1892, the *Western Reserve* departed Cleveland light under the command of Captain Albert Myers, en route to Two Harbors, Minnesota, to take on a load of ore. Aboard as a passenger for a summer holiday was Captain Peter Minch, who had succeeded his father as president of the shipping company. The Minch party also included his wife, their two children, his wife's sister—Mrs. Jacob Englebry—and Mrs. Englebry's young daughter. The holiday entourage was rounded out by the presence of Carl Myers, the captain's son.

Storm warnings had been posted when the *Western Reserve* departed the Soo on the afternoon of August 30, and while they were still in Whitefish Bay the ship had begun to roll in the growing seas. Captain Myers moved his ship out of the traffic lanes and dropped anchor, intending to ride out the storm "on the hook" and spare the passengers an uncomfortable ride on Lake Superior. When the wind and waves showed no signs of increasing in strength, Myers and Minch agreed that their ship could easily handle the seas. They weighed anchor and pressed on toward Two Harbors.

The storm grew in intensity as they passed Whitefish Point and made their haul toward the northwest. At about 9 p.m., all aboard heard a deafening roar and felt the ship quiver. Captain Myers looked out the rear windows of the pilothouse to see the deck of his ship cracking and tearing just forward of the stern cabin. He hurriedly sounded the alarm to abandon ship.

The next morning, personnel at the Deer Park lifesaving station near Grand Marais, Michigan, west of Whitefish Point, saw a lone man staggering down the beach toward them. It was Harry Stewart, a wheelsman from the *Western Reserve* and the only survivor of the tragedy played out on the storm-tossed lake the previous evening. Stewart reported that twenty-seven of the thirty-two people aboard the *Western Reserve* had managed to get off in the two lifeboats in the minutes after the ship started to break apart. The violent seas swamped one of the lifeboats almost immediately, however, and only two of its occupants managed to climb into the other boat, a small wooden yawl that was already overcrowded.

The nineteen people who found themselves crowded into the surviving lifeboat included Captain Myers, Captain Minch, all of the women and children, and eleven crewmembers, including Stewart. The *Reserve* sank as the survivors rowed away into the black night, their lifeboat battered incessantly by the huge waves. The small boat was in constant danger of being swamped by the seas, and half her occupants rowed while the other half bailed.

At daybreak they could see that they were only a mile offshore, and they rowed toward the beach with renewed strength. Then, as the nineteen cold, drenched survivors of the *Western Reserve* pulled steadily toward the safety of the shoreline, the small boat was swamped and capsized by a towering wave, and they were flung into the water. Stewart struggled to put on a cork-filled lifebelt that had floated free from the swamped boat. Looking about, Stewart saw that only he and Captain Myers's son were still afloat. Together, they started to swim toward the beach, but young Carl Myers soon tired and sank from sight. Alone, Stewart swam on.

The Minch freighters *Onoko* and *Western Reserve* both met tragic ends on Lake Superior. The *Onoko* sank near Duluth, while the *Western Reserve* went to the bottom just west of Whitefish Point. (Author's collection)

The bodies of Captain Minch, three of his family members, and eight crewmembers washed up on the beach in the aftermath of the unusually violent August storm. No other bodies were ever recovered. Lake Superior had claimed thirty-one lives.[16] The Great Lakes shipping community was rocked by word of the sinking of the *Western Reserve.* In Cleveland, the Minch and Steinbrenner families gathered to mourn the loss of their loved ones and the great steel ship they had all been so proud of.

Based on the detailed account of the sinking provided by Harry Stewart, industry officials initially thought the ship broke up because she was not carrying enough water ballast when she went out into the storm. Riding high in the water, the *Western Reserve* would have tended to teeter-totter on top of the huge waves, placing great stress on her hull. Shipbuilders and shipowners were still debating the cause of the sinking two months later when, on the night of October 28, the steel freighter *W. H. Gilcher* sank with all hands during an intense Lake Michigan storm. The *Gilcher* was virtually a twin of the *Western Reserve.* She had been under construction at Cleveland Ship Building when the Minch freighter had been launched.

Suspecting that the loss of the two ships under similar circumstances was more than merely a coincidence, investigators began to look closely at the steel that had been used in their construction. Testing eventually proved that the Bessemer steel was too brittle to stand up under the twisting and pounding a ship had to endure in heavy seas. Under stress, the steel plates and framing members would develop small cracks that could eventually lead to hull failure.

Some shipbuilders advocated abandoning steel altogether and returning to building iron ships. While many people in the industry had questioned the strength of iron, tests had shown that hulls like that of the *Onoko* were probably more resilient to bending, twisting, and deterioration than ships like the *Western Reserve* and *Gilcher* that were built of Bessemer steel.[17] Refinements in the steelmaking process soon produced plates and frames better suited to shipbuilding than those used on the two ill-fated freighters, but the problem of brittle steel continued to plague the industry until well after World War II. As late as 1966, the loss of the *Daniel J. Morrell,* a 600-foot freighter built in 1906, was attributed to structural failure resulting from brittle steel (See Chapter 16). Despite the ongoing problems caused by substandard steel, shipbuilders declined to return to the use of iron. As a result, the *Onoko* went into the record books as the only iron-built Queen of the Lakes.

Notes

1. Dana Thomas Bowen, *Memories of the Lakes* (Cleveland: Freshwater Press, 1969), 18.
2. James Clary, *Ladies of the Lakes* (Lansing: Michigan Department of Natural Resources, 1981), 105–106.
3. J. B. Mansfield, ed., *History of the Great Lakes*, vol. I (Chicago: J. H. Beers and Co., 1899; reprint, Cleveland: Freshwater Press, 1972), 408–409.
4. Ibid., 692.
5. Interestingly, the first iron passenger steamer built at Wyandotte was christened *Queen of the Lakes*, although it was only a diminutive 108 feet long—indicating that the title was not always associated with long ships, as it is today.
6. Gordon P. Bugbee, "The Life and Times of the Bessemer Fleet, Part I," *Telescope* 27, no. 2 (March–April 1978): 41.
7. Dates given for the *Onoko*, and those used throughout the book, represent the period during which the vessel was Queen of the Lakes, generally from their date of launching until the launching of the next longer ship.
8. Harry Benford, Kent Thornton and E. B. Williams, "Current Trends in the Design of Iron Ore Ships," paper presented at the meeting of the Society of Naval Architects and Marine Engineers, June 21-22, 1962, 19.
9. Gordon P. Bugbee, "Iron Merchant Ships - Part Two," *Telescope* 11 no. 3 (March 1962): 50.
10. Richard Wright, *Freshwater Whales* (Kent, OH: Kent State University Press, 1969), 5.
11. *Telescope* 15, no. 4 (April 1966): 82.
12. Mansfield, 408.
13. Ibid., 409.
14. Norman Beasley, *Freighters of Fortune* (New York: Harper and Brothers, 1930), 183.
15. *Telescope* 5, no. 6 (June 1956): 5–6.
16. James P. Barry, *Ships of the Great Lakes* (Berkeley: Howell-North Books, 1973), 145–47.
17. Dwight Boyer, *Great Stories of the Great Lakes* (New York: Dodd, Mead and Company, 1966), 63–68.

2

A Railroad Steamer

In some ways, the iron-hulled *Onoko* was the vestige of a bygone era even before her launching in February of 1882. Three years earlier, the first steel ocean vessel had been built in England. It had proved so successful that by 1880 ten percent of all British steamers under construction were being constructed of steel.[1]

On the Great Lakes, the first steel-hulled ship was built only after development of the Bessemer process made relatively low cost steel available around 1885. Once again, it was Globe Ship Building that brought the new technology to the lakes. The steel-hulled *Str. Spokane* was launched at Globe on June 6, 1886, for Captain Thomas Wilson and a group of investors. The ship was originally designed to be built of iron, although it had still not found favor with insurance underwriters. When Captain Wilson found out he could have the vessel built of steel without great additional cost, he authorized Globe to go ahead. Not wanting to take the time to redesign the ship, however, she was built to the specifications established for an iron hull, even though steel was considerably stronger. As a result, the *Spokane* was considered to have been about twenty percent stronger than steel-hulled ships built in subsequent years. At just over 264 feet in length and 1,741 gross tons, the *Spokane* was a little smaller than the *Onoko*, but the lines of her hull were much the same.

In 1892, the *Spokane* became the first steel ship on the lakes to be lengthened when a sixty-foot section was added to her cargo hold at Cleveland Ship Building. Placed in a drydock, the rivets in her hull were removed near midships so that the forward half of the hull could be winched ahead on greased ways. Nine-inch hawsers were attached to the bow section and run to winches at the forward end of the drydock, and two teams of horses were used to turn capstans supplying power to the winches. The new section increased the *Spokane*'s gross tonnage to 2,356, slightly more than that of the *Onoko*. While the innovative lengthening made the *Spokane* a little longer than the *Onoko*, she was never the Queen of the Lakes. Four years before the *Spokane*'s lengthening, the title had already passed to a series of package freighters launched at Buffalo, New York, by the Union Dry Dock Company.

In many ways, the package freighters were a cross between passenger steamers and bulk freighters. Like the passenger steamers, most of the package freighters were owned and operated by railroads as an adjunct to their rail lines that terminated at Great Lakes ports. They were designed for freight service, though a few had limited accommodations for passengers. Like the bulk freighters, the package freighters had hatches on their decks, though not as many. The deck hatches were augmented by gangways in the sides of their hulls, similar to those found on the passenger steamers, through which cargo could also be loaded. The history of the package freighter is somewhat obscure, but they date to at least 1871, the year the wooden package freighter *William H. Tweed* was launched at the Union Dry Dock Company in Buffalo. By the mid-1880's, most of the major shipyards around the lakes had experience in building wooden or iron package freighters.

It was natural for the Union Dry Dock Company to develop particular expertise in building package freighters. Not only was the shipyard located in Buffalo, the western terminus for many of the early railroads carrying freight and passengers to the Great Lakes region, but the Union Steamboat Company had purchased twenty-five percent of the shipbuilding operation in 1872. The Union Steamboat Company was a subsidiary of the New York and Erie Railroad and operated a number of passenger and freight steamers on the lakes.

Late in 1884, Union Dry Dock had launched the first iron-hulled package freighter on the lakes, the three-hundred-foot *Tioga*. Less than two feet shorter than the *Onoko*, she was built for the Erie Railroad Transit Line. Captain Marcus Drake, the shipyard superintendent, and his staff were justly proud of the *Tioga*, but by the time she was launched they were already involved in an even more significant project. Union had been hired by the Anchor Line, the lake shipping connection of the Pennsylvania Railroad, to design and build a mammoth steel package freighter for their important service between Buffalo and Duluth. George B. Mallory had drawn the lines for the new ship, and when Captain Drake saw them for the first time he was convinced she would be both the most efficient and the most beautiful package freighter on the lakes.

The steel freighter that soon took shape in the yard on the banks of Buffalo Creek was a masterpiece of size and perspective. She had none of the heavy boxiness of bulk freighters like the *Onoko* or *Spokane*, but was, instead, a lean, sleek-looking vessel. Like the bulk freighters, she had a cabin and wheelhouse forward, but they sat on the main deck, rather than being perched atop a forecastle deck. In fact, the ship had no raised forecastle, just a long flat main deck stretching from her gracefully tapered bow to her elliptical stern. The forward cabin was balanced by a cabin of similar size near the ship's stern, while a third, larger cabin occupied the midship area, which was over the engine room. The midship cabin was topped by an extremely tall and slightly raked smokestack. In profile, the vessel had an aesthetic symmetry that both Captain Drake and her designer thought was far superior to that of the bulk freighters.

On September 4, 1886, the new package freighter was ready to be christened and launched. Officials of the railroad had chosen the name *Susquehanna* for their new vessel, honoring the town in northeastern Pennsylvania and the river on which it was located. With the traditional baptism of champagne, the $220,000 ship slid into the water with an appropriately large splash and much applause and cheering from what was described as "an immense concourse" of onlookers.[2]

STR. SUSQUEHANNA

326'6"x40'x16'
Queen of the Lakes
September 4, 1886 to July 7, 1887

The *Susquehanna* was worthy of the applause. At 326 feet, 6 inches in overall length, she was the new Queen of the Lakes. With a beam of 40 feet and a depth of 24 feet, the new leviathan was rated at 2,500 gross tons. The *Susquehanna* even looked like a queen. Her sleek, black hull appeared lean and sinewy, like the torso of a panther, and her impressive length was accented by sparkling white cabins and a band of white capping the hull. At bow and stern, white gunwales rose about three feet above the deck level, and they were joined by an attractive metal railing running the length of the deck.

The *Susquehanna* carried two masts, one just aft of the forward cabin and the other just forward of the aft cabin, adding to her symmetry. From her forward mast flew a large Anchor Line pennant, while the stern mast was adorned with a large American flag and a pennant bearing the new vessel's name.

Among the innovations in her design, the *Susquehanna* had anchor wells, or boxes, built into the sides of her hull just back from her bow. The wells allowed her two large wood-stock anchors to be carried inboard, reducing the likelihood that they would foul on dock structures. They also reduced the clutter at the bow, as the anchors were barely visible. Anchor wells eventually became standard on all freighers on the Great Lakes, but not until the 1920s.

To facilitate cargo loading and unloading, the *Susquehanna* had five large hatches spaced along her deck, including one forward of the pilothouse and one between the after cabin and the ship's stern. She also had two gangways built into each side of her hull. Unlike bulk freighters like the *Onoko* that had a single large, open cargo hold, the *Susquehanna* had four holds, two forward of the engine room and two aft of it, and each hold had two decks. A between deck, referred to simply as a 'tween deck, rested on beams halfway between the floor of the cargo holds and the deck. ('Tween decks are still common on package freighters; they allow freight to be stowed more easily, since it doesn't have to be stacked as high.) The after cargo hold also had a shaft alley running along the floor of the hold, boxing in the long steel shaft that connected the engine and the propeller.

The *Susquehanna* was designed to carry twenty-nine crewmen. The captain and both mates were housed in the forward cabin, which adjoined the wheelhouse. The after cabin included a private room for the chief engineer and double-occupancy rooms for the two assistant engineers, two oilers, two wheelsmen, two watchmen, and two lookouts. The cook, six firemen, and eight other crewmembers shared rooms in the midship house, which also contained the galley and dining room.[3]

The engineering personnel oversaw the operation and maintenance of the ship's "double expansion, inverted, vertical, direct acting, jet condensing, three-cylinder, compound engine, the first installed on the lakes."[4] Later referred to simply as a triple expansion engine, the three cylinder "up and downers" became the standard means of propulsion until steam turbines made their debut just before World War II. The powerful steam engine generated 1,050 horsepower and pushed the *Susquehanna* along at a very respectable fifteen miles an hour.

While her title as Queen of the Lakes was passed on to an even larger package freighter in less than a year, the *Susquehanna* was an efficient carrier and a favorite of boatwatchers for over three decades. While bulk freighters like the *Onoko* called at only a limited number of loading and unloading ports, the diverse *Susquehanna* might show up at virtually any port on the lakes, loading or unloading bulk, bagged, or crated cargo. One photo of the ship shows her moored at Houghton, Michigan, preparing to take on a load of copper ingots and barrels of unsmelted copper.[5] She was an important vessel in the Anchor Line fleet that at the turn of the century included the passenger steamers *India*, *China*, and *Japan* and the steel freight steamers *Alaska*, *Lehigh*, *Clarion*, *Codarus*, *Schuylkill*, and *Mahoning*, in addition to seven smaller, wooden steamers.[6]

In 1917, after the U.S. had entered World War I, the aging *Susquehanna* joined a long line of freighters taken to saltwater to aid in the war effort. Too large to pass through the diminu-

The *Str. Susquehanna*, a package freighter launched in 1886 for the Pennsylvania Railroad's freight service between Buffalo and Duluth. The package freighters were developed by the railroads at a time when most of their rail lines extended no farther west than Buffalo. Large package freighters like the *Susquehanna* first appeared on the lakes about 1884, and most were gone by the end of World War I. (Institute for Great Lakes Research, Bowling Green State University)

The symmetrical profile of the *Susquehanna* is clearly evident in Stanton's drawing of the ship. While most of the bulk freighters built on the lakes after the 1869 debut of the *Hackett* had their engine rooms at the stern, the Anchor Line package freighter had a midship engine room. Stanton's drawing shows two gangways in the side of the hull that could be opened for use in loading cargo. The ship also had five hatches along her deck. (Author's collection)

tive locks of the Welland Canal, she was cut in half at the same yard where she had been built, then towed through the Welland to Lauzon, Quebec. At Davie Shipbuilding at Lauzon, the *Susquehanna* was rejoined, and she sailed under her own power out the St. Lawrence River to the Atlantic.[7]

After operating on the Atlantic for the American-flag Susquehanna Steamship Company for seven years, she was sold to Sunrise Steamship Company of London in 1923 and renamed *Papyrus.* While little information is available about her journeys under foreign flag, her new name suggests that she may have operated in the Mediterranean trade. In 1924, she changed hands again, purchased by the Antiva Shipping Company of Callao, Peru. Renamed *DeCosta,* she was operated in the South American trade for a year. In 1925, Antiva Shipping re-registered her at Halifax, Nova Scotia, and renamed her *Papyrus* for a second time.

In 1926, after serving under five different shipping companies and four flags, the former Queen of the Lakes bore evidence of more than four decades of service. Her diverse career came to an end under the shipbreaker's torch in Italy, far from the familiar waters of the Great Lakes that had first wetted her hull.[8]

Notes

1. Milo M. Quaife, *Lake Michigan* (New York: Bobbs-Merrill, 1944), 167.
2. "Susquehanna Launched," *Marine Record,* September 9, 1886.
3. Details on the design have been derived from the vessel's original plans, now part of the American Ship Building Collection at the Institute for Great Lakes Research, Bowling Green State University.
4. Ibid.
5. Frederick Stonehouse, *Keweenaw Shipwrecks* (AuTrain, MI: Avery Color Studios, 1988), 29.
6. J. B. Mansfield, ed., *History of the Great Lakes,* vol. I (Chicago: J. H. Beers and Co., 1899; reprint, Cleveland: Freshwater Press, 1972), 458.
7. She may also have been either shortened sixty feet or lengthened twenty-four feet at Lauzon. Reports differ, but it is more likely that she would have been shortened.
8. Ship Biography, Institute for Great Lakes Research, Bowling Green State University.

3

The Union Twins

If the plaudits that attended the launching of the *Susquehanna* seemed more subdued than usual for a Queen of the Lakes, it was probably because everyone attending the ceremonies had walked past the partially completed hulls of two ships that were actually bigger than the new Anchor Line freighter. Even the Anchor Line and Pennsylvania Railroad officials present for the launching appeared slightly uncomfortable, and several commented under their breaths that they felt as if they were in "hostile territory."

In a way, they were in the camp of the enemy. Union Dry Dock Company was partially owned by the Erie Railroad, the Pennsylvania Railroad's strongest competitor for the growing freight trade on the lakes. Prior to the launching of the *Susquehanna*, the largest package freighter in operation was the iron-hulled *Tioga*, owned by Erie's Union Steamboat Company. Since its launching in 1884, Erie officials had enthusiastically advertised the *Tioga* as the largest and most modern freight vessel serving the Great Lakes. It was a point of great pride for the railroad, and clearly an asset in attracting business for both its overland and steamboat services.

The ink had barely dried on the contract for construction of the *Susquehanna* before it was announced that the shipyard would be building not one, but two new package freighters for Erie's Union fleet. The ships would be virtually identical and, most importantly, they would be 24 feet, 1 inch longer than the *Susquehanna*. The significance of the announcement was not lost on anyone, least of all the other railroads and steamboat lines. It was a clear message: the Erie Railroad had not bought a twenty-five percent interest in a shipyard only to stand idly by while the yard built a record-breaking vessel for one of their competitors.

STR. OWEGO

350'7"x41'2"x13'7"
Queen of the Lakes
July 7, 1887 to December 3, 1892

The first of the two freighters was launched on July 7, 1887, less than a year after the *Susquehanna* made her debut. Christened *Owego* in honor of the city of Owego, New York, an important stop on Erie's railroad line, the grand new ship was just as sleek in appearance as the *Susquehanna*, despite its awe-inspiring dimensions. The *Owego* was 350 feet, 7 inches long and had a beam of 41 feet, 2 inches and a depth of 13 feet 7 inches. Wider, but several feet shallower, than the *Susquehanna*, the *Owego*'s gross tonnage was 2,615, compared to 2,500 for the previous Queen. Not only was she the biggest ship

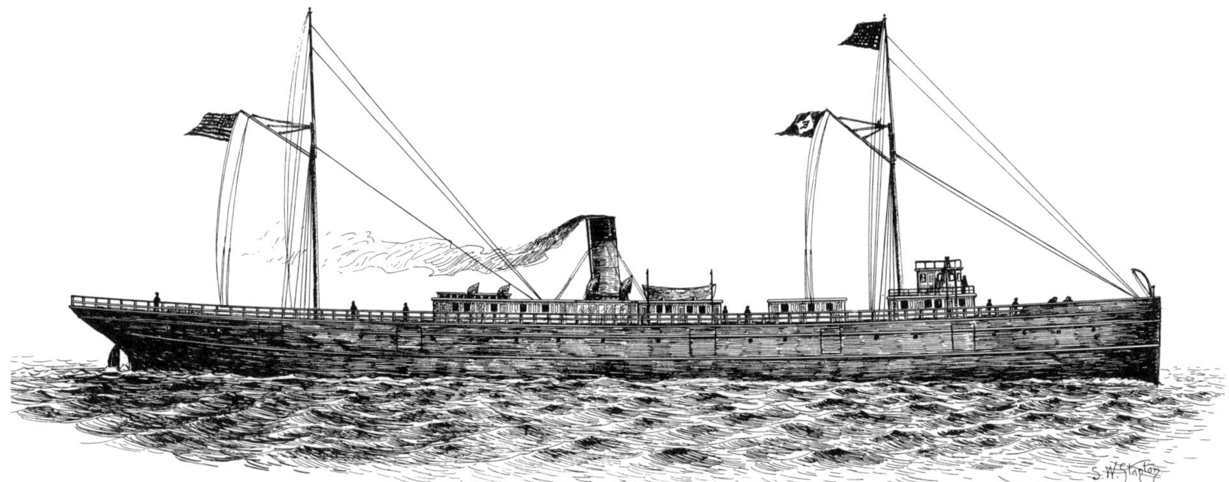

In 1887, the package freighter *Owego*, shown here in a Stanton drawing, replaced the *Susquehanna* as Queen of the Lakes. Built by the Erie Railroad for their Union Steamboat Company, the 350-foot steamer was easily identifiable because of the long sweep of its uncluttered fantail. While intended to operate in the grain trade between Chicago and Buffalo, the *Owego* proved to be too long to negotiate the upper reaches of the winding Chicago River. (Author's collection)

on the lakes, her sleek lines were more than merely pleasing to the eye. For almost a decade, the *Owego* and her sistership were generally regarded as the fastest freight vessels on the Great Lakes.[1] On a trip from Chicago to Buffalo, for example, the *Owego* set a record by averaging an astounding 16.4 miles per hour, a speed that few of today's bulk freighters could match.[2]

While the *Susquehanna*'s silhouette was pleasingly symmetrical, the cabins of the *Owego* had been pushed as far forward as possible on her deck. That resulted in more of a tapered look, with the mass of her structure tailing off into a long, clean afterdeck in the same way that the body of a fish narrows down toward its tail. The *Owego*'s design was much the same as that of the *Tioga*. Her wheelhouse was set atop the small forward cabin, well back from the bow. Just aft of the forward cabin was a second small cabin to house crewmembers. Over the midship engine room was a very large cabin, which included crew quarters, the galley, and the dining room. The midship house was topped by the eye-catching black and white striped smokestack, sloping gracefully backward like a dorsal fin. Like the *Susquehanna*, the *Owego* had two masts from which gaff-rigged sails could be set to provide auxiliary power.[3] Given her speed, it is likely that the sails were seldom set, but the masts would have done double-duty as booms for use in handling cargo.

It was a major marketing coup for the Union Steamboat Company to own the largest ship on the Great Lakes, but before the *Owego* went into the water company officials had discovered that big is not necessarily always best. The giant freighter had been intended to operate primarily in the grain trade between Chicago and Buffalo, but careful measurements made in the days just before her launching showed that the *Owego* would be too long to negotiate the narrow upper reaches of the river at Chicago where many of the grain terminals were located. Dismayed, and probably more than a little embarrassed by their *faux pas*, Union officials announced that the *Owego* would be placed in the grain and merchandise trade between Buffalo and Duluth, with only occasional trips to grain terminals at Chicago. The red-faced shipping executives also

The distinctive white-striped stack of the vessels operated by the Union Steamboat Company. At that time, most ships on the lakes had plain black smokestacks. (Author's collection)

ordered the shipyard to stop work on construction of the second freighter while they huddled to determine whether it would be feasible to shorten it forty feet. Work was already well underway on the second ship, however, and the decision was ultimately made to build her to the planned dimensions.[4]

STR. CHEMUNG

350'7"x41'2"x14'8"
Queen of the Lakes
February 29, 1888 to December 3, 1892

The *Chemung*, launched seven months after the *Owego*, on February 2, 1888, was named after the New York city and river of the same name. She was a twin of the *Owego*, except that she had a depth of only 13 feet, 7 inches, making her a little more than a foot shallower.

During the winter of 1897-98, the twins went back to the shipyard in Buffalo for rebuilding. Details of the rebuilding have been lost over time, but official documents updated when they went back into service in May of 1898 show that both had their net tonnage reduced by about 165 tons, although their gross tonnage was not affected.[5] The reduction is almost exactly the amount that would have resulted if the depth of their cargo holds had been reduced by one foot. That may suggest that the ships were originally built without 'tween decks, and the owners later decided to have them installed. Whatever changes were made, however, the cargo holds of both ships were slightly smaller after the rebuilding.

The *Chemung* went through another rebuilding during the winter of 1913–14. In addition to new boilers and a new draft system, she got a new propeller, a new electrical system, and her cabins were extensively refurbished. Before she went back into service in 1914, she was renamed the *George F. Brownell*, in honor of the attorney who served as vice president

A striking painting of the *Chemung*, sister ship to the *Owego*. Launched in 1888, the vessel was renamed *George F. Brownell* in 1914 after undergoing rebuilding. Both ships were sold off the lakes in 1915, when U.S. railroads were forced to dispose of their shipping lines. After being renamed the *Chemung* in 1916, the package freighter was sunk off the Spanish coast by an Austrian submarine during World War I. (The Great Lakes Historical Society)

of the Erie Railroad. This represented a departure from the traditional naming scheme the fleet had followed.

In 1914 and 1915, the federal government went on an anti-trust rampage that led to a provision being included in the Panama Canal Act of 1915 prohibiting railroads from owning steamship companies. Forced to divest themselves of their shipping line, the Erie Railroad sold both the *Owego* and *Brownell* off the lakes. They thus joined the Pennsylvania Railroad's *Susquehanna*, which had suffered the same fate. The *Owego* was purchased by Federal Operating Company, while the *Chemung* went to the Staten Island Shipbuilding Company, both of New York. The trip to the Atlantic Coast required that the ships be cut in half to transit the Welland Canal, a procedure carried out at Buffalo.

Both were subsequently rebuilt by their owners to deepen them for service on the oceans. The *Owego* came out on saltwater with a depth of just over twenty-four feet, while the *Chemung* was rebuilt to twenty-three feet. Interestingly, while the deepening raised the gross tonnage of both vessels to more than 3,060, their net tonnage actually dropped slightly. This means that the additional space within their hulls was not intended for cargo, at least not freight cargo.

While America managed to stay out of World War I until after the sinking of the *Lusitania* in the spring of 1917, many U.S. shipping companies were reaping healthy profits by carrying cargo for the various combatants. Return passages from Europe also presented them with opportunities to transport some of the thousands of people who were fleeing the war-torn continent, emigrés who were willing to pay premium rates for passage on any vessel bound for the U.S. or Canada. In all likelihood, the additional space created by deepening the *Owego* and *Browning* was devoted to passenger cabins.

After being rebuilt at Staten Island Shipbuilding, the *Brownell* was sold to the Harby Steamship Company of New York, which restored her original name. She went into service on the Atlantic in 1916 with the familiar name *Chemung* again painted on her bow and stern. Her service on the ocean would be short, however. On November 26, 1916, while crossing the Mediterranean on a voyage from New York to Genoa, Italy, the *Chemung* found herself in the sights of an Austrian submarine off Cabo de Gata, Spain. It was not a fair fight. The defenseless freighter came under attack by both gunfire and torpedoes from the U-boat, and in a matter of minutes her fate was sealed. Ignored by the submarine, the crew abandoned ship and watched the *Chemung* plunge to her watery grave as they rowed away from the scene.[6]

The *Owego* survived the war and continued to operate on the Atlantic under U.S. flag until sold in 1923 to Brewster and Company of Seattle, Washington. Taken through the Panama Canal to the Pacific, the *Owego* was reflagged by her new owners in China in 1924 and her name changed to *Yin Tung*. A prominent China trader for the balance of her career, she sailed under Brewster colors until 1927, when she was sold to the first of two Chinese shipping firms that would own her. They again changed her name, and she became the *Ting On*. Sometime prior to 1944, the aging former Queen of the Lakes changed hands for a final time, and with it came a fourth name. When they registered their new vessel in Shanghai, the Chi Ping Steamship Company called her the *Voo Yang*.

Records on the *Owego*'s service in China are scarce and somewhat contradictory. One report indicates that she sank in China in 1944, possibly a victim of World War II Pacific combat. A second source has her continuing in operation until being scrapped in 1955 after sixty-nine years of total service, including an astonishing thirty-nine years on saltwater. It is possible, of course, that the *Voo Yang* was sunk during World War II, but was subsequently salvaged and returned to service following the war.

If she went to the shipbreakers in 1955, it is unlikely that that any of those involved in dismantling her would have been aware of her colorful career.[7] They would not have known that until 1916 she had a twin sister, or that she had once been revered as Queen of the Lakes.

Notes

1. Rev. Peter Van Der Linden, ed., *Great Lakes Ships We Remember II* (Cleveland: Freshwater Press, 1984), 60.
2. John O. Greenwood, *Namesakes, 1900–1919* (Cleveland: Freshwater Press, 1986), 156.
3. Details derived from drawings in the American Ship Building Collection, Institute for Great Lakes Research, Bowling Green State University.
4. *Marine Record*, July 7, 1887.
5. Gross tonnage is really a volumetric measurement, not a weight. It is arrived at by calculating the total cubic footage of the vessel and dividing by 100, assuming that 100 cubic feet of space would contain one long ton of cargo (2,240 pounds). In calculating net tonnage, on the other hand, only those areas of the ship actually intended for the carriage of cargo are measured. Machinery spaces, passenger and crew quarters, storerooms, and spaces devoted to navigation of the vessel are not included in the net tonnage measurement; this dimension is, therefore, always smaller than a vessel's gross tonnage.
6. Greenwood, 154.
7. Ship Biographies, Institute for Great Lakes Research, Bowling Green State University.

4

A World's Fair Whale

The Chicago World's Fair, known officially as the Columbian Exposition, opened its gates on October 23, 1892. Over the next twelve months, millions of visitors would marvel at the diverse exhibitions comprising what came to be known as the "White City," a stunning celebration of the four-hundredth anniversary of Christopher Columbus's discovery of the New World.

Many new products were unveiled for exposition-goers, including caramel-coated popcorn, called Cracker Jacks, and Adolph Coor's Golden Select beer. Visitors could choose to eat at a variety of restaurants, including a unique self-service eatery that was being referred to as a "cafeteria."

There were attractions at the World's Fair to delight virtually all of the senses. One of the most popular was a giant Ferris wheel carrying riders 250 feet into the air, higher than most people had ever been off the ground before. More down-to-earth entertainment was provided by "Little Egypt," a dancer purportedly imported to the exposition from Persia. Women in the audience were shocked by her "hoochee-coochee dance," during which she made suggestive, undulating movements while waving a handkerchief in each hand. The reactions of the men in her audience were not recorded.

A centerpiece of the exposition was the display of full-size replicas of the three ships that had brought Columbus to America—the famous *Nina*, *Pinta*, and *Santa Maria*. While they were viewed as curiousities by those attending the Columbian Exposition, the three surprisingly small sailing ships proved to be less popular than an enormous steamboat built to ferry fair-goers from downtown Chicago to the fairgrounds at Jackson Park. So unusual was the new vessel that it rapidly became one of the highlights of the exposition.

Named, appropriately, the *Christopher Columbus*, the passenger ship was built for the World's Fair Steamship Company by the American Steel Barge Company of Superior, Wisconsin,[1] and reportedly cost $360,000.[2] When she was launched on December 3, 1892, the 362-foot steel steamer claimed the title Queen of the Lakes from the *Owego* and *Chemung*.

STR. CHRISTOPHER COLUMBUS

362'x42'x24'
Queen of the Lakes
December 3, 1892 to April 29, 1893

The American Steel Barge Company had been established in 1890 to build the unusual type of tow barges and steamers designed by Captain Alexander McDougall. McDougall had begun his sailing career at the age of sixteen as a deckhand aboard the schooner *Edith.* By the time he was twenty-six, the native of Scotland was appointed captain of the Anchor Line package freighter *Thomas A. Scott*, having worked his way up through the hawsepipe over his ten years on the lakes.

From 1878 to 1881, McDougall served as master on the wooden bulk freighter *Hiawatha*, operated by Captain Thomas Wilson's Wilson Transit Company. The powerful, 236-foot steamer often towed one or two barges behind it, a practice that had emerged first in the lumber trade as a way for shipowners to maximize the return on their investment in an expensive steam engine. The barges were not easy to tow, however. Their boxy hulls would often not follow cleanly in the wake of the ship towing them, tending instead to weave back and forth like an oversized sea serpent. During his service on the *Hiawatha*, McDougall conceived the idea for a new type of barge that would track well behind a steamer and offer little resistance to the sea. On May 24, 1881, he was granted a U.S. patent for a tow boat featuring a rounded deck and a tapered bow and stern.[3]

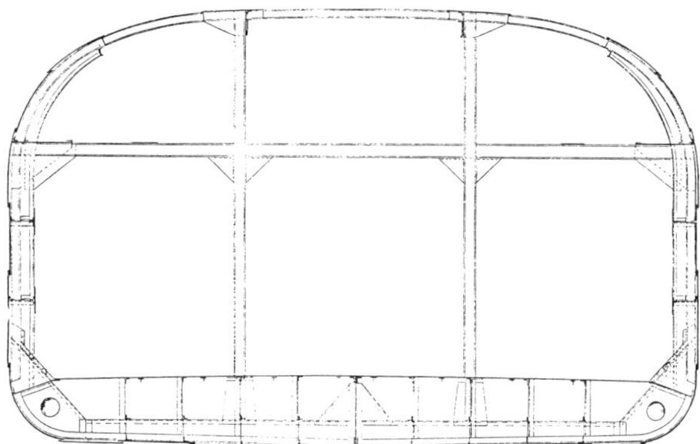

A midship section of one of Captain Alexander McDougall's patented whalebacks, clearly showing the rounded deck. Rounded decks, along with severely tapered bows and sterns, were designed to make the streamlined vessels cut through the water more cleanly. (Author's collection)

The shipping world did not beat a path to his door to take advantage of the new design, so in 1888, with the financial assistance of Captain Wilson, McDougall himself built a prototype barge at a cost of $40,000.[4] Launched at Duluth on June 23, 1888, the 191-foot steel barge was simply named *101.* It was the first large ship and the first steel vessel built at Duluth.[5] The *Duluth Evening Herald* proclaimed it a ship "destined to revolutionize the carrying of heavy lake freight."[6]

The *101* was described as "a great cigar of steel," and it was said that it resembled Captain Nemo's submarine *Nautilus* in Jules Verne's *20,000 Leagues Under the Sea* more than it did any Great Lakes ship.[7] Many people commented that the tapered bow of *101* looked like the snout of a pig, and all too often McDougall heard his sleek new barge referred to as a "pigboat." Others likened the curved deck to the back of an immense whale, a description that McDougall did not find altogether displeasing. In time, the term "whaleback" came into general use to describe the new type of vessel.

Below the water, the barge looked like the *Onoko* and other modern freighters of the day. Above the water, however, *101* was a genuinely unique creation. The deck of the barge was rounded, so that it looked like the top of a long steel cylinder. Instead of the normal rectangular deckhouses, McDougall's vessel had turrets near the bow and stern, each eight feet in diameter and seven feet high. The after turret served as the wheelhouse and was topped with a wooden pilothouse.[8]

McDougall hired the tug *Record* to tow the strange looking barge from Duluth to Two Harbors, Minnesota, where it loaded 1,200 tons of iron ore for delivery to Cleveland. Captain McDougall was an enthusiastic passenger on that maiden voyage. While he may have been pleased with the way *101* performed, he was undoubtedly taken aback by the derisive remarks that greeted his new invention all along its route.

With McDougall's last dollar sunk into construction of barge *101*, Captain Wilson arranged for him to travel to New York and present his plans for an even larger barge to Colgate Hoyt, an associate of John D. Rockefeller. In addition to owning Standard Oil Company, Rockefeller had extensive mining interests in the Lake Superior region. Aware that shipping companies on the lakes were having difficulty building enough new vessels to handle the increasing demand for ore, Rockefeller agreed to purchase McDougall's patents for the whaleback and set up the American Steel Barge Company. Captain McDougall received $25,000 in cash, twenty percent of the stock in the new company, a seat on the board of directors, and free rein to run the shipyard. Two whaleback barges were put into service in 1889, and two more were completed early in 1890. Then, on June 9, 1890, McDougall oversaw the launching of the first self-propelled whaleback, a 277-foot steel steamer named after Colgate Hoyt.

From the launching of *101* in 1888 until 1898, the shipyard flourished, turning out a total of forty whalebacks.[9] Among them were twenty-two barges that, as McDougall had predicted, were remarkably easy to tow. The *Colgate Hoyt* was one of seventeen steam-powered whaleback freighters built at the West Superior yard. They proved to be extremely seaworthy and seem to have handled better in heavy seas than any other vessels on the lakes.

The most unique ship ever built at the yard, however, was clearly the *Christopher Columbus.* McDougall's shipyard beat out several competitors for the right to build the passenger steamer for the Chicago World's Fair. It was a victory in which many residents of Duluth and Superior took great pride. They had long ago tired of the derisive nicknames attached to the unique whalebacks. "I wonder what the cranks, the kickers, the snarlers, and the new idea haters think of the success of whaleback managers now?" asked one resentful reporter from Superior when word came that McDougall had won the World's Fair contract.[10]

McDougall had actually won the competition with a flamboyant proposal to build a massive twin-screw whaleback steamer that would be fully 500 feet long—a mind-boggling 150 feet longer than the *Owego* and *Chemung.* But in the months between winning the right to build the World's Fair steamer and actually signing the contract for the *Christopher Columbus,* McDougall's plans were significantly scaled down, though we don't know why. It may have been the result of McDougall's realization of the enormous risks inherent in attempting to build a ship so large, or he may have bowed to pressure from the conservative financiers who were putting up the money to construct the boat. That syndicate included John D. Rockefeller and experienced shipping officials from Lehigh Valley Transportation Company, Union Steamboat Company, and Western Transit. Regardless of what, or who, changed McDougall's mind, he soon suggested that he might build two 350-foot boats, instead of the 500-foot gargantuan.[11]

When the contract between American Steel Barge and the World's Fair Steamship Company was finally signed on August 26, 1892, however, it provided for construction of a single 362-foot ship. American Steel Barge's architectural drawings identified the ship as a "World's Fair Passenger Steamer." The keel was laid on September 7, 1892, and with as many as six hundred workers employed in her construction, she was launched just three months later.[12]

The launching of the unusual passenger steamer on the afternoon of Saturday, December 3, 1892, was viewed as a major event in the twin ports of Duluth and Superior. The local newspaper reported that in addition to the hundreds of local residents who turned out to see the new ship slide into the water, eight special railroad cars brought dignitaries from New York, Milwaukee, Chicago, and Minneapolis. Those notables included "capitalists," World's Fair commissioners, and "prominent vessel, railroad, and elevator men."[13]

Winter comes early at the American lakehead, and there was about seven inches of ice in the slip adjacent to the shipyard where the *Christopher Columbus* was to slide into the water. The tug *Record* was hired to break up the ice on the morning of the launching, and the whaleback steamers *A. D. Thomson* and *Colgate Hoyt* used their propellers to churn the shattered ice out of the slip. The two freighters were then tied up bow to stern across the end of the slip to provide a platform from which McDougall and his guests would have an unobstructed view of the spectacular launching.[14]

When she went into service, the *Christopher Columbus* had a pristine white hull topped by two decks of cabins that were also painted white. Built with a midship engine room, her top deck was crowned by a massive cream-colored smokestack that belched clouds of coal-black smoke. Rather than sitting directly on top of the forty-two-foot-wide hull, the two decks of cabins were perched atop a series of seven steel turrets spaced down the middle of her main deck, looking like slices of a farmer's silo.[15]

Capable of carrying five thousand passengers at a time, the *Christopher Columbus* sported luxurious appointments rivalling the classic Greek architecture that dominated the Columbian Exposition. The *pièce de résistance* of her two passenger decks was a magnificant "Grand Saloon" furnished with velvet Wilton carpets and chairs and lounges covered in russet Turkish leather. Above the saloon deck was a promenade deck 287 feet long. The promenade deck cabin featured a remarkable skylight running down its center that was 151 feet long and 38 feet wide. At the forward end of the promenade deck was the wheelhouse and cabins for the captain and other officers.

Sixteen gleaming white lifeboats hung from davits atop the promenade deck for use in case of an emergency, although they would have been able to accommodate only a small percentage of the big ship's passengers. The *Christopher Columbus,* however, had been designed to be virtually unsinkable. She was built with a double bottom and thirty-two separate watertight compartments that would provide buoyancy and limit flooding if the hull were holed. Safety was a major consideration for her owners. Shipyard plans showing the watertight compartments bear a notation to the effect that the design would make her "practically indestructible by collision or fire."[16] The big steamer was also said to have been built with more frames and heavier steel than any boat in operation on the lakes. It is also reported that she was "a bewildering mass of straps, arches, and braces."[17]

At the core of the twenty-four-foot-deep hull of the *Christopher Columbus* were her powerful triple expansion steam engine and six massive Scotch boilers. With a total of 3,040 horsepower she moved through the water at about twenty miles an hour, an astonishing speed for that era. The steam engine also drove a generator that provided electricity for the ship's incandescent lighting system. At that time most ships still used kerosene lamps for lighting, but electric lights had

After the close of the Chicago World's Fair on October 30, 1893, the *Christopher Columbus* toured the lakes. The unique passenger steamer is shown here at Marquette. Tied up ahead of the whaleback is the *India*, a conventionally designed passenger steamer. The Marquette ore dock, the first chute-type loading dock on the lakes, can be seen to the left of the two steamers. (State Archives of Michigan)

been in use aboard a few ships since at least 1887, when they were first installed aboard Captain Wilson's *Yakima.*[18]

It is said that the unusual ship carried over two million passengers during her first year of operation. When the Columbian Exposition closed its gates in the fall of 1893, the popular vessel was purchased by the Hurson Line of Chicago to run day-excursions from Chicago to Milwaukee in competition with the Goodrich liner *Virginia.* When her new owners experienced financial difficulties, the *Christopher Columbus* was taken over by a group known as the Columbian Whaleback Steamship Company, and she continued on the Chicago to Milwaukee run.

Captain Charles Moody of Milwaukee commanded the whaleback steamer for an astonishing thirty-six years on the day-long trip up Lake Michigan. He had been sailing since the age of fourteen and had been a master on steamers since 1887. In 1896, Captain Moody went to work for Bessemer Steamship Company, and he soon developed into one of their favorite skippers. It is reported that he had "not cost the company one dollar while in service with them for damages."[19]

At nine o'clock each morning Captain Moody would gently maneuver the big ship away from her dock in Chicago and point her nose out onto the lake. She covered the eighty-five-mile trip in about five hours. Promptly at 4 p.m., after a two-hour layover at the dock in Milwaukee, Captain Moody sounded one short blast on the ship's deep-throated steam whistle—the signal to cast off her mooring lines for the trip back to Chicago. The voyages were always festive events for the throngs of passengers who crowded the decks of the *Christopher Columbus.* The ship generally carried a dance band, and there were a variety of deck games available to entertain those aboard. After the advent of motion pictures, films were regularly shown during the early evening passages back to Chicago.[20] It was not an expensive day's entertainment, either. Even in 1910, the average fare was only one dollar.[21]

In 1898, the *Christopher Columbus* was sold to Chicago and Milwaukee Transportation, a company set up by A. W. Goodrich of the well-known steamship company that bore his family's name. The famous passenger whaleback was subsequently chartered to the Goodrich Transportation Company.[22] During the winter of 1899–1900, Goodrich sent the *Christopher Columbus* to the shipyard at Manitowac, Wisconsin, to be overhauled and rebuilt. A third passenger deck was added, and she was painted in the familiar colors of the Goodrich fleet, with a black hull, white superstructure, and a brilliant red smokestack.[23]

In 1917, the career of the *Christopher Columbus* was marred by a tragic accident that occurred at Milwaukee. While departing that port on the afternoon of June 30, 1917, she was caught in the swift current at the junction of the Milwaukee and Menominee rivers and struck the dock on the far side of the river. Her long nose swept down the dock and rammed the steel supports for a hundred-foot-high watertower. The collision sheared off the legs of the tower, and the steel tank, filled with tons of water, crashed down on the deck of the *Christopher Columbus,* just forward of her pilothouse. A gaping twelve-foot hole was torn in the deck, and some passengers who were gathered on the foredeck to watch the departure from

Milwaukee were crushed by the impact. Others were washed overboard by the flood of water spilling from the tank. A total of sixteen persons were killed in the incident, while twenty others were seriously injured. The damaged ship went into drydock for repairs and did not return to service until the following season.[24]

Passenger service on the lakes dropped off during the Great Depression, and in 1931 the *Christopher Columbus* was laid-up. With the Goodrich fleet financially crippled by the Depression, three of their ships, including the passenger whaleback, were placed in a trustee's sale and auctioned off to a representative of the First Union Trust and Savings Bank of Chicago for the sum of only $512.90. At the time, the three ships were estimated to be worth two million dollars. In 1936, the results of the auction were set aside by another court, and the *Christopher Columbus* and one other Goodrich passenger vessel were subsequently sold to Manitowac Shipbuilding for the equally trivial sum of $6,500. Scrapping began almost immediately on the two ships, and the steel salvaged from their hulls was sold to Japan.[25]

After forty-four years, during which she undoubtedly carried more passengers than any vessel in the history of the Great Lakes, Alexander McDougall's strange-looking ship finally passed from the scene. It's likely that many of the millions of passengers who had ridden on the *Christopher Columbus* over the years remembered her nostalgically, and they no doubt mourned her passing.[26] While the giant whaleback steamer had been the longest ship on the lakes for less than five months, for many of those who had made passages on the unique vessel, she had been Queen of the Lakes throughout her many seasons of service.

Notes

1. Fraser Shipbuilding currently occupies the site, just down the shoreline from Barker's Island, where the last surviving whaleback, the *Meteor*, is now a marine museum.
2. John H. Wilterding, *McDougall's Dream: The American Whaleback* (Duluth: Lakeside Publications, 1969), 44.
3. Ibid., 4.
4. "In The Water," *Duluth Evening Herald*, June 23, 1888.
5. According to the *Marine Record*, February 9, 1888, the tapered ends for *101* were actually built in Cleveland by the firm of Pusey and Jones Co. The ends were then disassembled and shipped to Duluth for atttachment to the barge's midsection.
6. "The 101," *Duluth Evening Herald*, June 22, 1888.
7. "In The Water."
8. Ibid.
9. Two other whalebacks were built under McDougall's direction at Brooklyn, New York, and one at Everett, Washington.
10. "Talks Authoritatively," *Superior Daily Call*, May 2, 1892.
11. Ibid.
12. *Duluth Evening Herald*, December 3, 1892.
13. "Launching Tomorrow," *Duluth Evening Herald*, December 2, 1892.
14. Ibid.
15. Details on the design of the ship were found in drawings in the American Ship Building Collection, Institute for Great Lakes Research, Bowling Green State University.
16. *Duluth Evening Herald*, December 3, 1892.
17. It should be noted that virtually the same claim would be made for the White Star Line passenger steamer *Titanic*, launched two decades later. She sank on her maiden voyage after striking an iceberg in the North Atlantic, claiming over a thousand lives. Like the *Christopher Columbus*, the *Titantic* did not carry enough lifeboats for all of her passengers and crew.
18. Jewell R. Dean, "The Wilson Fleet, Freight Pioneers," *Inland Seas* 2, no. 3 (July 1946): 163.
19. J. B. Mansfield, ed., *History of the Great Lakes*, vol. I (Chicago: J. H. Beers and Co., 1899; reprint, Cleveland: Freshwater Press, 1972), 124.
20. James P. Barry, *Ships of the Great Lakes* (Berkeley: Howell-North Books, 1973), 157–58.
21. Wilterding, 44.
22. In 1909, she was sold to Goodrich Transportation.
23. Rev. Peter Van Der Linden, ed., *Great Lakes Ships We Remember* (Cleveland: Freshwater Press, 1979), 141.
24. Barry, 159.
25. Wilterding, 44.
26. Her powerful steam whistle was salvaged during scrapping and donated to the Manitowac County Museum Society. During World War II it was used as the City of Manitowac's air raid siren. Ironically, the scrap steel from the hull of the *Christopher Columbus* may have been used in the building of the aircraft carriers and airplanes that launched the surprise attack on Pearl Harbor and drew the U.S. into the war.

5

The Ore Boat Dynasty Begins

Iron ore mining was already an important industry in the Lake Superior region when the *Onoko* was launched in 1882. No one could have foreseen, however, the meteoric expansion the industry would experience over the next decade. In the *Onoko*'s inaugural season, total iron ore shipments from the Marquette and Menominee ranges in Michigan's Upper Peninsula amounted to just under two million tons. Production began at the Vermilion Range, west of Duluth, Minnesota, and the Gogebic Range, near Ashland, Wisconsin, in 1884, adding to the flow of ore off the northern lakes. In 1892, the first ore was shipped off the Mesabi Range, north of Duluth, which was destined to become the most productive in the world. Total shipments from the Mesabi mines in 1892 amounted to only 4,245 tons, literally a drop in the bucket in a year when total shipments on the Great Lakes approached nine million tons.[1]

The flow of iron ore through the St. Marys River became virtually "a river of red," and Orlando Poe, superintendent of the Soo Locks noted that, "the wildest expectations of one year seem absolutely tame the next."[2] In 1888, iron ore tonnages exceeded shipments of grain for the first time. After that, no other type of cargo ever approached the importance of iron ore for the Great Lakes shipping industry. The effect on the bulk fleets was profound. Both the number and size of ships engaged in the ore trade increased geometrically in the decade after the *Onoko* made her debut.

While the *Onoko*'s distinction as Queen of the Lakes passed to a succession of package freighters and then, in 1892, to the *Christopher Columbus*, she was also surpassed by many of the bulk freighters that followed her. Those ships, though smaller than the *Christopher Columbus* and package freighters like the *Owego* and *Chemung*, represent interesting and important chapters in the story of the continuing evolution of the Great Lakes bulk freighter that began in 1869 with the *Hackett*. While they missed, sometimes only by inches, the distinction of being Queen of the Lakes, they set the stage for the launching of bulk freighters that would eventually regain, and tenaciously hold onto, the coveted title.

In 1889, the Cleveland Iron Mining Company's *Str. Pontiac* succeeded the *Onoko* as the longest and largest bulk freighter on the lakes. Launched at the two-year-old yard of the Cleveland Ship Building Company, the steel-hulled *Pontiac* was 319 feet long, 41 feet wide, and had a depth of just over 12 feet. On her maiden voyage, she carried a record cargo of 2,849 tons of iron ore through the Soo.

Almost exactly a year after the launching of the *Pontiac*, a still-larger bulk freighter was completed at the Detroit Dry

Dock Company yard on the Detroit River at Wyandotte, Michigan. The *Maryland*, built for Inter Ocean Transportation of Milwaukee, was 332 feet long. With a beam of 42 feet and a depth of more than 20 feet, she was registered at 2,419 gross tons.

While the *Pontiac* had followed the lines of the *Hackett* and *Onoko*, the *Maryland* differed considerably. The Detroit Dry Dock Company had begun experimenting with ocean styling as early as 1871, and the *Maryland* contained elements of both ocean and Great Lakes designs.[3] The most obvious difference between the *Maryland* and the bulk freighters that preceded her was that her engine room was located almost amidships, rather than at the stern. In a very unusual arrangement, she also had five cabins spaced out along her deck, drastically reducing the amount of open deck area.

The following spring, Detroit Dry Dock launched yet another hybrid bulk freighter, one that was even larger than the *Maryland*. The *E. C. Pope* appears to have been built on speculation by the shipyard, but in September of 1891 she went into service for Eddy-Shaw Transit of Bay City, Michigan, managed by Lake Transit Company. The *Pope* was 332 feet long, 42 feet wide, and 24 feet deep, with a gross registered tonnage of 2,637. In her design, the engine room was moved nearer the stern than that of the *Maryland*, but she still had one hatch between her engine room and stern cabin. Relocation of the engine room allowed the center cabin to be eliminated, but she still had four cabins on her deck.

In many ways, the *Maryland* and *Pope* seem to be crosses between package freighters and bulk freighters, suggesting that the shipyard may have been attempting to develop a multipurpose vessel that could operate in both trades. In fact, like the *Susquehanna*, *Owego*, and *Chemung*, the *Maryland* and the *Pope* were both taken to saltwater during World War I and undoubtedly served there as package freight vessels.

By the early 1890s, more shipyards around the lakes were becoming involved in the construction of steel bulk freighters, but most were content to follow the more traditional styling that had been established with the *Hackett*. Minor design changes were regularly made, however, as the shipyards and shipowners attempted to perfect the bulk freighter, or at least make some modification that would make their vessels superior to those built by their competitors.

Several ships were launched in 1892 embodying one such design modification. The 350-foot *Maritana*, which became the longest bulk freighter on the lakes when she was launched on June 8, 1892, at Chicago Shipbuilding, belongs in this group. Built for the Minnesota Steamship Company of Duluth, the *Maritana* had the standard raised forecastle deck at her bow. Rather than having a forward cabin that adjoined or sat on top of the forecastle deck, however, her forward cabin was set back slightly from the forecastle, and there was a cargo hatch in the area in between.

The precise logic behind this design innovation is unknown, but it may have represented an attempt to increase the vessel's carrying capacity by allowing cargo to be stowed in the bow of the ship. Had the forward cabin adjoined the forecastle, the area within the bow would have been inaccessible. It may also have been considered desirable to move the pilothouse back from the bow in order to avoid its being battered by waves when steaming into heavy seas. Ships' decks were much lower to the water in those days, and a pilothouse perched atop the forecastle would certainly have taken a beating in a seaway. Once the decision had been made to move the pilothouse back from the bow, it would have been logical to place a hatch ahead of the pilothouse.

Regardless of its exact purpose, the forward hatch became quite common on ships built in the decade following the launching of the *Maritana*. The *Maritana*'s sistership, the *Mariposa*,[4] launched just eight days later at Globe Shipbuilding in Cleveland, followed the same design, which is not unusual given that Globe Iron Works owned both yards. On the same day that the *Mariposa* was launched, the F. W. Wheeler shipyard in West Bay City, Michigan, completed work on the *W. H. Gilbert*. It was two feet shorter than the *Maritana* and *Mariposa*, but it also had a hold forward of its wheelhouse cabin.

The *Maritana*, referred to as a "monster boat,"[5] immediately set a new cargo record, loading 4,800 tons of ore at Escanaba for delivery to Chicago—the largest cargo ever carried on the lakes at that time. This feat was made possible in part by the fact that she loaded at Escanaba; sailing from this port she could load to a deeper draft than vessels coming off Lake Superior and having to pass through the Soo Locks.

When the *Maritana* cleared Escanaba and her captain rang up "full ahead" on the engine order telegraph, the new ship began to shudder and heave. Thinking they might still be in shallow water, the captain cut back on her speed. Ten minutes later, when he was sure they were in deep water, he again signalled "full ahead," but the *Maritana* once more began to buck and jerk. To keep the big ship from shaking itself apart, the long trip down Lake Michigan had to be completed at half speed, a situation that did not please her irascible captain.

Shipyard personnel made some small adjustments in the *Maritana*'s engine while she was unloading, but after the vessel departed the dock and got up to full speed it was obvious to all aboard that the annoying problem had not been corrected. Most of the trip to Two Harbors, Minnesota, was made at reduced speed. There she took on a load of ore that would break the record for ships travelling through the Soo. When the ship limped into the Soo on the slow downbound journey to Lake Erie, the *Maritana*'s captain received a telegram ordering him to stop at Port Huron so that the ship could be examined by a team of marine designers.

After a careful inspection, the designers concluded that the *Maritana*'s 1,250-horsepower engine was too large for her light construction. Some corrections were eventually made, but she is reported to have been "jittery" throughout her long career, a source of great irritation for the captains and engineers who crewed her.[6] The *Maritana* was a testament to the fact that marine designers of the period were continually venturing into unproven territory. Through trial and error they gradually learned how to build bigger and better boats.

Before the shipping season began in 1893, a new bulk freighter had been launched at Detroit Dry Dock Company that was longer than the *Maritana* and *Mariposa.* The *Selwyn Eddy* was an addition to the Eddy-Shaw fleet that also included the *E. C. Pope.* The *Eddy* was 359 feet, 2 inches in length, more than 9 feet longer than the two Minnesota Steamship boats, but 2 feet shorter than the new *Christopher Columbus.* With a beam of 42 feet, 2 inches and a depth of almost 22 feet, she was measured at 2,846 gross tons. During the 1893 season she carried a record cargo of 3,686 tons of ore through the Soo,[7] breaking the record set previously by the *Maritana.* By that time, however, the *Eddy* was no longer the biggest bulk freighter on the lakes.

On April 29, 1893, a bulk freighter had been launched that regained the crown as Queen of the Lakes, the first such ship to hold it since the *Onoko.* From that auspicious day in 1893 until the present, that cherished honor has not been bestowed on any other type of vessel on the Great Lakes.

STR. S. S. CURRY

377'6"x45'x20'8"
Queen of the Lakes
April 29, 1893 to June 29, 1895

It was a Wheeler-built freighter that snatched the title away from the *Christopher Columbus* almost before the paint was dry on the passenger steamer's hull. The *S. S. Curry* was 377 feet, 6 inches long and measured at an almost astronomical 3,260 gross tons. Built for Hawgood-Avery Transit of Cleveland at a reported cost of $260,000, she was one of three sisters of the same length that would be launched at the West Bay City yard in 1893. The new freighter was named in honor of Captain S. S. Curry, president of the Metropolitan Iron and Land Company and head of the Norris Mine, then "the largest iron ore producing property in the world."[8]

Like the *Maryland* and *E. C. Pope* that were also built at the Wheeler shipyard, the *Curry* had her engine amidships. She was what saltwater sailors would call a "three-island" ship, with a cabin at her bow, a cabin and her stack amidships over the engine room, and a stern cabin. The forward house included the captain's and owner's cabins, said to have been "as handsome as those of the best passenger boats afloat on fresh water."[9]

The *Curry* was also one of the first ships on the Great Lakes to be equipped with power steering. Prior to the launching of the *Curry*, most vessels on the lakes, from small tugs right up to the largest passenger steamers and ore boats, used manual steering systems. Ropes, cables, or chains ran from a drum attached to the ship's wheel down each side of the ship to the rudder through a series of sheaves strung beneath the deck. As the wheel was turned, the drum would pay out cable on one side of the ship while taking up cable on the other, thereby turning the rudder to the desired angle. This manual steering system often involved a lot of manual labor. On a longer ship, the weight of the steering cables or chains, combined with friction occurring at every sheave, made it difficult to turn the heavy rudder. In a following sea, the force of waves against the rudder also required a strenuous effort by the wheelsman to hold the ship on course, and often the big spoked wheels could only be held steady by several seamen.

The *Curry*, however, was equipped with a Williamson steering engine that controlled the rudder by steam power, rather than by the physical force exerted by the wheelsman. The steam steering engine was connected to the shaft of the rudder by two heavy chains running from a drum on the steering engine through sheaves to each side of the tiller attached to the top of the rudder stock. When the steering system was activated by the wheelsman turning the wheel, the drum on the steam engine would turn one way or the other, paying out chain on one side of the tiller while taking up chain on the other. The brute force necessary to turn the heavy rudder was exerted by the steam engine, not by the wheelsman.[10] This innovation immediately found favor with shipping companies on the lakes, and steam steering systems rapidly became standard equipment.

STR. MERIDA

377'6"x45'x20'8"
Queen of the Lakes
May 1, 1893 to June 29, 1895

On May 1, the *Curry* was followed down the ways by the *Merida*, built to the same plans for the account of D. C. Whitney of Detroit. At the end of the summer, on August 31, they were joined by the *Centurion*, which had been built for Mark Hopkins of St. Clair, Michigan, and managed by brothers Mitchell and James Corrigan.[11]

The *Merida* was the most powerful of the three, and probably the most powerful bulk freighter on the lakes at that time. Her triple-expansion steam engine generated 1,700 horsepower. The *Curry* was rated at 1,100 horsepower, while the *Centurion* had only 1,000 horsepower. Even with her relatively low power, the *Centurion* was reportedly able to average twelve miles an hour on her maiden trip to Chicago.[12]

STR. CENTURION

377'6"x45'2"x21'9"
Queen of the Lakes
August 30, 1893 to June 29, 1895

The *Centurion* differed slightly from her two sisters in that her engine was at the stern and her stern cabin was slightly

The *S. S. Curry* was one of a number of giant steamers with midship engine rooms built at the Wheeler shipyard in West Bay City, Michigan, in the early 1890s. In 1904, the *Curry* was lengthened and her engine room moved to the stern. In this early photo, the deck officer navigating the ship—probably the captain—can clearly be seen on the flying bridge above the wheelhouse. (Institute for Great Lakes Research, Bowling Green State University)

larger. Many thought she was somewhat better looking than the *Curry* or *Merida.* She was reported to have had magnificant guest accommodations, "equal to those of any steam yacht on the lakes."[13]

While shipowners took great pride in putting their colors on ships the size of the *Curry, Merida,* and *Centurion,* there were times when a big ship was actually a disadvantage. On the *Centurion*'s maiden voyage, for example, she arrived at Chicago on September 20, 1893, to load 155,000 bushels of corn at the Armour "E" elevator on the south branch of the Illinois River. When she was about halfway up the river, however, the ship proved to be too long to negotiate a bend in the narrow channel. Pulled backward down the south branch by tugs, the *Centurion* attempted to take the north branch to the Armour "A" elevator. At the Halstead Street bridge she stuck fast and could go no farther. In frustration, she was finally taken to the Illinois Central "B" elevator, located nearer the mouth of the river. Unfortunately, the elevator was almost empty and the *Centurion* had to wait several days for corn to arrive by rail from Nebraska before she could begin loading. While waiting to load, Captain J. S. Dunham held a reception aboard the *Centurion.* In an address to his guests, he commented that "With every advance in the size of lake boats the cry has gone up that they are too big. Still they keep growing and what was a leviathan today is soon forgotten in the next newcomer."[14]

As a result of pressure by shipowners, the river channels and harbors around the lakes were gradually deepened and widened. In 1904, the owners of the eleven-year-old *Curry* decided that she needed to be lengthened if she was to compete with the latest generation of freighters. While a new seventy-two-foot section was being added to her midbody, the *Curry*'s engine was moved to the stern and her midship cabin was eliminated.[15] At some point her pilothouse was also moved to the top of her raised forecastle deck, possibly at the time she was being lengthened.

The *Merida* had the shortest career of the three sisters. During the "Black Friday" storm of October 20, 1916, she foundered in heavy seas about forty miles southeast of Long Point on Lake Erie. All twenty-three crewmembers were lost with their ship.

The *Curry* continued in service until 1935, but by then her name had been changed three times. In 1921, Interstate Steamship changed her name to the *Elmore.* When she was sold to the Valley Camp Steamship Company in 1922, they renamed her the *P. W. Sherman* and, in 1926, changed her name again to the *E. G. Mathiott.* In 1935, she was sold to Columbia Transportation, along with the rest of the Valley Camp fleet, but her new owners never operated her. After sitting idle for several years, she was finally scrapped at Fairport, Ohio, during the winter of 1936–37.

The *Centurion* outlived her sisters. Sold in 1917 to the Reiss Steamship Company of Sheboygan, Wisconsin, her name was changed to the *Alex B. Uhrig* in 1923. In 1943, her owners traded her to the U.S. Maritime Commission for new tonnage, but she continued to be operated by Reiss Steamship until the end of the war. When the war ended, the *Uhrig* was laid-up in Erie Bay at Erie, Pennsylvania, along with forty-six other outdated ships. In 1947 she was towed to Hamilton, Ontario, and scrapped by the Steel Company of Canada.[16]

While the careers of the three ships ranged from twenty-three to fifty-three years, they had been surpassed in length after only two years by a newer and larger vessel that became Queen of the Lakes. Over the years, they went from being the largest ships on the lakes to among the smallest. Indeed, while the *Centurion,* or *Uhrig,* lay rafted with other outdated ships at Erie at the end of World War II, she was passed frequently by ships that were more than two hundred feet longer than she was, with close to three times her carrying capacity.

The austere black stack of the *S. S. Curry* looked much like a stovepipe. Except for its slight rake, the stack was purely utilitarian, designed to carry boiler gases and hot ashes away from the ship. (Author's collection)

Notes

1. J. B. Mansfield, ed., *History of the Great Lakes,* vol. I (Chicago: J. H. Beers and Co., 1899; reprint, Cleveland: Freshwater Press, 1972), 567.
2. Walter Havighurst, *The Long Ships Passing* (New York: Macmillan, 1975), 222.
3. "A Short Historical Sketch of the Detroit Dry Dock Company," *Telescope* 15, no. 4 (April 1966): 86.
4. All of the ships in the Minnesota Steamship fleet had names that began with the letter "M" and ended with the letter "A."
5. *Telescope* 11, no. 8 (August 1962): 178.
6. Walter Havighurst, *Vein of Iron* (New York: World Publishing Company, 1958), 85–87.
7. John O. Greenwood, *Namesakes 1910–1919* (Cleveland: Freshwater Press, 1986), 25.

8. "The Largest Afloat," *Bay City Times*, April 30, 1893.
9. Ibid.
10. Ibid.
11. "Centurion Launched," *Bay City Times Press*, August 31, 1893.
12. Edward N. Middleton, ed., "Chicago's Always Had Bridges, Always," *Telescope* 27, no. 5 (September–October 1978): 135.
13. Ibid., 135–36.
14. Ibid., 136.
15. That same year, the *Merida*'s cargo hold was deepened by five feet, raising her gross tonnage to 3,329.
16. Ship Biographies, Institute for Great Lakes Research, Bowling Green State University.

6

The First 400-Footers

In 1892, a gala celebration was held at the Detroit Dry Dock Company shipyard at Wyandotte, not in conjunction with the launching of a ship, but to promote their imposing new graving dock. The 378-foot dry dock was the second largest on the lakes, and "vessel men thought [it] would be ample for a generation."[1] While the 362-foot *Christopher Columbus* and the latest freighters—such as the 332-foot *E. C. Pope* and the 359-foot *Selwyn Eddy*, both built at Detroit—were almost as long as the new drydock, shipyard officials confidently assured their guests that it would be many years before bigger ships would sail the lakes. Their argument was based on sound logic.

The draft of vessels operating on the lakes was severely limited to a maximum of fourteen feet, six inches by the shallowness of the harbors and river channels. For structural reasons, the length of a ship has to be proportional to the depth of the hull, so longer ships would have to wait until after a dredging program of Herculean proportions. The smug officials of Detroit Dry Dock were convinced that such an expensive undertaking was not in the offing.

Even if it were likely, however, longer and deeper ships would necessarily have higher sides, making it impossible for them to get under the chutes at ore loading docks on the upper lakes. And if that limitation were somehow overcome, harbor turning basins were clearly too small to accommodate longer ships. It was common knowledge that many of the current generation of vessels, like the *Centurion*, were finding it difficult, if not impossible, to negotiate the narrow and winding rivers in the system.

To those in attendance at the unveiling of the new dry dock at Detroit, the arguments presented by the shipyard officials were extremely persuasive. As Yogi Berra is reported to have said once, however, "It's hard to make predictions, especially about the future." Regardless of how reasoned the arguments against longer ships might have seemed, they were, of course, wrong.

The obviously risky move to still larger ships was led by Pickands Mather and Company, one of the giants of the iron mining and lake shipping industries. James Pickands, Samuel Mather, and Jay C. Morse had established the company in 1883 to mine, broker, and ship iron ore. In 1889, the trio joined with other investors to form the Minnesota Steamship Company. Their growing fleet already included some of the giant ore boats, including the *Maritana*, *Mariposa*, and *Merida*, but they were committed to building even larger ships.

In 1894, Washington I. Babcock and his staff of naval architects at Chicago Shipbuilding developed plans for a new bulk freighter that was revolutionary in its design. With drawings in hand, Babcock and his staff approached a number of shipping companies in an effort to land a contract to build a ship from the plans. It seems to have been an easy sale. Babcock and his associates returned to Chicago with not one, but two, construction contracts. One of the new ships would be built for Pickands Mather, while the second would join the fleet of American Steamship Company's "City Line."

Plans for both of the leviathans were finalized in succeeding months and their keels were laid early in 1895. The only vessels under construction at Chicago Ship Building at the time, they were the total focus of activities at the yard. The first was ready for launching on June 29.

STR. VICTORY

398'x48'3"x22'5"
Queen of the Lakes
June 29, 1895 to December 23, 1895

Pickands Mather had named the new ship *Victory*, and when she slid off the ways at Chicago she did indeed represent a victory for both her owners and builders. While generally referred to as the first of the 400-footers, she was actually 398 feet in overall length, with a beam of 48 feet, 3 inches and a depth of 22 feet, 5 inches. *Victory* was measured at 3,774 gross tons and, even more significantly, her unique construction gave her a net tonnage of 3,339, more than twenty-five percent greater than the *Curry*.

The construction of the *Victory* and her sister involved a building technique invented by a marine surveyor for the U.S. Standard Register of Shipping several years earlier. Used first at Chicago Ship in constructing the bulk freighter *Kearsarge* for Pickands Mather in 1893-94, the channel system of construction replaced traditional angle iron beams with U-shaped steel channels. The system produced ships that were both stronger and lighter in weight. The resulting savings in weight translated directly into greater carrying capacities for ships such as the *Kearsarge* and *Victory*.[2]

Like the *Maritana* and *Mariposa* that had also been built at Chicago, the design for the *Victory* and her sister included a

Stanton's drawing of Pickands Mather's *Str. Victory* that became Queen of the Lakes in 1895. The immense freighter was designed by Washington I. Babcock with a "submarine stern"; all of her aft accommodations were located below the level of the main deck. The smaller freighter in the foreground is not identified by Stanton, but is similar in size and design to the *R. J. Hackett*, the 1869-built ship that was the first steam-powered bulk freighter. The differences between the two vessels in the drawing vividly illustrate the dramatic progress made in shipbuilding on the lakes in a period of less than two decades. (Author's collection)

hatch between the forward cabin and the raised forecastle deck. According to a naval architect who started work at the yard the day the keel of the *Victory* was laid, the forward hatch eliminated reserve buoyancy in the bow of the ship and allowed cargo to be spread evenly throughout her hold.[3]

Later, when the available draft was increased from 14 feet, 6 inches to 16 feet, it created substantial excess buoyancy in the bow of the *Victory* and other ships built along her lines. The excess buoyancy caused the *Victory* to sag in the middle because there was less buoyancy there than at the bow and stern. This caused some of the steel beams in her main deck to buckle. Naval architects solved the problem by developing loading tables for use by the ship's officers. The tables told them how much cargo to put into each hatch to compensate for the excess buoyancy at the ends and reduce stress on the hull. Basically, more cargo had to be put into the outer hatchs to weigh down the buoyant ends of the ship. Loading tables similar to those developed for the *Victory* are still used today by deck officers responsible for loading the big freighters.[4]

In addition to the cargo hatch between the forward cabin and the forecastle, the *Victory* had ten other hatches spaced on twenty-four-foot centers down her long deck. She had no stern cabin, as her galley and crew accommodations were located below her main deck. The only protuberances at her stern were her tall smokestack, lifeboat davits, and several funnel-shaped vents for carrying fresh air to the engine room. The uncluttered "submarine stern" gave the *Victory* a particularly sleek profile, not unlike the earlier *Owego* and *Chemung* that had also been built at Globe in Cleveland.

To the delight of her owners, the *Victory* proved to be a prodigious carrier. On her maiden voyage under the command of G. B. Mallory, the senior captain in the fleet, she carried 3,689 long tons through the Soo on a draft of just over fourteen feet. When channels had been deepened sufficiently to allow her to operate on her maximum design draft of eighteen feet, she was ultimately able to move cargoes of as much as 5,200 tons.

Unlike many of the bulk freighters and package freighters that preceded her, the *Victory* had no intermediate 'tween decks in her hold. All of her cargo was carried directly on the floor of her cargo hold, referred to as her "tank tops," which was lined with three inches of wood planking. The planking protected structural members under the hold from damage by the mechanical unloaders that were then in use. Between her cargo hold and the bottom of her hull was a double bottom five and a half feet deep. The double bottom was subdivided into ballast tanks that could be filled with water to give the ship greater stability when she was running light.

The giant Pickands Mather vessel was powered by a 1,100-horsepower triple-expansion steam engine with Scotch boilers. Each of the two huge boilers was almost fifteen feet in diameter and more than thirteen feet long.

STR. ZENITH CITY

398'x48'3"x22'3"
Queen of the Lakes
August 16, 1895 to December 23, 1895

On August 16, the *Victory*'s twin sister was launched. Ships in the American Steamship Fleet were all named for cities around the lakes, and this new ship was christened *Zenith City* in honor of Duluth. Except for being two inches shallower and having slightly different boilers, the *Zenith City* was identical to the *Victory*. Where the *Victory* had the low pressure Scotch boilers that had been in use for a long time, the *Zenith City* was built with newer water tube boilers. In Scotch boilers, the hot gases from the burning of coal passes through tubes that give off heat to water surrounding the tubes. The water around the tubes is heated to the boiling point and gives off steam used to drive the pistons in the reciprocating engine. While Scotch boilers achieve steam pressures of about 220 pounds per square inch, the newer water tube boilers could generate as much as 500 pounds pressure. In them, the water is contained within the tubes and heated by gases that surround them. Because the water is contained, much higher temperatures and pressures can be achieved.[5]

Pickands Mather and American Steamship had gambled wisely. When the two companies signed contracts for construction of the new ships in 1894, 5.8 million tons of iron ore was shipped on the lakes. During 1895, the first year the *Victory* and *Zenith City* operated, ore tonnages exceeded 10 million tons for the first time in history, and totals would continue to climb.

The *Victory* and *Zenith City* played important roles in the growth of the iron ore trade on the Great Lakes. Both had long and impressive careers. In 1901, the *Zenith City* and other vessels in the American Steamship fleet were absorbed into the newly organized Pittsburgh Steamship Company, owned by United States Steel. She continued to be owned by the Pittsburgh fleet until 1942, when they traded her to the U.S. Maritime Commission with some other older freighters in exchange for new Maritime-class vessels. Although her ownership had changed, she continued to be operated by the Pittsburgh fleet until the war ended in 1945. When her services were no longer needed, the *Zenith City* was retired and laid-up in Presque Isle Bay at Erie, Pennsylvania, with other ships that had been traded to the Maritime Commission. In 1947, she was towed to Hamilton, Ontario, for scrapping.

The *Zenith City* led a rather uneventful life on the lakes, but the same was not true for her sister. In November of 1905, the *Victory* and her barge consort, the 379-foot whaleback *Constitution*, were downbound on Lake Superior on their last trip of the year. They weren't far out of Duluth when a terrible storm descended on the lake. In mountainous seas off the tip of the Keweenaw Peninsula, the towline connecting the two vessels parted, and the unpowered *Constitution* was adrift. Despite the heavy seas and blinding snow, the *Victory* searched for the *Constitution* for half a day, placing herself at great risk in the process. The dangerous exercise proved to be futile, however, and she eventually struggled on to the Soo. Days later the helpless barge was sighted off Keweenaw Point by crewmen aboard the *Str. C. W. Moore*, and they towed her to port before winter's ice closed down shipping on the lakes.

Throughout the storm, the crewmen on the *Victory* were unable to go out on deck, because the decks were constantly

The *Victory* later in her career. The first of the 400-footers originally had three masts that were used primarily to support rigging used to unload the ship. With the advent of more efficient shoreside unloading systems, one of the *Victory*'s masts was removed and the remaining two served mainly as flagstaffs and mounts for the ship's running lights. The *Victory* was built with a "submarine stern," clearly visible in the photo. Instead of a stern cabin housing crewmembers, accommodations were located below the spar deck to eliminate structures on the stern that might interfere with loading or unloading equipment. (Institute for Great Lakes Research, Bowling Green State University)

awash with waves that would have undoubtedly swept them overboard. The captain and other personnel who were housed at the bow of the ship were cut off from the stern, where the galley was located. Like deck crewmembers on most of the freighters caught out in the blow, the forward end personnel on the *Victory* went without food until they got into the sheltered waters of Whitefish Bay. At the same time, had it been necessary for them to abandon ship, they could not have gotten aft to where the lifeboats were located. After the 1905 storm, all ships on the Great Lakes were required to have fore-and-aft safety lines strung the length of their decks so that crewmembers could cross the decks even if they were awash.[6]

During the lay-up season at the end of 1905, the *Victory* was lengthened seventy-two feet at Superior Ship Building in Superior, Wisconsin. At the start of the 1906 shipping season, the *Victory* came out of the yard stretched to 470 feet in length, with a gross tonnage of 4,527. The lengthening raised her carrying capacity to 7,500 tons at maximum draft and greatly prolonged her life on the lakes.

In 1913, *Victory* was caught out in another of the famous November storms. The three-day blow that began on November 9 drove the big ship aground in the Livingstone Channel of the Detroit River, near where the river joins Lake Erie. While the *Victory* was lightered and released in the aftermath of the storm, virtually undamaged, many other ships were not so lucky. The 1913 storm is believed to have wrecked as many as thirty-two ships. About seventeen of the vessels were total losses, and two hundred and fifty people lost their lives as the hurricane-force winds tore their way across the lakes.[7]

That season, the *Victory* had become part of Pickands Mather's Interlake Steamship Company, which was formed to consolidate all of their vessel operations. The Interlake fleet was then second in size only to the giant Pittsburgh fleet. In 1940, Interlake sold the aging *Victory* to the Upper Lakes and St. Lawrence Transportation Company of Toronto, Ontario, which later became Upper Lakes Shipping. Placed under Canadian flag, she was renamed *Victorious*, after a famous racehorse owned by Canadian distiller Joseph Seagram.

Victorious operated mainly in the grain trade until she was laid-up for the final time at Toronto on December 6, 1968. The following year she was sold to the Toronto Harbour Commission, and on July 21, 1969, *Victorious* was sunk as breakwall in Humber Bay. Her career had spanned seventy-four seasons. Launched as the 398-foot Queen of the Lakes, by the time she met her end one Great Lakes shipping company was already in the process of building the first thousand- foot ore carrier. As the *Victory* and *Victorious*, she had seen shipments of iron ore grow from just over ten million tons a year in 1895 to more than eighty-six million tons in 1969. Few vessels in the history of shipping on the lakes had ever seen such changes. In retrospect, her names were wisely chosen.

Notes

1. "A Short Historical Sketch of the Detroit Dry Dock Company," *Telescope* 15, no. 4 (April 1966): 86.
2. Richard Wright, *Freshwater Whales* (Kent, OH: Kent State University Press, 1969), 8.
3. Dwight True, "Sixty Years of Shipbuilding," paper presented at the meeting of the Great Lakes Section, Society of Naval Architects and Marine Engineers, October 5, 1956, 11.
4. Ibid.
5. A. C. Hardy, *The Book of the Ship* (New York: Macmillan Company, 1949), 63.
6. Walter Havighurst, *Vein of Iron* (New York: World Publishing Company, 1958), 89–90.
7. Dana Thomas Bowen, *Lore of the Lakes* (Daytona Beach: Dana Thomas Bowen, 1940), 193.

7

Captain Wilson's Christmas Boat

The *Victory* and *Zenith City* joined a fleet on the Great Lakes that totalled 3,342 vessels in 1895. They were two of the 1,755 steam-powered ships that plied the lakes, and there were still 1,100 sailing vessels in operation, in addition to 81 barges and 406 canal-sized boats.[1] While the number of sailing vessels was continuing the decline that had begun at the time of the Civil War, the number of steamers would reach an all-time high during the 1896 season.

The steamers were not only growing in numbers, they were also growing in size. When the *Onoko* was launched thirteen years earlier, she was one of 1,101 steam vessels, but in 1882 the steamers in operation averaged only 265 gross tons. By 1895, the size of the steamships had increased to an average of about 489 gross tons, but at 3,774 gross tons, the *Victory* was still more than seven times larger that the average steam-powered boat on the lakes. It was a time of dramatic changes in the Great Lakes shipping industry, but the changes extended well beyond the ships themselves. After evolving slowly for more than two hundred years, the industry was suddenly growing much more sophisticated.

The first U.S. survey of the lakes did not begin until around 1850, and the first navigational charts were not issued until 1852. Prior to that time, captains truly guided their ships through the lakes by the "seat of their pants." There were crude, privately drawn maps available, but most of them showed only the major landforms of the region. Many of the reefs, shoals, peninsulas, and small islands were not plotted, and these claimed many ships each year. When the original U.S. survey was finally completed in 1882—the year the *Onoko* was launched—there were a total of seventy-six charts in the Great Lakes series, and navigation was much improved.[2]

The first lighthouses had appeared on the lakes in 1804. By 1895 the U.S. Lighthouse Service, a forerunner of the Coast Guard, maintained lighthouses and beacon lights at almost four hundred key locations around the lakes.[3] In 1837, the service also anchored a lightship in the Straits of Mackinac to mark the busy junction of Lake Huron and Lake Michigan. By 1895, there were close to a dozen lightships stationed at critical points on the lakes.[4]

In 1860, the fifteen-year-old son of the keeper of the lighthouse at the mouth of the Saginaw River devised the first system of range lights to guide mariners through the shoals and into the river channel. The rudimentary system consisted of two towers that young Dewitt Brawn erected in line with the river channel. At night, lanterns would be hoisted to the top of each tower so captains could line up on them when entering the river.

Channels were often also marked by buoys, usually consisting of anchored barrels or spars made from logs. Many of these were privately maintained by local mariners or dock owners, but in 1850 Congress had passed legislation to standardize buoyage.[5] Until 1895, the buoys were unlighted, so they were only of assistance to mariners during daylight hours.

During the 1895 Fourth of July celebration at Erie, Pennsylvania, officials of the Anchor Line arranged a demonstration of a lighted navigational buoy for Captain Charles Gridley, inspector in charge of the Tenth Lighthouse District. The Pintsch-type buoy was manufactured in Germany and contained a Fresnel lens that could be lighted by four gas jets. Gas to fuel the buoy was stored under pressure in the base of the massive buoy, which was over eight feet in diameter, twenty feet high, and weighed 5,860 pounds. Gridley was apparently impressed by the demonstration, because he immediately authorized purchase of the buoy. Two days later, it was installed outside the Erie harbor and became one of only 394 lighted buoys in operation worldwide. The following year, gas buoys were installed at Lansing Shoal, north of Squaw Island in Lake Michigan, and at Poverty Passage at the entrance to Green Bay.[6]

The growth in the iron ore trade had resulted in dramatic increases in traffic through the locks at Sault Ste. Marie. A new, larger lock had been opened in 1881, but within several years it became obvious to all that it would be inadequate to handle either the volume of traffic at the Soo or the size of the new iron and steel ships. Planning for another new lock began in 1887. That year, vessels journeying to or from Lake Superior logged only about 6,000 passages through the Soo. During the 1895 shipping season, when work on the new lock was finally nearing completion, ships made a total of 17,956 passages through the locks, seriously straining the system.[7] During the peak of the season, delays for the locks averaged nearly five hours.[8]

The new lock being built would not only cut delays at the Soo, but it would also accommodate larger ships. The 1881 lock was 515 feet long and 80 feet wide, dimensions that were more than adequate for that period, but it had a depth of only 13 feet, 6 inches over the sills. Ships like the *Victory* and *Zenith City* could not load to their maximum drafts if they had to pass through the lock. The new lock that would be brought on line in 1896 would be the largest in the world. It was 800 feet in length and 100 feet wide, with a depth over the sills of 18 feet. The deepening of the lock and connecting channels would have the greatest impact on the shipping industry. As Captain Joseph Sellwood noted at the time, "Every increase in the depth of our Great Lakes channels enlarges the mineral output, cheapens transportation, lowers prices, and benefits the whole people."[9]

Corps of Engineers personnel who had designed the new lock intended it to accommodate up to four ships at a time.[10] So rapidly did ships increase in size, however, that by the time the lock was ready to be flooded for the first time in 1896, only two of the biggest ships in operation would fit into the lock at once. The *Zenith City* had been in the water for only four months, for example, before she and the *Victory* lost their shared Queen of the Lakes title to an even longer ship.

STR. W. D. REES

413'x45'x23'6"
Queen of the Lakes
December 23, 1895 to February 22, 1896

The new behemoth was the 413-foot *W. D. Rees*, of 3,760 gross tons. The *Rees* was launched at Cleveland Ship Building on December 23, 1895, as part of the yard's gala Christmas party. On hand for the celebration was her owner, Captain Thomas Wilson of the Wilson Transit Company. The *Rees* operated under Wilson colors until sold in 1937 to Cargo Carriers of Chicago. After World War II, she again changed hands, purchased by Johnston Transportation of Grosse Ile, Michigan. Bulk freight tonnages dropped significantly after the wartime boom, however, and by then the *Rees* was too small to operate in the mainstream of trade of the lakes. During the winter of 1949–50, the *Rees* was converted to a combination bulk freighter and automobile carrier at Detroit. When she came out in the spring of 1950, she was operated by T. J. McCarthy Steamship Company of Detroit, carrying new automobiles up the lakes and iron ore on the return trip. She was one of many older ships engaged in the lucrative trade.

With the importance of Detroit to the auto industry, it is not surprising that the world's first auto carrying ships were developed on the Great Lakes. As early as 1914, cars were carried aboard the combination passenger and package freighters that had emerged on the lakes, like the *City of Cleveland.* By 1917, some companies were already experimenting with the first specialized auto carriers by refitting older vessels to carry cars.

The following year, the *Str. Spokane*, launched in 1887 as the first steel-hulled bulk freighter on the lakes, was converted for use in the auto trade. In addition to modifications to her cargo hold, the *Spokane* had an elevator installed on her deck to lower cars into her hold. She immediately proved to be an efficient auto carrier and moved more than five thousand cars between Detroit and Buffalo that season.

Quite a number of companies entered the auto trade following World War I. Among them was Tri-State Steamship Company, which later became Thompson Transit. Tri-State operated the *E. C. Pope* as an auto carrier between Detroit and

Cleveland and eventually controlled that route. Starting in 1922, the Minnesota-Atlantic Steamship Company of Duluth carried new cars on a number of the ships in their famous "Poker Fleet," including the *Ace*, *King*, *Queen*, and *Jack*. Their vessels generally carried autos up the lakes and either refrigerated or package cargo on the downbound leg.

A total of 32,883 cars were shipped on the lakes in 1920, and the number rose to almost 172,000 by 1928, a year in which the Nicholson Universal fleet of Detroit carried 70,000 new automobiles worth more than $100 million. Detroit was always the major loading port, but cars were also shipped from Chicago, Milwaukee, and numerous other small ports in Michigan and Wisconsin. The major receiving ports were Buffalo, Cleveland, Chicago, Milwaukee, and Duluth. From there the cars were shipped overland to markets throughout the U.S.

The Nicholson fleet increased the efficiency of loading and unloading operations by replacing the elevators with ramps built into the sides of its ships, similar to those used today on modern auto carriers. Eventually, Nicholson also installed "flight decks" above the main decks, increasing the ships' carrying capacity by about twenty-five percent. The largest Nicholson ships could carry as many as four hundred new cars per trip, making a round trip to Cleveland six days a week. They were paid $5.50 apiece for small cars, like Fords, and up to $22.50 for larger vehicles.

During the 1930s, the number of cars waiting to be

The stack of the *Rees* when the vessel was operated by Captain Thomas Wilson's Wilson Transit Company. Wilson was one of the premier shipping companies on the lakes until the fleet folded in the early 1970s after losing the Republic Steel contract. (Author's collection)

The *W. D. Rees* departing the Soo locks with a load of iron ore, later in her career. Her flying bridge has been removed and the original wooden hatch covers replaced by segmented, telescoping hatch covers that first appeared on the lakes in 1904. (Institute for Great Lakes Research, Bowling Green State University)

shipped and the lucrativeness of the trade led a number of companies operating bulk freighters to begin carrying cars on the decks of their ships on their voyages up the lakes. While cars loaded as deck cargo were more susceptible to damage than those carried aboard specially modified auto carriers, that practice continued through the early 1970s.

The specialized auto carriers began to fade from the scene during the 1950s, when railroads and trucking companies began to claim increasingly larger shares of the trade. The last auto carrier to operate on the lakes was the *Highway 16*, a converted Navy LST that went into service on Lake Michigan in 1948. The ship's unique name resulted from her service as the connecting link between terminuses of U.S. Highway 16 in Milwaukee, Wisconsin, and Muskegon, Michigan. She made her last trip on July 31, 1973, and with her lay-up the auto trade ended on the lakes after almost sixty years.[11]

The *Rees* was only involved in the auto trade for two seasons, however. With the coming of the Korean War and increased demand for bulk cargoes, she was reconverted to a bulk carrier at Great Lakes Engineering Works in River Rouge, Michigan, in 1951. Purchased by Bethlehem Steel, she was rechristened as the *Leetsdale* and operated as part of the steelmaker's fleet throughout the period of the conflict in Korea. By the end of the war she was too small to be economically viable, and in 1955 the *Leetsdale* was scrapped at Lackawanna, New York.

Although she served faithfully on the lakes for sixty years, the *Rees* is not well remembered today. Few realize that she was ever Queen of the Lakes. That is no surprise, though. She held the title for only eight weeks, and those came during the winter months of 1895–96 when no ships were operating on the lakes.

Notes

1. J. B. Mansfield, ed., *History of the Great Lakes*, vol. I (Chicago: J. H. Beers and Co., 1899; reprint, Cleveland: Freshwater Press, 1972), 439.
2. John W. Larson, *Essayons: A History of the Detroit District, U.S. Army Corps of Engineers* (Detroit: U.S. Army Corps of Engineers, 1981), 45.
3. Ivan H. Walton, "Developments on the Great Lakes, 1815–1943," *Michigan History Magazine* 27 (1943), 128.
4. Mansfield, 371.
5. Harlan Hatcher, *Lake Erie* (New York: Bobbs-Merrill, 1945), 354.
6. Robert J. MacDonald, "Captain Gridley and the German Gas Buoy," *Inland Seas* 15, no. 4 (Winter 1959): 288–90.
7. Grace Lee Nute, *Lake Superior* (New York: Bobbs-Merrill, 1944), 122.
8. Larson, 93.
9. Mansfield, 263.
10. Larson, 105.
11. Lawrence A. Brough, *Autos on the Water* (Columbus: Chatham Communicators, 1987).

8

Queens for Hanna and Rockefeller

Selecting a name for a new ship is always a serious matter for a shipping company. Many different naming schemes have been used, but new vessels are most often named for executives of the owning company or top officials of one of the shipping company's major customers. Only one name can go on any hull, so there will always be people who are very pleased with the choice, and others who will be disappointed. For that reason, while many people may be involved in suggesting names for a new ship, the final choice is always reserved for top-ranking corporate executives, who weigh their decision carefully. Well, almost always.

STR. CORALIA

432'x48'x24'
Queen of the Lakes
February 22, 1896 to August 8, 1896

The steamer *Coralia* was apparently an exception to the rule. Launched on February 22, 1896, it is said that her name was not picked until five minutes before she was launched.[1] Huddling in the moments before the launching, officials of the Mutual Transportation Company of Escanaba, Michigan, decided to name their new ship for Coralia Hanna, wife of fleet manager L. C. Hanna. In all likelihood, word of the name that had been selected spread rapidly through the crowd gathered at Globe Ship Building in Cleveland to see the giant vessel plummet sideways into the water. Their reaction upon hearing the chosen name was not recorded, but it is likely that many thought *Coralia* was a fittingly melodic name for the beautiful new freighter.

Even though she had been built with an extra stiff and strong hull and was longer than any other ship on the lakes, the experienced staff of designers and shipwrights at Globe had created a vessel that was truly a masterpiece of proportioning. Not since the launching of the *Onoko* fourteen years earlier had Globe built a record-breaking ship, and it appears as if the staff there had gone out of their way to insure that it would be a vessel worthy of the title Queen of the Lakes.

After the launching of the 350-foot bulk freighter *Globe* in the fall of 1894, the once highly respected shipyard had fallen on hard times. In the seventeen months that passed between the launchings of the *Globe* and the *Coralia*, the yard that had pioneered the construction of both iron and steel ships found its only work in the construction of a 90-foot canal towboat and seven barges, six of which were just 100 feet long. It must have been a difficult time for the talented staff at Globe, trying to find some modicum of satisfaction in building the utilitarian towboat and barges while other yards were launching impressive ships like the *Victory*, *Zenith City*, and *Rees*.

The opportunity to design and build the *Coralia* undoubtedly breathed new life into the Globe yard on the banks of the Cuyahoga. At 432 feet in overall length, she was fully 34 feet longer than *Victory*, which had been launched just eight months earlier, and 19 feet longer than the *Rees*, launched only two months before. At 4,330 gross tons, she was fifteen percent larger than the *Rees* or *Victory*, representing a phenomenal leap in size.

The forecastle deck on the *Coralia* was very low and did not extend as far back from the bow as was common on the ships immediately preceding her. This was achieved by eliminating the forecastle cabin and locating quarters for unlicensed crewmembers one deck down. The *Coralia*'s forward cabin was set well aft of the forecastle, making room for two hatches between the forecastle and the cabin structure. The blocky profile of the stern cabin was softened by beginning the stern gunwale at the forward end of the cabin, so that much of the cabin was concealed by the clean line of the black hull.

On her maiden voyage in 1896, *Coralia* established a new Great Lakes cargo record by loading 4,869 net tons of ore at Escanaba. Early in her career, it was also common to see her towing a barge, which further increased the amount of cargo she could move on a single trip.

The *Coralia* was actually the first of three sisterships built from the same plans. The other two vessels followed her into the water on May 9 and July 25, 1896. They were two of twelve new ships built for John D. Rockefeller's Bessemer Steamship Company, which had just been organized.

Rockefeller had decided in 1895 that it was critical for mine owners like himself to operate their own fleets, rather than to be at the mercy of shipowners. Because the amount of ore to be shipped was increasing so rapidly, Rockefeller had found that shipowners were often in an advantageous position

Mutual Transportation's *Coralia* preparing to load at a chute-type ore dock on the upper lakes. A chute has already been lowered into one of the forward hatches on the big freighter, and her wooden hatch covers can be seen stacked along the outboard wing of the deck. In 1901, the *Coralia* and the other ships in the Mutual fleet were purchased by U.S. Steel's Pittsburgh Steamship Company. (Institute for Great Lakes Research, Bowling Green State University)

when negotiating contracts with mine owners. Rockefeller cajoled Samuel Mather of Pickands Mather into helping him establish his new fleet. While Pickands Mather was in the shipping business and stood to lose some cargoes if mine owners had their own boats, Rockefeller informed Mather that he was committed to building a fleet and Mather could either help him or stand by while someone else earned the healthy fees for assisting with the $3 million project. With the situation expressed so boldly, Mather saw the light and agreed to help establish the Bessemer fleet.

Within months, each of the major shipyards around the lakes recieved letters from Pickands Mather asking them to bid on the construction of one or two ships or barges. All of the yards were eager to land new contracts, so each quoted the lowest possible costs, hoping to outbid the other yards for the work. Officials from all of the yards were subsequently summoned to Cleveland. One by one they were called in to meet with Sam Mather, and each and every one of them came out of the meeting with a signed contract. When the shipyard officials later compared notes, they were stunned. They found they hadn't really been bidding against each other at all. Mather had simply requested the bids as a ploy to cover the fact that he intended to have twelve vessels built simultaneously for Rockefeller, and to force the yards to quote realistic, rather than inflated, prices. If the yards had known in advance that they were going to get an order for one or two ships, they would undoubtedly have padded their prices. Once the yards became aware of the remarkable coup masterminded by Mather, they had to admit that the resulting contract prices were fair. What's more, they were glad to have the work.[2]

STR. SIR HENRY BESSEMER

432'x48'x24'
Queen of the Lakes
May 9, 1896 to August 8, 1896

The first of the two ships launched at Globe for the Bessemer fleet was the *Sir Henry Bessemer*, followed several months later by the *Sir William Siemens*. Within two years the fleet boasted ten steamers and eleven barges, all of which were named in honor of famous inventors. Together, the twenty-one vessels in the new Rockefeller fleet had a combined carrying capacity of 100,000 tons.[3] By 1901, the fleet had swelled to fifty-six vessels, making it the largest on the lakes.[4]

The stack of the *Coralia* when it was operated by Mutual Transportation, prior to 1901. (Author's collection)

STR. SIR WILLIAM SIEMENS

432'x48'x24'
Queen of the Lakes
July 25, 1896 to August 8, 1896

The three identical sister ships—*Coralia*, *Bessemer*, and *Siemens*—were united in 1901 when the holdings of the Mutual and Bessemer fleets became part of the new U.S. Steel Corporation. The vessels operated as part of the subsidiary Pittsburgh Steamship Company, often referred to as the "steel trust" fleet. Over one hundred vessels flew the Pittsburgh flag; it was the largest shipping company on the lakes and would continue as such for the next eight decades.

As part of the Pittsburgh fleet, *Coralia* often towed the barge *Maia*. The 395-foot *Maia* had been built in 1898 for the Minnesota Steamship Company, which had also been absorbed into the steel trust fleet. In May of 1906, the 455-foot freighter *Howard L. Shaw* made the mistake of trying to pass between the *Coralia* and the *Maia*, apparently not seeing the towline connecting the two vessels. The unfortunate *Shaw* was raked by the cable, which unceremoniously snapped off both of her masts and tore off her smokestack.[5] It was one of the few incidents that would blemish the *Coralia*'s long career.

Around 1920, the *Coralia* was rebuilt. Her pilothouse was moved atop her forecastle at that time, following a pattern that had by then become standard on the lakes. Like most of the ships built before the change from a two-watch to a three-watch system, the *Coralia* also needed additional accommodations for crewmembers. While most of the older ships were having "doghouse" cabins added on their decks to provide the necessary rooms, the *Coralia* had her doghouse placed atop the stern cabin instead. She may, in fact, have been the first ship with a two-story cabin at her stern. In time, the design became standard on the lakes.[6]

In 1927, *Coralia* was sold to Nicholson Universal Steamship Company of Detroit and, like the *Rees*, she was rebuilt for service in the automobile trade. When the demand for bulk cargoes increased and auto production dropped off during World War II, she was reconverted for the bulk trade. The shipping business dropped off after the war, and in 1949 the *Coralia* was sold to the T. H. Browning Steamship Company. Her new owners changed her name to *T. H. Browning* in 1950 and, again, to *L. D. Browning* in 1952. During the winter of 1953–54, her coal-fired boilers were modified to burn oil with the installation of burners that had previously been used on two other ships. In 1955, Browning sold her to the Continental Grain Company's Beta Lake Steamship Company, which used her as a storage barge at Buffalo for several years. No longer deemed to be an efficient carrier, she was finally sent to the shipbreakers at Hamilton, Ontario, in 1964, after sixty-eight years of service.[7]

The *Bessemer* and *Siemens* operated under Pittsburgh colors until the end of the 1928 season, when both were sold to the Paisley Steamship Company. In 1929, the *Bessemer* was renamed *Michael J. Bartelme*, while the *Siemens* became the *William B. Pilkey*. When Columbia Transportation Company was formed in 1935 by Oglebay-Norton, both ships were transferred into that fleet.

In 1941, Columbia had the *Pilkey* rebuilt as a crane vessel at the Fairport Machine Shop in Fairport, Ohio. Two large, movable, electromagnetic cranes were installed on her deck so that she could handle scrap steel and pig iron in addition to bulk cargoes. The addition of the cranes was not the first change in the appearance of the vessel, however. While still part of the Pittsburgh fleet, the flying bridge atop the *Siemens*'s wheelhouse was enclosed and became a pilothouse, while still retaining the old wheelhouse structure. After that, she looked as if she had a two-story pilothouse. The old wheelhouse was removed sometime before 1930, at which time the pilothouse was placed directly on top of the forward cabin and her bridge wings and cabin overhang were eliminated. Before that date, a doghouse had also been added on her deck, just forward of the stern cabin, to provide additional accommodations for crew. The doghouse had to be removed when she was converted to a craneship, for it would have interferred with operation of the cranes. At that time, a doghouse-type cabin was built just ahead of the ship's forward cabin, sitting atop the forecastle.

When she returned to service after being converted to a crane vessel, the former *Siemens* was renamed *Frank E. Vigor.* On the morning of April 27, 1944, the *Vigor* was downbound on Lake Erie in a dense spring fog, carrying a cargo of sulphur. It would be another year before the first radar would make its debut on the lakes, and the captain of the *Vigor* was feeling his way along slowly in the fog. Lookouts were posted, the ship's foghorn was being sounded regularly, and everyone on duty listened intently for an answering signal that would alert them to another vessel in the area. Despite the precautions, while negotiating the dangerous waters of Pelee Passage between Pelee Island and the Canadian mainland, she collided with the 500-foot steamer *Philip Minch.*

The *Vigor*, launched in 1896 as the *Sir William Siemens*, sank off Lake Erie's Long Point in 1944 after colliding in the fog with the *Str. Philip Minch*. The crane ship was carrying a load of sulphur at the time. (Author's collection)

She was holed badly, and it became immediately obvious that the *Vigor*'s fate was sealed. Her thirty-two crewmembers abandoned ship successfully and were picked up by the *Minch.* As her cargo hold and side tanks flooded, the *Vigor*, perhaps made slightly top-heavy because of her cranes, capsized and sank in seventy-five feet of water. She was the first of the three sisters to go, but she had by then given her various owners forty-eight years of faithful service. No doubt, the *Vigor's* hull and machinery would have been good for another decade or more, but not every ship on the lakes is fortunate enough to survive to its maximum longevity.

The *Bartelme*, the former *Bessemer*, had her name changed again in 1943, when Columbia renamed her *Wolverine.* She operated in the bulk trade through the end of the Korean War, when she was sold to a construction company for use as a floating warehouse. In 1955, while being used during the construction of the Mackinac Bridge that spans Michigan's two peninsulas, the hull of the *Wolverine* gave way, and she cracked badly amidships. Whether the hull failure was the result of age or improper loading is unknown, but the damaged hull was towed to a shipyard at Sturgeon Bay, Wisconsin. It was determined that the cost of repairing her could not be justified, so the *Wolverine* languished there until 1971, when her seventy-five-year-old hull was finally scrapped. She was the last of the three sisters to disappear from the lakes.

Notes

1. Rev. Peter Van Der Linden, ed., *Great Lakes Ships We Remember* (Cleveland: Freshwater Press, 1979), 144.
2. James P. Barry, *Ships of the Great Lakes* (Berkeley: Howell-North Books, 1973), 175.
3. J. B. Mansfield, ed., *History of the Great Lakes*, vol. I (Chicago: J. H. Beers and Co., 1899; reprint, Cleveland: Freshwater Press, 1972), 452–53.
4. Barry, 175.
5. Skip Gillham, "The Last of the Consorts," *Telescope* 25, no.6 (November–December 1976): 159.
6. Van Der Linden, 144.
7. Ibid.

9

Two Bessemer Queens

When Pickands Mather asked the major shipyards around the lakes to submit bids to build one or two ships for Rockefeller's new Bessemer Steamship Company, Globe wasn't the only shipyard that wanted to construct record-breaking vessels. Detroit Dry Dock proposed to build the two longest of the new ships, longer even than the *Bessemer* and *Siemens*. By the time the contracts were awarded, two ships were already under construction at the Detroit Dry Dock yard at Wyandotte for other customers, so construction of the Bessemer ships did not move ahead as fast as work did at Globe. As a result, both the *Bessemer* and *Siemens* were already in the water before the first of the Detroit-built ships was launched on August 8, 1896.

It's unlikely that Rockefeller or his agent, Sam Mather, was upset by the delays encountered in launching the two boats being built at Detroit. By the end of July 1896, shipping rates plummeted as the industry attempted to adjust to the dramatic growth in carrying capacity that was taking place in the Great Lakes bulk fleet. Iron ore was moving out of Duluth at only sixty cents a ton, well below the normal rate that ranged from ninety-five cents to a dollar and twenty-five cents a ton. Coal could be shipped from Lake Erie ports to Lake Michigan at twenty-five cents a ton, while the average rate during the prior year had ranged from thirty-six to fifty-nine cents a ton. Backhaul cargoes of corn were bringing shipowners only a penny a bushel, instead of the four cents a bushel that was considered normal. At ports from Buffalo to Duluth crews were being paid off and ships laid up because they were unable to operate profitably at the low rates.[1] Some of the newest and largest vessels on the lakes were idle, including Mutual Transportation's *Coralia*, which had gone into service only a few months earlier. "The *Coralia* made one trip at sixty cents," said Captain George McKay, manager of the vessel, "and she will not make another."[2]

STR. SIR WILLIAM FAIRBAIRN

445'x45'8"x27'8"
Queen of the Lakes
August 1, 1896 to April 13, 1898

Despite the temporary softness of the shipping market, a large crowd was on hand for the private ceremonies marking the launching of the first of the two Detroit-built ships, the longest vessel ever to enter the waters of the Great Lakes. Christened *Sir William Fairbairn* in honor of the English inventor who had pioneered the construction of iron ships and bridges some sixty years earlier, the $260,000 freighter was thirteen feet longer than the *Coralia* and the two Bessemer boats built at Globe.[3] Newspaper accounts were quick to point out, however, that the *Fairbairn* was "still not in the same class with the *Coralia* and *Bessemer*."[4] While considerably longer than the Globe-built boats, the *Fairbairn* was more than two feet narrower. The reduced beam resulted in lower gross and net tonnage measurements and, even more importantly, less carrying capacity. While the *Coralia* had already set a cargo record by carrying 4,869 net tons of ore on a draft of 14 feet, 6 inches, the *Fairbairn* would be limited to cargoes of only about 4,000 net tons on the same draft.

Nonetheless, the *Fairbairn* was rightly hailed as a "mammoth ship." Laid out in a straight line, the steel beams and angle iron used in her construction would stretch for more than seventeen miles. Laid end to end, the steel plates that formed her skin would span more than seven miles. Her framing and plates were held together by 415,553 rivets, which would stretch out for more than nine miles if placed in a line.[5]

The *Fairbairn* looked much like the Globe boats, though many observers thought her lines were not quite as refined. She had one hatch in the well formed between her raised forecastle deck and her forward cabin, and a catwalk bridge spanned the well and connected the two structures. Instead of having a long, clean deck, the *Fairbairn* had been built with a midship deckhouse containing cabins for firemen and deckhands. While many observers undoubtedly thought that the deckhouse sullied the appearance of the new freighter, industry insiders magnanimously applauded it as "a feature that will command itself to well-wishers of humanity." The unique deckhouse was the brainchild of shipbuilder Robert Wallace of Cleveland, a former engineer on the lakes who obviously remembered all too well the many unpleasant hours he had spent cooped up in damp and airless quarters located below deck.[6]

STR. ROBERT FULTON

445'x45'8"x27'8"
Queen of the Lakes
September 10, 1896 to April 13, 1898

Just over a month after the launching of the *Fairbairn*, on September 10, 1896, the second of the two identical ships slid into the water. Named the *Robert Fulton*, she honored the man credited with inventing the first successful steamboat. The only

The *Sir William Fairbairn* was one of the original ships built for John D. Rockefeller's Bessemer Steamship Company. This Pesha photo shows the empty ship on the St. Clair River. The doghouse at the after end of her deck was an original feature and housed firemen and deckhands. By the time this photo was taken, the *Fairbairn*'s flying bridge had been converted into a pilothouse, with the original wheelhouse still visible below the pilothouse. (Institute for Great Lakes Research, Bowling Green State University)

difference between the *Fairbairn* and *Fulton* was not obvious to onlookers. While the *Fairbairn* was powered by a 1,800-horsepower triple expansion engine, the *Fulton* engine was rated at only 1,600 horsepower.

Both of the new ships became part of the Pittsburgh Steamship Company when it was formed in 1901. The *Fairbairn* operated in the familiar colors of the steel trust fleet until 1936, when she was sold to the Buckeye Steamship Company. In 1959, she was purchased by Continental Grain's Gamma Lake Shipping Company and operated in the grain trade until 1962. In that year, ownership of the aging *Fairbairn* passed to Marine Salvage of Port Colborne, Ontario, a Canadian shipbreaker, although she remained at Buffalo, New York, as a storage hulk until the summer of 1964. On August 19, 1964, the tugs *America* and *North Carolina* towed the *Fairbairn* from her dock at Buffalo to Hamilton, Ontario, for scrapping.

The *Fulton* was owned by the Pittsburgh fleet until 1943, when she was traded to the U.S. Maritime Commission for new tonnage. She continued to be operated by Pittsburgh Steamship until the end of World War II, at which time she was mothballed at Erie. In 1948, the *Fulton* was scrapped at the Steel Company of Canada dock at Hamilton.

Of the original twelve vessels built for the Bessemer fleet, the *Siemens* was the first to disappear from the lakes, having sunk in 1944. The *Fulton* was the second to go, and the first to be cut up for scrap. The other ten vessels began their individual journeys to the shipbreakers in the 1960's, though one barge had a diesel engine installed in 1978 and avoided scrapping until 1984.[7]

Together, the twelve vessels built for the Bessemer fleet in 1896 operated for a total of 846 years, for a remarkable average lifespan of more than seventy seasons. While the 432-foot *Bessemer* and *Siemens* and the 445-foot *Fairbairn* and *Fulton* held the title of Queen of the Lakes for periods of from two weeks to twenty months in the 1896-98 period, three of the other original Bessemer ships were still operating on the Great Lakes during the 1970s and 1980s, when the industry was dominated by massive 1,000-foot freighters. In retrospect, the Bessemer boats may be better remembered for their staying power than their size.

Notes

1. "Rapidly Laying Up," *Detroit Free Press*, July 29, 1896.
2. "Nothing to Carry," *Detroit Free Press*, July 30, 1896.
3. "A Mammoth Launch," *Detroit Free Press*, July 31, 1896.
4. Ibid.
5. "Fairbairn Launched," *Detroit Free Press*, August 2, 1896.
6. "A Mammoth Launch."
7. Launched at the Wheeler shipyard in West Bay City, Michigan, on August 27, 1896, as the *James Nasmyth*, she was transferred to Canadian ownership in 1936 as the *Merle H.*. In 1949, she was renamed the *Pic River*. Converted to a motorship in 1952, her name was shortened in 1978 to *Pic R.* She served out her long career under the ownership of Ontario Paper Company's Quebec and Ontario Transportation Company and outlived all other consort barges on the lakes.

10

A Superior Freighter

The *Zenith City* of American Steamship Company's "City Line" had shared the Queen of the Lake title for only a few months at the end of 1895. For three years American Steamship officials had watched as the bragging rights that went with having the longest ship on the lakes passed first to Wilson Transit and then to Mutual Transportation and Bessemer. American Steamship then recaptured the title briefly in early 1898 with the launching of the *Superior City* for their Zenith Transit Company, managed by A. B. Wolvin.

STR. SUPERIOR CITY

450'x50'x24'7"
Queen of the Lakes
April 13, 1898 to July 31, 1898

The 450-foot freighter was the first ship built at Cleveland Ship Building's new shipyard near the mouth of the Black River at Lorain, Ohio. The town declared a holiday on April 13, 1898, and thousands crowded the waterfront to watch the giant freighter slide down the ways.[1] Not only was the *Superior City* the longest ship on the lakes, she was the first freighter built with a 50-foot beam. Her gross tonnage was also substantially larger than that of any other freighter then in service, and she had a carrying capacity of about 7,100 tons. The new ship was also among the most powerful bulk freighters. Instead of the common triple expansion steam engine, the new American freighter had a quadruple expansion engine rated at 1,900 horsepower.

While American Steamship officials and the residents of Lorain were delighted with the new ship, her reign as Queen of the Lakes lasted only a little more than three months. By midsummer, a still larger freighter was completed at the Wheeler shipyard at West Bay City, Michigan, for none other than the growing Bessemer fleet.

In 1901, the ships of the American Steamship fleet, along with those of the Bessemer fleet, passed into the ownership of U.S. Steel's Pittsburgh Steamship Company. Despite the grand ceremonies that attended her launching, if the *Superior City* is remembered at all today, it is most likely as a result of the relative brevity of her career and the tragic circumstances surrounding her unfortunate end.

Just over twenty-two years after she slid into the cold waters of the Black River, the *Superior City* met her end on Lake Superior's Whitefish Bay. She had loaded 7,069 gross tons of iron ore at Two Harbors, Minnesota, the previous day and set off on the long trip down the lakes. At 9:30 on the evening of August 20, 1920, she was on Whitefish Bay, just a few hours

The *Superor City* shortly after its launching on April 13, 1898. It was the first ship built at Cleveland Ship Building's new yard in Lorain, Ohio. A large crowd was on hand to observe the launching of the new Queen of the Lakes, including many who watched from rowboats. Much fitting-out work remained after the big Wolvin freighter was launched; note that it does not have a smokestack or masts yet. On the right is the tug *Cascade*, which towed the *Superior City* to its fitting-out berth. (Institute for Great Lakes Research, Bowling Green State University)

sailing time from the Soo Locks, when she was involved in a collision with the steamer *Willis L. King* that was upbound light at the time. The *Superior City* was punctured aft of amidships on her port side, and she began to settle in the water immediately as the result of the unrestrained flooding of her cargo hold. Roused by the collision, most of her crew rushed onto deck and began to launch the two lifeboats located on her stern above the engine room. As they strained at the davits, the *Superior City*'s two boilers suddenly exploded and unleashed a shock wave that hurled most of the crewmembers into the water.

The ship sank almost immediately after the explosion, plunging to the bottom in 265 feet of water. Despite the efforts of the crew of the *King*, other ships in the area—including a small yawl named the *Turner*—and personnel from the nearby lifesaving station at Whitefish Point, only four crewmembers were saved. One of those was boatswain Walter Richter, who had gone to his lifeboat station on the stern wearing only his underwear. The explosion of the boilers tore the underwear from Richter's body and blew him into the water. "I sank deep into the icy water, which evidently brought me to my senses," he recounted later. "I thought I would never reach the surface. I

The *Superior City* sank near the mouth of Whitefish Bay in 1920 after a collision with the *Str. Willis King*. Twenty-nine of the thirty-three persons aboard the freighter at the time went down with the ship. (Author's collection)

swam for about four minutes and up from the depths came a steamer's hatch cover upon which I climbed and hung onto for a half hour until the *Turner* arrived. I would not be surprised if most of the boys were blown to pieces from their places over the boiler house where they had lined up in order to get into the lifeboats."[2] Crewmembers on the *Turner* later told Richter that "wooden ports in the interior of the steel ship [had been] blown clear through the sides."[3]

Out of thirty-three persons aboard the *Superior City*, twenty-eight men and one woman died with their ship. In addition to Richter, the captain, second mate, and a wheelsman were pulled from the water. Among the dead was the wife of the second assistant engineer, who was making a summer trip with her husband.[4] Most of those who died must have been blown to pieces by the boiler explosion or trapped in the suction of the powerful whirlpool that resulted when the *Superior City* made her dive in two hundred feet of water. No bodies were ever recovered. Lake Superior does not easily give up her dead.

Notes

1. Dana Thomas Bowen, *Lore of the Lakes* (Daytona Beach: Dana Thomas Bowen, 1940), 226.
2. "No Trace Found of Crew of Lake Wreck," *Detroit Free Press*, August 22, 1920.
3. Ibid.
4. Ibid.

11

Bessemer Reclaims the Crown

As the nineteenth century drew to a close, it must have seemed to many people as if John D. Rockefeller and his Bessemer Steamship Company were intent on nothing less than the total domination of bulk shipping on the lakes. Through 1896 and 1897, most of the freighters launched by the major shipyards had the now-familiar Bessemer "B" on their stacks, and most were exceptionally large ships. From May of 1896 until the launching of the *Superior City* in April of 1898, one or more Bessemer ships either held or shared the title as Queen of the Lakes. A little over three months after the *Superior City* was launched for American Steamship Company, another Bessemer ship reclaimed the title.

STR. SAMUEL F. B. MORSE

475'x50'x24'
Queen of the Lakes
July 31, 1898 to January 20, 1900

The *Samuel F. B. Morse* was launched for the Bessemer fleet on Sunday, July 31, 1898, at the F. W. Wheeler shipyard at West Bay City, Michigan. The new Queen of the Lakes was 475 feet long, with a 50-foot beam, and measured at 4,936 gross tons. The *Morse* did not take to the water easily, and her launching proved to be a major embarrassment for Frank Wheeler.

The giant Bessemer freighter had been scheduled for launching on Saturday afternoon, July 30, and thousands of spectators ignored the stifling heat to gather at the shipyard and on lumber piles, tramways, and docks on the opposite side of the Saginaw River. Wheeler was eager that the launching go without a hitch, and by 10 a.m. his work crews had put a heavy coat of grease on the sloping ways down which the big ship would slide.

At 3 p.m., the time that had been set for the launching, Wheeler pushed a button to sound a bell. Along the hull of the *Morse*, teams of sweating workers wielding sledge hammers drove out the wooden blocks holding the freighter on the ways. On the opposite side of the keel, other workers worked in unison to drive stout wooden wedges under the keel to start the big ship on her slide into the water. Despite the efforts, the *Morse* would not budge from her perch. For more than an hour, the spectators waited patiently in the summer heat as Wheeler and his launch crew tried to break the freighter free. Finally, at 4:30 p.m., Wheeler threw in the towel. The flags flying from the *Morse*'s masts were lowered, and his crews went to work re-blocking the hull. The thousands of local residents who had gathered to witness the launching went home disappointed.

Wheeler found that the grease on the ways had melted in the midday heat. Without the lubricant, there was too much friction between the steel hull of the *Morse* and the heavy wooden timbers of the ways for the big freighter to slide.[1] Wheeler told his staff to be at the shipyard early the following morning to again attempt to launch the Bessemer steamer. At 9 a.m. on Sunday the *Morse* gave up her grip on the ways and slid into the water "as gracefully as a duck." Only Wheeler and his workers were present to cheer the launching of the new Queen of the Lakes.[2]

The *Morse* had all of the latest equipment aboard, including steam appliances, steam winches, steam capstan, and steam steering gear,[3] but "as in the case with the rest of the steamers of the Bessemer fleet, nothing in the shape of luxury of appointments [was] provided. These boats are made without regard for beauty of line, but are built for carrying large cargoes."[4] She could carry 7,500 tons of ore.

While she may not have been a beauty, the *Morse* had a unique appearance as the result of having twin smokestacks on her stern. The stacks exhausted gases from her powerful 2,700-horsepower quadruple expansion engine.[5] Like the *Superior City*, the new Bessemer freighter had a hatch between her pilothouse and raised forecastle and a catwalk spanned the resulting well. She also had a midship deckhouse.[6]

In the contract for construction of the *Morse*, Bessemer also hired Wheeler to build two large schooner consorts. The first of the consorts, the *John Fritz*, was actually launched before the *Morse*, on June 22, 1898. The second, the *John A. Roebling*, was completed on August 13, about the time shipyard workers had put the finishing touches on the *Morse* and the

Bessemer's giant *Samuel F. B. Morse* belching coal smoke from its unique twin stacks. The open-air flying bridge is shown clearly in the photo, as is her midship deckhouse. Hanging from the sides of the hull are timbers that were used as fenders to protect the hull when making a dock. (Institute for Great Lakes Research, Bowling Green State University)

freighter was ready to go into service. The barges were identical, each 456 feet long, 50 feet wide, and 24 feet deep. While their gross tonnages were less than that of the *Morse*, their carrying capacities were slightly greater.[7]

STR. DOUGLASS HOUGHTON

475'x50'x24'2"
Queen of the Lakes
June 3, 1899 to January 20, 1900

An identical steamer was launched for the Bessemer fleet the following year by Globe Ship Building. Construction of the ship, named the *Douglass Houghton*, had reportedly been slowed by a year-long shortage in the availability of shipbuilding steel.[8] The two ships and two barges had long careers on the lakes. In a way, all of them are still part of the Great Lakes industry.

The *Morse*, along with the other Bessemer boats, became part of the Pittsburgh fleet in 1901. She remained in Pittsburgh colors until 1954, when she was sold to Wyandotte Transportation, a division of Wyandotte Chemical Company. Wyandotte converted the *Morse* to a barge and renamed her *Wy Chem 105*. In 1955, the barge was purchased by a salvage company and sold to Merritt-Chapman and Scott of New York City. The construction firm used the hull as a temporary breakwater at the Clague Road water intake being built at Bay Village, Ohio. When the Bay Village project was completed, the barge was sold to Roen Steamship Company of Sturgeon Bay, Wisconsin. From 1958 until 1974, Roen used the hull as a breakwater or cofferdam in a number of construction projects around the lakes. In 1975, she was scrapped at Bay Shipbuilding in Sturgeon Bay, but a section of her midbody was retained for use as a yard barge. That portion of the old *Morse* remains in use at Bay yet today.[9]

The *Houghton* went into service for Bessemer in August of 1899. On September 5, the wheel chains that connected her steering wheel to her rudder failed while she was downbound with the barge *John Fritz* in the narrow Middle Neebish Channel of the St. Marys River. Despite the fact that the *Houghton*'s captain immediately reduced her speed to "dead slow" so that the unsteerable vessel could be anchored, the big vessel swung out of control, driving her bow twelve feet onto a limestone ledge alongside the channel. Caught in the current, the ship's stern was carried across the channel until it, too, grounded.

As if the ignominious grounding was not enough humiliation for the big new ship, her crew noticed almost immediately that the towline stretching between the *Houghton* and the *Fritz* had gone limp in the water, and the unpowered, heavily laden barge was bearing down on them. While the crew aboard the *Fritz* frantically scrambled to drop her anchors, the barge struck the ship lying helpless across the channel, "cutting through [her] plates like a tin can."[10] Badly holed and taking on a torrent of water, the heavily laden *Houghton* settled to the bottom almost immediately, blocking the busy channel and forcing vessels transiting the river to go to anchor. For the first time since the Soo Locks opened in 1855, Lake Superior was cut off from the other lakes and vital ore shipments ground to a halt, creating what some referred to as "the most appalling situation in lake freight traffic that has been experienced in a quarter of a century."[11]

From the standpoint of shipowners, the accident couldn't have occurred at a worse time. The Great Lakes shipping industry was experiencing unusually high demand for shipments that fall, and ore was moving out of Duluth at the very profitable rate of two dollars a ton.[12] Prior to the accident, freight was moving through the river at the staggering rate of a million tons every ten days. Even higher tonnages were anticipated as grain shippers tried to move the immense crop that had just been harvested.[13]

Salvage crews were hurriedly dispatched to the wreck site to refloat the *Houghton* and reopen the critical river channel. While salvors optimistically predicted that the operation would take only several days, some shipowners argued that it would make more sense for them to buy the sunken hulk of the big freighter and have it dynamited so that the river could be opened to traffic as soon as possible.[14]

The "Houghton blockade" became front page news across the Great Lakes region as scores of ships attempting to transit the river were forced to go to anchor. Owners of many of the ships caught below the blockade withdrew their ships from the Lake Superior iron ore trade and placed them in service on the less profitable routes on the lower lakes. James J. Hill and other officials of the Northern Steamship Company operating passenger ships between Buffalo and Duluth devised a creative system that enabled them to continue offering service to and from Lake Superior. The downbound steamer *North West* discharged her passengers on the shores of Neebish Island, just above the wreck site, and they walked along the shore to a spot below the *Houghton* where the upbound steamer *North Star* had docked. Passengers from the *North Star* similarly trekked up the river to reach the *North West*. Once the two groups of passengers had made the switch and their baggage and other cargo had been portaged overland, the two ships doubled back on their routes. While the system seemed highly innovative to many onlookers, others undoubtedly noted with some amusement that prior to the construction of the first locks at Sault Ste. Marie only a few decades earlier, *all* traffic between Lake Superior and the lower lakes involved a similar overland portage of passengers and cargo.[15]

Within two days, salvage officials announced that their divers had successfully placed a temporary wooden patch over the hole in the hull of the *Houghton* and efforts were underway to pump out the flooded cargo hold. As the water was being removed from the hull, a large crew of workers was taken to the wreck site to begin lightering cargo from the ship's hold to make it easier to refloat her. It was estimated that about two thousand tons of ore would have to be laboriously shovelled out of the hold before the vessel would float free.[16]

Five days after the ship had blocked the channel, salvage officials reported that pumping and lightering operations had managed to raise the bow of the *Houghton* more than forty inches, but they found that the ship was wedged tightly in a crevasse in the rocky bottom of the river channel. A decision was made to blast out the rock holding the ship, and drilling equipment was rushed to the site to bore holes into the rock ledge so dynamite charges could be set. A stout hawser twelve inches in diameter was run from the bow of the *Houghton* to a large tree on the shore to control the downstream swing of the bow once it was freed. The last thing the salvors wanted was for the big ship to float free, but out of control, and possibly ground itself again.[17]

The following day, Monday, September 11, lightering and pumping efforts had raised the bow of the *Houghton* by five feet and blasting operations began shortly after dawn. To the dismay of salvors and officials from Bessemer Steamship who were present at the site, the first blasts managed only to crack the sturdy rock ledge. Many additional charges had to be touched off before the rock was sufficiently shattered to allow the vessel to be pulled free of the ledge by four powerful tugs. After six days, the Houghton blockade had finally ended. Up and down the river, crews on more than two hundred ships idled by the blockade prepared to weigh anchor and get underway.

To avoid the chaos that would result by turning loose two hundred ships in the narrow confines of the river, vessel movements were tightly controlled by Captain A. H. Davis of the Revenue Service, a predecessor of the Coast Guard. Word went out to ships' captains that downbound vessels would get underway first, and they would be released from their anchorages in

The *Douglass Houghton*, wrecked in the St. Marys River in 1899. Alongside the sunken Bessemer freighter is a salvage barge from Soo Lighter & Wrecking. A pencilled note on the back of the original photo says that 332 ships were delayed when the *Houghton* blocked the critical shipping channel. (State Archives of Michigan)

the order in which they had arrived. One-third mile spacing was mandated between ships, resulting in a forty-mile-long procession winding its way down the river. Together, the ships in the convoy carried 300,000 tons of iron ore, 11,900,000 board feet of lumber, and 900,000 bushels of wheat.[18]

Only two ships in the convoy were involved in incidents during the carefully orchestrated procession down the river. The 300-foot package freighter *Northern Wave* grounded, but was easily released. Pickand Mather's 300-foot, wooden bulk freighter *Crete* ran onto the boulders behind the *Houghton* and was trapped for about two hours before being pulled free by tugs.[19]

The following day, large crowds gathered at Port Huron and Detroit, and at other points along the St. Clair and Detroit rivers, in the expectation that they would see an unprecedented procession of ships passing downbound. The first vessels to reach the lower rivers were the fast passenger steamers *North Star* and *North Land*, but they led no grand flotilla. The ships had become strung out during their voyages down Lake Huron. With the exception of a group of twenty-five freighters that passed Detroit at 9 p.m. on Tuesday, September 13, most of the ships freed from the blockade steamed past the gathered crowds of onlookers singly or in disappointingly small groups.[20]

Shipping officials and government leaders were relieved that the supplies of iron ore so vital to the U.S. economy were again flowing off the ranges bordering Lake Superior. At the same time, the *Houghton* incident vividly demonstrated that neither the industry nor the nation could afford to be totally dependent on a narrow river channel that could so easily be shut down. Within a few years after the sinking of the *Houghton*, construction began on a second channel around the west side of Neebish Island. Once the West Neebish Channel had been hewn through the solid rock between the island and the mainland, it became the downbound route, while the Middle Neebish Channel was limited to upbound traffic.[21]

In 1901, the *Houghton* and the other Bessemer vessels passed into the Pittsburgh fleet. Nine years later, she was reboilered and one of her two stacks was removed.[22] In the summer of 1945, both the *Houghton* and her nemesis, the *Fritz*, were sold to the Upper Lakes and St. Lawrence Transportation Company, the predecessor of today's Upper Lakes Shipping, and the two ships were registered as part of the Canadian fleet. They served their new owners for twenty-three years, making hundreds of trips through the St. Marys River, where the career of the *Houghton* had almost come to an end so many years earlier.

The *Houghton* and her barge were laid-up at Toronto in 1967, replaced by newer vessels with greater carrying capacities. In 1969, the *Houghton*'s cabins were removed and her hull was filled with stone and sunk to form a breakwater at Ontario Place, a government park. The *Fritz* and her twin sister, the barge *John A. Roebling*, had met the same fate the prior year. An observation platform now stands atop the *Houghton*'s forecastle, and her name is still visible on her bow.[23] To the crewmembers aboard the hundreds of ships that pass Ontario Place each year, she is a reminder of a long and proud era in the history of shipping on the Great Lakes.

Many people view the years of the launching of the *Morse* and *Houghton*, 1898 and 1899, as representing a major watershed in the history of the bulk freight industry. Prior to that time, ships were substantially unloaded by hand. Mechanical systems like the Brown Hoist had helped to speed up the process, but down in the holds of the freighters, buckets and barrels were still filled by sweaty laborers wielding shovels.

In 1898, most of the manual labor was eliminated when a Brown Hoist at Conneaut, Ohio, was fitted with a clamshell bucket designed by Hoover and Mason Company of Chicago. Lowered into the hold of a ship in the open position, the jaws would automatically close and scoop up cargo as the bucket was hoisted. Each clamshell bucket had a capacity of about five tons of cargo per bite. By using twelve hoists with clamshell buckets, the dock at Conneaut could unload ships at an average rate of about nine hundred tons an hour, meaning that the largest vessels on the lakes, ships like the *Morse* and *Houghton*, could be completely unloaded during a single eight-hour shift.

As ports around the lakes scrambled to install clamshell buckets on their hoists, a very different type of unloader was introduced in 1899 that totally revolutionized the unloading of bulk cargoes. Within a few years, the remarkably efficient "Hulett" made all other unloading systems obsolete.

George Hulett was an eccentric genius who wore baggy clothes and always seemed to have a wet plug of tobacco in his cheek. In 1899, he demonstrated a new type of unloader at the docks at Conneaut which was just as strange in appearance as he was. The Hulett unloader used a clamshell bucket, but it was attached to the end of a long steel arm, rather than being suspended from cables. The top of the arm was connected to a horizontal rocker arm that, in turn, was connected to the top of a movable platform housing a large hopper. Together, the system looked like a massive prehistoric beast.

Rather than being controlled by someone stationed on the dock, the Hulett steam-powered unloader featured an operator who rode in a cab mounted just above the bucket. From his vantage point, the operator would lower the arm into the hold of a ship and take a ten-ton bite of cargo. As the arm was raised out of the hold, it would automatically pivot toward the top of the platform on the dock until the bucket was stationed directly over the hopper. The operator would then open the jaws of the bucket and the cargo would drop into the hopper, from which chutes would carry it to waiting rail cars. Because the operator rode into the hold atop the bucket, the unloading system was about twice as fast as the hoists and did a better job of cleaning a ship's hold than any of the other equipment then in use.

Many of those who had gathered to watch the demonstration at the Carnegie Steel dock in Conneaut doubted that George Hulett's odd-looking contraption would work at all. They stood in stunned silence as they watched it take bite after bite of ore from the hold of the ship. They knew that what they were seeing was a glimpse into the future of their industry. The Carnegie Steel officials wasted no time in contracting with Hulett to have three of the new machines installed at their dock. They went into operation during the 1899 season, and a fourth was added in 1901, by which time dock officials at Cleveland and Erie had also placed orders for Hulett unloaders.[24]

George Hulett continually improved his unloaders. Starting in about 1911, he began producing electrically-driven Huletts with a bucket capacity of seventeen tons. Twenty-ton capacity Huletts were eventually installed at a number of ports, though the seventeen-ton electric model was always the backbone of the industry. In 1925, William Livingstone, long-time president of the Lake Carriers' Association, wrote that, "the thing which in my judgement most influenced the change in type and size of the bulk freighters on the lakes came about through the invention of the Hulett unloader . . . ."[25] George Hulett, the unlikely inventor, profoundly altered the course of the Great Lakes shipping industry. In time, even the ships would be changed so that they would better conform to the capabilities of the unloading machines.

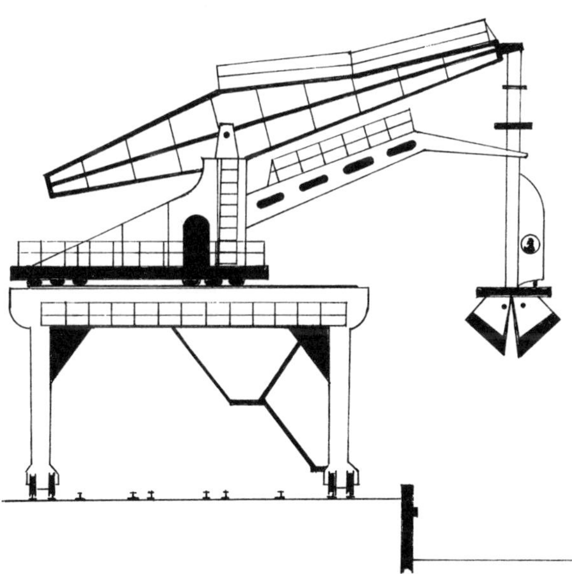

A drawing of a typical Hulett unloader, first demonstrated in 1898. The arm of the unloader can be lowered into the hold of a ship by the operator, who rides in a tiny cab just above the clamshell bucket. The ore, coal, or stone scooped out of the ship's hold can then be dropped into railcars positioned under the unloading rig. (Author's collection)

Notes

1. "She Did Not Slide," *Bay City Times*, July 31, 1898.
2. "She Slid Sunday," *Bay City Times*, August 1, 1898.
3. "She Did Not Slide."
4. J. B. Mansfield, ed., *History of the Great Lakes*, vol. I (Chicago: J. H. Beers and Co., 1899; reprint, Cleveland: Freshwater Press, 1972), 414.
5. "She Did Not Slide."
6. Ship Biography, Institute for Great Lakes Research, Bowling Green State University.
7. Mansfield, 453.v
8. Gordon Pritchard Bugbee, "The Life and Times of the Bessemer Fleet, Part 2," *Telescope* 27, no. 3 (May–June 1978): 73.
9. Ship Biography, Institute for Great Lakes Research, Bowling Green State University.
10. "Houghton is Wreck," *Detroit Free Press*, September 6, 1896.
11. "Navigation Situation Appalling," *Detroit Free Press*, September 7, 1899.
12. Ibid.
13. "Two Hundred Vessels," *Detroit Free Press*, September 10, 1899.
14. "Navigation Situation Appalling."
15. Ibid.
16. "Pumps Have Started," *Detroit Free Press*, September 8, 1899.
17. "Two Hundred Vessels."
18. "Dynamite," *Detroit Free Press*, September 11, 1899.
19. Ibid.
20. "Rush Last Night," *Detroit Free Press*, September 13, 1899.
21. Bugbee, 73.
22. The second stack on the *Morse* was also removed early in her career, probably when she had new boilers installed in 1903.
23. Rev. Peter Van Der Linden, ed., *Great Lakes Ships We Remember II* (Cleveland: Freshwater Press, 1984), 147.
24. James P. Barry, *Ships of the Great Lakes* (Berkeley: Howell-North Books, 1973), 178.
25. Harlan Hatcher, *Lake Erie* (New York: Bobbs-Merrill, 1945), 326.

12

Quad Queens

At the turn of the century, one astute observer of the bulk shipping industry paused to sum up the status of shipbuilding on the Great Lakes:

> For ten years past it has been impossible to get a strictly modern boat on the lakes. Size and style changed between laying of the keel and the launching of the ship. Nowhere in the world has the progress in marine architecture been so pronounced as on the Great Lakes, where a greater tonnage was launched in 1896 than in all the rest of the United States. There never has been a time when, nor a waterway where, progress has been so rapid as in the past half dozen years on the Great Lakes.[1]

The record of the previous six years had been genuinely astonishing. At the end of the period, ships were one hundred feet longer, and both beams and depths had grown by about five feet. The increased dimensions translated into gross tonnages that were fifty percent greater than they had been six years before and, even more importantly, they doubled the carrying capacity. Many who had watched the dramatic metamorphosis occur undoubtedly felt that freighters like the *Morse* and *Houghton* represented the culmination of the shipbuilder's art. They firmly believed that ships would change little in coming years, perhaps even decades.

Change is the only thing constant, however. Calendars had just rolled over to the new century when throngs of Lorain, Ohio, residents crowded into the shipyard just above the Black River bridge to witness the launching of the first 500-foot freighter. Many were disappointed by what they saw. "In appearance, this first of the 500-footers was the antithesis of the high and lordly *Morse*, *Houghton*, and *Poe*."[2] The forecastle of the new ship, the *John W. Gates*, was barely raised above the main deck, and there was no stern deckhouse at all. The pilothouse was diminutive and looked as if it had been built for a much smaller ship. A few of the knowledgeable boatwatchers in the crowd expressed the opinion that the design of the new vessel was a throwback to the *Victory* and *Zenith City* that had been built five years earlier.

STR. JOHN W. GATES

497'x52'x30'
Queen of the Lakes
January 20, 1900 to April 9, 1904

In fact, the lines of the *Gates* had been drawn by Washington I. Babcock, the same naval architect who had designed the *Victory* and *Zenith City*. It was his belief that structures on the deck of a freighter should be minimized so as not to interfere with the machinery used to unload it. Like the two earlier vessels, the *Gates* had only three masts and a tall black funnel to break the otherwise clean sweep of her deck astern of her pilothouse.[3]

Regardless of what the crowd of onlookers thought, Augustus Wolvin, who managed the American Steamship Company fleet, was not the slightest bit disappointed by the new addition to the fleet. Not only was the *Gates* the longest, widest, and deepest ship on the lakes, but her net tonnage was slightly higher than that of the *Morse* and *Houghton*, which meant she would have an excellent carrying capacity.

In christening the *Gates*, American had departed from the tradition of naming their vessels after important cities around the lakes. Instead, the new ship was named after the president of American Steel and Wire Company, one of American's important customers. John Gates was on hand for the launching of his namesake, and he was very proud that the new steamer had his name boldly emblazoned on her bow. Until his death in 1911, he would maintain an interest in the vessel far exceeding that normally shown by the corporate officials after whom the big freighters are named. It is said that he always demanded "spit and polish" for her, to the extent that crewmembers on the *Gates* soon dubbed her the "John W. Workhorse."[4]

STR. JAMES J. HILL

497'x52'x30'
Queen of the Lakes
January 24, 1900 to April 9, 1904

The *Gates* was the first of four, basically identical ships launched between January 20 and June 20, 1900. While they were, and are, referred to as the first 500-footers, they were actually only 497 feet long. The *James J. Hill* followed the *Gates* down the ways at Lorain on January 24. On May 5, the *Isaac L. Ellwood* was launched at the F. W. Wheeler yard at West Bay City, Michigan, followed on June 20 by the *William Edenborn.*

The *John W. Gates* waiting for a lock at Sault Ste. Marie. The two doghouses on her deck housed crewmembers who had to be added after the traditional two-watch system was replaced by the current three-watch system. Designed by Washington I. Babcock for the Wolvin-managed American Steamship fleet, the *Gates* and her three sister ships had submarine sterns like the earlier *Victory*. (State Archives of Michigan)

STR. ISAAC L. ELLWOOD

497'x52'x25'2"
Queen of the Lakes
May 5, 1900 to April 9, 1904

Originally, all four of the ships were to be built at the Lorain shipyard of Cleveland Ship Building, but in the spring of 1899 the company merged with the other major Great Lakes yards to form American Ship Building Company. Managers of the giant shipbuilding firm decided that it would be more efficient to split the contract for the four boats between the Lorain yard and the idle West Bay City yard that was also part of the new company.[5]

STR. WILLIAM EDENBORN

497'x52'x25'2"
Queen of the Lakes
June 20, 1900 to April 9, 1904

While all four of the ships had long, and largely unevent ful, careers, Wolvin and Gates must have been shocked to hear that the *Gates* had been damaged while on her maiden voyage. On April 30, 1900, while lying to behind Whitefish Point for weather with a number of other ships, the giant *Gates* sagged against the 292-foot steamer *Mariska*, owned by the Minnesota Steamship Company. The collision cracked several plates on the starboard side of the *Gates*, resulting in about $10,000 in damage to her hull. She went on to the lakehead, where temporary repairs were made before she set out on her return voyage. More permanent repairs would have to wait until she returned to the lower lakes, as there was no drydock on Lake Superior large enough to accommodate the new ship.

The *Gates* and her three sister ships were purchased by steel magnate Andrew Carnegie just after the turn of the century and became part of his famous Pittsburgh Steamship fleet. While the stack on the *Gates* was still little more than a stovepipe, it was considerably shorter than stacks on earlier ships. On vessels with steel hulls and superstructures, like the *Gates*, there was much less chance that a hot ash from the boilers would set the vessel afire, so their stacks did not have to be as tall as they had been on earlier wooden ships. (Author's collection)

The *Ellwood* and *Edenborn* were involved in an even more serious incident a few years later, after all four of the ships had become part of the Pittsburgh Steamship fleet. On November 28, 1905, the two ships departed Duluth in a convoy with the steamers *R. W. England* and *Mataafa*, and the *Mataafa*'s consort, the barge *James Nasmyth*. It had been a bad fall for the shipping industry. Two major storms had already swept across the lakes, and as the small convoy cleared the piers at Duluth, the sky turned black and winds increased as a violent northeasterly gale suddenly roared in off Lake Superior.

As if in unison, the captains of the four steamers brought their ships around to make a dash for the safety of the Duluth harbor. The frigid waters had already become a frenzy of waves and spray was washing over the decks of the five vessels. Buffeted by waves and wind, the *Edenborn* and *England* managed to negotiate the narrow opening between the piers. Once inside the harbor, though, the *England* was almost immediately driven onto the beach by the fierce winds.

As the *Ellwood* struggled toward the relative safety of the harbor, the wind and waves flung the massive ship against the concrete piers. Recovering, she managed to limp into the harbor. But the big freighter was taking on water, and before her crew could get the pumps started she sank to the bottom in shallow water.

As the *Mataafa* approached the piers, her deckhands managed to cast off the towline linking their ship to the *Nasmyth*. With torrents of driven snow making visibility difficult, the captain of the 450-foot freighter tried to get up enough speed to dash between the piers and into the harbor. When she was almost abreast of the piers, a giant swell lifted the big ship and threw her against the end of the north pier with an impact that knocked most of her crewmen to the decks. Before the *Mataafa* could regain headway, her bow swung around, heading back out to sea, and her stern crashed against the south pier, tearing off her rudder. Within seconds, the rudderless vessel was driven broadside into the rocky, shallow water along the shore, and under the relentless pounding of the wind and waves she broke in two.

Duluth is perched on a sprawling hillside that stands above the harbor. From everywhere in town, the residents have a view of the harbor and the west end of Lake Superior. In the waning light of that November afternoon, thousands saw the tragic events taking place at the harbor entrance and many began making their way toward the piers. The Duluth lifesaving crew was already on the scene, and they had used an eprouvette mortar to fire a light line out to the stranded *Mataafa*. They then attached a heavier hawser to the end of the line and signalled for those aboard the *Mataafa* to pull it out to their ship so a breeches buoy could be rigged to evacuate them from the wreck. As they took up a strain on the small heaving line, it rose out of the water, but the instant the cold wind hit the wet line it turned into a brittle icicle. As the crewmen heaved on the frozen line, it suddenly parted, and they crashed to the wet deck.

As night settled over Duluth, the thousands who had gathered on the beach in the driving snowstorm lit bonfires to keep warm and provide some beacon of hope for the crewmen stranded on the *Mataafa*. Temperatures plummeted to twenty below zero, with wind chills of more than fifty below. There was no source of warmth aboard the stricken freighter, except the little given off by the bodies huddled together at both ends of the ship. In the minutes after the *Mataafa* had broken in half, water flooding into her engine room had extinguished the fires in her boilers, and it wasn't long before the radiators in her cabins had grown as cold as the steel of her hull. At the forward end of the ship, the captain gathered deck crewmembers in his cabin, where they clustered together against the inboard wall to escape the torrents of water pouring through the broken portholes. At the stern, the chief engineer and the engine room and galley personnel weren't as lucky. The stern had settled in the water, and there was no dry place for them to gather.

In the morning, the weather abated a little, and a lifeboat was launched from shore to evacuate the crew of the *Mataafa*. They found the captain and other deck crewmembers in the forward cabin, cold, wet, and hungry, but alive. At the stern, the lifesaving crew found only nine dead bodies, including one totally encased in a shroud of ice. What had begun the day before as the last trip of the 1905 season had ended tragically as literally the last voyage for the *Mataafa* and nine of her crew.

The *Mataafa* was the victim of one of the worst storms to ever sweep across the lakes. Thirty vessels were wrecked on Lake Superior alone, including fourteen that had been driven ashore by winds gusting as high as eighty miles an hour at the height of the storm. For years, the killer storm of 1905 and the tragic loss of the *Mataafa* were commemorated in a very unusual way. An enterprising cigar manufacturer profited from the disaster by producing "*Mataafa* Cigars," which bore a picture of the ill-fated ship on their bands.[6]

The *Ellwood* and *Edenborn* lived to sail another day. In fact, the four sister ships that had begun their careers within months of each other were all to end their careers in the same

The wrecked hull of the *Mataafa* the morning after she was driven onto the beach at Duluth and broken in half by a violent November storm in 1905. Nine crewmembers at the stern of the ship froze to death during the ordeal. The hull of the *Mataafa* was later salvaged and returned to service. Launched in 1899 as the *Str. Pennsylvania*, the ship was finally scrapped in Germany in 1965. (State Archives of Michigan)

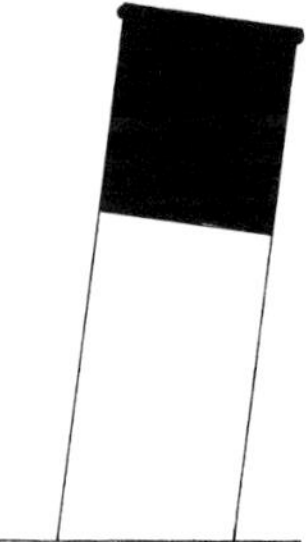

The *John W. Gates* and her three sister ships operated on the lakes until 1961. By that time Andrew Carnegie's Pittsburgh Steamship Company had become part of U.S. Steel's Great Lakes Fleet. Ships in the giant steelmaker's fleet had silver stacks with a black cap and were often referred to as "silverstackers" or "tin stackers." Later, a white U.S. Steel logo was added to the black cap. (Author's collection)

year. The *Edenborn* and *Hill* were both sunk in 1961 to form a breakwater at Gordan Park in Cleveland. The *Gates* and *Ellwood* were scrapped the same year at Conneaut.

The launching of the *Gates* and her three sisters was evidence of the fact that despite the incredible changes in Great Lakes bulk freighters during the last six years of the nineteenth century, the process of evolution had not come to a halt. Those who witnessed the *Gates* slide into the waters on that cold January day in 1900 could not possibly have foreseen the developments that would occur during the first six years of the twentieth century.

Even those few who were bold enough to predict further growth in the size of ships could not, in their wildest imaginations, have envisioned that ships would grow by another hundred feet in the next six years, or that carrying capacities would leap by another fifty percent. The efficiency of bulk freighters on the lakes had already surpassed everyone's wildest expectations. In 1900, for example, a ship like the *Gates* could haul wheat from Chicago to Buffalo for 4.42-cents a bushel. It would cost 9.98-cents—more than twice as much—to move that same bushel by rail, even though the overland trip was much shorter than the circuitous water route. Shipping iron ore, coal, or stone by water resulted in similar savings.

Shipowners were masters of the principles of economies of scale. They knew that if they built a ship with a larger carrying capacity they could carry more cargo with basically the same crew and operating costs. Larger ships, then, allowed them to attract more cargo by offering shippers better rates. At the same time, not all of the savings were passed on to shippers. The shipowners, too, realized larger profits by operating larger ships. Thus the die was unalterably cast: shipowners would forever seek bigger vessels.

Notes

1. J. B. Mansfield, ed., *History of the Great Lakes*, vol. I (Chicago: J. H. Beer and Co., 1899; reprint, Cleveland: Freshwater Press, Cleveland, 1972), 357–59.
2. Gordon Pritchard Bugbee, "The Life and Times of the Bessemer Fleet, Part 2," *Telescope* 27, no. 3 (May–June 1978): 78.
3. Ibid.
4. Ibid.
5. American Ship Building Company was formed by the merger of Cleveland Ship Building, Ship Owners' Dry Dock Company, Globe Iron Works, American Steel Barge Company, Detroit Dry Dock Company, Chicago Ship Building, and Milwaukee Dry Dock Company on March 16, 1899. F. W. Wheeler and Company joined in June of 1899, followed in April of 1900 by the Union Dry Dock Company. A Canadian subsidiary, Western Ship Building of Port Arthur, Ontario, was incorporated in 1909, and the Delta Shipbuilding Company of Toledo, Ohio, was acquired in 1945.
6. Walter Havighurst, *The Long Ships Passing* (New York: Macmillan, 1942), 245–47.

13

The Magnificent Yellow Kid

Testifying before the U.S. Congress in 1904, William Livingstone, president of the powerful Lake Carriers' Association, declared: "Fifteen years ago a 2,000-ton ship was considered large. Today, I would not take a 2,000-ton ship as a gift, provided I had to keep her in condition and run her."[1] Quite literally, small ships constituted an endangered species. While there were still hundreds of small vessels operating on the lakes, they had been on the road toward extinction since the 1882 launching of the *Onoko*. The shift to the use of iron and then steel in ship construction had removed the inherent size constraints limiting shipbuilders during the long era of wooden ships. It also had the effect of reducing the amount of variation in the size of ships in the Great Lakes bulk fleet.

Although the trailblazing *Onoko* was the longest ship on the lakes when it was launched in 1882, less than two decades later she had been dwarfed by the *Gates* and her sisters that were two hundred feet longer, with almost triple the gross tonnage. As ships grew larger, with greater carrying capacities, economies of scale gradually pushed freight rates downward. Simply put, big ships could carry cargo cheaper than small ones. At the same time, the higher costs incurred in constructing large, steam-powered iron and steel ships made it impossible for many owners of wooden ships to make the transition to iron or steel vessels. Wooden ships had commonly been owned by individuals, many by the captains that sailed them, but the big iron and steel freighters generally operated under the corporate flags of the relatively few firms that dominated the iron mining and shipping industries.

From the launching of the iron-hulled *Onoko* in 1882 until the end of the 1903 shipping season, 239 iron, steel, and composite-hull bulk freighters were launched by shipyards on the Great Lakes. Only 38 of them had gross tonnages of 2,000 or less, and most of those were built during the decade immediately following the debut of the *Onoko*. Of the 169 ships built in the eleven years between 1893 and 1903, only 8 were under 2,000 gross tons; 161 were over 2,000 gross tons, 145 were over 3,000 gross tons, 95 were over 4,000 gross tons, and 19 of the newest freighters were over 5,000 gross tons.

In the years following William Livingstone's Congressional testimony in 1904, only *one* steel-hulled bulk freighter of less than 4,000 gross tons was launched by U.S. shipyards on the lakes, and that was the *Str. Calcite*, a self-unloader of 3,996 gross tons.[2] By 1904, owners of ships in the 2,000 gross ton range were finding that their little vessels were no longer economically viable. Big steel freighters were dominating the major bulk cargo trades on the Great Lakes, and the small freighters were left to try and eke out an existance on the fringes of what had become the world's premier bulk industry.

Even large corporate fleets found it difficult to keep pace with the rapid growth in the size of ships. Vessels that were on the cutting edge of shipbuilding technology when they were launched were often found to be too small to compete efficiently only a few years later. Most of the ships had hulls and machinery that would be serviceable for several more decades, but their small size made them economically obsolete. To prolong the lives of many of these vessels, shipping companies often had them lengthened, or "stretched," to increase their carrying capacities. Typical was the lengthening of M. A. Hanna Company's *Str. Republic*, which was lengthened at American Ship Building's Cleveland yard during the winter of 1903–04. The 310-foot freighter had been launched in 1890 and was measured at 2,316 gross tons. By lengthening the *Republic*'s cargo hold by 72 feet, the vessel's carrying capacity was increased by 1,300 tons per trip; the cost was only about $70,000, far less than her owners would have paid to build a new ship. During an average season, the lengthened vessel's earning power was increased by about $13,000, representing a significant return on their investment.[3] With increased carrying capacity, the *Republic* was able to avoid the shipbreaker's torches, and she continued operating on the lakes until 1917.[4]

While the *Republic* was undergoing lengthening at American Ship Building's Cleveland yard, workers at the AmShip yard in nearby Lorain were putting the finishing touches on an innovative new ship that would forever alter the techniques used to construct Great Lakes bulk freighters. At 560 feet in length, the *Str. Augustus B. Wolvin* would also wrest the title Queen of the Lakes from the *Gates* and her three sisters. Launched on April 9, 1904, and celebrated with a chicken salad and champagne luncheon in the yard's mould loft, the new ship was built for A. B. Wolvin's Acme Steamship of Duluth.

Born in Cleveland in 1857, Wolvin had started his marine career as a ten-year-old cabin boy on the Great Lakes, and by the time he was twenty-one he had worked his way up to captain. After a brief detour into the produce business, Wolvin went to Duluth in 1888 to work in the general vessel commission business. He remained in that position until 1895, when he left to start the five-boat Zenith Transit Company and manage other vessels, including American Steamship's "City Line." When U.S. Steel's Pittsburgh Steamship fleet was formed in 1901, it absorbed the fleets managed by Wolvin, and he played a major role in the creation and management of what became the largest fleet on the lakes. By 1904 he was vice president and general manager of Pittsburgh Steamship, which then operated 116 vessels, and the latest addition to the fleet was christened in his honor.[5]

STR. AUGUSTUS B. WOLVIN

560'x56'x32'
Queen of the Lakes
April 9, 1904 to April 8, 1905

While the size of ships generally tends to inch upward incrementally, with each new generation of vessels being only modestly larger than the preceeding generation, the *Wolvin* represented a major stride forward in size. The *Wolvin* was so long, in fact, that the drydock and building berth at the Lorain shipyard had to be lengthened before she could be built. Designed under the leadership of James C. Wallace, vice president of American Ship Building, the new freighter was fully sixty-three feet longer than the *Gates*, *Hill*, *Ellwood*, and *Edenborn* launched just four years earlier. She was also four feet wider and two feet deeper, and her gross tonnage was ten percent higher. Even more importantly, the *Wolvin*'s net tonnage was almost twenty percent higher than the *Gates* and her sisters. Net tonnage is the key determinant in how much cargo a ship will be able to carry.

On the outside, the *Wolvin* looked much like the flush-decked *Gates* and the earlier *Zenith City* designed by Washington Babcock. There was no raised forecastle deck forward, and at the bow the main deck held only the pilothouse and a small cabin for the captain. At her stern, the galley and all cabins were located below the spar deck. The clean lines of her deck were broken only by thirty-three hatches, coamings around the various engine and boiler openings, the smokestack, and a skylight above the dining room. Most steamboat aficionados agreed that she was nowhere near as pleasing to the eye as ships like the *Morse* or *Houghton*.

While her exterior design may have been a throwback to an earlier era, it was beneath her steel skin that James Wallace and his staff had worked their magic. The *Wolvin* was the first freighter built without main deck beams and hold stanchions. Until the *Wolvin*, construction techniques for iron and steel ships differed little from those used for wooden ships. The timbers that supported the decks of wooden ships were not strong enough to span the width of the vessel without support, so the middle of each timber rested on a vertical hold stanchion running from the keel of the ship up to the timber beam supporting the deck planking. The hold stanchions were spaced every twelve or twenty-four feet down the center of the cargo hold, and they were an obstacle to the rapid unloading of ships by means of Huletts or other automated unloading systems. Not only did the stanchions get in the way of the unloading operators, they were often damaged by the unloading buckets.

Framing on steel freighters built before the *Wolvin* was almost identical to that on wooden ships, except that I-beams had been substituted for timbers and steel plates replaced wooden deck planking. On the *Wolvin*, however, a heavy arched deck support replaced the traditional deck beams; it bore the weight of the deck without being supported by hold stanchions. The cargo hold of the *Wolvin* was a great, open cavern—409 feet long, 43 feet wide at the top, and 24 feet wide at the bottom—perfectly suited to being unloaded by the automated systems then in use. After touring the freighter, one writer remarked that "When you stand at the bow of this ship and look aft through her unobstructed hold, gracefully arched over by its steel girders at the hatches, you feel as though you were in the Detroit-Windsor tunnel, and that at any minute an automobile may come whirring out of the dunnage deck and race down the vast tube into the darkness at the engine room bulkhead."[6]

The *Wolvin* was also one of the first ships built with her hatches on twelve-foot centers, instead of the more common twenty-four-foot spacing. Because chutes on the upper lakes ore loading docks were spaced twelve feet apart, when a ship with hatches on twenty-four-foot centers was being loaded every other chute would be lowered, and ore held in the pockets would slide down into the cargo hold. Then the boat would move twelve feet down the dock and the remaining chutes would dump their cargo. The shift to twelve-foot hatch spacing allowed ships like the *Wolvin* to load without shifting at the dock. Although this saved some time, it created other problems. Hatch openings had to be narrower when spaced on twelve-foot centers, making it more difficult to negotiate the buckets of unloading rigs into or out of the hatches. It also left little room on deck between the hatches for deckhands to work, creating both an inconvenience and a safety hazard.

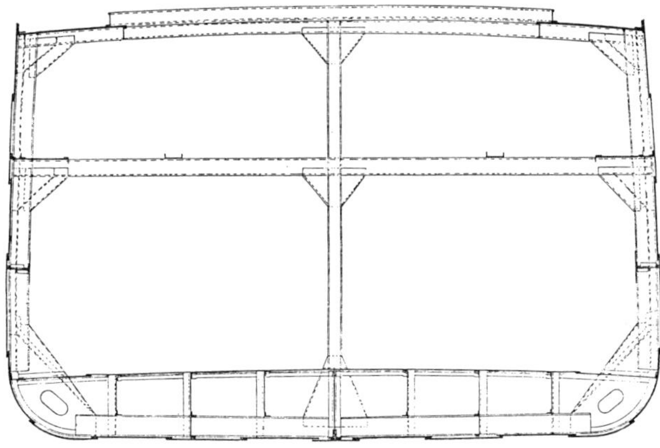

The framing on steel and iron freighters built between 1882 and the launch of the *Augustus B. Wolvin* in 1904 was very similar to that used on wooden ships. Wooden knees had been replaced by steel angles, but hold stanchions were still used to support the main and 'tween decks. (Author's collection)

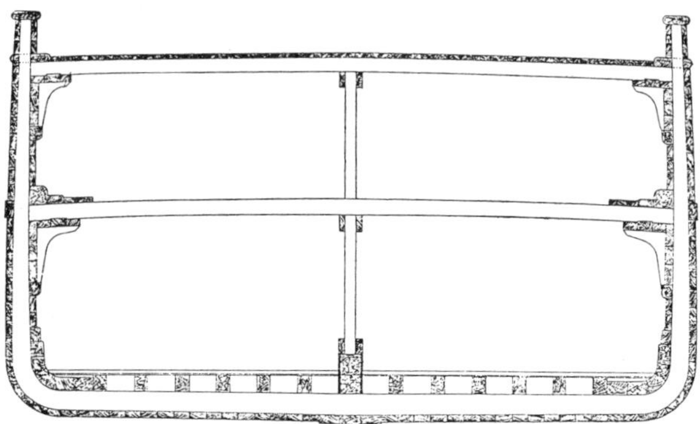

The hold of a typical wooden ore freighter, featuring a 'tween deck. Cargo was stowed both on the 'tween deck and on the bottom of the hold. The 'tween deck and main deck rest on wooden knees where the decks join the hull framing and stanchions support the center of both decks. (Author's collection)

In addition, the *Wolvin* was the first ship to be equipped with ballast tanks along her sides, sandwiched between the hull plating and the cargo hold below the deck arches. Ballast tanks allowed large ships to take on weight—water—so that they would float deep enough to get under the chutes at loading docks, virtually all of which had been designed to service smaller ships. Water ballast also helped stablize a ship when she was running without cargo in heavy seas. Until the *Wolvin*, water ballast was always carried in what is referred to as the "double bottom," the space between the outer hull of the ship and the bottom of the cargo hold, or "tank tops." The first ships with double bottoms appeared at the time of the *Onoko*, but the practice of carrying water ballast did not become popular until about 1890. After that it was almost univeral within the Great Lakes fleet. The side tanks on the *Wolvin* allowed the ship to carry much more water ballast, which was necessary to get the thirty-two-foot depth of the hull under the loading rigs.

The side tanks also made unloading easier. On ships built before the *Wolvin*, a portion of the cargo hold was located under the deck wing, the space between the hatch opening and the side of the ship. It was difficult for the buckets on the unloading rigs to reach cargo under the deck wing, and shovellers often had to be employed to clean cargo out of those recesses. On the *Wolvin*, however, the sidetanks forming the walls of the cargo hold sloped inward so that the bottom edge was almost directly below the ends of the hatch openings. As a result of this design innovation, unloading rigs were able to remove almost all of the cargo from the hold, greatly reducing the need to use shovellers for cleanup.

Subsequent to the *Wolvin*, all bulk freighters were built with arched deck beams and sidetanks, although the configuration of the sidetanks varied somewhat based on the types of cargo that would be carried. Vessels built primarily to haul grain or coal—relatively lightweight cargoes—generally had smaller sidetanks that increased the volume of cargo they could haul. While the shape of sidetanks has changed over the years, those on today's most modern freighters are very similar to those on the *Wolvin*, and they continue to perform the same functions.[7]

The *Wolvin* was also the first ship equipped with telescoping steel hatch covers instead of the traditional wooden hatch covers. It was an innovation that would win high praise from every deckhand who sailed the lakes. Until the *Wolvin*, deckhands had to lift the heavy wooden hatch covers off at every loading and unloading dock, then replace them again before clearing port. This long, backbreaking task added greatly to turnaround time in port. By contrast, hatch covers on the *Wolvin* were composed of overlapping leaves of steel that could be slid back to the outboard ends of the hatch opening by using deck winches. As the winches took up slack on cables attached to pad eyes at the center of each hatch cover, the leaves would slide over the top of each other until they were neatly stacked and the hatch was open and ready for loading or unloading. The telescoping hatches caught on quickly and were used on almost all ships built after the *Wolvin*—until single-piece steel hatch covers were pioneered on the *Str. William C. Atwater* in 1925.[8] A few ships continued to be built with wooden hatch covers until at least 1906, and vessels with wooden hatch covers could still be found on the lakes as late as the 1930s. Today, only a handful of older ships still employ telescoping hatch covers.

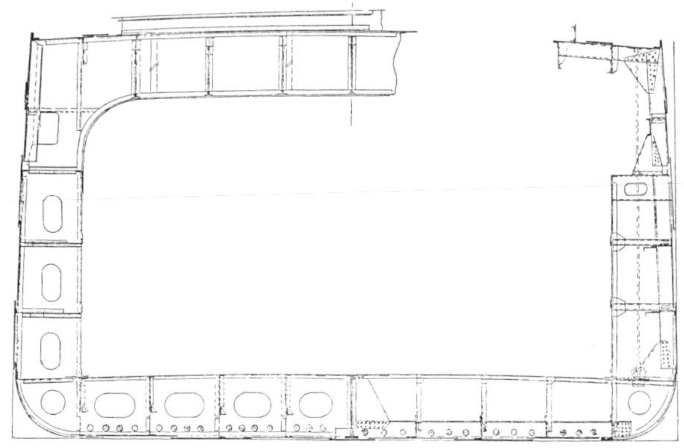

A view of hold framing similar to that used on the *Augustus B. Wolvin*. The use of arch construction allowed the elimination of hold stanchions and revolutionized ship construction. Sidetanks were sandwiched between the hull and the inside of the cargo hold and used for water ballast. The top right portion of the drawing has been cut away to show how deck and side framing were joined by triangular steel gussets, similar to the wooden knees that had been used previously. (Author's collection)

While the *Wolvin* embodied significant design innovations that would impact on the industry even after her long career on the lakes had ended, she was probably best known for her unique paint job. While the hulls of most lake freighters were painted utilitarian black, grey, or rust-red, the *Wolvin* was coated in vivid yellow above her waterline and bright green below it. She was almost immediately nicknamed "The Yellow Kid."

There is always risk in innovation, and the *Wolvin* was the most innovative bulk freighter to enter service on the lakes since McDougall launched his first whaleback in 1888. But any concern that Augustus Wolvin or the shipbuilders might have had was quickly dispelled when the unique new vessel went into service. On her maiden voyage, the *Wolvin* established a Great Lakes cargo record by loading 10,694 net tons of ore at Two Harbors, Minnesota. The *Wolvin* also proved to be a stalwart ship, operating on the lakes for more than six decades.

Only a few months after the big freighter was launched, Augustus Wolvin left his position with Pittsburgh Steamship, ending a distinguished maritime career that had spanned thirty-seven years. Starting as a ten-year-old cabin boy, Wolvin had climbed his way up through the hawsepipe until he managed the largest fleet to ever sail on the Great Lakes. Wolvin left the Pittsburgh fleet to accept a position as president of Zenith Furnace Company of Duluth, a blast furnace operation largely controlled by Pickands Mather. Wolvin still held major interests in seven ships of what was generally referred to as the "Wolvin fleet," even though the ships operated under flags of the Acme, Peavy, and Provident steamship companies. He played a role in the operation of the three fleets until Pickands Mather took over management responsibilities for all of the Wolvin vessels in 1906.

In 1913, the *Wolvin* and the other ships in the Acme, Peavy, and Provident fleets, along with four vessels of the Mesaba Steamship Company, two from the Interlake Company, two from the Huron Barge Company, and seven ships of the Lackawanna Steamship Company, were organized under the umbrella of the new Interlake Steamship Company, a subsidiary of Pickands Mather. Shortly after Interlake was formed, it also purchased seventeen ships from the Gilchrist Transportation Company. With a total of thirty-nine vessels flying the Pickands Mather house flag and sporting the familiar rust-red hulls with gleaming white superstructures, Interlake Steamship became the second largest fleet operating on the lakes.[9]

Sailors tend to be a little superstitious, and if any Pickands Mather officials were looking for some omen to indicate that they had made a wise decision in forming their new fleet, they got mixed messages during that 1913 season. On one hand, 1913 was an exceptionally busy year on the lakes. By the end of the season, bulk cargo shipments had exceeded the 100-million-ton mark for the first time ever. On the other hand, the industry was devastated by a horrible four-day storm of hurricane proportions that struck the lakes that November. Thirteen freighters were totally destroyed, including Interlake's *Argus* and *Hydrus*. If their experiences during that initial season were to presage the future of the Interlake fleet, Pickands Mather officials would have had to conclude that they could expect a mixed bag in future seasons. Such a conclusion would have been accurate.[10]

Augustus Wolvin died in 1932, but the ship that bore his name operated as part of the Interlake fleet for a remarkable fifty-three years. On two separate occasions the *Wolvin* underwent major renovations. In 1938, the water tube boilers that supplied steam to her 2,000-horsepower, quadruple expansion engine were replaced. At the same time, her cargo hold was rebuilt and a cabin constructed on her deck just forward of the stern. Then, in 1946, her twelve-foot center hatches were replaced with new hatches built on twenty-four foot centers, which had become standard on the lakes. During that modernization, the bow of the *Wolvin* was also substantially rebuilt: she received a raised forecastle deck and a new forward cabin and pilothouse. To balance the changes made at the bow, an updated smokestack, shorter than the original, was installed at the stern. The stack bore the familiar Interlake markings, a horizontal band of orange on a background of black.[11]

The *Augustus B. Wolvin* waiting to offload at Ashtabula, Ohio. The ship has been positioned under a battery of bridge cranes that will be used to unload the big freighter. Several Hulett unloaders can be seen in the background. The hull of the *Wolvin* is in the process of receiving a new coat of paint, which ends just aft of the bow section. (Institute for Great Lakes Research, Bowling Green State University)

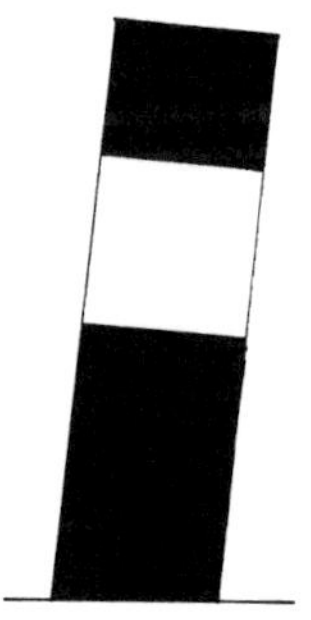

The original stack of the *Augustus B. Wolvin* in the familiar Halloween colors of Interlake Steamship. The black stack is girdled by a band of bright orange. (Author's collection)

After she lay idle at Erie, Pennsylvania, from 1961–65, ownership of the aging freighter was transferred in early 1966 to the Labrador Steamship Company, a Canadian subsidiary of Pickands Mather. During that season, the *Wolvin* operated in the grain and ore trades on the St. Lawrence Seaway, carrying grain out the seaway and backhauling ore from the iron ranges of Labrador to steel mills on the Great Lakes.

Her long career on the lakes finally came to an end in June of 1967, when she scraped a bank while rounding a bend in the Welland Canal and suffered extensive bottom damage. Following the grounding, the *Wolvin* was declared a constructive total loss, and a month after the incident she was sold to a Canadian salvage firm for scrapping. She was subsequently sold to Spanish shipbreakers, and on August 27, 1967, the *Wolvin* and the *Str. Saskadoc* departed Hamilton, Ontario, under tow. On September 24, 1967, they arrived in Santander, Spain, and went under the shipbreaker's torches.[12] The distinguished career of the former Queen of the lakes—one of the most innovative ships ever built on freshwater—was over.

When the *Wolvin* was renovated in 1946, it received a new smokestack that was much shorter and stouter than the original. Instead of looking like a stovepipe, the new stack resembled a barrel. (Author's collection)

Notes

1. Norman Beasley, *Freighters of Fortune* (New York: Harper and Brothers, 1930), 221.
2. These figures do not include canallers built for trade through the Welland Canal; these boats were restricted in size by the dimensions of the locks in the canal.
3. Richard Wright, *Freshwater Whales* (Kent, OH: Kent State University Press, 1969), 158.
4. With the outbreak of World War I in 1917, the *Republic* was sold to a Canadian firm and put into service on the Atlantic as the *North Pine*. She was scrapped in 1924 at Danzig, Poland.
5. John Greenwood, *Namesakes II* (Cleveland: Freshwater Press, 1973), 359.
6. Harlan Hatcher, *Lake Erie* (New York: Bobbs-Merrill), 328.
7. Harry Benford, "Sixty Years of Shipbuilding," paper presented at the meeting of the Great Lakes Section of the Society of Naval Architects and Marine Engineers, October 5, 1956, 13–34.
8. Rev. Peter Van Der Linden, ed., *Great Lakes Ships We Remember, II* (Cleveland: Freshwater Press, 1984), 419.
9. Walter Havighurst, *Vein of Iron* (Cleveland: World Publishing, 1958), 99.
10. Ibid.
11. Van Der Linden.
12. Ibid.

14

Four Giant Tin-Stackers

Before the *Wolvin* first slid into the water at Lorain, U.S. Steel had already contracted for the construction of four ships that would embody many of the design innovations pioneered by the big Acme freighter and would reclaim the Queen of the Lakes title for the Pittsburgh Steamship fleet. The four were also the first new boats built for the U.S. Steel fleet, which had been formed in 1901.

Two of the ships were to be built at Chicago Ship Building in Chicago, and one each at Superior Ship Building, in Superior, Wisconsin, and West Bay City Ship Building, in West Bay City, Michigan. All three of the yards were subsidiaries of American Ship Building, which had designed and built the *Wolvin*. The total contract for the four ships amounted to $1,650,000, or an average of just over $400,000 per ship.[1]

STR. ELBERT H. GARY

569'x56'x26'5"
Queen of the Lakes
April 8, 1905 to April 26, 1906

It was a busy spring and summer of 1905 for Miss Jennie Jewell Powell, the daughter of L. W. Powell, an officer of the Oliver Iron Company of Duluth. Miss Powell travelled first to Chicago on April 8 to christen the *Str. Elbert H. Gary*, the first of the new ships to be launched. On June 24 she was again in Chicago, this time to christen the *Str. William E. Corey*, the new flagship of the giant Pittsburgh fleet. Two days later Miss Powell was back in Superior, across the harbor from her Duluth home, to preside at the June 26 christening of the *Str. George W. Perkins.*

STR. WILLIAM E. COREY

569'x56'x26'5"
Queen of the Lakes
June 24, 1905 to April 26, 1906

While it had been a great honor for the young Miss Powell to be involved in the gala activities planned in conjunction with the launchings of the *Gary* and *Corey* at Chicago—occasions said to have "brought together probably the largest representation of steel interests ever gathered at a similar event"[2]—she was undoubtedly much more excited at the prospect of christening the *Perkins*, which had literally been built in her backyard. Most residents of Duluth and Superior had report-

The *Elbert H. Gary*, the first new ship built for the giant U.S. Steel fleet after it was formed in 1901. The freighter is shown entering a lock at Sault Ste. Marie on a journey up the lakes. A group of crewmembers can be seen gathered at the forward end of the deck for the trip through the locks. (Institute for Great Lakes Research, Bowling Green State University)

edly become quite blasé about launchings, however. In the eighteen years that had transpired since the opening of Alexander McDougall's American Steel Barge Company in 1888, fifty-eight large ships had been put into the water at shipyards in Duluth and Superior. Initially, the launchings were very popular events. It was not unusual for thousands of local residents to turn out to watch a new freighter slide off the ways, as had been the case with the launching of the passenger steamer *Christopher Columbus* in 1892. In recent years, however, attendance at the launchings had been sparse.[3] Miss Powell and the officials of Pittsburgh Steamship must have been delighted, and possibly a little surprised, when they arrived at the Superior shipyard on that Monday afternoon and found that thousands of spectators had gathered to watch the launching of the *Perkins*. It was, according to a local newspaper, the biggest event since the launching of the *Christopher Columbus*.[4]

STR. GEORGE W. PERKINS

569'x56'x26'5"
Queen of the Lakes
June 26, 1905 to April 26, 1906

Two months later, the *Str. Henry C. Frick* was launched at West Bay City, without the aid of Miss Powell. In a simple ceremony, Mrs. E. R. Collins, wife of the Pittsburgh fleet's traffic manager, broke the traditional bottle of champagne on the bow of the "last of the big four" as the freighter plunged into the water. Mrs. Collins was assisted by Captain Neil Campbell, "as canny a Scot as ever came across," who had been selected to be master of the *Frick* during her maiden season on the lakes. Unlike the other three new Pittsburgh ships, all of the *Frick*'s machinery had been installed prior to the launching, so she was ready to go into service immediately after sea trials.[5]

STR. HENRY C. FRICK

569'x56'x26'4"
Queen of the Lakes
August 26, 1905 to April 26, 1906

Those attending the launching reported that the *Frick* was "magnificantly furnished." According to one writer, "her appointments could not be more luxuriant and costly were they ordered for a millionaire's private yacht." Rooms aboard the *Frick* had individual toilets and bathrooms, electric call bells, telephones that could be used to call various parts of the vessel, electric fans, electric lights, and unusually fine woodwork. The dining room, according to one report, "was a symphony in the woodworker's art."[6]

By the time the *Frick* went into the water at West Bay City, the final outfitting of the *Gary* had been completed, and this magnificent new addition to the giant tin-stacker fleet had gone into service. Early reports on her performance undoubtedly thrilled fleet officials. Measured at 6,331 gross tons and 4,988 net tons, she proved capable of carrying in excess of 10,500 long tons of iron ore. At the same time, while her triple expansion steam engine was rated at only 1,800 horsepower and many thought she was underpowered for her size, the *Gary* was actually making better speed than her designers had anticipated. While they had predicted that the *Gary* would be able to average ten miles an hour when loaded, she averaged an impressive twelve miles an hour between the Straits of Mackinac and South Chicago on the down-bound leg of her maiden voyage.[7]

The four ships were almost carbon copies, with a few exceptions. Most notable was the fuller Texas deck cabin[8] and deckhouse installed on the *Corey*, the new flagship of the Pittsburgh fleet. The enlarged Texas deck cabin was necessary to accommodate a suite of five passenger cabins for use by guests of the vessel's owners.[9] The deckhouse, located where the other three ships had their number two hatch, housed deck department personnel, augmenting the normal accommodations in the forecastle.

The *Corey* and her three sister ships had long and distinguished careers on the lakes. The *Corey*, *Gary*, and *Frick* each operated for more than six decades, while the fourth, the *Perkins*, saw a remarkable seventy-six seasons before going to the shipbreakers. For a few days in 1905, however, Pittsburgh Steamship officials weren't certain that their new flagship was going to make it through her first season.

On November 28, only a little over three months after she made her first trip on the lakes, the *Corey*'s career almost came to an end on Gull Island in the Apostle Island system at the west end of Lake Superior. Under the command of Captain F. A. Bailey, the *Corey* was running for cover from an unusually fast moving northeasterly gale of extreme intensity when she was driven hard aground on Gull Island Reef. The big Pittsburgh flagship wasn't the only Great Lakes ship travelling in harm's way that day. Off the Keweenaw Peninsula, Pickands Mather's *Str. Victory* was separated from her consort, the barge *Constitution*, and limped on to the Soo alone. At the entrance to Duluth harbor, the Pittsburgh fleet's *Isaac L. Ellwood* and *Mataafa* were fighting for their lives as they tried to reach the safety of the harbor. At Fourteen Mile Point on the Keweenaw, the 430-foot freighter *Western Star* was driven aground so high and dry that after the storm was over people could walk all the way around her without getting their feet wet.[10]

When Harry Coulby, president of Pittsburgh Steamship, received word that his fleet's new flagship was aground, he personally rushed to the scene to supervise salvage operations. Coulby found the *Corey* intact, but in a dangerously exposed position. If it could not be pulled off the reef before another storm struck the lakes, the stranded vessel would be battered into a pile of scrap metal by the force of the sea. Even if Lake Superior was spared from any more late season storms, the mercury was steadily moving downward, and in a matter of weeks heavy ice would begin to form in the shallow waters of the Apostles. Once ice set in, salvage efforts would be futile, and the *Corey* would spend the long northern winter locked in the grinding ice pack. By spring there would be little left.

Coulby spared no expense in the effort to free the *Corey.* The tugs *Crosby, Edna G.*, and *Gladiator*, three of the most powerful on Lake Superior, were already at the site and working feverishly to pull the freighter off the reef. When their valiant efforts failed to budge the *Corey*, Coulby sent out orders for four of the Pittsburgh ore boats to steam to the site and join the salvage effort. Within days, the *Houghton, Manola, Marina*, and *Sir William Siemens* arrived at the site and were harnessed to their recalcitrant flagship with stout hawsers. The reef's grip on the torn and battered hull of the *Corey* was finally broken, and she began to move astern slowly, gradually sliding back toward deep water. Finally, twelve days after she was driven onto the reef, the *Houghton* and *Marina* managed to pull her completely free, and the crippled ship was taken in tow to the shipyard at Superior for repairs. Before she was ready to resume service the next spring, her owners spent $100,000 to erase the damages caused by the grounding, amounting to almost a quarter of her original cost.[11]

It wasn't the only repair bill that came into the Pittsburgh Steamship offices in the aftermath of the late November storm. The *Corey* was just one of eleven Pittsburgh vessels damaged in the blow. At Duluth, the *Mataafa* was broken in half, and her barge, the *Nasmyth*, was damaged. A few miles down the shore, their steamer *Crescent City* had blown ashore. Near Two Harbors, the *Lafayette* was driven on the rocks and broke in two. The already crippled ship was further damaged when her barge, the *Manila*, crashed into her. The *William Edenborn* was beached at Split Rock and her consort, the barge *Madeira*, was broken in two. The *Cornelia* and her barge, the *Maia*, had been driven ashore at Point Isabelle, while the steamer *German* grounded at Glencoe.[12]

The *Str. William E. Corey*, which almost had its career ended by a killer storm that struck the lakes only five months after the big U.S. Steel freighter was launched. The twin to the *Gary* is shown here just after being launched at Chicago on June 24, 1905. Cables were attached to the seven temporary masts that lined the deck of the *Corey* and tied off to bollards adjacent to the launching ways to prevent the ship from rolling over when it splashed into the water. The ship's smokestack has not yet been installed. (Institute for Great Lakes Research, Bowling Green State University)

Sailors on the Great Lakes always look toward November with great trepidation. It is the month of killer storms, and seldom are the lakes spared the fury of at least one good blow. Even by Great Lakes standards, though, that November of 1905 was exceptionally brutal. The lakes were torn by three furious storms in the *Corey's* first season. In their aftermath, seventy vessels had been wrecked and 149 lives lost.[13]

While the late November storm marred the *Corey's* debut on the lakes, she and her crew were luckier than many. The *Mataafa* was in two pieces at Duluth, and nine of her crewmembers had frozen to death. The *Str. Ira Owen*, which had been downbound from the American lakehead with a cargo of 116,000 bushels of barley, vanished in the storm. Crewmembers from the *Str. H. B. Nye* reported that they had caught a glimpse of the *Owen* at the peak of the storm, about forty miles off Outer Island in the Apostles. She was laboring heavily in the furious seas and blowing distress signals. The *Nye* was itself in jeopardy of sinking and could lend no help. When the storm had abated, the 280-foot freighter and her nineteen crewmembers had disappeared from the face of the lake. Several days later, a steamer reported finding floating wreckage from the *Owen*, including marked life preservers, east of Michigan Island, near where the ill-fated freighter was last seen.[14] Such vessel disappearances were not at all uncommon in the days before ships were equipped with radio equipment.

It was not the last Lake Superior storm that the *Corey* would have to weather, nor the last damage she would sustain. Lake Superior never treated the *Corey* very well. In May of 1917, she was blown ashore on Gros Cap Reef and sustained $25,000 in damage. During the night of October 22-23, 1929, while downbound with a load of ore from Two Harbors, the *Corey* was again battered by a killer storm, causing damage of $3,500.[15] In comparison, the *Corey*'s three sisters had relatively uneventful careers. The *Gary* and *Frick* escaped involvement in any serious casualties, while the *Perkins* ran aground in the fog near Two Harbors in 1908 and suffered relatively minor damage in a collision with the *Str. William P. Snyder, Jr.*, in Duluth Harbor in 1918.[16]

The unfortunate *Corey* was also the first of the four to be sold by the Pittsburgh fleet, and the first to have her career ended. In 1963, following several years of declining cargo tonnages on the lakes, the *Corey* was declared excess by her owners and sold to Upper Lakes Shipping of Toronto. Her Canadian owners renamed her *Ridgetown* in honor of the hometown of the firm's president. Until 1969, she operated in the iron ore and grain trade on the Canadian side of the lakes. At the end of that season she was laid up at Toronto with a load of storage grain, and the former Queen of the Lakes was never to sail again.

In the spring of 1970, the *Ridgetown* was sold to Canadian Dredge and Dock, which was then involved in the construction of harbor facilities at Nanticoke, on the north shore of Lake Ontario. They sunk her as a temporary breakwater at Nanticoke during the summer of 1970. Raised later, the *Ridgetown* was towed to Port Credit, Ontario, for use in another construction project. Loaded with stone, she was sunk to form a portion of the breakwater at the entrance to the Port Credit harbor. The retired freighter is still there today, just off the shipping lanes she sailed for sixty-five seasons.

Only months after the *Corey* was sold to Upper Lakes Shipping, the Pittsburgh fleet conveyed the *Gary* to Kinsman Marine Transit, successor to the historic Minch fleet. Renamed the *R. E. Webster*, she was put into service in the grain trade between Duluth-Superior and Buffalo. By the end of the 1972 season, the freighter's hull and machinery were badly showing the wear that accumulates after sixty-seven seasons. Unable to justify the expense of bringing the *Webster* into compliance with Coast Guard inspection standards, Kinsman officials decided to send the vessel to the shipbreakers. Sold to Marine Salvage of Port Colborne, Ontario, the *Webster* was towed out of her berth at Toledo, Ohio, on June 9, 1973, by the Canadian tugs *Helen McAllister* and *Salvage Monarch*, en route for Quebec. On June 15, the Polish tug *Jantar* took the *Webster* and the former Wilson Marine Transit freighter *A. E. Nettleton* in tow for the long trip out the St. Lawrence and across the North Atlantic. They arrived in Santander, Spain, on July 5, 1973, and scrapping operations commenced soon afterward on the two freighters.[17]

The Pittsburgh fleet sold the *Frick* and *Perkins* in 1964. The *Frick* was purchased by Providence Shipping of Nassau in the Bahamas, and she was managed and operated by Algoma Central Marine of Sault Ste. Marie, Ontario. Renamed the *Michipicoten*, she was used mainly in the Canadian ore trade until October 27, 1972, when she passed through the Welland Canal carrying her final cargo, a load of salt bound from Goderich, Ontario, for Trois-Rivières, Quebec. Sold to Spanish shipbreakers, the *Michipicoten* departed Quebec in tow of the Polish tug *Koral* on November 15, 1972. On November 17, she broke adrift in heavy seas in the Gulf of St. Lawrence and split in two off Anticosti Island.

Word of the drama at the mouth of the St. Lawrence flashed back to the lakes. At ports from Montreal to Duluth and aboard scores of freighters plying the trade routes the *Frick* had travelled for so many seasons, hundreds of her former crewmembers listened intently for news of the historic ship's desperate struggle. As darkness settled over the lakes, word came that the bow of the *Michipicoten* had sunk, but the stern section remained afloat. The old ship was putting up a valiant fight against overwhelming odds. Former crewmembers and thousands of boatwatchers on both sides of the lakes clung to the hope that tugs would be able to take the stern section in tow and at least a part of the ship would survive her last bout with a November storm. Their hopes were dashed the following day when news broadcasts solemnly reported that the stern section had flooded and sunk to the bottom.[18] Some would conjecture that the old ship simply refused to leave the Great Lakes and St. Lawrence system that she had been such a vital part of for so many years. A few even celebrated the sinking, pleased that the once proud vessel had deprived the shipbreakers of irreverently picking over her bones.

The loss of the *Michipicoten* left the *George W. Perkins* as the only survivor of the four Pittsburgh steamers launched in 1905. Sold in 1964 to a Canadian holding company, she was renamed the *Westdale* and operated primarily in the parcel grain trade between Georgian Bay and Goderich, Ontario, under management of Westdale Shipping. In 1977, ownership of the vessel passed to the Soo River Company, and she was renamed the *H. C. Heimbecker*. Her new owners operated her in the Canadian grain trade until 1981, when they traded the seventy-six-year-old ship to Triad Salvage in exchange for the fifty-eight-year-old *Maxine*.[19] On November 3, 1981, the *Heimbecker* arrived at Triad's dock in Ashtabula, Ohio, and scrapping operations began.[20] The last of the *Gary*-class ships finally disappeared from the lakes.

Notes

1. Gary S. Dewar, "A Forgotten Class," *Telescope* (March–April 1989): 31–39.
2. "The Corey Launched," *Duluth Evening Herald*, June 24, 1905.
3. "Christen Ship," *Duluth Evening Herald*, June 24, 1905.
4. "Perkins Goes In," *Duluth Evening Herald*, June 26, 1905.
5. "Is Queen of Fresh Water," *Bay City Tribune*, August 27, 1905.
6. Ibid.
7. *Duluth Evening Herald*, June 21, 1905.
8. The Texas deck is located one deck above the main deck or spar deck at the bow. The cabin area on main deck at the bow is generally referred to as the forecastle. For a distance back from the

bow, the sides of the hull are extended some distance above the main deck, an aid in keeping water off the deck when the vessel is heading into a sea. Those extensions of the hull form the outer bulkheads for the forecastle cabin. At the stern, the deck above the main deck is referred to as the poop deck.

9. "The Corey Launched." Unlike many of their saltwater counterparts, freighters on the Great Lakes do not carry paying passengers, although many have what are alternately referred to as passenger, guest, or owner's quarters. Most of the guests carried on the bulk freighters are influential officials from companies that are customers of the shipping line.
10. William Ratigan, *Great Lakes Shipwrecks and Survivals* (Grand Rapids, MI: Wm. B. Eerdmans, 1960), 273–74.
11. Julius F. Wolff, Jr., "Grim November," in Walter Havighurst, ed., *The Great Lakes Reader* (New York: Macmillan, 1966), 319.
12. Ratigan, 274.
13. Frederick Stonehouse, *Went Missing, II* (AuTrain, MI: Avery Color Studios, 1987), 50.
14. Wolff, 317–18.
15. Ship Biography, Institute for Great Lakes Research, Bowling Green State University.
16. Ibid.
17. Ibid.
18. Rev. Peter Van Der Linden, ed., *Ships We Remember* (Cleveland: Freshwater Press, 1979), 195.
19. Rev. Peter Van Der Linden, ed., *Ships We Remember, II* (Cleveland: Freshwater Press, 1984), 263.
20. The *Maxine* had been launched in 1923 as the *William H. Warner*, a standard 600-footer. In 1934, the ship had been purchased by International Harvester, the maker of farm equipment, and renamed *The International.* That company operated the ship in the iron ore trade, serving its steel mill in South Chicago, Illinois, until the firm withdrew from the shipping business in 1977.

15

The Standard 600-Footers

While the four *Gary*-class boats were being readied to get underway for their second season, workers at Chicago Ship Building were preparing for the launch of their hull number sixty-eight. When it was christened as the *J. Pierpont Morgan* and plunged into the cold waters of the Calumet River on April 26, 1906, it displaced the *Gary* and her sisters as the longest ship on the Great Lakes. The *Morgan*'s reign as Queen of the Lakes would be a relatively short one, however, and she is best remembered today not for her length, but as the prototype for what would become the largest class of ships ever to operate on the inland seas.

STR. J. PIERPONT MORGAN

601'x58'x27'4"
Queen of the Lakes
April 26, 1906 to August 18, 1906

Prior to the launching of the *Morgan*, it was unusual for more than three or four ships to be built from the same set of plans. Particularly since the launching of the first iron and steel vessels in the early 1880s, the size and design of ships had changed so rapidly that by the time three or four ships had been built from a set of plans they were outdated. Many times, before naval architects completed drawings for a new ship, new developments would force them to go back to their drafting tables and revise the plans they had just finished. There were even instances where significant changes were made after construction had begun.

For the Great Lakes shipbuilding industry, the design of the *Morgan* represented a plateau of perfection in the endless evolution of the bulk freighter. Vessels would continue to grow in length, width, and depth, and designs would be continuously modified, but between 1906 and 1930 the basic plan of the *Morgan* would be followed in the construction of between fifty-six and seventy-six ships. They were the "standard 600-footers," and for thirty years they were the backbone of the world's most efficient bulk shipping industry.

There were three principal reasons for the popularity of the standard 600-footers. The first was their low cost. Shipping companies saved a lot of money by using a standard, off-the-shelf plan, rather than having naval architects custom design a ship. At the same time, major shipyards around the lakes soon became proficient at building the 600-footers and were able to keep their costs to a minimum. Within a few years, shipowners found that the standard 600-footers were the least expensive vessels being built on the lake on a ton-for-ton basis. Whereas shipbuilding costs generally rose each year, in 1909 a shipping

The historic *J. Pierpont Morgan*, the first of the standard 600-footers, as it looked on a trip down the St. Marys River in 1955. The billboard lettering on the side of the ship makes the ownership of the big freighter clear to all onlookers. Once common on the lakes, billboard lettering proved to be difficult to maintain, and most fleets have since abandoned the practice. (Institute for Great Lakes Research, Bowling Green State University)

company could have a standard 600-footer built for no more than Pittsburgh Steamship had paid for the *Gary* in 1905.[1] In the world of shipbuilding, the standard 600-footer was the first "economy model."

Second, the ships could be built in an incredibly short period of time. It took three to four months to build the first of the standard 600-footers, but as the yards became more accustomed to building them, that time was cut to as little as six to eight weeks.[2] The abbreviated construction period allowed fleets to put new ships into service rapidly to meet their changing needs, and they did not have to tie up capital for a long time waiting for a new ship to be delivered and put into service.

Third, the standard 600-footers were highly versatile freighters. Their carrying capacities were among the highest of any ships on the lakes, which translated into higher profits for their owners and reduced costs for shippers. At the same time, with the aid of tugs, they were still small enough to negotiate even the serpentine Cuyahoga River at Cleveland. In fact, until the 621-foot *Cadillac* went up the Cuyahoga in 1961, the 600-footers were considered to be the longest ships capable of servicing steel mills on the river. The standard 600-footers were really the first of what we would refer to today as river-class freighters.[3]

STR. HENRY H. ROGERS

601'x58'x27'4"
Queen of the Lakes
June 16, 1906 to August 18, 1906

The *J. Pierpont Morgan* was the first of six standard 600-footers built in 1906. The *Morgan* and three sister ships were fabricated at Chicago Ship Building for Pittsburgh Steamship. On June 16, workers at Chicago launched the *Henry H. Rogers*, followed on August 18 by the *Norman B. Ream*. The fourth freighter, christened the *Peter A. B. Widener*,went into the water on October 20, but by that time a new Queen of the Lakes, the *Str. Edward Y. Townsend*, had been launched at Superior Ship Building for Bethlehem Steel's Great Lakes Steamship Division. Interestingly, the new Bethlehem freighter was also a standard 600-footer, one of two they ordered that year, but it had been stretched one foot to make it the longest ship on the lakes. It was launched on August 18, 1906, the same day as the *Ream*. The second Bethlehem 600-footer, the *Daniel J. Morrell*, went into the water at West Bay City Ship Building four days later.[4]

STR. NORMAN B. REAM

601'x58'x27'4"
Queen of the Lakes
August 18, 1906

The launch of Bethlehem's *Townsend* underscored an irony about the standard 600-footers: they weren't standard, nor were they necessarily 600 feet long. The standard 600-footer was really the "Ford" of the maritime industry on the lakes. They came in several different models, models changed from year to year, and their owners could customize them by the selection of different options. In the same way that it is often hard to tell one make of car from another, it is sometimes difficult to determine whether a particular ship was a standard 600-footer or not. The *Morgan* and *Townsend* are both considered to be standard 600-footers, yet the *Morgan* had a keel length of 580 feet, while the *Townsend* was 586 feet along her keel. The *Morgan* was 601 feet in overall length, compared to 602 feet for the *Townsend.* The *Morgan* was 27 feet, four inches deep, while the *Townsend* was 32 feet deep. The *Morgan* was measured at 7,161 gross tons and 5,530 net tons, compared to 7,438 gross tons and 5,673 net tons for the *Townsend.* Machinery and cabin arrangements varied even more dramatically. They were both standard 600-footers, having been built from the same basic American Ship Building plans, yet they weren't very standard and they weren't necessarily 600 feet long.

There is general agreement within the maritime community that the *Morgan* was the first standard 600-footer and that the *Rogers, Ream, Townsend, Morrell,* and *Widener* belonged to the same class. Beyond that, there is substantial room for disagreement over which ships were standard 600-footers. The total number of standard 600-footers ranges from a low of fifty-six ships to an upper limit of about seventy-six vessels built between 1906 and 1930.

A total of twenty-five ships built between 1906 and 1916 had the same basic dimensions as the *Morgan,* with keel lengths of 580 feet and beams of 58 feet. While they varied in overall length from 601 to 604 feet, they are probably the purest of the standard 600-footers. Beginning in 1916, all of the ships built with 580-foot keels had their beams increased to 60 feet.[5] From 1916–30, thirty-five vessels were built to those dimensions, and they are generally also considered to fall within the standard 600-footer-class. The last ship of that size built was Pittsburgh Steamship's *Thomas W. Lamont.* Launched in 1930 at AmShip's Toledo yard, the *Lamont* is widely viewed as the last of the standard 600-footers.

It could easily be argued that the only ships that can rightly be called standard 600-footers were the sixty vessels built with keel lengths of 580 feet. Unfortunately, that list wouldn't include the *Townsend,* which had a keel length of 586 feet, yet we know that the Bethlehem freighter was merely a stretched version of the *Morgan.* The *Townsend* and fifteen other ships built between 1906 and 1927 are often referred to as standard 600-footers, even though their keel lengths ranged from 580 feet, 9 inches to 596 feet. Regardless of whether there were fifty-six or seventy-six standard 600-footers, or some number in between, the *Morgan* and the other ships in her size range had become the backbone of the U.S. fleet on the Great Lakes by the time of World War I, and they continued in that role until World War II.

The *Morgan* had a long and relatively uneventful career as one of the workhorses of the Pittsburgh Steamship fleet. In 1965, she was sold to a Canadian firm. Renamed the *Heron Bay,* she operated from 1965-78 in the colors of Quebec and Ontario Transportation. Retired from service in 1978, the seventy-two-year-old freighter was sold to Union Pipe and Machinery of Montreal, and her name was shortened to *Heron B.* On March 30, 1979, scrapping operations began on the *Heron B.* at Davie Shipbuilding in Lauzon, Quebec.

The *Henry H. Rogers* operated as part of the giant Pittsburgh Steamship fleet for its entire career. By 1974, the *Rogers* was considered to be excess tonnage, and on November 21 the second of the standard 600-footers was towed to the Hyman-Michaels dock in Duluth for scrapping. By the summer of 1975 scrapping was complete.

Of the original 600-footers, the *Norman B. Ream* had the longest career. Like the *Morgan,* the *Ream* left the Pittsburgh Steamship fleet in 1965, sold to the Steinbrenner-owned Kinsman Marine Transit fleet. Renamed the *Kinsman Enterprise* in 1965, the third of the standard 600-footers spent the balance of her active sailing career in Kinsman colors, although the Kins-

When the *Norman B. Ream,* a sister ship to the *Morgan,* was purchased by Kinsman Marine in 1965, its U.S. Steel stack markings were painted over in Kinsman colors. The black stack bears a dark green band with white borders and a block "S"; this signifies that the fleet is owned by the Steinbrenner family, which took over the former Minch fleet in the early 1900s. (Author's collection)

man fleet became S&E Shipping in 1975. The Kinsman/S&E fleet is one of the last independent U.S. vessel operators on the Great Lakes, not owned or controlled by a steel or mining firm. The fleet, which is a successor to the famous Minch fleet that had operated the historic *Onoko* and the ill-fated *Western Reserve*, is primarily involved in transporting grain from the American lakehead at Duluth and Superior to elevators in Buffalo owned by General Mills, Pillsbury, and International Multifoods. The *Enterprise* operated in the grain trade until 1979, when S&E sold the seventy-three-year-old freighter to the Economic Development Corporation of Port Huron, Michigan, for use as a dock face and storage facility on the St. Clair River. From 1979 until 1990, the former *Ream*, with her name and Kinsman stack markings painted out, sat idle at the dock just south of Port Huron. In 1990, the eighty-four-year-old hulk was sold for scrapping in Turkey and was towed out of the lakes. She was the last of the original standard 600-footers that had been launched in 1906.[6]

Notes

1. Herbert C. Sadler, *Some Points in Connection with Shipbuilding on the Great Lakes, U.S.A.* (London: Institute of Naval Architecture, 1909), 9.
2. Ibid.
3. Today, ships of up to 635 feet in length regularly make the five-mile trip up the winding Cuyahoga without the aid of tugs. Their increased maneuverability results from the installation of such things as bow and stern thrusters, diesel engines, pilothouse control of engines, and twin screws.
4. The last standard 600-footer to operate on the lakes was launched for the Pittsburgh Steamship fleet in 1910 as the *William B. Dickson*. Purchased by Kinsman Marine and renamed the *Merle M. McCurdy* in 1969, she operated in the grain trade until 1985. In addition to being the last operating standard 600-footer, the *McCurdy* was the first ship on the Great Lakes to be named after an African American. The vessel's namesake was a former Cleveland lawyer who was appointed as a U.S. attorney in 1962.
5. The first ship built with a beam of sixty feet was the *Str. William G. Mather*, launched in 1905 as the flagship of the Cleveland-Cliffs fleet.
6. Ship Biographies, Institute for Great Lakes Research, Bowling Green State University.

16

A Queen Named Edward

On the same hot, humid day that officials of Pittsburgh Steamship gathered in Chicago to observe the launching of the *Norman B. Ream*, the third of their new standard 600-footers, a major celebration was underway in Superior, Wisconsin. A large and exuberant crowd of onlookers was on hand at Superior Ship Building on August 18, 1906, to watch the *Str. Edward Y. Townsend* slide off the ways and into the waters of Lake Superior for the first time. At 602 feet in overall length, a miserly one foot longer than the Pittsburgh fleet's *Morgan*, *Rogers*, and *Ream*, the *Townsend* was the new Queen of the Lakes.

STR. EDWARD Y. TOWNSEND

602'x58'x32'
Queen of the Lakes
August 18, 1906 to December 29, 1906

The *Townsend* had been built for Cambria Steamship Company, the marine subsidiary that Cambria Steel Company had formed earlier that year. A second Cambria ship, the *Str. Daniel J. Morrell*, was nearing completion at West Bay City Ship Building, in West Bay City, Michigan, and it would follow the *Townsend* into the water on August 22. Like the three new Pittsburgh steamers that had already been launched, the *Morrell* was a foot shorter than the *Townsend.* Both of the new Cambria freighters were to be operated under contract by the M. A. Hanna Company, one of the most experienced vessel management firms on the lakes. The *Morrell* and *Townsend* entered service painted in Hanna colors, with black hulls, white forecastle and cabins, and a black stack with a white shield bearing the Hanna fleet logo.

Two months later, on October 20, 1906, the last of the six original standard 600-footers was launched at Chicago. Christened the *Peter A. B. Widener*, it joined its three virtually identical sisters in the Pittsburgh Steamship fleet.

The careers of the first three 600-footers, the *Morgan*, *Rogers*, and *Ream*, were surprisingly uneventful, particularly given the fact that they operated for the first thirty years of their careers without radios or radar. It is actually quite remarkable

Although owned by Cambria Steel, the *Townsend* and its sister ship, the *Daniel J. Morrell*, were managed by the M. A. Hanna Company and their black stacks bore the Hanna fleet logo. (Author's collection)

Cambria Steel's *Edward Y. Townsend* downbound at Port Huron, with the historic Fort Gratiot lighthouse in the background. Although generally considered to be one of the first standard 600-footers, the *Townsend* was one foot longer than the *Morgan*. Launched in 1906, the *Townsend* was a familiar sight on the lakes until it suffered fatal damage in a severe storm in November of 1966. (Institute for Great Lakes Research, Bowling Green State University)

that over a period of seven decades, none of those ships were involved in serious casualties. The experience of the other three original standard 600-footers was to be quite a different story. The *Townsend, Morrell,* and *Widener* are best remembered today for having been unwitting participants in epic battles for survival waged against the fury of November storms on the inland seas.

No month is completely safe on the lakes, but November has come to be the archenemy of countless generations of sailors who have crewed the big freighters. Mention November to a sailor and he, or she, will tell you a story about a storm. The mood on the ore boats changes markedly when the calendars are turned over to November. A heavy pall of apprehension descends on the ships, mirroring the blanket of dirty grey clouds that covers the lakes throughout most of the month. Tempers grow short, and patience is a scarce commodity. Consumption of alcohol goes up, and, in the privacy of their rooms, crewmembers who normally scoff at the frequent lifesaving drills hang their lifejackets and survival suits where they can get at them in a hurry. It's not an issue of whether there will be a storm in November, only a question of when it will come. And it's likely that there will be more than one.

Around the first of November, the stationary high pressure systems that bring the warm days of Indian summer retreat in the face of cold fronts moving down from the Arctic. Where the two conflicting weather systems meet, the cold air mass forces its way under the warm, lighter air. The barometric pressure drops where the two air masses make contact, establishing a low pressure system with winds swirling around it in a counterclockwise pattern. Fed by warm moist air, most often from the Gulf of Mexico or the Pacific Ocean, the low continues to deepen as it begins to track to the east or northeast, carried by the prevailing westerly winds. The result is what meteorologists refer to as an extra-tropical cyclone. These cyclones are common on the lakes, especially during the month of November. Before the freighters were equipped with radios and the National Weather Service began issuing marine weather forecasts, a captain was often unaware of the approach of a major storm until the bottom began to drop out of his barometer. By then it was often too late to find a safe haven.

In the waning light of the afternoon of November 16, 1926, Captain Henry T. Kelley paced nervously in the pilothouse of the *Str. Peter A. B. Widener* as he watched the mercury in the barometer drop lower and lower in the glass. Overhead, the sky was a dirty black, and the steadily increasing winds were beginning to pile the waters of Lake Superior into fearful black waves that buffeted his ship. With winds building out of the north-northwest, Captain Kelley abandoned the established courseline to Duluth and headed for the north shore of the lake, planning to sneak up behind Isle Royale and beachcomb along toward the American lakehead in the sheltered lee of the land.

At 8:45 a.m. on November 17, the *Widener* passed the east end of Isle Royale, and Captain Kelley ordered his wheelsman to make the haul for Duluth. The wheelsman put the big wood-spoked wheel over to ten degrees of left rudder to start the turn, but the long ship wouldn't come around. He tried twenty degrees, then put the wheel over to hard left, but the *Widener* showed no sign of making the turn. Captain Kelley passed word to the chief engineer that the ship's steering system was malfunctioning and he feared that the wheel chains that ran to the rudder had parted. After a hurried inspection, the chief made a rare personal appearance in the pilothouse to notify Captain Kelley that his inspection showed that the wheel chains were still intact, but the rudder itself had fallen off!

Kelley's mind flashed back to events at Conneaut, Ohio, three days earlier. While maneuvering to enter the harbor at Conneaut, the stern of the *Widener* had nudged the breakwall. Fearing damage to his ship, Kelley had hired divers to make an underwater inspection of the stern. They reported that they could find no damage. Now Kelley knew there had been damage, an unseen crack in the stout shaft of the rudder. The incessant action of the heavy seas encountered when the *Widener* crossed Lake Superior had undoubtedly widened the crack until the shaft was no longer able to support the weight of the rudder. One final wave had hurled tons of water against the big slab rudder and it had dropped off.

Captain Kelley told the chief to stop the ship's engine. With no radio on which to broadcast a distress signal, Kelley ordered a crewmember to fly the U.S. flag upside down from the mast that towered above the pilothouse. At the same time, he told the mate of the watch to begin blowing the distress signal with the ship's steam whistle to catch the attention of any vessels in the area.

The *William E. Corey*, flagship of the Pittsburgh Steamship fleet, was a few miles ahead of the *Widener*, and crewmembers on watch in the pilothouse heard the distress signal. The captain immediately ordered the wheelsman to haul the ship around and steam toward the *Widener*. In less than half an hour, the *Corey* steamed slowly past the *Widener* as crewmembers attempted to determine the exact nature of the *Widener*'s difficulties. Captain Kelley struggled out onto the *Widener's* bridge wing with one of the large megaphones that ship personnel used for ship-to-ship and ship-to-shore communications in the days prior to radio. The fierce wind buffeted the megaphone when he put it to his mouth to shout his message across the raging waters separating the two Pittsburgh steamers. On the *Corey*, crewmembers could barely make out Kelley's shouts above the unremitting roar of the storm: ". . . lost . . . rudder." With an exaggerated nod, the captain of the *Corey* acknowledged that he understood the message.

The *Corey* wasn't the only vessel responding to the *Widener's* distress signal. In short order, the Pittsburgh flagship was joined by the steamers *J. Pierpont Morgan*, *J. P. Morgan, Jr.*, *Samuel F. B. Morse*, and *Maricopa*. While the presence of the other ships, all Pittsburgh Steamship freighters, must have been reassuring to the crewmembers aboard the *Widener*, there wasn't much that could be done for them because of the severity of the storm. The *Morgan* and *Morgan, Jr.*, attempted to steam close enough to the *Widener* to pass tow lines, but the combination of strong winds and high seas made the efforts impossible.

Eventually, the six Pittsburgh ships were joined by Reiss Steamship's *William K. Field*, the newest ship on the lakes. The *Field* was equipped with a radio, and word of the *Widener*'s precarious situation was transmitted to the Duluth office of Pittsburgh Steamship. Personnel in the Duluth office immediately notified officials at the company's headquarters in Pittsburgh. After a crisis session in which they evaluated the sketchy information available to them, a call went out from Pittsburgh to Fort William, Ontario, ordering that a tug be sent to aid the *Widener*. Fort William, later consolidated with the adjacent community of Port Arthur to form the present-day city of Thunder Bay, was the port closest to the *Widener*'s location. The tug operators knew they would be very generously compensated if they could rescue the crippled freighter, but despite a gallant effort they never got past the great sleeping giant of Welcome Island at the mouth of Thunder Bay. To go farther onto the raging waters of Lake Superior would have put their little vessel and its crew in serious jeopardy.

With the faint grey light of day waning in the late afternoon of November 17, messages were shouted back and forth between the six ships that had been shadowing the movements of the *Widener*. With darkness settling over the lake, it was dangerous for all of the vessels to remain with the *Widener*. There was nothing they could do to help the stricken ship, and in the storm-tossed darkness there was always a risk that the ships would collide with one another. In turn, the *Field*, *Morgan, Jr.*, *Morse*, and *Corey* each blew a whistle salute to the crippled *Widener* and left the storm-battered flotilla. The *Morgan* and *Maricopa* continued to maintain their vigil, staying within sight of the *Widener* and poised to mount a rescue effort if the ship foundered and its crewmembers had to go into the frigid waters.

Aboard the *Widener*, Captain Kelley knew that the fate of his ship was in his hands. He had spent most of his life on the lakes, and the stark facts were painfully clear to him: nobody was going to miraculously rescue his ship and crew. The storm was worsening, and it was unlikely that the wallowing ship would survive the night. If he and his crew were forced to abandon their ship, it was likely that many lives would be lost. Kelley knew that it would be virtually impossible to launch the *Widener*'s two lifeboats in the high seas, and with temperatures well below zero crewmembers wouldn't survive long if they had to go into the water.

Mustering all the knowledge gained in his long career as a merchant seaman, Captain Kelley ordered the engineers to pump out all the ship's ballast tanks except the afterpeak. As the ballast was removed, the *Widener* rose in the water until her bow was almost clear of the waves. As more and more freeboard was exposed to the onslaught of wind and waves, the big freighter rolled so badly that it was impossible to stand up in the pilothouse without holding onto something immovable. The ship and its crew were taking an unmerciful pounding. To continue to wallow so violently would only hasten the breakup of the *Widener*. No ship could long endure such a beating.

But Captain Kelley had no intention of spending the night wallowing in the high seas. With the ballast out, the hull and superstructure of the *Widener* acted like a huge steel sail: Kelley intended to half-sail, half-steam toward Duluth. At 5 p.m., he rang up "ahead slow" on the engine order telegraph, and the *Widener* got underway. Without a rudder, the clockwise rotation of the ship's massive propeller gradually pushed the ship into a slow right turn, bringing her up into the wind and waves. Just before his ship was headed straight into the seas, Kelley threw the indicator on the engine order telegraph to "stop." Once headway was taken off, the wind against the sail-like hull of the *Widener* pushed the ship back to the left until it was once again wallowing in the troughs. Then Kelley signalled "ahead slow" and repeated the procedure again: steam slowly ahead until the ship swung up into the seas, then take off way and allow it to be pushed back down. Throughout the night of November 17 and on into the following day, Captain Kelley and his ship cautiously crabbed their way down the shore toward Duluth.

Off Two Harbors, tugs alerted to the plight of the *Widener* again attempted unsuccessfully to take the stricken ship in tow. At 7:30 p.m. on November 18, Captain Kelley and the crippled *Widener* arrived off Duluth, still in the teeth of a storm of immense severity. Within sight of the safe haven of Duluth harbor, they were forced to ride out the storm for thirty-six more hours until winds and seas abated enough for two tugs to get lines to the *Widener*. After the vessel was towed into the shipyard at Superior, a careful inspection showed that several thousand of the ship's rivets had snapped off during the long siege on Lake Superior. Captain Kelley was greeted as a hero by residents of the twin ports, but he graciously gave credit for saving the *Widener* to God, his chief engineer, and his crew. Having spent seventy-two consecutive, sleepless hours at the helm of his ship, the short, stocky captain modestly summed up the harrowing experience with the words, "It's all in a day's work."[1]

Forty years after the incident involving the *Widener*, the *Morrell* and *Townsend* also fell victims to a November storm on the lakes. By then, the two steamers were operating in the colors—red hulls, white superstructures, and light yellow stacks—of Bethlehem Steel's Great Lakes Steamship Division, which had been formed in the 1930s. The *Morrell* and *Townsend* unloaded iron ore at Buffalo, New York, on November 26, 1966. The *Morrell* cleared the Buffalo breakwater just before midnight, and the *Townsend* followed her out at about three o'clock the following morning. Both vessels were bound for the ore-loading dock at Taconite Harbor, Minnesota, on the north shore of Lake Superior, to take on their final loads of the season.

Crewmembers were jubilant that the season was coming to an end and they would be home with their families for Christmas. Many of them had gone "up the street" to celebrate while the two ships were unloading, and three crewmembers missed the boat when it departed the dock in Buffalo. One of them was Dennis Hale, a twenty-six-year-old watchman from Ashtabula, Ohio. Hale had gone home to Ashtabula while the boat was unloading.

The weather was deteriorating as the *Morrell* crossed Lake Erie, and when the ship entered the Detroit River in the late afternoon of November 27, Captain Arthur Crawley decided to go to anchor for the night. The *Townsend*, under the command of Captain Thomas Connelly, steamed past its anchored sister ship just after 11 p.m. that night. The two captains talked on the radio at that time, and Connelly reported that he intended to anchor the *Townsend* in the upper St. Clair River until weather conditions were more favorable.

The *Morrell* got underway again just before 7 a.m. on November 28. About an hour later, the ship docked at the Consolidation Fuel Dock in Windsor, Ontario, where it took on 221 tons of stoker coal. Waiting on the dock when the *Morrell* got tied up was Dennis Hale, the watchman who had missed the ship at Buffalo. Hale told Captain Crawley that his car had broken down on the way from his home in Ashtabula back to Buffalo. By the time the car was repaired, it was too late to catch the boat at Buffalo, so he had gone on to Windsor, knowing that the *Morrell* was to fuel there. Hale signed back onboard and went about his duties, pleased that he hadn't lost his job or the big bonus he would get for finishing out the sailing season.[2] By 7:30 a.m., the *Morrell*'s bunkers were full, and the ship departed for the trip north to Taconite Harbor. Captain Crawley made a radio call to the company's office in Cleveland at about

9 a.m., notifying the dispatcher on duty of his ship's position. Company policy required all vessels in the Bethlehem fleet to report their positions to the Cleveland office each morning during the early spring and late fall sailing seasons when delays were common.

At 1 p.m., the *Morrell* passed the *Townsend*, which was still at anchor just below Stag Island in the St. Clair River. Winds at that time were light, although gale warnings had been posted and the noon marine weather broadcast predicted that winds would increase to thirty to fifty miles an hour over the next twenty-four-hour period. Two hours later, Captain Connelly again talked to Captain Crawley on the radio. By that time, the *Morrell* had left the river at Port Huron and was in the vicinity of the Lake Huron lightship, which marked the juncture of the shipping lanes at the lower end of Lake Huron. Crawley reported that winds were westerly, varying from six to twenty-eight miles an hour. After the radio conversation, the *Townsend* weighed anchor and followed the *Morrell* north.

On Lake Huron, both the *Morrell* and *Townsend* followed the normal upbound courseline.[3] The two captains talked on the radio at about 11 p.m. By that time, the *Townsend* was off Harbor Beach, near the tip of Michigan's thumb. The *Morrell* would then have been some twenty miles north of the *Townsend*. Crawley and Connolly again discussed the weather, which was rapidly deteriorating. The wind had shifted around to the north, blowing about fifty miles per hour. Waves were about twelve feet high and the *Townsend* had begun to pound and roll. Fearing that his ship might broach in the growing seas, Captain Connolly restricted the movement of personnel between the forward and after ends of the vessel. For the next twenty-four hours, deck crewmembers housed in the forward end of the ship were cut off from the galley, which was located at the stern.

Just before midnight, Captain Crawley again called the *Townsend* on the radio, but an abrupt Connolly said that he would have to call him back. When Captain Connolly returned the call about twenty-five minutes later, he told Crawley that the *Townsend* had started to broach just as the call came over the radio. He said that his ship had fallen off to starboard about twenty-two degrees before he could bring it back onto course by putting on full left rudder. Crawley told Connolly that the *Morrell* had just had a similar experience.

By 2 a.m. on November 29, winds had increased to about sixty-five miles an hour and seas had built to twenty-five feet. On the *Townsend*, Captain Connolly reduced speed in an effort to lessen the pounding his ship was taking as it drove headlong into the towering black waves. Occasionally he had to order the engines to "full ahead" in order to keep the bow from falling off into the troughs. As the *Townsend* pitched and rolled in the furious seas, its big propeller regularly came out of the water. When that happened, the propeller spun wildly and engineers quickly cut back on the throttles to prevent damage to the propeller and propulsion equipment. As the *Townsend* slowly worked its way north on Lake Huron, winds diminished to between fifty and fifty-five miles an hour, but Captain Connolly could not recall having experienced such seas in all the years he had sailed on the Great Lakes.

On two separate occasions during the early morning hours of November 29, Captain Connolly tried unsuccessfully to make radio contact with the *Morrell*. He assumed that the *Morrell* was having some sort of radio problems. At about two in the afternoon, Connolly called the dispatcher in Cleveland to report his ship's position. The dispatcher asked if Connolly had heard anything from the *Morrell*, which had not been in contact with the Cleveland office since Captain Crawley transmitted his morning position report on November 27. Connolly told the dispatcher that he had last talked to the *Morrell* around midnight, but hadn't been able to raise her since. No doubt the *Morrell* was having radio problems, added Crawley.

After reaching the sheltered waters of the St. Marys River on the morning of November 30, the battered *Townsend* stopped to fuel at the Lime Island fuel dock. While the ship was taking on fuel, crewmembers discovered that some of the rivets securing the steel plates on the vessel's main deck were loose. A more detailed examination showed a crack in the steel deck plating at the corner of number ten hatch, about half way down the *Townsend*'s deck. A substantial amount of water had also been discovered in the ship's cargo hold: it was about forty-five inches deep at the after bulkhead.

Captain Connolly called the Bethlehem office in Cleveland to advise them of the damage to his ship. Chief dispatcher Arthur Dobson seemed unusually glad to hear from Connolly. Dobson told Connolly that he and the other office personnel had been very concerned about both the *Townsend* and the *Morrell*. There had still been no word from the *Morrell*. Dobson had spent most of the previous afternoon and evening trying to locate the missing ship. After he had talked with Connolly the previous afternoon, Dobson put in a call to personnel on the Bethlehem steamer *Arthur B. Homer*, which was then also on northern Lake Huron, requesting that they attempt to make radio contact with the *Morrell*. The *Homer* called back early in the evening to say they had been unable to raise the *Morrell*. The captain of the *Homer* thought the *Morrell*'s radio antenna may have been damaged during the storm. Dobson had also called the marine radio station in Rogers City, Michigan, on northern Lake Huron. Radio operators there said they had heard nothing from the *Morrell* on either the AM or FM radio frequencies they constantly monitored, but they told Dobson that heavy snows had disrupted AM radio transmissions throughout much of the storm.

Shortly after noon on November 30, Bethlehem officials contacted the Coast Guard's rescue coordination center in Cleveland to report that the *Morrell* had not been heard from for thirty-six hours. An immediate radio broadcast went out to all ships on the lakes to keep a lookout for the missing freighter. At the same time, a Coast Guard airplane commenced an aerial search for the *Morrell*.

At 1:12 p.m. on November 30, less than an hour after receiving the call from Bethlehem officials, the Coast Guard rescue coordination center received word that the *Str. G. G. Post* had sighted a body wearing a lifejacket eight miles north of Harbor Beach. The lifejacket was stencilled with the name *Daniel J. Morrell*. The Coast Guard immediately launched an intensive search in the waters of Lake Huron north of Harbor Beach. Seven Coast Guard vessels, including the icebreaker *Mackinaw* and the buoy tenders *Bramble* and *Acacia*, along with numerous helicopters and fixed-wind aircraft from the air stations at Traverse City, Michigan, and Detroit, were dispatched to the scene.

At 4 p.m., a Coast Guard thirty-foot patrol boat and two helicopters reported recovering seven bodies from the waters north of Harbor Beach. Minutes later, a call came in that a helicopter had discovered the *Morrell*'s forward life raft on the beach about three miles below Huron City, Michigan, fifteen miles north-northwest of Harbor Beach. The helicopter crew reported that at first they thought the raft held four dead bodies, but as they approached closer one of the bodies raised its arm and head. The survivor was Dennis Hale, the burly twenty-six-year-old watchman from Ashtabula. Clad only in undershorts, a peacoat, and his lifejacket, the bruised and battered Hale was flown immediately to a nearby hospital.

The Coast Guard search continued until December 4, 1966, by which time the bodies of twenty-two crewmembers had been found. Six crewmembers were still missing and presumed dead. Dennis Hale was the only survivor. The hull of the sunken ship was found and positively identified on January 6, 1967, lying in about two hundred feet of water, sixteen miles almost due north of Pointe Aux Barques and northwest of Harbor Beach.

From his hospital bed, Dennis Hale related the fearful story of the last hours of the *Daniel J. Morrell*. Watchstanders on lake freighters stand two four-hour watches each day, with eight hours off in between. Hale was on the four-to-eight watch,

The *Daniel J. Morrell* disappeared in a furious storm that struck the lakes in late November of 1966. The sunken hull was later located just north of Michigan's thumb. The only survivor of the disaster was found in the ship's life raft, washed up on the shore north of Harbor Beach, Michigan. (Author's collection)

and shortly after going to work at about four o'clock in the afternoon on November 28, he was sent to inspect the three cargo holds of the *Morrell* to check for any damage that might have been caused by the buckets on the unloading rigs at Buffalo. The buckets commonly bang into the side tank slopes and the bottom of the cargo hold during unloading, often punching holes through the steel. In the first and second holds, Hale found that three small holes in the skin of the side tanks were spurting water, but he was not able to enter the ship's number three hold because a substantial amount of free surface water was sloshing around in it. The water extended from the after bulkhead to about the midway point of the hold. He estimated the water to have been about eighteen inches deep at the bulkhead. Hale believed the water had probably come from holes in the sidetanks, and he reported his findings to Captain Crawley.

Hale got off watch at 8 p.m. and went back to the galley to eat. It was snowing, but the weather was not too severe, and the ship seemed to be riding well. By the time he crawled into his bunk at about 9:30 p.m., however, the weather had worsened considerably. His room was on the main deck level near the bow, and he could hear the anchors banging in their wells as the ship pitched and rolled in the growing seas. Hale had been sailing for three years, and, like most sailors, he was used to the cacophony of noises aboard ship and had no trouble falling asleep.

Hale was awakened at about 2 a.m. the following morning by what he described as a loud bang. Lying in his bunk, he heard another bang, and the books on the bookshelf in his room were thrown to the deck as the ship rolled. Alarmed, Hale tried to switch on the light above his bunk, but it wouldn't work. Right at that instant, the ship's general alarm bell began clanging. Hale leaped out of his bunk, grabbed his lifejacket, and ran out into the passageway outside his room, clad only in his undershorts.

Looking out the doorway at the rear of the passageway, Hale could see that the forward end of the *Morrell* was dark, but the lights at the stern were still on. As he looked down the long deck, he noticed that the center of the deck appeared to be higher than the bow or stern, as if the ship was hogging badly. Feeling the bite of the cold wind on his almost naked body, he went back into his room to look for his pants. In the darkness and excitement of the moment he couldn't find them, but he did find his heavy wool peacoat. He slipped into the peacoat, and pulled the bright orange lifejacket on over the top of it as he hurried out on deck to where the forward liferaft was located. Once outside, he could hear the sounds of metal tearing and steel grinding against steel coming from the midships area of the deck.

The forward liferaft was located between number three and number four hatches on the main deck, and most of the crewmembers from the forward end of the ship appeared to already be at the raft by the time Hale got there. Someone exclaimed, "get on the raft and hold on tight," and Hale and his shipmates did just that, although normal procedure would have called for them to throw the raft over the side of the ship before boarding it. Instead they sat on the raft on the deck of the *Morrell* and waited for their ship to sink out from under them.

From his vantage point on the raft, Hale could clearly see that the ship had cracked badly amidships. As the bow and stern sections rolled and twisted in the high seas, sparks were given off in the area of the crack as metal grated against metal and steam billowed from broken heating lines. Then the ship broke cleanly in two, and the stern section, still seemingly under power, began to ram and push the bow section. Gradually, the seas and the ramming action of the stern pushed the bow around until it was perpendicular to the stern. The two sections of the *Morrell* finally parted, and the bow began noticeably to settle in the water. Within moments, waves rolled up the deck and washed the raft off the ship, spilling the crewmembers into the frigid waters of Lake Huron. Only about eight minutes had passed since the general alarm bells had sounded.

Hale came to the surface about ten feet from the raft and swam for it in the violent waters. Two deckhands and a wheelsman also reached the raft, and the four helped each other crawl aboard the bobbing platform. The only other crewmember Hale saw after climbing onto the raft was a lone figure still on the forecastle deck of the *Morrell*. The others who had gone into the water when the raft was swept overboard had all been wearing lifejackets, but they simply vanished in the turbulent water. About fifteen minutes later, Hale and the three crewmen aboard the raft watched in silence as the bow of their ship settled into the water and sank out of sight. The stern section was then between a half-mile and a mile from the raft and appeared to be steaming away into the darkness. It, too, would later sink. Hale knew that other ships were supposedly in the area, and he used the signal pistol from the raft's emergency locker to fire several parachute flares into the night sky.

The four shipwrecked sailors huddled together on the open raft trying to stay warm. None were dressed for a night on the stormy lake, and the cold winds and frigid water rapidly took a terrible toll on them. At about six in the morning, the two deckhands died. Later that afternoon, the wheelsman quietly told Hale that he was going to "throw in the sponge," and he rolled over and died.[4] Dennis Hale was suddenly the loneliest man in the world. He burrowed beneath the bodies of his three dead shipmates in an effort to keep warm. During the next twenty-four hours he would pass in and out of consciousness and experience a variety of hallucinations. Against all odds, Hale lived through the night, but when daylight came on the morning of November 30, he knew that it wouldn't be long before he joined his dead shipmates.

Sometime that morning Hale felt the raft drifting in the surf and banging against rocks as it finally came to rest on the beach. Lifting his head, he could see the lights of a farmhouse in the distance, but the hours of brutal cold had literally paralyzed his body. Unable to move, Hale yelled until he was exhausted. Later he managed to shoot off the last of his parachute flares, hoping that someone would see it and come to his aid. At four o'clock in the afternoon, he heard the sounds of a helicopter and somehow managed to raise his head and wave an arm. Minutes later he was bundled in warm blankets and being whisked to the hospital. He was suffering from exposure, and his feet and right hand were frostbitten. Within days he was on his way home to his wife and four children in Ashtabula. Hale still lives there today, but he never sailed again.

Coast Guard officials conducted a lengthy inquiry into the sinking of the *Morrell*. Their findings, issued more than a year after the sinking, concluded that the Bethlehem freighter had broken in two as the result of structural failure in a hull girder in the midships area. The steel used in construction of the *Morrell* and most other ships built before 1948 was brittle, particularly when cold. After sixty seasons on the lakes, and while being brutally assaulted by one of the worst storms to occur during those sixty seasons, a tiny fracture developed in a stringer in the vicinty of hatch number eleven. The small crack gradually lengthened and widened as the *Morrell* rolled and pounded in the heavy seas, until the hull had lost so much of its strength that it just came apart.

When the ship broke in half, the electrical cables, steam, and water lines connecting the bow and stern sections of the vessel were torn apart. The only auxiliary power supply on the forward end of the *Morrell* was from batteries that supplied backup power for the general alarm system, so lights and radio equipment were unusable. There had been no way for Captain Crawley to broadcast a distress call in the terrible moments before his ship sank.

Structural damage on the *Morrell* was very similar to that discovered on the *Townsend* when a team of Coast Guard inspectors went over it at a Sault Ste. Marie, Ontario, dock on December 2. A thirteen-inch crack, one-eighth of an inch wide, was found running from the corner of the *Townsend*'s number ten hatch toward the side of the ship. At the forward corners of number ten and eleven hatches, rivets in the deck strapping showed signs of working. Loose rivets and other cracks were also found in the *Townsend*'s doublebottom and side tanks in the midships area.

The Coast Guard immediately withdrew the *Townsend*'s certificate of inspection and ordered that the ship be drydocked for a more complete inspection and repairs before operating again. The Coast Guard specified that the seriously damaged vessel would have to be towed to a shipyard as a "dead ship," with no crewmembers aboard.[5] After careful consideration, Bethlehem fleet executives decided to withdraw the *Townsend* from service. She remained at the Algoma Central Railway dock in Sault Ste. Marie, Ontario, until 1968, when the hull was sold to a U.S. saltwater fleet so that it could be traded to the U.S. Maritime Commission for a newer ship. The Maritime Commission sold the *Townsend* to a Canadian shipbreaker, and in early October of 1968 the former Queen of the Lakes passed out of the St. Lawrence Seaway on her way to be scrapped in Spain.

The *Townsend* and the Canadian steamer *Dolomite* were under tow by the Dutch tug *Hudson* on October 7, 1968, when they encountered an Atlantic storm about four hundred miles southeast of St. Johns, Newfoundland. The *Townsend* broke loose from the tug and foundered in the raging seas. Before the tug could get a line on the wallowing freighter, it broke in half and sank.[6] It had obviously sustained critical—terminal—damage in the November storm on Lake Huron that had claimed the *Morrell*. A few more hours of unrelenting punishment in that killer storm and the *Townsend*, too, might have broken in half and sunk. Two huge steamers built from the same plans, launched within days of each other, their careers ended by the same storm.

Notes

1. John J. Kelley, "An Historic Thirty-Six Hours of Superior Seamanship," *Inland Seas* (Summer 1984): 82–88.
2. Crewmembers who finish out the sailing season aboard freighters on the Great Lakes normally receive a bonus amounting to ten percent of the gross pay they earned during the sailing season. The bonus program is a longstanding tradition on the lakes. It predates the establishment of unemployment compensation and was originally instituted in an effort to insure that seamen would have enough money to live during the winter months when they were unemployed. While sailors today are covered by unemployment insurance from layup to fitout, the bonus program has been continued as an incentive for sailors to finish out the sailing season. If they didn't have bonuses to look forward to at layup, many sailors would undoubtedly quit their jobs in the late fall when the weather gets bad or when Thanksgiving and Christmas come and they face the unpleasant prospect of spending the holidays away from their families and friends.
3. Separate upbound and downbound courses had been established for all lakes by the Lake Carriers' Association in the days prior to the advent of radar; this separation of courses was intended to reduce the number of vessel casualties resulting from collisions.
4. Death certificates for the three listed the cause of death as drowning, with exposure listed as an antecedent cause. Today, we would undoubtedly have cited hypothermia as the cause of death.
5. *Marine Casualty Report, SS Daniel J. Morrell* (Washington, DC: Department of Transportation, 1968), 1–34.
6. Ship Biography, Institute for Great Lakes Research, Bowling Green State University.

17

The Weston Triplets

Bulk freighters were a sound investment at the time the first standard 600-footers came out, especially those with high carrying capacities. While new ships like the *J. Pierpont Morgan* and *Edward Y. Townsend* were rated at more than 7,000 gross tons, the average for the more than five hundred vessels enrolled with the Lake Carriers' Association was only 3,714 gross tons. Most ships operated by fleets belonging to the association were about the size of the *Str. Victory*, which had been launched more than a decade earlier. It had a carrying capacity of less than 4,000 tons per trip, compared to more than 10,000 tons for the standard 600-footers like the *Morgan* and *Townsend.*

While the *Victory* could still be operated profitably, there were hundreds of ships around that survived only because there weren't enough big freighters around to handle the tonnages that had to be moved on the lakes each year. The small ships were gradually being displaced by larger, more economical freighters, but the process was a slow one. Vessels like the *Morgan* and *Townsend* represented significant investments for their owners, each costing in excess of $400,000—$30–40 million in today's inflated dollars. Even though owners of big ships could expect to realize handsome profits, the high cost of building a freighter limited the number of new ships that could be put into operation each year. In 1906, for example, forty new freighters had been launched on the lakes. They had an average per trip carrying capacity of over 9,000 tons, more than double that of most ships then operating.[1] The forty ships built in 1906 could probably have displaced more than a hundred of the older, smaller vessels, except that growth in cargo tonnages allowed many of the small boats to survive on the fringes of the industry.

The early years of the twentieth century were a time of dramatic economic growth and prosperity in the United States. J. Pierpont Morgan formed U.S. Steel in 1901, the same year that huge oil deposits were found in Texas. In 1902, International Harvester was formed to manufacture farm machinery, Gustavus Swift and J. O. Armour opened their huge National Packing Company plant in Chicago, and J. C. Penney established a nationwide retail clothing chain. In 1903, Henry Ford produced the first Model A automobile in Detroit, and Orville and Wilbur Wright successfully flew their first airplane. Bethlehem Steel was formed in 1904, the same year that a drastic cut in steerage fares on steamboats operating between Europe and the U.S. made it possible for tens of thousands of badly needed workers to emigrate to the states. Construction of the Panama Canal began in 1905, linking the Atlantic and Pacific oceans. In 1906, U.S. Steel created Gary, Indiana, as a new steelmaking center on lower Lake Michigan.

This unprecedented economic growth both helped and hindered the modernization of the bulk fleet on the Great

Lakes. While increased demand for iron ore, coal, stone, and grain made new ships a sound investment, the shipping industry had to compete for investment dollars with other business activities, many of which promised even higher profits. The availability of investment dollars could not keep pace with the opportunities for the construction and operation of efficient new ships. Most of the ships built during the period were owned by established Great Lakes shipping companies, but new fleets occasionally appeared on the scene.

STR. WILLIAM B. KERR

605'9"x60'2"x32'
Queen of the Lakes
December 29, 1906 to May 1, 1909

In 1906, a group of investors formed the Weston Transit Company of North Tonawanda, New York. They immediately contracted for the construction of three ships that would displace the *Townsend* as the longest on the lakes. The first of the three giant freighters was launched at Chicago Ship Building on December 29, 1906. Christened the *William B. Kerr*, the new freighter was 605 feet, 9 inches in overall length, close to four feet longer than the *Townsend*.[2] With a beam of sixty feet, the *Kerr* was also two feet wider than the early standard 600-footers. The new Weston freighter was measured at 7,769 gross tons, compared to 7,438 gross tons for the *Townsend* and 7,161 for the *Morgan*.

STR. LEGRANDE S. DEGRAFF

605'9'x60'2"x32'
Queen of the Lakes
June 1, 1907 to May 1, 1909

The new Queen of the Lakes went into service at the start of the 1907 shipping season. On June 1, 1907, a second Weston steamer was launched at American Ship Building's yard in Lorain, Ohio. Virtually identical to the *Kerr*, the new freighter was launched in a downpour of rain and christened the *LeGrand S. deGraff*. Exactly a month later, the Lorain shipyard launched the third of the new ships, named the *William M. Mills* in honor of the manager of the Weston fleet.

STR. WILLIAM M. MILLS

605'9"x60'2"x32'
Queen of the Lakes
July 17, 1907 to May 1, 1909

In appearance, the *Kerr*, *Mills*, and *deGraff* were very similar to the standard 600-footers. In the years since the launching of the *R. J. Hackett* in 1869, shipbuilders had experimented with many design innovations. In trying to improve on the design pioneered by the *Hackett*, they had built ships with engines amidship, flush sterns, no raised forecastle deck, a hatch between the bow and the forward deckhouse, and so on. With the design of the *Morgan* and the other standard 600-footers, builders had reverted to the basic design of Captain Eli Peck's *Hackett*. The forward deckhouse sat atop a raised forecastle deck. The engine was placed at the stern, and there was a deckhouse on the stern deck, topped by the smokestack. The *Kerr*, *Mills*, *deGraff*, and most other freighters built between 1906 and 1973 followed that same design.

The *Kerr*, *Mills*, and *deGraff* operated in Weston colors until 1910, when the fleet was purchased by U.S. Steel's giant Pittsburgh Steamship Company. All three of the ships were promptly renamed to honor officials of U.S. Steel. The *Kerr* became the *Francis E. House*, the *deGraff* was rechristened as the *George C. Crawford*, and the *Mills* became the *William J. Filbert*.

The three sisters operated in the familiar colors of the tin-stacker fleet for more than five decades. At the start of the 1966 shipping season, U.S. Steel sold the *House* to Kinsman Marine, the fleet owned and operated by the Steinbrenner family. Henry G. Steinbrenner personally selected the name for his new ship, choosing to call it the *Kinsman Independent*. The name signified that the Kinsman fleet was a family operation, one of the few shipping companies on the lakes not controlled by mining or steel interests. Kinsman Marine had a portion of the contract to supply iron ore to the Republic Steel mills on the upper Cuyahoga River at Cleveland. The fleet was also one of the last U.S. fleets actively involved in the grain trade between Duluth-Superior and Buffalo. The largest ship in the Kinsman fleet, the *Independent* participated in both the ore and grain trades.

The *Kerr/House* had a relatively uneventful career on the lakes for more than six decades, a remarkable feat given the fact that her early years predated radio communications, radar, and marine weather forecasts. Only once had she received any serious damage, that coming on September 1, 1908, when she was struck by the *Str. Buffalo* while lying at anchor in Duluth harbor. Even then, repairs had cost only $10,000. Luck seemed to leave her in her later years, however. On July 18, 1970, the *Independent* was loading ore at the Burlington Northern dock in Superior, Wisconsin, when the *Filbert* approached the same slip. Caught in the current that eddied at the end of the dock, the *Filbert* collided with her former sister ship. The repair bill for the *Independent* totalled $100,000, almost a quarter of her original cost and probably more than the sixty-four-year-old ship was worth at that time.

If the 1970 damage to the *Independent* had not been covered by U.S. Steel's insurance, the old freighter's career might have ended right then. She went on to operate for three more years, however. On August 21, 1973, the *Independent* developed steering problems while negotiating the West Neebish Channel of the St. Marys River—the "Rock Cut" that had been excavated after the infamous *Houghton* blockade of the Middle Neebish Channel in 1899. Miraculously, the *Independent* managed to make it through the narrow channel without colliding with the rock walls, but it ran aground just after clearing the cut. Having suffered substantial damage, the old ship was towed to Lorain, Ohio, and laid-up for a last time. Repair costs could not be justified, and the *Kinsman Independent* was sold for salvage the following year. She arrived in Santander, Spain, for scrapping on July 21, 1974, making her last voyage in a tandem tow with the *Str. James Davidson.* Scrapping operations began on October 1, 1974.

Approaching the end of seven decades of operations on the lakes, the *Crawford* and *Filbert* were declared excess by the U.S. Steel fleet in the mid-1970s. The *Crawford* went to the shipbreakers in 1975, followed the next year by the *Filbert.*[3]

It is unlikely that the three ships attracted much attention during their final years on the lakes, except, perhaps, from the most avid of boatwatchers or a few aging sailors. The three freighters were relics of a bygone era. Where once people had lined the riverbanks to catch a glimpse of them, the *Independent*, *Crawford*, and *Filbert* now passed almost unnoticed. After 1972, the crowds along the riverbanks waited to see the *Stewart J. Cort*, the first of the thousand-footers that would dominate the industry on the Great Lakes in the future. The *Cort* was more than four hundred feet longer and forty-five feet wider than the three former Weston ships, and it could carry four times as much cargo per trip. As the three ships neared the ends of their long careers, it is unlikely that many remembered they had once been Queens of the Lakes.

Built in 1906 for Weston Transit Company, the *William B. Kerr* was sold to U.S. Steel in 1910 and renamed the *Francis E. House.* By the time the *Kerr* was launched, the designs used for freighters on the lakes had been all but standardized; the *Kerr* looked very much like the *Townsend*, *Morgan*, and *Gary* that preceded her. The basic design would remain standard on the lakes until the early 1970s. (Institute for Great Lakes Research, Bowling Green State University)

Notes

1. *1907 Annual Report* (Cleveland: Lake Carriers' Association, 108), 94.
2. The *Kerr* and the two identical Weston freighters launched in 1907 had keel lengths of 585 feet, five feet longer than that of the early standard 600-footers.
3. Ship Biographies, Institute for Great Lakes Research, Bowling Green State University.

18

The Regal Shenango

William Penn Snyder, president of Shenango Furnace Company of Sharpsville, Pennsylvania, beamed with justifiable pride on Saturday, May 1, 1909, as he presided over the launching ceremonies for the newest ship in the growing Shenango fleet. The foundry company he headed was not the largest or best known in the iron and steel industry, and many of the six thousand people who had gathered to watch the launching had probably never heard of Shenango Furnace before. But Snyder felt the new ship that sat regally on the ways at Great Lakes Engineering Works' shipyard in Ecorse, Michigan, would clearly establish his firm as a leader in the Great Lakes shipping industry.

Snyder had hired special railroad cars and brought many of his friends and business associates the more than four hundred miles from the Pittsburgh area to share the historic moment with him. Next to Snyder on the raised platform that had been built directly in front of the bow of the new ship was Miss Sarah Chaplin of Sewickley, Pennsylvania, who was to have the honor of christening the new freighter. She, too, made the long train trip from Pittsburgh to Ecorse, bringing along twelve girlfriends to share the special moment with her.

The exuberant crowd of onlookers hushed when the signal was given to launch the ship. At the very instant that the massive vessel began its slide down the ways and into the water, Miss Chaplin raised a bottle of champagne wrapped in a silk American flag and swung it vigorously at the steel hull. Fearing that the bottle would not break, a common occurrence at launchings, Miss Chaplin had gripped the bottle with both hands and used every ounce of energy in her young body to smash it against the bow of the freighter. She accomplished her task admirably, except that when the bottom of the bottle shattered from the force of her blow, the frothy champagne spewed out and into her face—and into the face of William Penn Snyder. Temporarily blinded, neither the owner of the ship nor its young sponsor saw the vessel slide into the water. By the time they dried their eyes and regained their vision, the 606-foot *Shenango* rocked gently upon the waters of the launching slip as the immense crowd of onlookers boisterously cheered the newest Queen of the Lakes. Snyder graciously made light of the incident later at a luncheon he hosted aboard the *Str. Wilpen*, which had been tied up at the shipyard for the festivities.

The 579-foot *Wilpen* had been the second ship built for the Shenango Furnace fleet after Snyder had taken over the company in 1906. The first Shenango ship, a 552-foot freighter, Snyder had named after himself. The *William P. Snyder* had been launched at Ecorse in 1906, while the larger *Wilpen* came out of the same yard in 1907. Both were large, modern freighters, but smaller than some of their contemporaries. The little

The *Shenango*, shown here in American Steamship colors, just inside the famous aerial bridge that marks the entrance to the busy harbor at Duluth, Minnesota. The big freighter is carrying a deck load of new cars—1953 Chevrolets—a common practice during the period. Originally built for the Shenango Furnace Company, the *Shenango* and the other freighters in the company's fleet were hailed as being among the most elegant on the lakes. After fifty years in Shenango colors, the *Shenango* was subsequently owned by American Steamship, Wilson Transit, Kinsman Marine, S&E Shipping, Soo River Company, and P&H Shipping, before being scrapped in 1984. (State Archives of Michigan)

they might have lacked in size, they more than made up for in the extraordinary craftsmanship that had gone into their construction.

By the time the $450,000 *Shenango* went into the water, the fleet had established a reputation as having some of the finest ships in operation on the Great Lakes. While many fleets cut every corner when they built new ships, turning out spartan, utilitarian vessels totally devoid of any hint of luxury, Snyder spared no expense on his ships. Vessels in the Shenango fleet had many frills that other fleets normally reserved only for their flagships. All of them had extravagant passenger quarters, providing accommodations as fine as could be found in any of the best hotels around the lakes. On the *Wilpen*, for example, guests who gathered for the luncheon following the launch of the *Shenango* were entertained by music played on the pipe organ installed in the passenger lounge. Several members of the Snyder family were proficient organists, and organs were included on two of the Shenango boats so they could entertain themselves and guests during their frequent trips aboard the freighters. The many added touches included on the Shenango vessels added significantly to their cost, but Snyder felt the extra outlays were justifiable. The boats projected an image of quality, just the kind of reputation that Snyder wanted to build for his company. To make sure that people would recognize his magnificent ships, Snyder departed from traditional painting schemes used for Great Lakes freighters—black or rust-red hulls—and had his ships painted a striking green.

STR. SHENANGO

606'x58'2"x33'
Queen of the Lakes
May 1, 1909 to July 1, 1911

While some Great Lakes shipowners were probably put off by what they would have considered the many unnecessary expenses that Snyder had borne in the construction of the Shenango boats, they would have at the same time been impressed by their carrying capacities. Measured at 8,047 gross tons, the *Shenango* could haul more than 12,000 tons of iron ore or an astonishing 488,000 bushels of wheat. It would take the total yield of 19,500 acres of wheat to fill the immense cargo hold of the *Shenango*. A freight train three miles long would be needed to move the wheat to the loading docks. Ground into flour, a single cargo of wheat hauled by the big freighter would allow bakers to produce thirty million loaves of bread.[1]

It took two months after her launching for shipyard workers to finish fitting out the *Shenango.* She finally made her maiden voyage on the lakes in early July under the command of Andrew Peterson, fleet captain. Among those occupying the big freighter's lavish passenger quarters on that first trip were Snyder; Harvey Brown of Cleveland, a well known vessel owner and general manager of Northwestern Transportation Company, the fleet founded more than thirty years earlier by Captain Eli Peck; the attorney for Shenango Furnace; and a Mr. Black, described as "the Pittsburgh steel man." After loading ore at Duluth, the *Shenango* departed for Erie, Pennsylvania, where the ore would be carried overland by train to the Shenango foundry at Sharpsville.[2]

The record-breaking *Shenango* operated in the fleet's eye-catching colors for almost fifty years. Her machinery underwent a major upgrading in 1952, when the original 1,900-horsepower triple-expansion steam engine was replaced by a 4,400-horsepower steam turbine. In 1957, the ship was sold to American Steamship Company. Renamed the *B. W. Druckenmiller* and with her hull repainted black, the former Queen of the Lakes was operated by Boland and Cornelius, managers of the American Steamship fleet.[3]

After fifty-five seasons on the lakes, the still serviceable freighter was purchased by Wilson Marine Transit in 1963 for $300,000. The new Wilson freighter was immediately sent to a shipyard for installation of automatic boiler controls and a bow thruster.[4] Bow thrusters were a new development on the lakes, designed to aid the big ships in maneuvering at docks or in the narrow and winding river channels that they frequently had to negotiate. The bow thruster is a propeller set into a tunnel running transversely through the bow of the ship, just below the waterline. The thruster is driven by an electric motor powered by a diesel engine installed in the ship's forepeak. When activated by controls in the pilothouse, the thruster can be used to push the bow of the ship to the left or right. The thrusters were intended to reduce the ships' reliance on tugs when maneuvering in constricted waters. With a major contract to haul ore to the Republic Steel mills on the serpentine Cuyahoga River at Cleveland, Wilson was one of the first fleets on the lakes to install bow thrusters on their vessels.

Renamed the *A. T. Lawson,* the former Shenango freighter went into service for Wilson Transit at the start of the 1965 shipping season. She operated as part of the large Wilson fleet until 1972, although her ownership changed twice during that period. In 1967, the Wilson vessels were sold to Ingalls Ship Building of Pascagoula, Mississippi. In 1968, both the Wilson fleet and Ingalls Ship Building became part of Litton

Ships in the Shenango Furnace fleet had black stacks with red lettering in a white diamond. (Author's collection)

Industries, a diverse, multinational corporation. Litton had decided to make a major investment in shipping on the Great Lakes. In addition to their acquisition of Wilson Marine Transit, Litton announced plans to construct a modern shipyard at Erie, Pennsylvania. That yard would go into the record books a few years later when it turned out the first of the 1,000-foot ore carriers, the *M/V Stewart J. Cort* and the integrated tug-barge *Presque Isle.* Under Litton ownership, the ships continued to operate in Wilson colors, capped off by their familiar black stacks bearing the large, white block "W."

The shipping industry on the lakes was not as profitable as Litton officials had thought it would be. After struggling financially for several seasons, the death knell of the Litton-owned Wilson fleet was sounded in 1970 when Republic Steel announced that after the 1971 season Cleveland-Cliffs would carry most of their ore. Industry insiders knew that without the lucrative Republic contract, it was unlikely that the Wilson fleet could continue operating. Wilson had grossed about $8.5 million during the 1969 shipping season. The Republic contract represented $5.5 million of that total, while shipments for Jones and Laughlin Steel (J&L) amounted to almost $2 million, and the balance of Wilson's customers brought in another $1 million. To add insult to injury, Litton soon found out that they had lost the J&L contract to Pickands Mather's Interlake Steamship Company.

Cleveland-Cliffs, knowing that they would need to augment their fleet in order to handle the giant Republic contract —the largest ever awarded to a Great Lakes shipping company —made a proposal to buy the Wilson fleet. Litton officials rejected the offer. We have no way of knowing whether that decision was based on an optimistic belief that they would be able to pick up additional contracts to offset the loss of the Republic tonnage, or whether it was merely a "sour grapes" reaction to having been bested by Cliffs in bidding for the Republic contract. Regardless, it proved to be a poor business decision. Officials at Cleveland-Cliffs immediately negotiated to buy two ships from Interlake.

It didn't take the officials at Litton long to realize that they had made a serious error in rejecting the offer from Cliffs.

By that time, however, Cliffs had reached agreement to purchase two large ships from Interlake, and they were no longer interested in the Wilson boats. With Litton's marine operations tottering on the brink of bankruptcy, a group of long-time Wilson employees attempted to purchase the fleet. Their offer was summarily rejected.

On August 15, 1972, after negotiations that had spanned more than twelve months, Litton agreed to sell the Wilson fleet to George Steinbrenner's American Ship Building Company for $4,300,000. The Wilson boats would become part of Steinbrenner's Kinsman Marine Transit, a wholly-owned subsidiary of AmShip. The *Lawson* and the other Wilson vessels went into service as part of the Kinsman fleet in 1972.

Throughout much of the period during which Steinbrenner was negotiating with Litton for the purchase of the Wilson fleet, there had been rumors that if the sale was consummated the U.S. Department of Justice would bring an anti-trust action against American Ship Building. Other Great Lakes shipyards strongly objected to the potential sale, arguing that control of the Wilson fleet by AmShip would cost them business. They knew that it was unlikely they would ever see another Wilson ship in their yards if ownership of the fleet passed to American Ship Building. The ink on the contract between Litton and AmShip had barely dried before the federal government intervened.

Under threat of an anti-trust suit that might totally set aside the purchase of the Wilson boats, Steinbrenner acquiesced in 1974 to Department of Justice demands that he reduce the size of his fleet. Under terms of the agreement, Steinbrenner would sell three of the former Wilson ships, sell or scrap six others, and operate a total of not more than twenty vessels. As a result of the agreement, the *Lawson* was sold in 1974 to S&E Shipping.[5] Interestingly, Steinbrenner was a major owner of S&E, and the S&E vessels were managed by Kinsman personnel, as they are yet today.

In 1975, the *Lawson* was purchased by Roech Transports, a Canadian shipowner. Renamed the *George G. Henderson*, it went into service in the Canadian grain trade, managed by Soo River Company. In 1978, the freighter was rechristened as the *Howard F. Andrews*. In 1982, the seventy-three-year-old freighter was purchased by P&H Shipping, another Canadian fleet, and renamed *Elmglen*. After two more seasons in the grain trade, operating primarily between Thunder Bay, Ontario, and ports on the upper St. Lawrence River, the tired old ship was finally sent to the boneyard at Port Maitland, Ontario. Shipbreakers began cutting up the former Queen of the Lakes on November 1, 1984.[6]

The Great Lakes shipping industry had changed dramatically during the long career of the *Shenango*. When the giant ore boat first went into service, it was part of a U.S. fleet on the lakes that totalled 597 ships. Like the *Shenango*, all but a handful of the freighters were straight-deckers that needed to be unloaded by shoreside equipment.[7] As shipbreakers turned the *Shenango* into a pile of scrap metal, the U.S. fleet had shrunk to only 113 ships. Of those, fully 65 were self-unloading freighters—only 39 were traditional straight-deckers, and most of those were slated to follow the *Shenango* to the shipbreakers over the next few years. Included among the self-unloaders were 13 gigantic thousand-footers with carrying capacities of around 60,000 gross tons each, more than four times the capacity of ships like the *Shenango*.[8]

Once the Queen of the Lakes and the pride of the Shenango fleet, the old freighter had weathered more than seven decades, travelled hundreds of thousands of miles, and carried millions of tons of iron ore and grain. Few of the newest, most modern freighters would ever achieve such a record. She made an incalculable contribution to the growth and development of North America and, in the end, the *Elmglen*, née *Shenango*, could go to the shipbreakers with the same pride that she had when she first slid down the ways.

Notes

1. "Largest Bulk Carrier on the Great Lakes Taking to the Water at the Ecorse Shipyard," *Detroit Free Press*, May 2, 1909.
2. "Big Freighter Arrives," *Duluth Evening Herald*, July 8, 1909.
3. Ship Biography, Institute for Great Lakes Research, Bowling Green State University.
4. Alexander C. Meakin, *Master of the Inland Seas* (Vermilion, OH: Great Lakes Historical Society, 1988), 274.
5. Ibid., 323–37.
6. Ship Biography.
7. *1907 Annual Report* (Cleveland: Lake Carriers' Assocation, 1908), 94.
8. *1985 Annual Report* (Cleveland: Lake Carriers' Association, 1986), 67–74.

19

Shenango Retains the Crown

Shenango Furnace Company expanded dramatically under the leadership of William Penn Snyder. Snyder was an experienced and respected steel executive long before he joined Shenango. He had been named president of Clairton Steel Company in 1904, but left that company in 1906 when it was taken over by U.S. Steel. During his career in the steel industry, Snyder amassed a personal fortune through his holdings in ore mining operations, blast furnaces, coke ovens, and coal mines. Those diverse assets were consolidated under Shenango Furnace when he took over the foundry firm in 1906. Later that year, Shenango also expanded into the shipping industry with the launching at Ecorse, Michigan, of the *William P. Snyder*. It was clear to all onlookers that the aggressive and talented Snyder intended to make Shenango Furnace a major force in the U.S. steel industry.

Creating a diversified steel company is an expensive proposition, however, and after launching the record-breaking *Shenango* in 1909, Snyder found that a shortage of capital was threatening to delay his expansion plans. He badly wanted to add several more freighters to the Shenango fleet, but company accountants advised him that funds were not available to finance construction. Undaunted, Snyder used his ingenuity and reputation to put together one of the most creative ship financing plans in the history of the industry.

Snyder first approached Jones and Laughlin Steel with his plan. Snyder told J&L officials that the Shenango fleet would carry ore for them in exchange for enough plate steel to build two large ships. The J&L executives grabbed at the opportunity. It allowed them to move a substantial amount of ore without any cash outlay. The plate steel they needed to provide really represented what might otherwise have been excess production at their mills. With the J&L agreement in his pocket, essentially representing Shenango's down payment for two ships, Snyder floated a bond issue to cover the construction and machinery costs. The bonds, which promised an attractive rate of return for investors, were to be repaid out of the profits made by the new ships. The bonds sold rapidly. Investors showed great confidence both in Snyder's dynamic business acumen and the profitability of the Great Lakes shipping industry. With the plate steel from J&L and the revenue from the construction bonds, Shenango contracted with Great Lakes Engineering Works in Ecorse for the delivery of two giant bulk freighters.

The first of the new ships went into the water just before noon on Saturday, July 1, 1911, in what local newspapers hailed as "one of the prettiest launches that ever has taken place in a local yard." Gretchen V. Schoonmaker christened the vessel that had been named in honor of her father, Colonel

The Shenango freighter *Col. James M. Schoonmaker* being unloaded by Huletts. Below the pilothouse is an observation lounge for use by the many guests who were carried aboard the finely outfitted freighter. Behind the *Schoonmaker* is the *Charles S. Hebard*, a 1906-built freighter that was sunk along with the *Str. Amasa Stone* to build a pier at the Medusa Cement dock at Charlevoix, Michigan, in 1965. The hulls of the two freighters can be seen there yet today. (Institute for Great Lakes Research, Bowling Green State University)

James M. Schoonmaker, vice president of the Pittsburgh and Lake Erie Railroad and a veteran of the Civil War. Several hundred adventurous persons stayed aboard the new ship as it roared down the ways and dropped into the water for the first time.

STR. COL. JAMES M. SCHOONMAKER

617'x64'2"x34'2"
Queen of the Lakes
July 1, 1911 to April 14, 1914

The shipyard hosted a luncheon following the launching at the Hotel Pontchartrain in downtown Detroit. The distinguished list of guests included the Schoonmakers; Mr. and Mrs. William P. Snyder; twenty-two-year-old William P. Snyder, Jr., who had just gone to work for Shenango Furnace; and many family friends and business associates from the Pittsburgh area. Photos taken at the luncheon show the women attired in long, pastel-colored summer dresses and the broad-brimmed, flowery hats that were fashionable during that period. The men were all dressed in business attire: conservative, dark-colored, three-piece suits that might have been better suited for wear in a stodgy board room than at the festive events taking place that hot summer day in Detroit. Perhaps the men saw the launching less as a gala social affair than as an important business function. They weren't there to launch a yacht, a toy for the idle rich. The ship they watched slide into the water that day was a machine, a cog in the great wheel of American industry. Above all else, the *Str. Col. James M. Schoonmaker* was a workboat, the largest bulk freighter in the world.

Built at a cost of about $400,000, the *Schoonmaker* was 617 feet in overall length, 11 feet longer than the *Shenango.* Stood on end, the green-hulled ship would have towered ten feet above the Singer Building, the second tallest structure in New York City, and it would have dwarfed any building in Detroit. When it went into service in September of 1911, the big ship would carry an estimated 14,000 tons of iron ore from the ore fields of the Lake Superior region to the docks at Ashtabula, Ohio, the Lake Erie terminus of the Pittsburgh and Lake Erie Railroad. On back-hauls up the lake, the *Schoonmaker* would carry coal brought by rail to Ashtabula from the coal fields of Appalachia.[1]

Like the earlier *Shenango,* the new Queen of the Lakes looked much like the *J. Pierpont Morgan* and the other standard 600-footers. Her basic design followed the plan pioneered by Captain Eli Peck when he built the *R. J. Hackett* in 1869—pilothouse forward, engine room aft. Power was supplied by a quadruple-expansion steam engine rated at an impressive 2,600 horsepower.[2] Once the *Schoonmaker* went into service in the fall of 1911, it didn't take long for the big freighter to fulfill the high expectations of her owners. Before the 1911 season ended, the *Schoonmaker* had established cargo records for iron ore, coal, and rye.[3]

STR. WILLIAM P. SNYDER, JR.

617'x64'2"x34'2"
Queen of the Lakes
January 27, 1912 to April 14, 1914

The twin to the *Schoonmaker* was launched at Ecorse at 11:30 a.m. on Saturday, January 27, 1912, without special ceremony.[4] Several hundred people, mostly shipyard employees, watched as Miss Elizabeth Russel, daughter of John Russel, vice president and treasurer of Great Lakes Engineering Works, christened the new freighter as the *William P. Snyder, Jr.* There is no explanation for why the Snyder family and Shenango officials didn't play a greater role in the launching of the new ship. Perhaps it was because the *Snyder, Jr.*, did not set any new size records for Great Lakes ore boats, as the *Schoonmaker* and *Shenango* had. Or maybe the Snyders had merely tired of participating in the frivolities that went along with the launchings. On the other hand, the downscaled christening activities may have been due to the fact that the ship was launched in the middle of the winter, when the weather in Detroit was not very conducive to outdoor events.

Through the balance of the long Michigan winter, workers at Great Lakes Engineering finished fitting out the new freighter so that it would be ready to go into service at the start of the 1912 shipping season. Its engine and machinery were virtually identical to that installed on the *Schoonmaker,* but its Texas deck passenger quarters were slightly more lavish. Like the *Wilpen,* the *Snyder, Jr.*, had a pipe organ installed in its passenger quarters. Interior bulkheads in the passenger quarters were also panelled in mahogany and "prolifically finished with lavish moldings in the style of the day." Like the other Shenango ships, the *Snyder, Jr.*, was a prodigious carrier. While she could not top the records set by the *Schoonmaker,* the *Snyder, Jr.*, did establish a cargo record for wheat during her second season. On July 10, 1913, the big freighter loaded 464,000 bushels of wheat at Duluth for shipment to Buffalo.[5]

Built from the same plans, the two Shenango ships had careers that closely paralleled each other. In 1950, the *Snyder, Jr.*, was repowered with a five-cylinder Skinner Unaflow engine, rated at 5,000 horsepower. At the same time, her original Scotch boilers were replaced by more efficient water tube boilers. The *Schoonmaker* was repowered in 1952, receiving a 4,950 horsepower steam turbine engine and new water tube boilers. Both ships were also converted to burn oil rather than coal. Around 1954, the forward cabins on both ships were modernized. On the *Snyder, Jr.*, the organ was removed and the Texas deck passenger lounge was converted to a recreation room for crewmembers.[6] Both ships also received new pilothouses.

Like virtually all ships built before World War II, the *Schoonmaker* and *Snyder, Jr.*, originally had "flying bridges" on top of their wheelhouses. The flying bridge was the domain of the captain or the mate of the watch who navigated the ship. Early on, the flying bridge was really nothing more than a railed-in area on top of the wheelhouse where the captain or mate stood while on duty. The open air bridge provided the navigational personnel with totally unobstructed vision and hearing, so critical to safe navigation in the days before radar. From their perch high atop the forward superstructure, the captain or mate could see lighthouses or the lights of approaching ships and hear foghorns or ship's bells sounding across the water. A speaking tube allowed the officer on the flying bridge to give orders to the wheelsman who was in the enclosed wheelhouse below. The wheelhouse was heated, to keep the steering mechanism and other equipment from freezing up during cold weather, but there was no heat on the flying bridge. On some ships, such as the 1895 *Zenith City,* bridge wings extended out from each side of the flying bridge so that the captain could see around the smokestack and cabin at the stern and get a better view of how far his ship was from a dock or pier.

Over time, efforts were made to make the flying bridges a more hospitable environment for the deck officers. An awning was often installed over the bridge to protect the captain and mates from sun, rain, and snow. Later, canvas windscreens enclosed the area below the railing as a wind barrier. Even with the modifications, watches stood on the flying bridges were often punishing ordeals for deck officers. In an article that appeared before the turn of the century, a writer for *Midland* magazine asked readers to "Imagine yourself standing in a little coop, perhaps eight feet square, with no shelter other than a canvas fence chin high, with a bleak, howling wind, and the snow, sleet, and spray encasing you in a rigid frozen mold; there to be tossed up, down, and sideways."[7] It's no wonder old sailors are often described as having "weathered" faces.

On some ships, the flying bridges were converted to pilothouses, with the canvas awnings and windscreens replaced by wooden walls and ceilings. Even then, open areas were left at eye level all the way around the pilothouse so that the vision and hearing of the deck officer on duty wouldn't be diminished. Ships were built with flying bridges as late as 1946, but when radar sets began to be installed on commercial ships at the end of World War II, they were soon replaced by pilothouses like those we find on contemporary ships.

A drawing of the bow section of a typical pre-World War II lake freighter, copied from a drawing in the American Ship Building collection at Bowling Green State University's Institute for Great Lakes Research. Shown is the open-air flying bridge from which the captain and mates navigated the ship; from this vantage point their vision and hearing would not be obscured. One deck below the flying bridge is the enclosed and heated wheelhouse where the wheelsman steered the ship. Wheelhouses were enclosed to protect the steering machinery from rain and snow. Deck officers on the flying bridge had no such protection. (Author's collection)

On the *Schoonmaker* and *Snyder, Jr.*, the flying bridges were replaced by pilothouses that stood above the old wheelhouses on top of the forward cabin. When they were rebuilt, the ships looked like they had two wheelhouses, one stacked on top of the other. It might have been simpler to convert the existing, enclosed wheelhouse into a pilothouse, but deck officers were used to navigating from the higher vantage point afforded them from the top of the wheelhouse, and they were loath to change. With the emergence of the modern pilothouse, deck officers no longer stood their watches alone in the open air. The wheelsman now stands on a platform toward the back of the pilothouse, raised so that he can see past the officer of the watch, who generally takes up a position in the center window, directly behind the steering pole jutting out from the bow of the ship. Many an old wheelsman will tell you that it was a sad day in the annals of Great Lakes shipping when they were first forced to share their domain with the often haughty deck officers.

With their new pilothouses and engine machinery, the *Schoonmaker* and *Snyder, Jr.*, continued to operate in Shenango colors until 1965. That year the *Schoonmaker* was chartered out to Wilson Marine Transit. While she retained her original name, the *Schoonmaker* was repainted in Wilson colors for the duration of the charter, which lasted until the end of the 1966 season when that fleet was taken over by Litton Industries and the ship reverted to Shenango. During the 1966 season, the *Snyder, Jr.*, was chartered out to Pickands Mather's Interlake Steamship Company. The following year brought the death at age seventy-eight of William P. Snyder, Jr., who had succeeded his father at the firm's helm in 1918. Even before his passing, Shenango executives had decided to sell the three ships remaining in their fleet and contract with other shipping companies to haul their raw materials.

The *Snyder, Jr.*, and the 710-foot *Str. Shenango II*, which had replaced the original *Shenango* in 1959, were sold to Interlake early in 1967. Their unique green hulls were covered over with a fresh coat of Interlake's rust-red hull paint before they went into service with Interlake during the 1967 season. In 1969, Interlake also purchased the *Schoonmaker*, the last of the Shenango vessels. Renaming it the *Willis B. Boyer* in honor of the president of Republic Steel, Interlake operated the ship under charter to Republic from 1969–72.

In 1971, Cleveland-Cliffs was scheduled to take over the lucrative Republic Steel ore contract from Wilson Marine. It was obvious to all industry insiders that Wilson would not survive the loss of the Republic tonnage. Cliffs was in need of additional ships to fulfill their new contract commitments, and they attempted unsuccessfully to purchase the Wilson fleet from Litton Industries. Their offer rejected by Litton, Cliffs' officials negotiated with Interlake Steamship and struck a deal to buy the *Snyder, Jr.*, and *Boyer*, the former *Schoonmaker*. Once again, the twin freighters were repainted. Like the other ships in the growing Cleveland-Cliffs fleet, the *Snyder, Jr.*, and *Boyer* went into service in 1971 with black hulls and pea-green cabins. Their black smokestacks now bore the radiant orange "C" that was the logo of the Cliffs fleet.

The Cleveland-Cliffs fleet was one of the most successful on the lakes during the 1970s. Buoyed by the giant Republic Steel contract, the largest ever awarded on the lakes, the fleet grew to more than twenty ships. In addition to their ore contracts, managers of the Cliffs fleet secured a major contract to supply coal to power generation plants on the lakes. There was even serious talk that the fleet would build a thousand-footer to augment their coal-carrying capacity. Then, in 1980, Cleveland-Cliffs lost the critical Republic Steel contract to Interlake Steamship. Like Wilson, Cliffs would not survive the loss of their largest contract. They managed to hang on until 1984, but seldom could they find enough cargoes to operate more than two ships. Between 1980 and 1984, most of the Cliffs fleet lay idle at docks around the lakes. Some of the older, smaller vessels began to be sent to the shipbreakers, while Cliffs executives scrambled to try to find cargoes for ships like the *Snyder, Jr.*, and *Boyer*.

In 1983, both of the former Shenango freighters were sold to American Bulk Shipping of Los Angeles. That firm hoped to revamp the two ships to carry container cargoes. Containers ultimately destined for shipment overseas would be loaded at major U.S. ports on the lakes and hauled to Canadian ports on the St. Lawrence Seaway. From there the containers would be transferred to ocean vessels for overseas shipment. While the plan sounded very feasible to many within the Great Lakes shipping community, it was found that water transportation of containers could not compete with rates offered by the railroads.

In 1986, the *Boyer* was purchased by the city of Toledo, Ohio, for her scrap value. City officials intended to convert the former Queen of the Lakes to a museum ship that would attract visitors to the riverfront area along the Maumee River.[8] That plan never reached fruition, however, and the weatherbeaten hulls of the *Boyer* and *Snyder, Jr.*, still sit idle at Toledo. There is virtually unanimous agreement within the Great Lakes maritime community that neither ship will ever see service again and that they are but a short step away from the shipbreakers' torches.

Notes

1. "Largest Steel Bulk Freighter in the World Is Successfully Dropped Off at Ecorse Shipyard," *Detroit Free Press*, July 2, 1911.
2. Ship Biography, Institute for Great Lakes Research, Bowling Green State University.
3. John O. Greenwood, *Namesakes of the Lakes* (Cleveland: Freshwater Press, 1970), 208.
4. A third identical freighter was built in 1922 for the Franklin Steamship Company of Duluth. The *Fred G. Hartwell* was sold to Hanna in 1946, and in 1951 they renamed her the *Matthew Andrews*. In 1962, the *Hartwell* was sold to Misener Transportation, a Canadian shipping company, and she entered service for them as the *George M. Carl*. The *Carl* was scrapped in Spain in 1984-85.
5. Christine Rohn Hilston, "A Queen in Limbo," *Telescope* 31, no. 5 (Sept.-Oct. 1982): 117.
6. Ibid., 118.
7. J. B. Mansfield, ed. *History of the Great Lakes*, vol. I (Chicago: J. H. Beers and Co., 1899; reprint, Cleveland: Freshwater Press, 1972), 481.
8. Ship Biographies, Institute for Great Lakes Research, Bowling Green State University.

20

Canadian Royalty

The shipping industry on the Great Lakes has had a binational character dating back to 1755, when the first British vessels built at Oswego, New York, first shared Lake Ontario with the small, preexisting French fleet. After the British took control of Canada in 1763 and the U.S. gained its independence from England in 1783, vessels flew either the British ensign or the stars and stripes of the new nation south of the lakes until 1867. In that year, Canada was granted dominion status, and ships in the large Canadian fleet began operating under their own national flag.

Ships flying the national ensigns of the U.S. and Canada shared the busy shipping lanes of the Great Lakes after 1867, yet from the debut of the iron-hulled *Onoko* in 1882 through the launchings of Shenango's *Schoonmaker* and *Snyder, Jr.*, in 1911 and 1912, the successive heirs to the Queen of the Lakes title had always been U.S. ships. Trading mainly between ports on the upper lakes and urban and industrial centers on Lake Ontario and the lower St. Lawrence River, the Canadian ships were limited in size by the dimensions of the locks in the Welland Canal, which first connected Lake Erie and Lake Ontario in 1829. Although the canal had been modernized in 1850 and again in 1867, in the second decade of the twentieth century the locks could still only accommodate ships of up to 270 feet in length.[1] Because of the importance of the trade to Lake Ontario and the lower St. Lawrence, most Canadian shipowners were hesitant to build ships too large to transit the Welland.

STR. W. GRANT MORDEN

625'x59'2"x27'9"
Queen of the Lakes
April 4, 1914 to June 23, 1926

The long U.S. monopoly of the Queen of the Lakes title finally came to an end on Tuesday, April 4, 1914, at Port Arthur, Ontario. Thousands of excited residents of Port Arthur and neighboring Fort William joined with many of their country's top shipping executives and government officials at Western Ship Building and Dry Dock Company two days after Easter to watch the launching of the *Str. W. Grant Morden*. At 625 feet in length and 8,611 gross tons, the *Morden* was the largest ship ever built in Canada, the longest ship on the Great Lakes, and the first Canadian Queen of the Lakes.

The *Morden* had been built for Canada Steamship Lines (CSL), Canada's oldest and largest shipping company. CSL could trace its colorful history back to the formation in 1845 of

La Societé de Navigation de la Rivière Richelieu, the Society for the Navigation of the Richelieu River. The historic company had been formed by a group of farmers who lived along the banks of the Richelieu River in St. Charles, Quebec, and who were interested in finding a way to transport their produce to markets in Montreal. A collection taken at the organizational meeting of the society financed the fleet's first vessels, the *Str. Richelieu* and its barge consort, the *Sincennes*. The grassroots venture proved to be highly successful, and the Richelieu fleet eventually combined with a number of other Canadian shipping companies to form CSL in 1913. That same year, CSL contracted with Western Ship Building, a subsidiary of American Ship Building, to construct the *Morden* for their upper lakes trade.[2]

In addition to its record-breaking length, the *Morden* is remembered as having been one of the early Great Lakes freighters built on the Isherwood system.[3] Developed by Sir Joseph W. Isherwood, a British naval architect, the system involved the use of longitudinal rather than transverse side framing. The main advantage of Isherwood's technique was that ships built with longitudinal framing were much lighter. The biggest negative was that ships with longitudinal framing were exceptionally flexible and tended to undulate in a seaway.

James G. Wallace, president of American Ship Building, thought the Isherwood system was perfectly suited to the peculiarities of shipping on the Great Lakes.[4] Because longitudinal framing reduced a ship's weight, it resulted in a vessel that could carry more cargo than a conventionally framed ship of

The *W. Grant Morden* of Canada Steamship Lines, the first Canadian Queen of the Lakes, discharging a cargo of coal at Port Arthur, Ontario, one of two neighboring communities on the rugged north shore of Lake Superior that later merged to form the thriving city of Thunder Bay. Built at Western Shipbuilding in Port Arthur, and launched on April 4, 1914, the *Morden* was one of the few ships on the lakes built according to the Isherwood system of longitudinal framing. The *Morden* was too large to fit through the diminuitive locks of the Welland Canal that connected Lake Erie and Lake Ontario. (Institute for Great Lakes Research, Bowling Green State University)

equal size operating at the same draft. Drafts on the lakes have always been severely limited by the shallowness of river channels and harbors, and the ratio of depth to length on bulk freighters has always been extremely high. At a time when the accepted rule of thumb for ocean ships was to make the length ten times the depth, Great Lakes ships had lengths that were routinely eighteen times their depth.[5] In 1910, AmShip signed a licensing agreement with Isherwood giving them exclusive rights to use his system on the Great Lakes. Although it was in vogue for four or five years, the Isherwood system fell from favor with shipowners not long after construction of the *Morden*.[6]

Another early Isherwood-framed ship was the *Str. Renown*, launched at AmShip's Lorain yard on May 20, 1911. Owned by Standard Oil Company, the 390-foot vessel was the first U.S. tankship on the Great Lakes. The world's first tankship, the *Glaukauf*, had been built in England in 1886 for the German-American Petroleum Company. While Imperial Oil Company of Canada employed several vessels to haul liquid petroleum products as early as 1902, the first real tanker on the lakes was their 200-foot, English-built *Imperial*, which went into service in 1910. The following year, a second tanker, the 243-foot *Impoco*, joined the *Imperial* in moving oil products from Imperial's refinery at Sarnia, Ontario, to ports throughout Canada.

In the same way that most U.S. bulk freighters on the lakes were significantly larger than their Canadian counterparts until the *Morden* came along, the *Renown* dwarfed the two Imperial tankers. It had a carrying capacity of 44,000 barrels—1,800,000 gallons—of liquid bulk products.[7] By the time the *Morden* made its debut, tankships were well-established in the growing liquid bulk trade on the lakes.

The *Morden* looked much like the big Shenango freighters, except that she had an unusually high forecastle deck at her bow. Another minor difference that undoubtedly went unnoticed by most boatwatchers was the presence of anchor wells. In 1926, most ships on the lakes didn't have anchor wells. The stocks of their anchors pulled up into the round hawseholes in their hulls, while the flukes of the anchors hung outside the hulls. On the *Morden*, the anchor flukes pulled up into an anchor box set into the side of the hull. In that way, the anchor flukes did not protrude beyond the lines of the hull and could not foul on anything or be damaged when the ship was dockside.

The *Morden* was far from the first ship to be built with anchor wells. They dated back to at least 1886, when the *Str. Susquehanna*, then the Queen of the Lakes, was built with anchor wells to accommodate her large wood-stock anchors. The practice did not catch on with shipbuilders or shipowners, however, until after the turn of the century. One of the early bulk freighters equipped with anchor wells was the 545-foot *Str. Harvey D. Goulder*, launched in 1906 at AmShip's Lorain yard. Even then, the standard 600-footers that also came out in 1906, and ships like the *Schoonmaker* and *Snyder, Jr.*, of 1911 and 1912, were built without anchor boxes. The innovation became slightly more common during the second decade of the twentieth century and gained fairly wide acceptance during the 1920s. While the *Morden* had been built with anchor wells, CSL continued to build ships without them as late as the 1950s, although they had by then become standard on U.S. bulk freighters.

The red-hulled *Morden* went into service two months after its launching. On June 15, 1914, it loaded its first cargo of iron ore at Escanaba, Michigan, and set sail for Port Colborne, Ontario, at the Lake Erie entrance to the Welland Canal. There the cargo was off-loaded for transfer to smaller, canal-size freighters that would carry the ore through the Welland to steel mills on Lake Ontario.

That first cargo was far from a record, however. Even though the *Morden* was the longest ship on the lakes, it was more than four feet narrower and had less carrying capacity than Shenango's *Schoonmaker* and *Snyder, Jr.* While it smashed all previous Canadian cargo records, the big CSL freighter did not set a Great Lakes record until it was well into its fourth decade of operation. On April 30, 1947, the first Canadian Queen of the Lakes finally got into the record books when it loaded 589,844 bushels of barley at Fort William for shipment to Kingston, Ontario. By then, the name of the ship had been changed, so it was the *Donnaconna*, not the *Morden*, that established the record. CSL executives had adopted the new name in 1926 to honor an Indian chief who had been taken to France by Jacques Cartier in 1535.[8]

While tankships were the newest breed of vessels on the lakes when the *Morden* was launched, a second new type came out two years later. In 1916, Huron Cement had the small bulk freighter *Samuel Mitchell* rebuilt as the first bulk cement carrier on the Great Lakes.[9] Like the tankers, the "cement boats" rapidly carved out a niche for themselves. While they continue to play an important role in Great Lakes shipping, the tankers or cement boats are commonly called on to deliver cargoes to terminals that can only be served by relatively small vessels. As a result, tankships and cement boats have never been contenders for Queen of the Lakes honors. In fact, among the tankers and cement carriers that have operated on the lakes, the largest is the 552-foot *Str. Medusa Challenger*, owned by Medusa Cement. Converted for the cement trade in 1967, the *Challenger* can haul 11,600 tons per trip, enough to build over ten miles of two-lane highway or make 6,700,000 concrete blocks.[10] Like most cement boats, the *Challenger* is a converted bulk freighter. It predates the launch of the *Donnaconna*, née *Morden*, having originally been built in 1906 as the *William P. Snyder*, the first ship in the Shenango Furnace fleet.

On December 16, 1964, the pilothouse and forward quarters of the *Donnaconna* caught fire while the ship was downbound on Lake Huron, north of Port Huron. Extensively damaged, the ship was taken in tow to Walkerville, Ontario, by the tugs *Maine* and *Superior*. There, during the winter of 1964-65, the fire damage was repaired, and a totally new pilothouse was installed.

Five years later, CSL decided to scrap the fifty-five-year-old freighter. Decades of service on the lakes, combined with her light construction, had taken a toll on the *Donnaconna*. On July 12, 1969, the first Canadian Queen of the Lakes arrived in Bilbao, Spain, in tandem tow with the sixty-seven-year-old U.S. freighter *Ben E. Tate*, for scrapping.[11]

The historic CSL freighter was the longest ship on the Great Lakes for eight years, from 1914 until 1926, longer than any previous ship had held the Queen of the Lakes title. At the same time, because of her narrow beam, the *Morden* could never equal the carrying capacities of the older *Schoonmaker* and *Snyder, Jr.*, or that of the *Fred G. Hartwell*, a near-identical sister to the *Schoonmaker* and *Snyder, Jr.*, that was launched in 1923. In 1924 and 1925, four new freighters with carrying capacities greater than the CSL ship were added to the fleet on the lakes.

The first of the four new giant carriers were the *Str. Joseph H. Frantz* and the *Str. Edward J. Berwind*, both launched in 1924. The *Berwind* was 612 feet long, while the *Frantz* was slightly longer at 618 feet. They were joined the following year by the *Str. John A. Topping*, 621 feet, 9 inches long, and the *Str. William G. Mather*, which was identical in size to the *Frantz*. All four were built at Great Lakes Engineering Works' new shipyard at River Rouge, Michigan. The *Berwind* was owned by Hanna Mining, while the *Frantz* and *Topping* were built for Oglebay Norton's Columbia Transportation Division, which had been formed in 1920. The *Frantz* was to be that fleet's new flagship. Similarly, the *Mather* was built as the new flagship for the Cleveland-Cliffs fleet. The three new freighters had 62-foot beams, and, while a few feet shorter than the *Morden*, they could carry about 13,900 gross tons per trip, compared to only 13,500 for the pride of the Canadian fleet. Interestingly, all fell short of the 14-15,000 gross tons that could be carried by the smaller *Schoonmaker*, *Snyder, Jr.*, and *Hartwell* with their 64-foot beams.[12]

Ships like the *Schoonmaker*, *Snyder, Jr.*, *Hartwell*, *Berwind*, *Frantz*, *Topping*, and *Mather* produced record profits for their owners. According to figures used by the Lake Carriers' Association in a federal income tax dispute, during the 1916–20 period the average ship capable of carrying 10,000 gross tons of cargo generated gross revenues of about $5.95 per mile. With expenses of about $3.87 per mile, they earned their owners $2.08 per mile in profits. By comparison, the average freighter capable of carrying in excess of 10,000 gross tons of cargo brought in income of $7.56 per mile. Their operating expenses were only slightly higher than those of the smaller ships—$4.48 per mile—so owners of the biggest boats recorded profits of $3.08 per mile. The average ship with a cargo capacity of more than 10,000 tons per trip generated profits for its owners that were more than fifty percent higher than profits from ships that could carry only 10,000 tons, and more than seven times the profits from a ship that carried only 5,000 tons.[13] It is no wonder that shipowners and shipyards were constantly trying to build ships with ever increasing carrying capacities. The economies of scale that exist within the industry ensured that the owners of the biggest ships would make the healthiest profits.

Several other major developments of note occurred on the lakes while the *Morden* was the reigning Queen. In 1915, passage of the LaFollette Act brought an end to the two-watch system for the U.S. merchant marine. Until then, crews aboard U.S. ships had always stood two six-hour watches each day, with six hours off in between. The federal legislation mandated that in the future, crewmembers would work no more than eight hours in any twenty-four-hour period. The two-watch system was replaced by a three-watch system, with crewmembers standing two four-hour watches each day, with eight hours off in between each watch. The Coast Guard granted exceptions where there were shortages of officers, however, and some officers were still standing six-and-six watches as late as 1936. The shift to the three-watch system added about eight additional people to the crews aboard most ships, creating a "housing shortage." In some cases, shipping companies converted passenger quarters for use by the extra crewmembers or replaced the standard double berths with triple-tier bunks. On many ships, the owners solved the problem by installing deckhouses. The deckhouses, referred to commonly as "doghouses," were generally installed in between hatches on the main deck or on top of the stern cabin.[14]

In 1925, the 604-foot *Str. William C. Atwater*, built at Great Lakes Engineering Works at River Rouge for Wilson Transit, became the first ship with full-size hatches to have single-piece, steel hatch covers.[15] The heavy hatch covers were lifted by means of an electric hatch crane that straddled the hatches and could be moved up and down the deck on a set of tracks. Once lifted off the hatch coamings, the covers were stowed in the open deck areas between the hatches while loading or unloading.

The single-piece hatch covers had several advantages over the telescoping hatch covers that had become standard on the ore boats after they first appeared on the *Str. Wolvin* in 1904. Because they didn't leak like the telescoping ones did, they did not have to be covered with tarps during inclement weather. In addition, they could be removed or replaced much faster than telescoping hatches. In short, the new hatch covers were much less labor-intensive than telescoping hatch covers. Most new ships built after 1925 had single-piece hatch covers, and many owners of ships built before that time converted their vessels from telescoping to single-piece covers. Today, there are only a couple of ships left on the lakes still using telescoping hatch covers.

Canadians were justly proud of their first Queen of the Lakes. Many hoped that its launching had marked a turning point for the Canadian shipping industry. Like their counterparts on the American side of the lakes, they were infatuated by such giant freighters as the *Donnaconna.* Thc little canallers that had been the mainstay of the Canadian industry for so many years were workhorses, to be sure, but they were not as awe-inspiring as ships that were more than six hundred feet long. Those who yearned for the Canadian industry to make the transition to big freighters must have been delighted when the *Donnaconna*'s title as Queen of the Lakes was passed on to another Canadian freighter in 1926.

Notes

1. Jacqueline Rabe, "The Four Welland Canals," *Telescope* (Nov.–Dec. 1985): 147–51.
2. In 1916, CSL purchased Western Ship Building from its American owners.
3. *The American Ship Building Company* (Cleveland: American Ship Building, 1915), 24.
4. Richard Wright, *Freshwater Whales* (Kent, OH: Kent State University Press, 1969), 175.
5. *American Ship Building Company*, 36.
6. Wright, 175.
7. Fred Landon, *Lake Huron* (New York: Bobbs-Merrill, 1944), 361.
8. Gary S. Dewar, "The Steamer *William G. Mather* and Her Contemporaries," *Inland Seas* 46, no. 2 (Summer 1990): 100.
9. Robert E. Lee, "The Green Fleet," *Telescope* 10, no. 7 (July 1961): 124.
10. *Medusa Challenger* (Detroit: Mcdusa Cement, 1967), 2-3.
11. Ship Biography, Institute for Great Lakes Research, Bowling Green State University.
12. Dewar, 100-03.
13. Lawrence A. Pomeroy, Jr., "The Bulk Freight Vessel," *Inland Seas* 2, no. 3 (July 1946): 197.
14. Harry F. Myers, "Remembering the 504s," *Inland Seas* 44, no. 2 (Summer 1988): 89–90.
15. The whaleback barges and freighters built between 1888 and 1898 by Captain Alexander McDougall had single-piece steel hatch covers, but those hatches were much smaller than covers on conventional freighters. The hatch covers on the whalebacks were small enough to be moved on and off the hatches by crewmembers.

21

A Canadian Successor

Canada Steamship Lines was already the largest of the Canadian fleets when it launched the *W. Grant Morden* on a chilly spring day in 1914. The historic firm's growth was far from over, however. In 1925, CSL acquired a shipyard, the Davie Shipbuilding and Repairing facility at Lauzon, Quebec. Then, in 1926, CSL further expanded its holdings by acquiring Midland Ship Building and the Great Lakes Navigation Company from Georgian Bay shipbuilder and shipowner James Playfair.

After amassing a personal fortune in the booming lumber business, the Scottish-born Playfair razed his mill at Midland, Ontario, in 1916 and built a shipyard on the site. World War I was still raging in Europe, and the first ships built at the yard were saltwater freighters contracted for by the Imperial Munitions Board. At the end of the war, Playfair made the shift to building bulk carriers for service on the lakes, several of which were assigned to his own shipping companies.

During the summer of 1926, Playfair invited a number of his friends to join him for the initial trial run of the newest ship built for his Great Lakes Navigation fleet. Launched at his shipyard at Midland on June 23, 1926, the *Glenmohr*[1] was the largest ship ever built there. At 633 feet in length, the pride of the Playfair fleet was also the longest ship on the Great Lakes. To it passed the title of Queen of the Lakes that had been held by CSL's *Morden* since 1914.

STR. GLENMOHR

633'x70'x29'
Queen of the Lakes
June 23, 1926 to April 9, 1927

Playfair walked the decks of the beautiful new ship with his guests as crewmembers put her through the required series of turns and stops that had to be conducted before it could receive a Coast Guard certificate and go into service. This must have been a bittersweet moment for Playfair. In the weeks that had passed since the *Glenmohr* first went into the water, the aging Scotsman had sold his shipyard and fleet to Canada Steamship Lines. As the big freighter was put through its paces on the calm, azure waters of Georgian Bay, the host of the sea trial party was himself but a guest on a ship he no longer owned. In fact, the ship no longer even bore the name he had selected for it. Even before the sea trials began, the *Glenmohr* had been renamed the *Lemoyne* in honor of the summer residence of William H. Coverdale, president of Canada Steamship Lines. It was a ship whose name would soon be etched boldly in the record books of the Great Lakes fleet, but few would remember that it began its career as James Playfair's *Glenmohr*.[2]

Unlike the *Morden*, the *Lemoyne* was not just the longest

The *Str. Lemoyne* became the second Canadian Queen of the Lakes when it went into service for Canada Steamship Lines in 1926. Built by James Playfair at his shipyard in Midland, Ontario, as the *Glenmohr*, the ship was sold to CSL even before it set sail for its sea trials. It is seen here at Sault Ste. Marie. (State Archives of Michigan)

ship on the lakes; it was also the biggest. While only eight feet longer than the *Morden*, the *Lemoyne* was one of the first vessels built with a seventy-foot beam. The giant CSL ship was more than ten feet wider than the former Queen and more than six feet wider than the *Schoonmaker*, *Snyder, Jr.*, and *Hartwell*, vessels that had amassed most of the Great Lakes cargo records during the 1911–26 period. The *Lemoyne*'s awe-inspiring dimensions translated into a gross tonnage of 10,480, over 1,000 gross tons more than any other ship on the lakes.[3]

It didn't take the *Lemoyne* long to flex her steel-hard muscles. She established her first cargo record in August of 1926, loading 15,415 net tons of soft coal at Sandusky, Ohio, on her maiden voyage. A second record was set on September 21, when her cavernous hold was filled with 518,000 bushels of wheat at Fort William.[4] During the 1928 season, her name also went into the record books alongside the world's record grain cargo of 555,000 bushels.[5]

The *Lemoyne* operated primarily in the coal and grain trades until World War II. When the wartime demand for raw materials led the American government to allow eight Canadian shipping companies to place thirty-five ships in the domestic U.S. iron ore trade, the *Lemoyne* promptly smashed the records previously set by the biggest American freighters. She carried three record cargoes during a single nine-day period in 1942,[6] shattering the previous iron ore record by loading 17,253 gross tons at Superior, Wisconsin, for delivery to a steel mill at Hamilton, Ontario.[7] While her iron ore record fell later that season to one of the "supers" of Pittsburgh Steamship's *Fraser*-class that came out in 1942, the *Lemoyne* still held seven Great Lakes cargo records at the end of 1943.[8]

Vying for tonnage records along with the *Lemoyne* and the supers of the tin-stacker fleet were two other U.S. freighters launched in 1927. Inland's 621-foot *L. E. Block* and Interlake's 631-foot *Harry Coulby* were strong contenders for the iron ore cargo record from 1927 until the launching of Inland's 678-foot *Wilfred Sykes* in 1949. Like the *Lemoyne* and the *Fraser*-class boats, both the *Block* and *Coulby* were prodigious carriers.

In case there was anyone around who didn't know who owned the record-breaking *Lemoyne*, the owners of CSL solved that in 1927 when they boldly painted CANADA STEAMSHIP LINES on the side of her hull in large block letters, as they did on all 115 vessels in their fleet. CSL wasn't the first fleet on the lakes to use the sides of ships as immense billboards. The practice actually dated back to 1917, when the *Belgium* had BUY WAR SAVINGS BONDS emblazoned on the sides of her hull. James Playfair adapted the practice in 1921 or 1922, when he had the names of his ships painted in large letters along the sides of their blue-gray hulls. In 1926, the Chicago-based Construction Materials Corporation had its corporate name painted on the sides of the hulls of its two sandsuckers, but the lettering was not very large.

After Canada Steamship Lines painted the fleet name on

the sides of the hulls of its ships, many other fleets followed suit. Eventually, most of the large fleets on the lakes adopted the practice, including Pittsburgh Steamship Company, Columbia Transportation, and Cleveland-Cliffs. Boland and Cornelius took a slightly different tack. In 1932, the Buffalo, New York, shipping company adopted the practice of naming ships for important clients, such as Consumers Power, Detroit Edison, Dow Chemical, and United States Gypsum. Lest its customers somehow overlook the honor that Boland and Cornelius had bestowed on them, fleet officials ordered that the names of the ships be painted on the sides of their black hulls in huge white letters. Most of the fleets discontinued the practice during the 1950s and 1960s, but Canada Steamship Lines continues the practice yet today.[9]

The *Lemoyne* operated in CSL colors throughout her career. During the winter of 1968–69, she was laid up at Kingston, Ontario, and her owners announced that the ship which had once been the pride of their fleet was being retired from service. After being stripped of much of her equipment, she was sold to shipbreakers. The *Lemoyne* departed the lakes in early June of 1969 in a tandem tow with the *Str. Goudreau.* The two freighters arrived in Santander, Spain, on June 27 and were soon dismantled.[10] Even as she went to the scrap pile, the *Lemoyne* set yet another record. She was the newest and largest Great Lakes freighter to be scrapped, a dubious distinction that would remain on the record books until the scrapping of the *William Clay Ford* two decades later.[11]

The CSL stack markings on the *Lemoyne* featured a black stack with an orange cap and a white band. (Author's collection)

Notes

1. Most of the ships in the Playfair fleet had names that began with the prefix "Glen."
2. James P. Barry, *Ships of the Great Lakes* (Berkeley: Howell-North Books, 1973), 199–200.
3. Ship Biography, Institute for Great Lakes Research, Bowling Green State University.
4. Fred Landon, *Lake Huron* (New York: Bobbs-Merrill, 1944), 316.
5. Arthur Pound, *Lake Ontario* (New York: Bobbs-Merrill, 1945), 324-25.
6. Milo M. Quaife, *Lake Michigan* (New York: Bobbs-Merrill, 1944), 168.
7. John O. Greenwood, *Namesakes II* (Cleveland: Freshwater Press, 1973), 123.
8. Landon, 316.
9. Gary S. Dewar, "Billboard Lettering on the Great Lakes," Inland Seas 44, no. 1 (Spring 1988): 21–25.
10. Ship Biography.
11. Barry, 200.

22

Rogers City's Big Self-Unloader

With few exceptions, U.S. ships on the Great Lakes don't really have home ports. While the freighters are owned by shipping companies with headquarters in port cities like Buffalo, Cleveland, Chicago, or Duluth, the ships themselves are vagabonds. During the operating season, they may never call at the port where their fleet is headquartered. When they are ordered into lay-up at the end of the shipping season, they may spend the winter months at any port around the lakes where their owners can rent suitable dock space. One year they might be tied up in the Maumee River at Toledo, while at the end of the next season they're sent to a dock at Duluth or Milwaukee. Attached to most ships on the lakes, the term "home port" would clearly be a misnomer.[1] That was not the case in 1927 for ships of the Bradley Transportation Company.

In every respect, Rogers City, Michigan, had been home port for the Bradley boats since the fleet was formed in 1912.[2] Located on the northern shore of Lake Huron, the community of less than four thousand residents was adjacent to U.S. Steel's Calcite Plant, one of the world's largest limestone quarries. The "plant," as it was known locally, was the major employer for residents of Rogers City and the small farming settlements in eastern Presque Isle County, most of whom were of German or Polish descent.

It is well known that during the late nineteenth and early twentieth centuries, millions of rural Americans abandoned their family farms and migrated to the growing industrial cities of the Midwest in search of wage-paying jobs. Young people, in particular, flocked to cities like Chicago, Detroit, Cleveland, and Buffalo to work in steel mills and auto factories. To them, working as a laborer in a mill or factory was a more attractive and exciting prospect than trying to eke out a meager living on a farm.

What many people don't realize, however, is that the farm-to-factory migrations weren't just limited to the great smokestack cities. In the rural areas around the northern lakes, for example, thousands left farming to take jobs in the growing mining industry. On Michigan's Keweenaw Peninsula, they were drawn to Houghton, Ishpeming, and Negaunee by jobs in the copper mines and mills. At Marquette, Iron Mountain, and Norway, Michigan, and in Ashland, Wisconsin, they stood in line to apply for jobs in the iron mines or at the ore docks where the big freighters were loaded. In the north woods of Minnesota, young men left their dairy farms and wheat fields and gathered at mine offices "up on the range" north of Duluth. And at Rogers City farm boys from Posen, Hawks, Metz, and Moltke put their names on waiting lists for jobs at the Calcite Plant. Descendants of families that had tilled the soils of Europe and North America for untold centuries became drill operators, blasters, mechanics, mill-wrights, steam shovel operators, truck drivers, locomotive engineers, crusher operators, and dockworkers at the sprawling limestone quarry.

When the Bradley fleet was formed in 1912 with the launching of the *Str. Calcite*, many young men who would normally have gone to work in the quarry took jobs as seamen. The jobs aboard ship paid better than those in the quarry, and seaman had the added opportunity to travel to ports around the Great Lakes. Compared to working on a farm or in the quarry, sailing was an exciting vocation for young men, many of whom had never been out of Presque Isle County before.

From its beginnings in 1912, the Bradley fleet grew steadily. In 1915, the *Str. W. F. White* was added to the fleet, followed in 1917 by the *Str. Carl D. Bradley*. The *Str. B. H. Taylor* was launched in 1923, and it was joined by the *T. W. Robinson* in 1925. With five freighters operating out of the port at Calcite, several hundred residents of the small community were employed on the boats during the sailing season. Despite the good wages and the opportunities to travel, however, many of those attracted to the boats didn't stay for more than a season or two. The sailing season was a long one, eight or nine months from fitout to lay-up, and there were no vacations in those days. Many could not adjust to being away from families and friends for such extended periods. Most of those who went to work on the boats eventually left to take jobs in the quarry or with other local businesses. They settled down, got married, and began families, but they never forgot the thrill they felt when they first signed articles on one of the Bradley boats or first cast off the mooring cables and steamed out of the harbor onto the waters of the Great Lakes. They were proud to have been "steamboaters."

By 1927, it's safe to say, everyone in Rogers City was either a sailor, a former sailor, or the friend, relative, or family member of a sailor or former sailor. The boats were a part of everyday life in the small community, and local residents were immensely proud of "their" fleet. In every sense, Rogers City was "home port" for the Bradley freighters. A major point of pride for residents of Rogers City was that the Bradley fleet was unique on the lakes. It was the first fleet composed entirely of self-unloading ships. While the vast majority of the freighters then in operation were "straight deckers," ships that needed to be unloaded by shoreside equipment, the Bradley boats were self-unloaders.

The first Great Lakes self-unloader was the *Str. Hennepin* of the Lake Shore Stone Company of Milwaukee. A 220-foot, wood-hulled package freighter launched in 1888 as the *George H. Dyer*, the *Hennepin* was converted to a self-unloading bulk freighter at Sturgeon Bay, Wisconsin, in 1902. The *Hennepin* was a scraper, or pan-type, self-unloader. Her conversion involved rebuilding the cargo hold above a box-like tunnel running the length of the hold. The sides of the cargo hold sloped inward toward the top of the tunnel so that cargo in the hold would slide down toward a series of gates, or trap doors, located along the top of the tunnel. When the gates were swung open by crewmembers, cargo would fall from the hold into the tunnel. At each end of the tunnel a large steel scraper, or scoop, could be pulled through the tunnel by a system of chains and cables. The scrapers scooped up cargo that had fallen into the tunnel and carried it to an opening in the tunnel near the middle of the cargo hold. From there a vertical bucket elevator carried the cargo up to the level of the main deck. On the main deck was a skeleton-like conveyor boom housing an endless rubber belt that ran on rollers. The end of the boom over the bucket elevator was hinged, and the boom could be raised and swung over the side of the ship by a system of cables. In that way, cargo dumped onto the conveyor belt by the bucket elevator would be carried the length of the boom and spill off the end and onto a dock. While information on the *Hennepin* is scanty, it is unlikely that the little self-unloader could carry more than a thousand tons of cargo. With her primitive scraper system, cargo would probably not have been unloaded at more than 100-200 tons per hour.

Compared to traditional straight-deckers, the *Hennepin* was an odd-looking affair, and it was widely ridiculed. Critics claimed that the self-unloader was just another sea-going aberration that would never catch on within the industry. Shipping executives were quick to point out that in order to make room for the tunnel and sloping sides of the cargo hold, a lot of cargo space had to be sacrificed. As a result of those modifications, the *Hennepin* could carry far less cargo than straight-deckers of her size. Since shipowners were paid based on the amount of cargo their ships carried, they weren't about to install equipment that would reduce the carrying capacities of their vessels. Besides, unloading equipment was available at all of the major ports around the lakes.

While many quickly dismissed the *Hennepin*, her owners were very pleased with their pioneering self-unloader. For the first time, it allowed them to transport cargoes of stone to hundreds of small ports around that lakes that did not have Huletts or other unloading systems. The *Hennepin* opened vast new markets for Lake Shore Stone.

Despite the utility of the *Hennepin*, self-unloaders did not catch on rapidly within the Great Lakes shipping industry. A few other small freighters were converted to self-unloaders after the *Hennepin* went into service, but it was not until the launching of the *Str. Wyandotte* on July 2, 1908, that many people in the industry began to take them seriously. The 286-foot, steel-hulled *Wyandotte* was the first ship designed and built as a self-unloader. The 2,095 gross ton vessel was owned by the Wyandotte Chemical Company, which had built a major manufacturing plant on the Detroit River. Company officials were looking for a way to bring shiploads of raw materials into the plant, primarily limestone, without going to the expense of installing expensive shoreside unloading rigs. George Palmer, head of engineering at Wyandotte, spent a great deal of time studying the efficiency of the few crude self-unloaders then in service. He also held extensive discussions with a firm that specialized in building conveying systems. With all of the data he gathered in hand, Palmer recommended to Wyandotte executives that the company commission a self-unloading freighter. Built at Great Lakes Engineering Works in nearby Ecorse, Michigan, the *Wyandotte* could carry 2,000 tons of cargo. The unloading equipment, an updated version of the system used on the *Hennepin*, could discharge cargo at a rate of about 500 tons per hour.[3]

By the time the first of the Bradley self-unloaders was launched in 1912, naval architects and conveyor system designers had decided to abandon the midship-mounted vertical elevator and unloading boom. On the *Calcite*, the boom and elevator apparatus were installed at the forward end of the cargo hold, directly behind the forward deckhouse. It was raised and lowered by means of cables running to it from a massive steel A-frame that towered above the forward end of the boom. The practice of placing the boom and elevator at the forward end of the cargo hold became quite universal on self-unloaders on the lakes after 1912, and the basic layout continued to be followed until the 1970s.

By the time the *Str. Charles C. West* was built for the Rockport Steamship Company of Sheboygan, Wisconsin, in 1925, self-unloading equipment had gone through a dramatic metamorphosis. Instead of a scraper-type conveying system, the 470-foot *West* had two forty-inch-wide rubber conveyor belts in the tunnels beneath her cargo hold. They carried cargo to the forward end of the hold where two inclined rubber belts replaced the previously used bucket elevators to move the cargo up and out of the hold to a hopper that fed the boom on deck. The *West* could carry 8,000 tons of cargo, and with its updated unloading system, it could discharge that cargo at the impressive rate of 1,800 tons per hour.[4]

While it was a state-of-the-art vessel, the *West* was not the largest self-unloader on the lakes in 1925. Honors for having the largest self-unloaders went to the Bradley fleet of Rogers City. All of the Bradley ships except the *Calcite* were bigger than the *West*. The newest Bradley boat, the 588-foot *Str. T. W. Robinson* launched the same year as the *West*, was more than a hundred feet longer than the Rockport self-unloader. Although the Bradley freighters were not suited to the important iron ore trade, fleet executives were from the very beginning committed to building boats that could, in every other respect, operate in the mainstream of shipping on the Great Lakes.[5] If the proud residents of Rogers City found it at all necessary to be defensive about their boats, it was only because their size still lagged behind that of the big straight-deckers then in operation.

STR. CARL D. BRADLEY

640'x65'2"x30'2"
Queen of the Lakes
April 9, 1927 to June 28, 1949

Any inferiority the people of Rogers City might have felt vanished completely at eight o'clock in the morning on July 28, 1927, when the *Str. Carl D. Bradley*[6] first poked its nose around Adams Point and steamed grandly into the harbor at Calcite. Built at Lorain, Ohio, by American Ship Building, the mammoth self-unloader was a record-breaking 640 feet long. In the stillness of that warm summer morning, hundreds of plant workers and local residents joined with officials of the Bradley fleet to welcome the new Queen of the Lakes to her home port.

Few ships in the history of the lakes have been greeted with such enthusiasm. Quarry operations were suspended for several hours so that all of the employees could attend the gala welcoming ceremonies. "Hundreds of flags placed on the numerous buildings, locomotives, trucks, etc., fluttered in the morning breeze and the whole affair presented a holiday appearance." The new harbor tug *Rogers City* carried the community band and Mrs. Carl D. Bradley and her guests out to meet the *Bradley* "and escorted her into the loading slip amid the shrieking of whistles and the waving of flags by spectators." Once the massive grey-hulled freighter had been docked, the village president formally greeted the *Bradley* and its crew on behalf of the citizens of Rogers City, stressing "the warm interest of the community in the [fleet] and its welfare." Carl D. Bradley, the president of Bradley Transportation and namesake of the new ship, also addressed the exuberant crowd. He thanked them for the warm welcome they had given the new freighter and described in detail its many attributes. The new Queen was, according to Bradley, "the last word in freighter construction."[7]

Seven feet longer than the Canadian *Lemoyne* and eighteen feet longer than Columbia's *John A. Topping*, the next largest U.S. ship on the lakes, the *Bradley* had a beam of just over sixty-five feet and a hull depth of more than thirty feet. She was measured at 10,028 gross tons, just a few hundred tons less than the wider *Lemoyne.* She was also one of the most powerful bulk freighters ever built. Her turbo-electric engine was rated at an impressive 4,800 horsepower,[8] almost twice that of the standard triple-expansion engines that were then being installed on most freighters.[9] The bottom line for shipowners, though, is carrying capacity, and during her early seasons on the lakes the *Bradley* set a number of new records for the stone trade. She carried her largest cargo during the summer of 1929, when she loaded 18,114 tons of limestone at Calcite for shipment to the U.S. Steel mills at Gary, Indiana.[10]

When the U.S. entered the Great Depression following the "Black Tuesday" stock market crash on October 29, 1929, the *Bradley* was one of 410 U.S. freighters owned by forty-two fleets.[11] Together, the ships had a combined single-trip carrying capacity of just over three million tons. As the U.S. economy ground to a virtual standstill, tonnages shipped on the lakes plummeted. After transporting more than 138 million tons during the 1929 season, less than 42 million tons was hauled in 1932 during the depths of the Depression. If all of the U.S. ships had been in operation that year, they could have hauled the total tonnage by making just fourteen trips each. By comparison, they would have been expected to make forty-five or fifty trips in a normal season. Of the forty-nine freighters

Engineering drawings of the self-unloading system and cargo hold of the *Charles C. West*, built at Manitowoc, Wisconsin, in 1925 for the Rockport Steamship Company. Cargo fell through gates at the bottom of the hopper-shaped hold and onto two rubber conveyor belts that carried it to a bucket elevator at the bow of the ship. From there, the elevator carried the cargo up to the self-unloading boom on the main deck. Today's self-unloading systems are very similar to that designed by Stephens-Adamson for use on the *West*. (Author's collection)

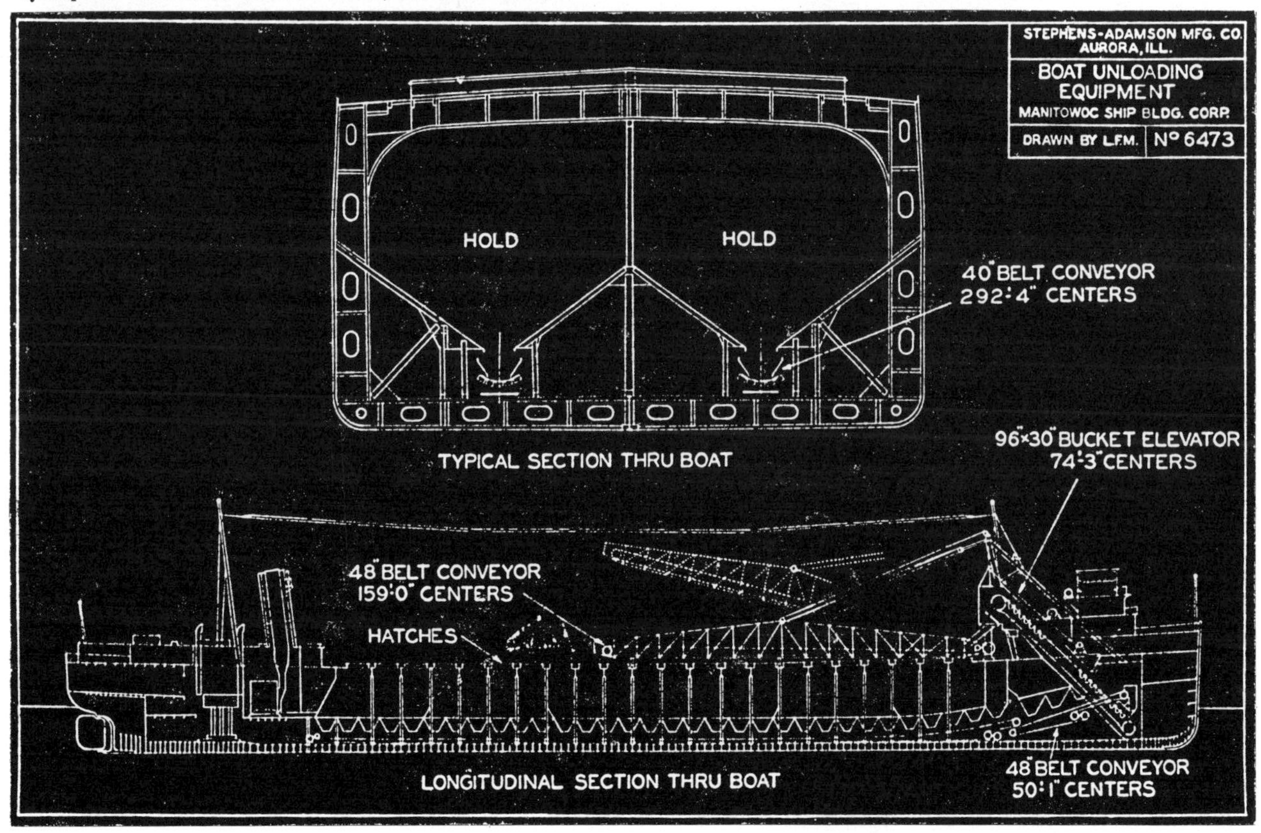

The *Carl D. Bradley* was the first self-unloader to hold the Queen of the Lakes title. Shown at the Soo Locks on its first trip to Lake Superior in 1927, the grey-hulled ship is flying a large pennant bearing its name. The *Bradley* sank in a killer storm that swept across the lakes on November 18, 1958. (State Archives of Michigan)

owned by Interlake Steamship Company, second only to Pittsburgh Steamship among the U.S. fleets, only thirty vessels operated in 1932. Together, they carried just over three million tons of cargo, mainly coal. During a normal season, that tonnage could have been carried by just eleven ships operating full-time.

Needless to say, most of the thirty Interlake boats that saw service during 1932 did not operate for the full season. Some were, in fact, in commission for as little as twelve days, just long enough to insure that their equipment received minimal maintenance attention. Fleet employees with enough seniority to hold a job were shifted from one boat to another. Most of the crewmembers holding unlicensed jobs aboard the Interlake boats were actually licensed officers. In better years they had sailed as mates and assistant engineers, but during the 1932 season they were glad to have work as deckhands or wipers in the engine room.[12]

Shipbuilding ground to a halt on the lakes by 1930. It wasn't until 1937 that a new U.S. ship came off the ways at a Great Lakes shipyard, that being the tanker *Amoco Indiana.* It was followed later that year by three new dry bulk freighters built for Pittsburgh Steamship, while a fourth Pittsburgh freighter was launched on Janary 8, 1938. The *William S. Irvin, Ralph H. Watson, Governor Miller,* and *John Hulst* were 610–611 feet long and measured at 8,200–8,300 gross tons. Smaller than the *Bradley,* they are best remembered as the first ships to have direct-drive, steam turbine engines and enclosed passageways, or "tunnels." The tunnels ran down each side of the ship, sandwiched between the sidetanks and the main deck in an otherwise unusable area of the cargo hold. The tunnels connected the engine room at the stern with the forepeak area at the bow and provided a way for crewmembers to travel between the fore and aft cabin areas and work spaces without going out on deck during inclement weather.

When caught out on the lakes in a storm, crewmembers often found it impossible to move between the bow and stern areas of their ships. That was a particular annoyance for members of the deck department. While they were housed at the bow, the galley was at the stern. In a bad storm, the galley might as well have been on the moon, for there was no way for deck crewmembers to get aft to eat. During the November 1926 storm in which the *Str. Peter A. B. Widener* lost its rudder, deck crewmembers couldn't get aft to the galley for three days. It's likely that they had some food stashed forward, but nothing to compare with the generous quantities of delicious hot food turned out by the galley crew. The tunnels that first appeared on the *Irvin, Watson, Miller,* and *Hulst* proved to be very popular with crewmembers, especially those in the deck department. Almost immediately, these tunnels became standard features on lake freighters.

The four new Pittsburgh Steamship vessels joined a Great Lakes fleet that had been decimated by the Depression. Only twenty-one fleets, with just over three hundred ships, were still operating in 1938.[13] Between 1929 and 1938, twenty-one U.S. fleets had disappeared from the lakes, along with over a hundred ships.[14] The owners of low-capacity steamers and sailing vessels that had hung on at the periphery of the industry for decades failed to survive the depression years. The ships still in operation averaged a very respectable 8,572 gross tons, slightly larger than the *Schoonmaker* and *Snyder, Jr.*, that had been launched in 1911–12. For the Great Lakes shipping industry, the Great Depression was sort of an unplanned "urban renewal" program. Small, inefficient vessels were forced out of business, making room for the construction of big new ships like the *Irvin, Watson, Miller,* and *Hulst* that began to appear in the post-Depression years.

The next notable class of ships to make their appearance after the Depression were the five "supers" of World War II that were launched in 1942 for Pittsburgh Steamship. The latest generation of tin-stackers were just inches short of the *Bradley*, but they were almost two feet wider and had slightly higher gross tonnages. Their carrying capacities were similar to those of the *Bradley* and *Lemoyne.*

The first of the "supers" was the *Str. Leon Fraser*, launched on February 28, 1942, at the River Rouge, Michigan, shipyard of Great Lakes Engineering Works. In April, two more of the big freighters went into the water, the *Enders Voorhees* at River Rouge and the *Benjamin Fairless* at AmShip's Lorain, Ohio, yard. The fourth and fifth ships were both launched on May 22. The *Irving S. Olds* came off the ways at Lorain, while the *A. H. Ferbert* went into the water at River Rouge. In design, the *Fraser*-class ships were very similar to the earlier *Irvin*-class boats, and they were also powered by steam turbine engines.

The *Fraser*-class freighters were the last privately-built ships launched on the lakes during World War II. In the 1940s, the government took control of the vital shipyards and redirected their efforts to support the U.S. war machine. During the war years, U.S. yards on the lakes turned out cargo ships, submarines, frigates, landing craft, motor torpedo boats, and minesweepers. To meet the heavy wartime demand for iron ore and other raw materials needed by the steel industry, the U.S. Maritime Commission also contracted for the construction of sixteen new bulk freighters for service on the lakes.

The first of the sixteen virtually identical Maritime-class boats was launched on September 19, 1942, at Great Lakes Engineering Works' shipyard in River Rouge. Christened the *Adirondack* at her launching, the new freighter was 620 feet long, with a 60-foot beam. Between September of 1942 and the end of 1943, fifteen other Maritime boats were built at yards around the lakes. The *Adirondack* and five other boats were built at the Great Lakes Engineering Works at River Rouge, while three more boats were turned out at their facility in Ashtabula, Ohio. American Ship Building constructed a total of six Maritime boats, four at Lorain, Ohio, and two at Cleveland. After launching, the new freighters were turned over to Great Lakes fleets. By the end of 1943, Maritime-class boats were being operated by Bethlehem, Boland and Cornelius, Columbia, Interlake, Reiss, Wilson, and Pittsburgh Steamship.

Smaller than the *Bradley* and the ships of the *Irvin* and *Fraser* classes, the *Adirondack* and the Maritime boats that followed her could carry only 16–17,000 tons at maximum draft. Their propulsion systems were also slightly out-of-date. Since all of the diesels and steam turbine engines built in the U.S. during the war years were earmarked for use on military vessels, the *Adirondack* and her sisters were outfitted with 2,500-horsepower, triple-expansion steam engines. While they weren't exactly state-of-the-art vessels, the sixteen Maritime boats added greatly to the carrying capacity of the fleet during the war years.

By the time the war ended in 1945, the U.S. fleet on the lakes stood at 404 ships, with a combined single-trip carrying capacity of 3,352,000 tons. By comparison, in 1945 the Canadian fleet was made up of 212 ships with a total single-trip carrying capacity of only 842,000 tons.[15]

Tonnages levelled off after the war, and there was little new U.S. construction at yards on the lakes. The few ships that came out were smaller than the *Bradley*, and she would retain her title as Queen of the Lakes for a record twenty-two years, until the launching of the *Wilfred Sykes* in 1949. She continued

The white "L" on the stack of the *Carl D. Bradley* stood for limestone, the cargo most often carried by ships in the Bradley fleet. Most of the limestone carried by the Bradley self-unloaders was mined at Rogers City, Michigan, which was also home port for the fleet. (Author's collection)

to be the longest self-unloader on the lakes until the *Str. John G. Munson* joined the Bradley fleet in 1952. Unfortunately, the *Carl D. Bradley* is most often remembered today not for having been the longest reigning Queen of the Lakes, but as the tragic victim of a vicious storm that raged across the inland seas on November 18, 1958.

There's a special telephone number you can call in Rogers City to hear a tape-recorded report of scheduled boat arrivals and departures at the Calcite Plant. Had you called the tape on the morning of Tuesday, November 18, 1958, as family members of many of the *Bradley*'s crew did, you would have heard that the big self-unloader was scheduled to arrive at Calcite at 2 a.m. on Wednesday and go into lay-up. In Rogers City and the nearby communities of Onaway and Posen, many wives of *Bradley* crewmembers set about cleaning house and making shopping lists for the trips they would make to the grocery store later in the day. A few made babysitting arrangements so they could meet the boat when it arrived during the night, while others planned to drop their cars off at Calcite in the evening so their husbands could drive themselves home. The *Bradley* had been into its home port more than forty times during the season. While crewmembers were usually able to run home to see their families for at least a couple of hours while the boat was being loaded, this trip into Calcite would be different. For the crew of the *Bradley*, the 1958 shipping season would end when the boat arrived at Calcite on November 19. For the next four months, the sailors on the *Bradley* would be reunited with their families and friends.

The *Bradley* finished unloading a cargo of limestone at Gary, Indiana, and departed the dock at 10 p.m. on Monday, November 17, 1958, bound for Rogers City. Moderate southerly winds were blowing, but the latest weather forecast called for winds to increase to gale force and shift around to the southwest, so fifty-two-year-old Captain Roland Bryan set a course up the west shore of Lake Michigan, to stay in the lee of the land. Winds increased steadily after the *Bradley* passed Milwaukee at 4 a.m. on Tuesday, and Captain Bryan instructed engineering personnel to take on the maximum amount of water ballast so the ship would ride better in the growing seas. After hugging the Wisconsin shoreline all day, the *Bradley* altered course late in the afternoon to angle across northern Lake Michigan toward the Straits of Mackinac at the top of the lake.

There wasn't much traffic out on the lake that afternoon. As the wind and seas had intensified, most freighters had sought out sheltered anchorages where they could safely ride out the storm. Captain Bryan, who had been sailing since he was a lad of fourteen and a captain for the past seven seasons, was apparently undaunted by the storm. We have no way of knowing what went on in his head that afternoon—why he chose to take his ship out onto the northern reaches of Lake Michigan when so many others were going to anchor. Earlier the bachelor captain had written a letter to his girlfriend in Port Huron, Michigan, in which he said that the thirty-one-year-old *Bradley* was "pretty ripe for too much weather." To another friend in Port Huron, Bryan wrote that "the hull is not good," adding that he had to "nurse her along."[16] Maybe he underestimated the severity of the storm, or maybe he was just in a hurry to get back to Rogers City and lay-up the boat. Sailors have a tendency to be very impatient at the end of the season, and Bryan knew that in just a few hours his ship would pass through the Straits and into Lake Huron. From there they could safely beachcomb their way down the shore to Rogers City in the shelter of the lee of the land. There are no rules that help a captain to decide whether to sail or go to anchor. The captains alone make those decisions.

At 5:31 p.m., as the *Bradley* was being buffeted by 20–25 foot waves, Captain Bryan and the mate and wheelsman on watch in the pilothouse heard a loud thud. The ship shuddered, like ships often do when pounding in heavy seas, but there was something different about it this time, and the three men in the pilothouse instinctively realized that their vessel was in trouble. Looking aft, they saw that the stern of the *Bradley* was sagging. Without hesitation, Captain Bryan sounded the general alarm. Throughout the ship, loud bells rang, alerting crewmembers that they should don their lifejackets and hurry to the two lifeboats located on top of the stern cabin. Bryan immediately began to blow the steam whistle, seven short blasts and one long one, the terrifying signal for crewmembers to abandon ship.

"Mayday, mayday, mayday," First Mate Elmer Fleming spoke into the microphone on the ship's radio set. "Mayday, mayday, mayday! This is the *Carl D. Bradley*, about twelve miles southwest of Gull Island. The ship is breaking up in heavy seas. We're breaking up. We're going to sink. We're going down!"[17] The mayday message was heard by many ships and Coast Guard stations in the area that maintained a radio watch on the international distress channel.

In the conveyor room, deep inside the bow of the ship,

watchman Frank Mayes heard the disturbing thud. He, too, realized that the vessel was in serious trouble. Even before the general alarm bells sounded, Mayes ran for the ladder leading topside.

There was yet another loud thud, and crewmembers in the pilothouse stared in shock as they saw a crack appear across the deck of the *Bradley*. Simultaneously, the lights went off and the radio went dead as the power cables running the length of the ship were torn apart. As crewmembers hurried toward the lifeboats at the stern or the life raft behind the pilothouse, the bow section lurched and settled deeply into the water, the main deck awash in the furious seas. In an instant, the bow listed to port, rolled over, and sank. The stern settled on an even keel until it too lost buoyancy and plunged beneath the storm-tossed surface.

A German cargo ship, the *M/V Christian Sartori*, was downbound on Lake Michigan at the time, about four miles from the *Bradley*'s location. Struggling almost directly into the high seas, the little *Sartori* was making forward progress of only about two miles an hour. Crewmembers in the pilothouse had picked up the approaching *Bradley* on the radar scope and were able to see her lights across the water. Just after 5:30 p.m., they noticed that the lights on the bow of the *Bradley* had gone out. Several minutes later, they were startled when the sky in the vicinity of the *Bradley* was illuminated by what appeared to be a massive explosion.[18] Checking their radar, they found that the "blip" indicating the *Bradley*'s position had disappeared from the screen. Although he had not heard the *Bradley*'s mayday call, the master of the *Sartori* knew the freighter was in serious trouble. He immediately altered his ship's course and headed for the location of the explosion.

The *Bradley* sank during the late afternoon hours of November 18, 1958, while trying to cross the northern reaches of Lake Michigan in a violent storm. Most of the thirty-three crewmembers who died in the disaster were from the *Bradley*'s home port of Rogers City, Michigan, a small community on the north shore of Lake Huron. (Author's collection)

Despite the angry seas, the Coast Guard Cutter *Sundew* and a thirty-six-foot lifeboat got underway from their moorings at Charlevoix, Michigan, shortly after they monitored the *Bradley*'s distress call. A forty-foot lifeboat from the Coast Guard station at Plum Island and the *Hollyhock*, a cutter stationed at Sturgeon Bay, Wisconsin, were also ordered to go to the assistance of the freighter. Because of the severity of the storm, the two smaller boats were recalled about an hour after they set out. The Pittsburgh Steamship Maritime-class steamer *Robert C. Stanley*, anchored in the lee of Garden Island near the top of Lake Michigan, heard the distress call from the *Bradley* and got underway about an hour later.

The *Christian Sartori* was the first vessel to arrive at the scene. Battered by brutal seas, the German freighter began to crisscross the area, searching for survivors. At about 10:30 p.m., it was joined by the *Sundew*. The *Stanley* joined the search at midnight, while the *Hollyhock* arrived on the scene several hours later. Throughout the night, crewmembers aboard the search vessels maintained a constant vigil as they put themselves and their ships at risk to run search patterns in the turbulent waters where the *Bradley* had gone down. It was a terrifying night for those aboard the search vessels, but no one complained. They were seamen, and they knew that out there among the towering black seas other seamen were fighting for their lives in the frigid waters of Lake Michigan.

After searching in vain throughout the long night, the *Sundew* recovered the *Bradley*'s life raft at 8:25 a.m. on November 19. Clinging to the raft, battered, bruised, and suffering from exposure . . . but alive, were First Mate Elmer Fleming and watchman Frank Mayes.

Word that two survivors had been found was flashed to the waiting world. In Rogers City, Bradley fleet officials and the friends and family members of the *Bradley* crewmembers—virtually everyone in the small community—had maintained their own vigils through the agonizingly long night. Even before word came that Fleming and Mayes had been picked up by the *Sundew*, the people of Rogers City were confident that their loved ones would survive the tragedy. They believed that the sailors would be found in the ship's lifeboats, or on one of the many islands dotting the northern stretches of Lake Michigan.

They refused to give up hope. When word came that two survivors had been picked up, it merely reinforced their belief that all of the *Bradley* crewmembers would eventually be found.

An hour after recovering Fleming and Mayes, searchers found one of the *Bradley*'s two lifeboats, but it was empty. As the day progressed, searchers began to find the lifejacket-clad bodies of crewmembers who had not survived the sinking. As the bodies were recovered and identified, teams of management personnel from the Calcite Plant had the onerous task of notifying family members that their loved ones were dead. Surprisingly, many of the children of the *Bradley* crewmembers had gone to school that morning. It was almost as if they believed that to break their normal routine would be bad luck. By going to school, as they would on any other day, they demonstrated their confidence that their fathers would be found safe. Their optimism was buoyed that morning when the school principal enthusiastically announced over the intercom system that two survivors had been found. As the day wore on, however, one child after another was called out of class by the principal. From the look on his face, it was obvious to all that he was not delivering good news.

During the day, searchers recovered a total of eighteen bodies from the waters north of where the *Bradley* had gone down. Elmer Fleming and Frank Mayes were the only survivors from the crew of thirty-five. Fifteen bodies, including that of Captain Roland Bryan, were never recovered. Rogers City went into mourning.

Twenty-three of the thirty-three seamen who died on the *Bradley* were from Rogers City, while five others were from the

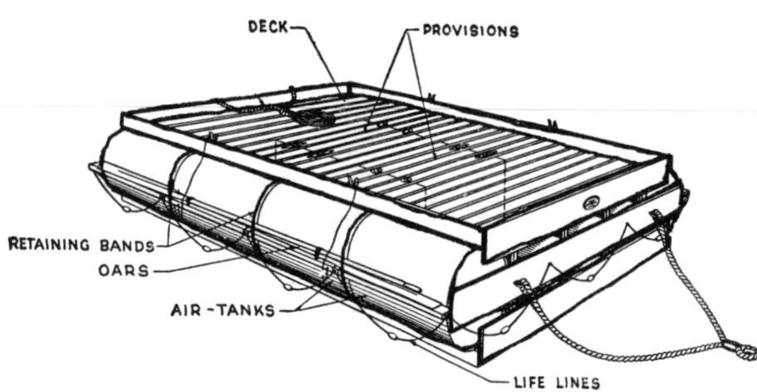

Frank Mayes and Elmer Fleming, the only crewmembers to survive the sinking of the *Bradley*, spent the night on a double-sided life raft. The massive waves that rolled across Lake Michigan that night flipped the raft over many times, and Mayes and Fleming had to struggle in the frigid waters to climb back aboard. Rigid rafts like the one carried aboard the *Bradley* have since been replaced by inflatable life rafts enclosed by a canopy to provide occupants much more protection. (Author's collection)

nearby communities of Posen and Onaway. The recovered bodies of the dead seamen were returned to their home port, and a mass wake was held in the gym at Rogers City High School, the only facility in town large enough to hold the caskets of the dead and accommodate the thousands who wanted to pay their respects. Funeral services for most of the sailors were held at noon on Saturday, November 22. The town virtually closed down while the services were going on.

At ports around the lakes, the other eight Bradley freighters broke with tradition by halting operations. From fitout in the spring until they reach the lay-up docks at the end of the season, ships in the Great Lakes fleets normally never stop operating. Not even on Easter Sunday, the Fourth of July, Thanksgiving, or Christmas do they take a break. The big ships operate twenty-four hours a day, seven days a week from fitout to lay-up. But at noon on November 22, 1958, the remaining eight, grey-hulled freighters of the fleet were tied up out of respect for those who had died on the *Bradley*. Four ships were docked at Calcite, while the others were at ports around the lakes. The *Myron C. Taylor* was at Conneaut, Ohio, the *T. W. Robinson* was at Buffalo, New York, the *Rogers City* was in South Chicago, Illinois, and the *Cedarville* docked at Port Huron. Local clergymen went aboard each of the four ships to conduct memorial services at the same time that services were being held in Rogers City.[19] While far distant from their home port, the crewmembers aboard the four ships had an opportunity to pay their final respects to their colleagues.

Even before the *Bradley* dead were buried, the Coast Guard had launched a massive inquiry into the sinking. Their findings, released the following summer, concluded that the casualty had been due to excessive hogging stress that the vessel had endured during the storm. The unrelenting pounding the ship took in the hours before her sinking may have aggravated a structural weakness existing prior to the storm. In her thirty-first season on the lakes, the *Bradley* was no more than middle-aged as lake freighters go. All freighters take a beating during the operating season, though, and it's common for them to undergo extensive repairs at least every five years. The *Carl D. Bradley* was scheduled for such repairs during the winter of 1958–59. As a result of the wear and tear she had suffered during the previous seasons, the *Bradley* was scheduled to have many loose or broken rivets replaced and her cargo hold almost completely rebuilt at the end of the 1958 season. Unfortunately, the former Queen of the Lakes would never keep that appointment at the shipyard.[20]

Notes

1. And don't be misled by the hailing port painted on the stern below the vessel's name. Most U.S. ships on the lakes claim distant Wilmington, Delaware, as their hailing port. They are documented there so they can qualify for tax breaks. Of all the ships in the U.S. Great Lakes fleet, the *M/V Presque Isle* has the distinction of having the hailing port farthest from the lakes. It uses Los Angeles, California, headquarters for its owners, Litton Industries.
2. Originally known as the Calcite Transportation Company, its name was changed to Bradley Transportation Company in 1923.
3. Letter from R. W. Frederick, Stephens-Adamson Division of Allis-Chalmers, Canada, August 12, 1987.
4. "S. S. Chas. C. West," *The Labor Saver*, no. 147 (October 1925): 3–8.
5. The early self-unloaders operated only in the stone, coal, and salt trades. Natural iron ore tended to hang up in the cargo hold, so it was generally not carried by self-unload ers until after the development of pelletizing processes in the 1950s. Grain, on the other hand, flowed too fast and could not be elevated out of the cargo hold by inclined conveyor elevators. The lightweight grains would simply spill off the elevators. In the 1970s, some Canadian fleets began carrying grain on self-unloaders with modern bucket elevator systems.
6. The first *Carl D. Bradley* had been launched in 1917 for the Bradley fleet. Named for the firm's president, it was renamed as the *Irvin L. Clymer* in 1927 when the new *Bradley* came out. The *Clymer* operated on the lakes until it was retired during the 1991 season.
7. "1927—Do You Remember?" *Michigan Limestone Screening (Winter 1958-59): 16–17.*
8. Ship Biography, Institute for Great Lakes Research, Bowling Green State University.
9. The *Bradley*'s sister ship, the *T. W. Robinson*, built in 1925, was the first vessel on the lakes equipped with a turbo-electric engine. In both the *Bradley* and *Robinson* a steam turbine generator produced electricity to drive electric motors that actually propelled the ship. Few ships were equipped with the complicated propulsion systems.
10. Dana Thomas Bowen, *Lore of the Lakes* (Daytona Beach: Dana Thomas Bowen, 1940), 229.
11. Pittsburgh Steamship was the largest fleet on the lakes, with eighty-four vessels, followed by Interlake Steamship, which owned forty-nine.
12. Walter Havighurst, *Vein of Iron* (New York: World Publishing, 1958), 169.
13. Jacques LesStrang, *Cargo Carriers of the Great Lakes* (New York: American Legacy Press, 1977), 72.
14. Pittsburgh Steamship, with seventy-nine boats, was still the largest of the U.S. fleets, followed by Interlake Steamship, with forty-five.
15. *1945 Annual Report* (Cleveland: Lake Carriers' Association, 1946), 46–48.
16. William Ratigan, *Great Lakes Shipwrecks and Survivals* (Grand Rapids, MI: Wm. B. Eerdmans, 1960), 18.
17. Ibid., 24.
18. While they didn't know it at the time, the crewmembers in the pilothouse of the *Sartori* had witnessed the explosion of the steam boilers aboard the *Bradley*. The boilers exploded when cold water from the lake flooded into the engine room.
19. "1927—Do You Remember?" 18.
20. Unless otherwise indicated, details regarding the sinking of the *Bradley* are from Marine Casualty Report: SS Carl D. Bradley (Washington: U.S. Coast Guard, 1959).

23

Inland's Beautiful Queen

The story of Inland Steel's *Str. Wilfred Sykes* actually began with the design of a new class of ships for U.S. Steel's Pittsburgh Steamship Company. In 1947, officials of the Pittsburgh fleet announced tentative plans to build several new freighters, and they contracted with American Ship Building to develop the design for the new vessels. The staff at AmShip was delighted with the prospect. Shipbuilding on the lakes had ground to a halt in the aftermath of World War II. As tonnages fell off from the record levels moved during the war years, U.S. fleets found that the 404 ships afloat in 1945 were more than adequate to handle the post-war tonnages. Rather than adding new vessels, the fleets were actually disposing of many older ships.

In the months after signing the contract with the Pittsburgh fleet, the design team at AmShip developed construction schemes and specifications for the new class of tin-stackers. The resulting plans were based loosely on the designs used for the four ships of the *Irvin*-class that had been launched for the Pittsburgh fleet in 1938. The design that was finally unveiled to officials of the Pittsburgh fleet, however, was for a class of ships substantially larger and more powerful than the *Irvin* and her three sisters. In addition, plans for the new ships showed lines which were much more refined than those of any ships that had appeared on the lakes before.

While Pittsburgh Steamship officials were impressed with the proposed designs, they informed AmShip that they had decided to indefinitely delay their plans to build the new ships because they were uncertain about the future of the steel and shipping industries. Disappointed, officials at AmShip shelved their innovative plans.[1] For hundreds of laid-off shipyard workers at Lorain, the news was devastating. Many of them were second- and third-generation shipbuilders. They and their families had been turning out magnificant ships at the Lorain yard since before the turn of the century. But as the bitter winds of winter descended on the lakes in late 1947, they began to seriously question whether they would ever build another ship.

STR. WILFRED SYKES

678'x70'2"x32'3"
Queen of the Lakes
June 28, 1949 to 1952

The pall of gloom that descended over the shipbuilding community at Lorain was to be shortlived. Only a few months after Pittsburgh Steamship's decision to delay construction of the new class of ships, Inland Steel signed a contract with AmShip to design a new ore boat for their fleet. The laid-off shipyard workers in Lorain were ecstatic when they heard details of the contract. Inland's instructions to AmShip were simple: they wanted the yard's staff to design the largest possible freighter that could operate on the lakes, within the size restrictions imposed by the loading docks on the upper lakes, the locks at Sault Ste. Marie, and the drydocks then available. Inland wanted to see plans for "the best vessel the design department could conceive, without regard for tradition or past practice."[2] Seldom had naval architects been given such a free hand in the design of a new ship. Even cost wasn't an overriding consideration for the designers. What Inland Steel wanted was not just plans for the biggest ship on the lakes, but plans for the ship of the future.

In the design rooms at American Ship Building, teams of naval architects dusted off the designs they had previously prepared for Pittsburgh Steamship. The work they had put in on those plans would not go to waste after all. They would be useful as a rudimentary starting point for the design of the Inland ship. The designs they had developed for the Pittsburgh fleet were the equivalent of plans for a 1948 Ford automobile. What Inland wanted were plans for a 1960 Cadillac. The innovative plans subsequently presented to Inland officials were just that.

By April of 1948, Inland had approved the plans and specifications, and contracts had been drafted. Construction orders were released in June, and the keel of the sophisticated new ship was laid at the Lorain yard on November 1.[3] Captain Henry Kaizer, senior captain in the Inland fleet, served as the owner's representative at the shipyard. Kaizer was scheduled to take command of the new ship when it was ready to go into service.[4]

Among those who watched the new vessel take shape at Lorain during the winter and spring of 1949 was fifty-year-old George Fisher, an Inland captain who lived in Akron, Ohio. Fisher was an American success story. Born in 1898 in Ukraine, Fisher had emigrated to Canada in 1914, during the early days of World War I. His first job was at the shipyard in Port Arthur, Ontario, passing rivets during construction of the passenger steamer *Noronic*. Fisher worked ten hours a day for twenty cents an hour. The following year, the young immigrant moved to Minnesota to live with an uncle. After trying his hand at a number of different, rather menial jobs he signed on the Pittsburgh steamer *James A. Farrell* during the 1920 sailing season.

On his first trip on an ore boat, Fisher shovelled coal in the *Farrell*'s stifling hot boiler room, deep in the bowels of the ship, while the vessel rocked and rolled its way down the lakes in a major storm. The twenty-two-year-old fireman was no heavy-weather sailor, and he attempted to quit his job just as soon as the freighter returned to Duluth. Short on personnel, the captain of the *Farrell* refused to pay Fisher off, demanding that he make one more trip. Not wanting to lose the pay he had worked so hard for, and probably not understanding that under the law he had every right to quit the job and still get paid, he reluctantly agreed to make a second trip on the Pittsburgh freighter. The weather on that second passage must have been better, because Fisher finished out the 1920 season in the firehold of the *Farrell.*

Sailing proved to be more agreeable to Fisher than any employment he had been able to find on the beach, and he returned to the boats in the 1921 season. He had his fill of the long watches in the firehold, however, and shipped out as a deckhand on the *Str. Australia.* By 1924, Fisher had worked his way up to wheelsman. After writing the difficult Coast Guard exams during the winter of 1926-27, he obtained his license as a deck officer and sailed the following spring as a mate. After the Great Depression struck the shipping industry in 1930, thirty-two-year-old Fisher found that he didn't have enough seniority to hold a job as a mate. In fact, with most of the ships in the Great Lakes fleet lying idle at docks around the lakes, there were years when he was happy to land an occasional job as a relief deckhand.

A big break came in 1936, when he was able to find a permanent job as a mate with the Inland Steel fleet. That first season with Inland, Fisher sailed aboard Inland's *Philip D. Block*, a standard 600-footer very similar to the *Farrell*, on which he had first shipped as a coalpasser. His move to the Inland fleet came at an auspicious time. As the industry began to rebound from the Depression, Fisher moved up rapidly. During the 1941 season, he was appointed to his first command as captain on the *N. F. Leopold.*[5] By the time construction began on the *Sykes* in 1948, the fifty-year-old Fisher was one of Inland's senior captains. As he watched the magnificent *Sykes* taking shape at Lorain, it was with the full knowledge that one day in the not too distant future he would probably have an opportunity to command the big freighter. Ship assignments are normally based on seniority, with the most senior captain getting his choice of vessels. Fisher was near the top of Inland's seniority list, and when the day came when he could claim command of any ship in the fleet, he would definitely choose the *Sykes.*

Fisher was out on the lakes when the *Sykes* was launched at Lorain at 11:35 a.m. on June 28, 1949. With Captain Henry Kaizer looking on, Mrs. Wilfred Sykes broke a bottle of champagne on the bow of the new Queen of the Lakes, named in honor of her husband. Like Captain Fisher, sixty-five-year-old Wilfred Sykes was an immigrant. Born in New Zealand in 1883, he had come to the U.S. via Germany, joining Inland Steel in 1932 as an electrical engineer. From then on, Sykes's career can only be described as meteoric. After just nine years with the Chicago-based steelmaker, Sykes was named president of Inland in 1941. In the same year that the big freighter that bore his name was launched, Wilfred Sykes reached retirement age and stepped down from the presidency of Inland.[6] Despite his remarkably successful career, few of the spectators who gathered at Lorain on June 28, 1949, recognized the namesake of the big steamer that went into the water that day. He was one of the anonymous giants of American industry. With the launching of the giant Inland freighter, however, Wilfred Sykes's name became virtually a household word around the Great Lakes. In many respects, the new Queen of the Lakes represented the capstone of his brilliant career.

Unlike Wilfred Sykes, Captain George Fisher hadn't yet reached the zenith of his career. As the shipping season of 1949 drew to a close, he was just another obscure steamboat captain, commanding a relatively nondescript ship. As Captain Fisher returned to his home in Akron, Ohio, to begin his long and much-needed winter vacation, Captain Henry Kaizer was finishing putting the *Sykes* through her sea trials in the waters off Lorain. Taking his new command out of the Black River and into Lake Erie for the first time must have been an exceptionally memorable occasion for Kaizer. During the preceding year, the Inland fleet's senior captain had commanded only a desk. The only thing that had made the long months on the beach bearable for Kaizer was the fact that he could look out the window of his office each day and see the *Sykes* slowly taking shape on AmShip's building berth.

The *Sykes* was *his* ship. It had been his ship when it was only a thick stack of blueprints. It had been his ship when it was nothing more than scattered piles of steel plate and beams in the AmShip yard. Even after the Inland Steel logo had been put on the massive streamlined stack and Wilfred Sykes's name had been painted on its bow and stern, it was still Henry Kaizer's ship. If the naval architects, shipfitters, welders, and rivetters at AmShip had any impression that the new vessel was theirs, it was totally dispelled on November 28, 1949, when the sturdy steel mooring cables were cast off for the first time and Captain Kaizer carefully inched the *Sykes* out onto Lake Erie. Even before the giant ship cleared the piers at the entrance to the Lorain harbor, it was clear to all that the *Sykes* was Henry Kaizer's ship.

As he signalled the engine room to bring the *Sykes* to full lake speed for the first time, Captain Kaizer reached the pinnacle of his career. He was the master of the largest ship ever to sail the Great Lakes, a ship which had received an unparalleled amount of attention from the news media. And while captains of lake freighters normally go about their jobs in relative obscurity, command of the *Sykes* had brought Henry Kaizer an almost unprecedented degree of notoriety. The distinguished, elderly captain was often quoted in news reports, and everywhere he went people were eager to question him about the *Sykes*. On January 12, 1950, personnel at American Ship Building finished fine-tuning the new freighter's machinery and officially turned the ship over to its owners. Captain Kaizer happily cleared out his desk at the shipyard and left Lorain, knowing that in less than three months he would be returning to fit out his ship for her first season of operations on the lakes.

Personnel who work on Great Lakes freighters seldom have any contact with their fleet offices during the winter months. After they leave their ships at the lay-up docks, they normally don't hear anything from the fleet office until they receive their vessel assignment and fit-out notice in the spring. George Fisher was probably somewhat surprised, therefore, when he received a telephone call from Inland's fleet manager well in advance of the 1950 sailing season. The call brought the shocking news that Captain Henry Kaizer had died and that he, George Fisher, would command the *Sykes* during the coming shipping season.[7]

Captain Fisher experienced mixed emotions when he reported to Lorain in late March of 1950 to assume command of the *Sykes*. He wished that his assignment to command the new Inland freighter had come as a result of different circumstances. Despite that, Fisher was thrilled with his new assignment and eager to get the season underway. It would be his thirty-first season on the lakes, his fifteenth with the Inland fleet. He had already achieved far more than he had ever thought possible when he first set foot on North American soil in 1914. Even after he had settled on a career as a merchant seaman, Fisher never for a moment thought that he would someday command his own ship, much less the newest, largest, and finest ship on the Great Lakes. The day he first walked aboard the *Sykes* at Lorain he must have known that he had made the right decision when he left his native Russia, that he had been right when he stayed on the *Farrell* for that second trip in 1920, when he shifted to the deck department the following season, and when he joined the Inland fleet in 1936. His years of hard work and plodding persistence had paid off handsomely. In 1950, he was captain of the *Str. Wilfred Sykes*, the Queen of the Lakes.

The $5 million *Sykes* had no equal on the lakes. At 678 feet in overall length, the new Inland freighter was thirty-eight feet longer than the *Carl D. Bradley*, the former Queen of the Lakes. Also wider and deeper than the big self-unloader, the *Sykes* was measured at a record 12,729 gross tons, compared to only 10,028 gross tons for the *Bradley*. The most powerful and fastest ship on the lakes, she quickly proved to be a superb carrier. Early in the 1950 season, Captain Fisher's ship established a new cargo record for iron ore, then broke that record on two other occasions that same season. The *Sykes* set other cargo records during the 1951 and 1952 seasons, including a personal best of 21,223 tons of iron ore loaded at the Great Northern Railway's dock near Superior, Wisconsin, on August 27, 1952.[8]

The *Sykes*'s greatest contribution to the Great Lakes shipping industry was not the size of her engines, her speed, her size, or even her carrying capacity, however. In 1952, her title as the longest ship on the lakes passed to Hanna's *Str. Joseph H. Thompson*, a converted saltwater cargo vessel, which was also more powerful and faster than the *Sykes.* The following year, the cargo record set by the *Sykes* was broken by another new freighter. Since then, the dimensions and carrying capacity of the *Sykes* have been exceeded many times. Today, it is actually one of the smaller ships in the U.S. fleet. Yet the Inland freighter is still highly revered within the shipping community. The most enduring attribute of the *Sykes* proved to be her design. She is today esteemed as having been the prototype for virtually all of the ships launched on the lakes from 1950 until 1971.

The traditional Great Lakes bulk freighter pioneered by Captain Eli Peck with the launching of the little *R. J. Hackett* in 1869 reached perfection in the design of the *Wilfred Sykes.* While the new Inland freighter was clearly a descendant of the *Hackett* and the many generations of lakes ships built with their pilothouses at the bow and engine rooms at the stern, the lines of the *Sykes* were highly refined. To say that the *Sykes* was "streamlined" may be a bit of an overstatement, but it was certainly more streamlined than any conventional bulk freighter preceding it on the lakes. The most obvious example of streamlining in the design of the *Sykes* was the way in which her aft cabins were incorporated into the lines of her stern.

The stately *Wilfred Sykes* being turned by steam-powered tugs in the outer harbor at Lorain, Ohio, on November 26, 1949, as it sets out for sea trials on Lake Erie. The massive Inland freighter was then under the command of Henry Kaizer, the senior captain in the fleet, who had personally supervised construction of the record-breaking ship. Kaizer died prior to the start of the 1950 shipping season, however, and when the streamlined *Sykes* departed on its maiden voyage up the lakes it was under the command of George Fisher. (Institute for Great Lakes Research, Bowling Green State University)

Until the *Sykes*, virtually each freighter on the lakes had a deckhouse that sat on top of the main deck at the stern, above the engine room. Within the stern deckhouse was the galley, dining rooms for the officers and unlicensed crewmembers, and cabins for galley and engine room personnel. On those vessels, the stern deckhouse did not extend all the way out to the bulwark,[9] so the structure was surrounded by a walkway. All of the rooms in the deckhouse had doors opening onto the main deck, and crewmembers had to go out on deck when going to or coming from rooms located at the stern. That could be uncomfortable during periods of inclement weather and dangerous when seas were breaking over the deck.

On the *Sykes*, the stern deckhouse extended all the way out to the sides of the ship, and the hull plating was carried up to the top of the cabins to form the enclosed stern cabin. Rooms within the enclosed cabin area opened onto passageways within the deckhouse, so crewmembers did not have to go outsidc during bad weather. Since the forward deckhouse also had interior passageways and the bow and stern sections were connected by tunnels running below the main deck, it was possible for crewmembers on the *Sykes* to go anywhere on the ship without having to go outside. At the same time, because the hull plating was carried up one deck higher than normal at the stern, the ship was less likely to be damaged by heavy seas, particularly following seas. A second, slightly smaller cabin was located atop the stern on the poop deck level. It housed mainly the galley, crews' messroom, officers' dining room, owners' dining room, and a stateroom for the steward. The poop deck cabin was surrounded by open deck where the ship's two lifeboats were located. All of the traditional-style freighters built after the *Sykes* imitated the unique design of her enclosed stern.

The enclosed stern and poop deck house helped to balance the structures at the bow. By comparison, the enclosed forecastles and cabin structures on the forward end of most ships built before the *Sykes* made their bows look much more substantial than their sterns. The naval architects at AmShip who had designed the *Sykes* also used the smokestack to help give further balance to the bow and stern sections of the ship. The smokestack installed on the *Sykes* was a massive, sleek-looking structure. It was encircled by a distinctive, wide band of stainless steel that bore the Inland logo, and the ship's whistles were neatly recessed into the stack.

The streamlined stack of the *Wilfred Sykes* bears the red Inland Steel logo on a band of polished stainless steel. The large stack casing used on the *Sykes* was intended as a visual balance to the mass of the pilothouse located at the bow. (Author's collection)

At the bow, the stem was raked forward more than usual, while the forward end of the pilothouse and its overhanging roof were sloped gracefully backward. The masts at the bow and stern were similarly sloped backward, and both were freestanding, while the masts on most ships were supported by stays. The ladder that led to the top of the after mast was recessed into the mast itself, giving it an unusually clean look. AmShip designers had gone to extraordinary lengths to eliminate the clutter normally seen on lake freighters. To the maximum feasible degree, the array of stays, pipes, tanks, ventilators, and ladders that normally muddle the decks were incorporated into the major structural elements of the ship, contributing to the streamlined appearance of the *Sykes*.

Her sleek lines were further accentuated by a new painting scheme developed by Inland and first used on the *Sykes*. A narrow, white, sheer-stripe band ran the entire length of the hull at the main deck level, topping off the rust-red hull. The bulwarks at the bow and stern that rose above the main deck were painted grey, topped by a second band of white at the bow. The cabins were painted a brilliant white. AmShip officials had at first balked at the mandated painting scheme, which was much more elaborate than that used on other ships. They argued that crewmembers would probably not be able to maintain the bands of grey and white and recommended instead that the entire hull be painted red right up to the top of the bulwarks.[10] To the surprise of the people at AmShip, and to the delight of officials at Inland, the crews aboard the *Sykes* and their other vessels in the Inland fleet seemed to readily adopt the new "white stripe" painting scheme. It is still used aboard Inland's ships today and remains the most distinctive painting scheme on the lakes.

While Captain George Fisher has long since left the lakes, the *Sykes* is still in operation. It is accorded special deference by both sailors and boatwatchers, although many rue the fact that Inland had the *Sykes* converted to a self-unloader during the winter of 1974-75. The addition of the self-unloading equipment destroyed the effect of the unusually high degree of streamlining achieved by her designers.[11] The long sweep of the *Sykes*'s deck was broken by the installation of a self-unloading boom and the massive, boxy casing of the vertical elevator that carries cargo out of the hold and up to the level of the boom. Unlike configurations on the *Bradley* and most other self-unloaders on the lakes at that time, the vertical elevator and boom on the *Sykes* are located at the after end of her cargo hold, instead of directly behind the forward deckhouse. To accommodate the unloading machinery under the cargo hold and still maintain the maximum carrying capacity, the *Sykes*'s last two hatches were also raised high above the level of the deck, forming what is referred to as a "trunk," located just ahead of the stern deckhouse. The elevator casing and unloading boom are located on top of the trunk, with the boom extending forward, well above the level of the main deck.

Between 1973 and 1975, Kinsman Marine, American Steamship, Litton Great Lakes, and Columbia Transportation had built a number of new ships with stern mounted, self-unloading systems. All of the U.S. ships converted to self-unloaders prior to the *Sykes*, however, had their unloading systems in the traditional location just behind the forward deckhouse. All of the ships converted to self-unloaders since 1975 have had their unloading equipment at the stern.

The self-unloading system installed on the *Sykes* also included several other innovations. Instead of the traditional bucket or conveyor elevator systems, the *Sykes* was equipped with a highly efficient loop belt elevator. Developed by Stephens-Adamson of Belleville, Ontario, a subsidiary of Allis-Chalmers Canada, the first loop belt system had been installed in 1971 on CSL's *J. W. McGiffin*. Before the conversion of the *Sykes*, the *Henry Ford II* was the only U.S. ship with this system. In the loop belt system, cargo is sandwiched tightly between two conveyor belts rising vertically out of the hold of the ship. The loop belt elevator takes up less hold space than other elevator systems and operates at higher unloading rates. With the loop belt elevator system, the *Sykes* could unload at six thousand tons per hour, far in excess of even the most efficient shore-based unloading equipment.

The unloading boom installed on the *Sykes* was of tubular steel construction, rather than angle iron. Tubular steel booms had made their debut on the lakes in 1965, used first in the conversions of Columbia's *Joseph H. Frantz* and Gartland Steamship's *Nicolet*. The tubular booms were substantially lighter than those built of angle iron. Like booms on the *Frantz* and *Nicolet*, the thirty-ton boom on the *Sykes* was elevated and moved laterally by hydraulic cylinders that replaced the more traditional A-frames and complex systems of cables and winches. Tubular booms and hydraulic positioning systems were used on all subsequent self-unloaders.[12]

Somewhat facetiously, the decade of the 1950s has been identified with "the coming of the whales" on the Great Lakes.[13] Not only was the *Sykes* the first of those whales, but the many elements of her unique design had a great impact on the ships launched after her. Few of the fleets launching new ships were willing to go to the added expense that Inland had done to make their new vessels aethetically pleasing, but all of them borrowed at least some design elements from the innovative *Sykes*. She was indeed a ship for the future.

Notes

1. Pittsburgh Steamship finally decided to go ahead with the construction of four new ships in 1949, about the time that the *Sykes* was ready for launching. Pittsburgh's AAA-class steamers, the *John G. Munson*, *Arthur M. Anderson*, *Cason J. Calloway*, and *Philip R. Clarke*, came out in 1952.
2. Walter C. Cowles, "A Decade of Great Ships: 1948–1958," *Inland Seas* 45, no. 3 (Fall 1989): 197.
3. E. B. Williams, Kent C. Thornton, W. R. Douglas, and Paul Miedlick, "Design and Construction of Great Lakes Bulk

While use of the term "streamlined" to describe the *Wilfred Sykes* may be stretching things a little, the Inland freighter was much sleeker in appearance than any previous laker. Designers of the unique ship managed to eliminate much of the clutter normally seen on the decks of freighters. While the basic design of the *Sykes* became a model for most conventional ore boats built after her, few shipping companies were willing to bear the extra expense that Inland accepted in order to build a ship that was both functional and aesthetically attractive. (Author's collection)

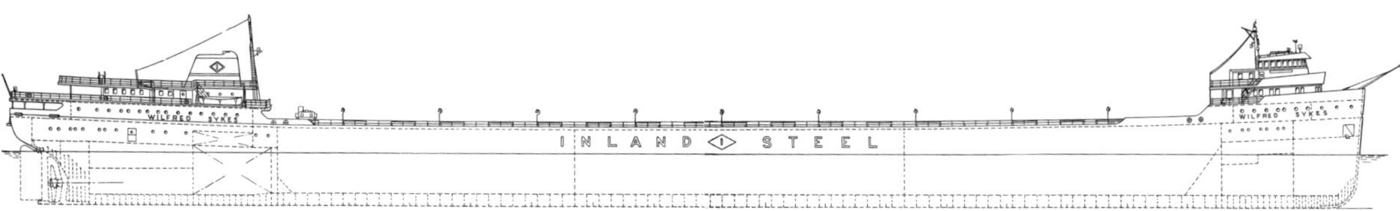

Freighter *Wilfred Sykes*," reprint of an article that originally appeared in *Marine Engineering and Shipping Review* (June 1950), 5.

4. Cowles, 197.
5. The *Leopold* was renamed the *E. J. Block* in 1943. After the 1945 season, the *Block* was almost totally rebuilt. When the ship came out of the yard on September 18, 1946, it had a new diesel-electric engine, new fore and aft deckhouses, and all new auxiliary equipment and deck machinery.
6. John O. Greenwood, *Namesakes of the Lakes* (Cleveland: Freshwater Press, 1970), 200.
7. Cowles, 197.
8. Greenwood, 200.
9. The bulwark is a section of hull plating that extends above the main deck level, forming a sort of solid railing around the stern.
10. Cowles, 197.
11. Inland Steel still operates one straight-decker, the *Str. Edward L. Ryerson*. Launched in 1960, the *Ryerson* is even more aesthetically pleasing than the *Sykes* was when she was launched, and Inland officials have so far rejected proposals to convert her to a self-unloader.
12. *Telescope* 14, no. 8 (September 1965): 210.
13. Richard Wright, *Freshwater Whales* (Kent, OH: Kent State University Press, 1969), 254.

24

A Saltwater Successor

From the launching of the *Onoko* in 1882 through the debut of the *Wilfred Sykes* in 1949, all of the ships that held the Queen of the Lakes title were new vessels built at shipyards around the lakes. In 1952, for the very first time, a ship claimed honors as the longest vessel as the result of being lengthened. It was also an adopted member of the bulk industry on the lakes, having been built at a shipyard on the East Coast.

STR. JOSEPH H. THOMPSON

714'3"x71'6"x38'6"
Queen of the Lakes
1952 to 1957

The *Marine Robin* had been launched at Sun Shipbuilding and Dry Dock in Chester, Pennsylvania, early in 1944. Built for the U.S. Maritime Commission for use in World War II, the C4-class cargo carrier had participated in the D-Day invasion of Normandy on June 6, 1944. Following the war, the 515-foot *Marine Robin* was laid up as part of the James River Reserve Fleet in Virginia.

In June of 1950, communist troops from North Korea crossed the thirty-eighth parallel and invaded South Korea. Within days, President Harry Truman committed U.S. ground, air, and naval forces under the command of General Douglas MacArthur to support our South Korean allies against the communist insurgence. By October, military forces of the United Nations Command had pushed the North Koreans back across the Yalu River at the thirty-eighth parallel, and MacArthur predicted that the troops under his command would conquer North Korea and unite the country by Thanksgiving. U.S. hopes for a speedy victory in Korea were dashed on November 26, when an estimated 550,000 Chinese soldiers came to the aid of their North Korean allies and drove MacArthur's troops back across the Yalu. It was then obvious to all observers that the United Nations forces were embroiled in what would be a protracted conflict.

On the home front, the Office of Defense Mobilization called for increases in U.S. steel production. On the lakes, shipments of iron ore needed to support higher steel production rose from 69.5 million tons in 1949 to more than 78 million tons in 1950, with similar increases in stone and coal movements. By 1953, iron ore shipments would reach almost 96 million tons, reflecting an increase of thirty-seven percent over 1949 levels.[1]

U.S. fleets on the lakes struggled to find enough ships to meet the increasing demands placed on them by the war effort. By the time the Chinese troops entered the war late in 1950, all of the U.S. shipbuilding capacity on the lakes had been reserved, and new freighters were under construction at all of the yards. Fleet executives soon realized that the Great Lakes shipyards would not be able to react fast enough to meet the escalating demands for shipments of ore, coal, and stone. They needed more ships immediately.

Shortly after the Chinese entered the war, officials of Cleveland-Cliffs conceived the idea of contracting with the Maritime Commission for the purchase of the *Notre Dame Victory.* The ship was one of the famous Victory-class cargo ships built by the government during World War II. Like the *Marine Robin*, the *Notre Dame Victory* had been laid up after the war as part of the reserve fleet moored in the James River. Cliffs had the *Victory* towed to Bethlehem Shipbuilding in Baltimore, Maryland, for lengthening and conversion for use on the lakes. The ship was rebuilt in less than ninety days, and on March 21, 1951, the vessel was rechristened as *Cliffs Victory.* Too large to fit through the locks on the St. Lawrence River, the 620-foot freighter was towed on a circuitous, three-thousand-mile voyage to the lakes via the Mississippi River, entering Lake Michigan through the ship and sanitary canal at Chicago. On June 4, 1951, *Cliffs Victory* went into service on the lakes.

Even before the *Victory* had reached the lakes, three other fleets had followed Cliffs's lead and purchased mothballed cargo ships from the Maritime Commission. Nicholson-Universal Steamship Company, seventy percent owned by Republic Steel, bought the *Louis McHenry Howe*, *Scott E. Land*, and *Mount Mansfield.* After lengthening and conversion at Maryland Drydock Company, they entered service on the lakes as the *Tom M.Girdler*, *Troy H. Browning*, and *Charles M. White*, respectively. Amersand Steamship Company, partly owned by American Steamship, bought the *Marine Angel* and rechristened her as the *McKee Sons.* Hansand Steamship Company, partly owned by M. A. Hanna Company, purchased the *Marine Robin*, which they renamed the *Joseph H. Thompson.* All five ships had originally been built as C4-S-A4-class ships; these were slightly longer and wider than vessels of the Victory-class. While the steam turbines that drove *Cliffs Victory* were rated at 8,500 horsepower, the C4s boasted 9,900 horsepower steam turbines. All six of the former saltwater ships were more powerful than any ships then in operation on the lakes. Prior to the arrival of the former saltwater vessels, the *Sykes*, with only 7,000 horsepower, was the most powerful ship on the lakes.

The three ships converted by the Nicholson fleet were all intended to operate on the Cuyahoga River, serving Republic's mills on the winding waterway that bisects Cleveland. They were lengthened to 600 feet, what was then considered to be the maximum size limit for ships negotiating the Cuyahoga. *Cliffs Victory* came out of the Bethlehem shipyard at Baltimore

The *Joseph H. Thompson* was launched in 1944 as the *Marine Robin*, a C-4 cargo carrier built for the U.S. Maritime Commission. Before it was ready to go into service on the lakes in 1952, the ship underwent a dramatic transformation. The top silhouette is of a C-4, outfitted with armament for use during World War II. On the bottom is a silhouette of the *Thompson* after her conversion to a lake freighter. (Author's collection)

slightly longer, at 620 feet. The *McKee Sons*, the only one of the saltwater ships to be converted to a self-unloader while being rebuilt for service on the lakes, was lengthened to 633 feet. The longest of the converted ships was the *Thompson.* She was intended to operate primarily in the ore trade between Lake Superior and National Steel's mills on the Detroit River. Her owners were more concerned about maximizing her carrying capacity than they were about ending up with a ship that would be too long to negotiate some of the narrow river channels around the lakes. The *Thompson* was stretched 199 feet, 3 inches to a new overall length of 714 feet, 3 inches. The Hansand freighter was then too long to fit through the locks on the Mississippi and the canal at Chicago, so it had to be towed into the lakes in two halves. When the two sections were rejoined at American Ship Building's yard in South Chicago, the *Thompson* became the longest freight vessel in the world and the new Queen of the Lakes.

Even before final touches had been put on the *Thompson* at South Chicago, Great Lakes shipyards had begun to turn out the first of the new freighters ordered at the outset of the Korean War. The first of the new ships was the *Philip R. Clarke*, built at AmShip's Lorain yard for the Pittsburgh Steamship fleet of U.S. Steel. Launched on November 26, 1951, the *Clarke* was the first of what was to become known as the Pittsburgh-class or AAA-class.[2]

The *Clarke* and the seven ships that followed her down the ways over the next eighteen months were basically built from plans developed by AmShip for the Pittsburgh fleet in 1947. When officials of the Pittsburgh fleet decided to delay building any boats from those plans, AmShip used them as the starting point for the design of the *Sykes.* With the coming of the Korean War, Pittsburgh officials had finally placed an order for three ships to be built from the plans. AmShip designers tried to talk officials of the Pittsburgh fleet into incorporating some of the features of the *Sykes* into their new ships, but "the Pittsburgh technical staff was rather more conservative than Inland and many of the more innovative design features of the *Sykes* were modified."[3] In other words, officials of the Pittsburgh fleet were cheaper than their colleagues at Inland. Two of the new Pittsburgh freighters were to be built by AmShip, with the third constructed at Great Lakes Engineering Works. AmShip was designated as the lead yard for the project, and they supplied plans to Great Lakes Engineering.

The *Clarke* and the other AAA-boats were 647 feet long, 31 feet shorter than the *Sykes* and 67 feet less than the *Thompson.* That had been judged to be the maximum length vessel that could be turned in the basin at Conneaut, Ohio, a major railhead for shipments of both iron ore and coal. Beams for the new ships were set at 70 feet, believed to be the widest width of vessel that could be loaded at the chute-type ore docks on the upper lakes.

The original 1947 plans for the Pittsburgh boats called for them to be powered by 4,500-horsepower steam turbine engines. Before construction began, a decision was made to install turbines rated at 7,000 horsepower, the same size used on the *Sykes.* Like the *Sykes,* the *Clarke* and the other AAA-class freighters proved to be slightly overpowered and all have experienced vibration problems throughout their careers. Model basin tests conducted later showed that the full hull form of the ships was not well suited to the new high power engines. The water just ahead of the propeller circulated and eddied, causing flow separation. As a result, the propeller operated in disturbed water and transmitted varying lateral and vertical forces to the propeller shaft. The annoying vibrations that result could be felt throughout the stern areas of the ships.

The stern cabin arrangement of the new Pittsburgh ships was substantially the same as that on the *Sykes.* In this scheme, main deck cabins were enclosed within the heightened bulwarks of the stern, topped by a poop deck cabin. On the Pittsburgh boats, however, the galley and dining rooms were located in the main deck cabin, while the poop deck house contained staterooms for engineering officers. In most other respects, the *Clarke* and the other AAA-class boats mimicked the *Sykes,* except that many of the aesthetic details were missing. They looked like the "poor cousins" of the beautiful Inland ship.[4]

At about the same time that Pittsburgh Steamship placed

The *Joseph H. Thompson* in Hanna colors on the St. Marys River. The 714-foot freighter was the first Queen of the Lakes built at a non-Great Lakes shipyard. The *Thompson* was constructed at Sun Shipbuilding in Chester, Pennsylvania, in 1944 for the U.S. Maritime Commission. Originally christened the *Marine Robin,* the ship participated in the D-Day invasion at Normandy. It was converted for use on the lakes during the Korean War. (State Archives of Michigan)

its order for the three AAA-class boats, it also ordered a fourth new ship for its fleet. Built at Manitowac Shipbuilding in Manitowac, Wisconsin, and launched two days after the *Clarke*, the *John G. Munson* was a big self-unloader that would become a sister ship to the *Carl D. Bradley* in U.S. Steel's Bradley Transportation Division at Rogers City, Michigan.[5] When it was launched, the *Munson* was the largest self-unloader on the lakes. In terms of overall dimensions, it was also the biggest ship on the lakes. The giant, grey-hulled self-unloader was just over 666 feet long, 72 feet wide, and 36 feet deep. She measured at 13,143 gross tons, compared to 11,623 gross tons for the *Clarke* and 12,729 for the *Sykes*. Although her gross tonnage set a new record for the lakes, the *Munson*'s net tonnage was slightly less than that of the *Clarke* and other ships in the AAA-class. While the *Clarke* had a boxy cargo hold typical of straight-deckers, the *Munson*'s hold was slightly smaller because she was built as a self-unloader. Her hold was hopper-shaped so that cargo would slide down the sides of the hold to the conveyor belt system located below it. The *Clarke* was measured at 8,690 net tons, while the longer, wider, and deeper *Munson* was rated at just 8,116 net tons.

All four of the new Pittsburgh boats were built to be prodigious haulers. Each of them had net tonnages larger than that of the *Sykes*, which measured at 7,875 tons. The *Munson*, for example, dominated the stone trade on the lakes for more than a decade. On July 4, 1953, she established a record by loading 21,011 gross tons of limestone at her home port of Calcite. That record stood for thirteen years.[6]

Shortly after the Pittsburgh fleet placed its order for the *Clarke* and its two sister ships, Cleveland-Cliffs placed an order with American Ship Building for a new flagship for their fleet. Launched on January 10, 1952, at AmShip's Toledo yard and christened the *Edward B. Greene* in honor of the president of Cleveland-Cliffs, the new freighter had been built from the same basic plans as the *Clarke*. From her main deck down, the *Greene* was virtually a twin of the *Clarke*, but her cabin arrangement was slightly different. Designed to be the fleet's "Board of Directors' ship," the *Greene* had an extra deck of cabins at her bow. The additional deck accommodated four single staterooms and two large double staterooms for use by Cliffs's executives and their guests. The deck above the staterooms included a large observation lounge for use by passengers, as well as an office and stateroom for the captain. As on the *Sykes*, the *Greene*'s galley, dining rooms, and quarters for the steward, or chief cook, were located in the poop deck cabin at the stern. The main deck cabin at the stern provided rooms for the other engineering and galley personnel.[7]

The two sisters to the *Clarke* were launched shortly after the *Greene*. The *Arthur M. Anderson* went into the water on February 16, 1952, at AmShip's Lorain yard. The *Cason J. Calloway* was launched on March 22, 1952, at the River Rouge, Michigan, shipyard of Great Lakes Engineering.

Following the lead of the Pittsburgh fleet and Cleveland-Cliffs, Columbia Transportation, Ford Motor Company, and Interlake Steamship also placed orders for AAA-class vessels to help meet their wartime cargo commitments. Interlake's *J. L. Mauthe* was launched at River Rouge on June 21, 1952. Five months later, on November 15, 1952, Columbia's *Reserve* took to the water at River Rouge, followed in early 1953 by the launching of their *Armco* at American Ship Building's Lorain yard. The last of the eight AAA-class vessels was launched for the Ford fleet in August of 1953 at River Rouge and christened the *William Clay Ford*.

The AAA-class freighters weren't the only boats built at Great Lakes yards during the Korean War, however. On November 19, 1952, workers at AmShip's Lorain yard who were putting the finishing touches on the hull of the *Armco* took time out from their activities to watch the launching of a ship that was even larger than the AAA-boats. Built for the National Steel fleet, the *Ernest T. Weir* was 690 feet in overall length. Like the *Thompson*, the *Weir* would be managed by Hanna. While the *Weir* was not as long as the *Thompson*, it did displace the *Munson* as the longest ship actually built on the lakes.

Another large freighter joined the Hanna fleet on October 5, 1954, with the launching at Lorain of National Steel's *George M. Humphrey*. The *Humphrey* was the longest and widest ship ever constructed at a Great Lakes yard. It was 710 feet long, with a beam of 75 feet, 9 inches. With a gross tonnage of 14,034 and net tonnage measured at 10,528, the massive *Humphrey* had the greatest carrying capacity of any ship on the lakes. On October 21, 1954, she set a new Great Lakes cargo record by loading 22,605 gross tons of iron ore at the docks in Superior, Wisconsin. That record would stand until 1960.

While her Queen of the Lakes title passed to a slightly longer ship in 1957, the *Joseph H. Thompson* continued to operate in Hanna colors until the bottom fell out of the industry in the early 1980s. After being laid up at a slip on the Detroit River for several years, the former salty entered another phase of its colorful career in 1984, when it was sold to Upper Lakes

When the AAA-class *William Clay Ford* was launched in 1953, the Ford name on its stack was in block lettering. It was later placed by the more familiar oval logo of the Detroit-based automaker. (Author's collection)

Towing Company of Escanaba, Michigan. Upper Lakes Towing operated the tug *Olive Moore* and the 524-foot barge *Buckeye* in various bulk trades on the lakes, and they announced their plans to convert the *Thompson* to a barge.

The converted *Thompson* reentered service in the 1991 season as a self-unloading barge, pushed by the tug *Joseph H. Thompson, Jr.* She had once again undergone a dramatic metamorphosis. Her fore and aft cabins had been removed, and a notch was cut into the stern to accommodate the bow of the pusher tug. The self-unloading rig installed near her stern is typical of those found on many other ships, but it has a bucket elevator rather than the more common loop belt or inclined belt normally used on U.S. vessels. The bucket elevator, while slower than belt elevators, can handle a greater variety of cargo. Many Canadian self-unloaders also use bucket elevators because of their flexibility. They have even been used to offload grain, a cargo that cannot easily be handled by belt-type elevator systems.

Upper Lakes bought the *Thompson* at bargain-basement prices. While they have made a substantial capital outlay to convert her to a self-unloading barge, they still have far less invested in the vessel than other operators have in their self-unloading ships. At the same time, as a barge the *Thompson* can operate with far less crewmembers than are required on self-propelled vessels. With tonnages rising on the lakes and the downsized U.S. fleet struggling to meet demand, combined with the barge's lower overhead and operating costs, the *Thompson* should represent a profitable venture for her owners. While she operates today at the periphery of the industry, the former Queen of the Lakes has had her life significantly extended through conversion to a barge. The *Weir* left the Hanna fleet even before the *Thompson*. In 1978, she was sold to Oglebay Norton's Columbia Transportation Division. Renamed the *Courtney Burton*, she was converted to a self-unloader in 1981 and continues to operate on the lakes today.

But not all of the Hanna boats were as fortunate as the *Thompson* and *Weir*. In the mid-1980s, Hanna and National Steel made the decision to abandon their shipping operations after more than 125 years. With tonnages shipped on the lakes dropping to their lowest levels since the Great Depression of the 1930s and scores of freighters lying idle at docks around the lakes, the ships of the Hanna fleet were put up for sale. All of the fleets had excess vessels at that time, however, and there were no buyers. One by one, the Hanna ships were towed off to the shipbreakers.[8] Even the thirty-two-year-old *Humphrey*, in the prime of her life by Great Lakes standards, was tabbed for the cutting torches. On August 13, 1986, the *Humphrey* departed her dock on the Detroit River under her own power and crewed by Hanna office personnel and former Hanna sailors for a nostaligic last trip out the St. Lawrence Seaway. At Quebec City, the Hanna personnel bid farewell to the big freighter, and it was taken under tow by a Dutch tug, bound for scrapping in Taiwan.

Most of the AAA-class boats fared better than the ships in the Hanna fleet. After the 1,100-foot long and 110-foot wide Poe Lock was opened at Sault Ste. Marie in 1968, all of the AAA-boats except Interlake's *Mauthe* were lengthened by 120 feet to increase their carrying capacity. The lengthening operations involved installing a new 120-foot section of midbody, bringing their overall lengths to 767 feet. The *Munson* was also lengthened, but by only 102 feet, bringing her overall length to 768 feet. Between 1981 and 1983, all but two of the AAA-class vessels were also converted to self-unloaders.

Only Interlake's *J. L. Mauthe* and Ford's *William Clay Ford* remained as straight-deckers in an industry that was rapidly being dominated by self-unloaders. The *Mauthe* was involved in the grain trade between the American lakehead and terminals in Buffalo, New York. Had she been lengthened or converted to a self-unloader, her owners would have had to withdraw her from that trade. Ford, on the other hand, was operating two other straight-deckers in addition to the *William Clay Ford*. Those vessels were unloaded by bridge cranes at Ford's Rouge Steel complex in the Detroit suburbs. Like those of Pittsburgh Steamship, Inland Steel, and Bethlehem Steel, the Ford vessels were part of a "captive fleet." They were involved almost solely in carrying Ford cargoes of ore, stone, and coal to the Rouge plant. In that respect, they were not in competition with other fleets, and there was little impetus to convert them to self-unloaders.

By the fall of 1984, however, Ford executives decided to compete for cargoes from other shippers. At that time, straight-deckers like the *William Clay Ford* put the fleet at a serious disadvantage. The majority of cargo moving on the lakes was destined for ports where there was no shoreside unloading equipment. To overcome that obstacle, Ford negotiated with Cleveland-Cliffs for the purchase of the AAA-class *Edward B. Greene* and the *Walter A. Sterling*, an 826-foot former saltwater tanker that Cliffs had brought into the lakes in 1961. The *Greene* and *Sterling* were the last two ships being operated by Cliffs. Like Hanna, the 125-year-old company had decided to get out of the marine shipping business and concentrate its efforts on more profitable ventures.

With the purchase of the two self-unloaders from Cliffs, Ford decided to liquidate its fleet of straight-deckers, keeping only the self-unloader *Henry Ford II*. The 642-foot *Ernest R. Breech* was sold to George Steinbrenner's S&E Shipping, the Kinsman Marine fleet, for operation in the grain trade. Steinbrenner renamed the vessel the *Kinsman Independent* and placed it in the grain trade. The other Ford ships, the 644-foot *Benson Ford* and the *William Clay Ford*, were scrapped. The *Clay Ford*, the last of the AAA-class to be built, had the dubious distinction of being the first to go to the shipbreakers.

Notes

1. *1981 Annual Report* (Cleveland: Lake Carriers' Association, 1982), 21.
2. Many people puzzle over the AAA-class designation that was eventually attached to the new ships. The AAA identification was an internal U.S. Steel accounting code used to classify the various types of vessels in their fleet for use in computing the pay of shipboard personnel. In those days, pay for deck and engine officers varied based on the size of the ship and the type of propulsion system it had. The larger and more powerful the ship was, the more the officers were paid. Other accounting designations in use at the time included AA for the supers of the Fraser-class, AM for their Maritime-class boats, AT for turbine-powered vessels, AO for ships with hand-fired reciprocating engines, AS for boats with stoker-fired reciprocating engines, B for barges, and C for towboats.
3. Walter C. Cowles, "A Decade of Great Ships: 1948–1958," *Inland Seas* 45, no. 3 (Fall 1989): 199.
4. Ibid., 195–201.
5. While the *Munson* was technically not from the same class as the *Clarke* and the other AAA-boats, she was close to their size and classified as AAA by U.S. Steel's accounting office.
6. John O. Greenwood, *Namesakes of the Lakes* (Cleveland: Freshwater Press, 1970), 372.
7. Cowles, 199–201.
8. Unable to find a buyer for the *George A. Stinson*, a modern thousand-footer launched in 1978, Hanna and National decided to continue operating that one vessel.

25

Victory

In 1957, the *Joseph H. Thompson* became the longest ship on the lakes as a result of being lengthened while undergoing conversion from a saltwater vessel to a Great Lakes bulk freighter. She was the first ship to become Queen of the Lakes as the result of being lengthened. The vessel that succeeded the *Thompson* as Queen of the Lakes took an even more circuitous route to the title.

Cliffs Victory was launched at Oregon Shipbuilding Corporation in Portland, Oregon, in 1945 as the *Notre Dame Victory*, one of scores of the famous Victory-class cargo ships launched during World War II. Built late in the war, the 455-foot Maritime Commission vessel saw little service before the war ended, and very early in her career she was retired to the James River reserve fleet. There the *Notre Dame Victory* rapidly faded into obscurity, becoming just another nondescript hull in an idle fleet made up of scores of similarly nondescript hulls. The fresh coat of grey paint applied to her hull before her launching initially distinguished her from most of the other mothballed cargo ships—many of which bore the clear scars of battle. It was soon dulled, however, by the unrelenting exposure to sun and rain. For five long and uneventful years, the *Notre Dame Victory* languished amidst the idle flotilla, her career seemingly ended virtually before it had begun.

Then, in 1950, the guns of war were once again unleashed, and the U.S. became embroiled in the escalating conflict on the Korean peninsula. Many vessels from the reserve fleet were recommissioned and placed back in service by the Maritime Commission to ferry troops and supplies to the war zone. Yet, the *Victory*, small by the standards of the shipping industry in 1950, was not one of the vessels earmarked for a return to government service. She might well have ended her days in the reserve fleet had the war not resulted in an acute shortage of cargo ships on the Great Lakes.

The stepping up of steel production to support the war in Korea accounts for only part of the increases in shipping that occurred on the lakes during the early 1950s, however. It was also a period of immense prosperity in the states. Spurred on in part by the war effort, the U.S. economy burgeoned in a frenzy of unparalleled consumerism that also increased demand for raw materials shipped on the lakes.

Between 1950 and the end of the Korean War in 1953, total shipments of bulk cargoes on the Great Lakes increased by more than twenty million tons. With the largest and most modern lake freighters capable of carrying about one million tons of cargo in a season, it immediately became obvious to shipping officials that they needed to expand their fleets in order to keep up with the rapidly growing demand. U.S. Steel, Columbia Transportation, Interlake Steamship, Ford Motor Company, and Cleveland-Cliffs rapidly placed orders for AAA-class boats. Almost overnight, order books at all the major Great Lakes shipyards were filled.

Cleveland-Cliffs had signed a contract with American Ship Building for construction of an AAA-class freighter that would become the fleet's new flagship. It would not be ready for service until 1952, however, and Cliffs's officials saw a more immediate need to add tonnage to their fleet. In what can only be viewed as a classic example of successful problem-solving, fleet executives in Cleveland carefully studied their options and determined that it would be possible to convert an idle saltwater ship for use on the lakes. As the highly successful 1950 shipping season approached its end, officials from Cliffs negotiated with Admiral Cochrane, head of the Maritime Commission, to purchase a vessel from the reserve fleet and convert it for use on the lakes.

When word of the negotiations leaked out, many in the Great Lakes industry merely shook their heads and branded the venture a boondoggle that would bring nothing but grief to Cliffs. It seemed patently obvious to the coterie of naysayers that saltwater cargo ships were totally unsuited to operation on the lakes: few had carrying capacities comparable to freighters on the lakes, their engines and pilothouses were in the wrong place—amidships—they didn't have sufficient ballasting capability to get under the rigs at the loading docks or to weather a November storm on the lakes, their flared bows would get tangled up with the loading rigs when they attempted to make a dock, their hatches were all wrong, and so on. The list of reasons why a saltwater ship was unsuited for service on the lakes was long and impressive.[1]

STR. CLIFFS VICTORY

716'3"x62'x38'
Queen of the Lakes
1957 to June 7, 1958

Undaunted, Cliffs proceeded with their novel plan and contracted with the Maritime Commission for purchase of the *Notre Dame Victory.* The ink was barely dry on the contracts before Cliffs had arranged to have the long-idle ship towed from its berth in the James River to Bethlehem Ship Building's Key Highway Yard at Baltimore, Maryland. By the time Great Lakes sailors sat down to their Christmas dinners in 1950, shipwrights at the Bethlehem yard were already at work on the

***Cliffs Victory* was the first large ocean freighter converted for service in the bulk trade on the Great Lakes. It was launched in 1945 as one of the famous Victory-class ships of World War II, shown in the top silhouette. When the Korean War broke out in 1950, Cleveland-Cliffs purchased the mothballed cargo ship and had it rebuilt to augment their cargo carrying capacity on the lakes. The bottom silhouette shows the *Victory* after her conversion. With one cargo hold located aft of her midship engine room, the *Victory* had a unique profile. (Author's collection)**

complicated task of converting the *Victory.* The project included removal of the ship's midship superstructure, the top deck of which was the pilothouse, and construction of two new sets of cabins. One, which would later be installed over the engine room, where the original superstructure had been, would house the galley and accommodations for engine and galley personnel. The second set of new cabins, three decks high, would be set atop the vessel's forecastle deck at the bow. It included accommodations for deck department personnel, including a suite for the captain, and was topped by the pilothouse.

The *Victory*'s hull was split apart forward of the midships engine room to allow the installation of a new section of cargo hold that would lengthen the ship by 165 feet, 6 inches and greatly increase her carrying capacity. Simultaneously, the cargo hold was rebuilt along the lines that had long since become standard on the lakes. A double bottom was constructed, and sidetanks were installed between the outer hull of the vessel and the walls of the cargo hold to provide sufficient ballasting capability.

On deck, workers removed the Victory ship's large saltwater hatches and replaced them with the narrower hatches used by lakers. The original wooden hatch covers were discarded and replaced by single-piece steel lids. The heavy steel hatch covers would be lifted on and off the hatch coamings by a hatch crane, or "iron deckhand." Because *Victory* had one cargo hold with five hatches located abaft of her midship engine room and cabins, two hatch cranes had to be installed, one to handle the hatches covering the four cargo holds between her forward cabins and her engine room and a second for use on the hatches located between the engine room and the stern.

To the astonishment of many in the industry, the massive conversion project was completed in less than ninety days. By comparison, it had taken more than a year to build Inland Steel's *Wilfred Sykes*. On March 21, 1951, in ceremonies at the yard in Baltimore, the refitted vessel was rechristened by proud officials from Cleveland-Cliffs as *Cliffs Victory*. The name made the ship's new ownership clear to all, while retaining a tie to the vessel's historic roots. At the same time, it made a bold statement about Cliffs's decision to abandon a hundred years of tradition and acquire a saltwater vessel for use on the lakes. The acquisition and conversion of the ship was indeed a victory for Cleveland-Cliffs.

The odyssey of *Cliffs Victory* was far from over that spring day in 1951, however. Ahead of her lay a three-thousand-mile journey down the Atlantic coast, around the peninsula of Florida, across the Gulf of Mexico, and up the Mississippi River to her new home on the Great Lakes. She made the entire voyage as a "dead ship," under tow of tugs, with only a skeleton crew aboard. Because the *Victory* would encounter a number of low bridges on the trip up the Mississippi and through the Illinois River and the Chicago Sanitary and Ship Canal to the lakes, her fore and aft masts, stack, and cabins were removed and stowed either on deck or deep inside the cargo hold. Even then, one bridge was cleared by only a matter of about five inches.

The *Victory* also had to pass through nine locks, and the last of the nine presented a particularly tricky obstacle for those overseeing the ship's passage to the lakes. The lock at Chicago that would lift the vessel to the level of Lake Michigan was only 600 feet long; after her lengthening *Victory* was 620 feet long. Under the watchful eye of the experienced lock operators, the big freighter was winched slowly into the lock. It was like trying to shoehorn a size ten foot into a size nine shoe. Sailors aboard the *Victory* paced nervously on deck, not at all convinced that their massive ship could be squeezed through the undersized lock. When *Victory* had been moved tight against the forward lock gate, her stern still sticking out of the rear gate, the lockmaster signalled for the forward gate to be opened. As the doors of the gate parted, a torrent of tens of thousands of gallons of water from Lake Michigan rushed into the lock, buffeting the *Victory* and threatening to tear her loose and carry her uncontrollably downstream. The powerful winches on her deck strained, and the steel cables that held her in the lock groaned under the awesome strain, but they held. With crewmen holding their breaths, *Victory* was carefully winched forward until the rear gate of the lock could be shut. As the huge gate swung closed, shutting off the deluge of water, *Victory* settled comfortably in the lock. The beaming lockmaster signalled the relieved and elated crewmembers aboard *Victory* that they could move their big ship out of the lock. The way was clear for them to proceed to Lake Michigan.[2]

Victory was towed to the Chicago yard of American Ship Building, where the freighter was made ready to go into service for Cleveland-Cliffs. On June 4, 1951, less than six months after work had begun on her conversion, she steamed out of the shipyard and headed up Lake Michigan, bound for Marquette to take on her first load of iron ore. Onlookers lined the banks of the St. Marys River at Sault Ste. Marie when she passed upbound through the Soo Locks for the first time, eager to get a look at the distinctive ship. Her colors were familiar. *Victory* had a stark black hull topped by cabins painted in a peculiar, some would say ugly, olive green. Over her engine room, the streamlined black stack bore the big orange "C" of the Cleveland-Cliffs fleet. At first glance, she looked like the scores of other freighters that had been turned out at Great Lakes shipyards for almost a hundred years. But closer scrutiny revealed the telltale flare to her bow that marked her as a saltwater ship, and as she drew abreast, onlookers could plainly see that her engine room and after cabins were not at the stern, where they would have been on a conventional laker, but almost amidships. And behind the after cabin trailed a long expanse of deck that looked like the tail of a crocodile. In profile, *Victory* was easy to distinguish from any other ship operating on the lakes.

On that maiden voyage, *Victory* also sailed into the record books of the Great Lakes shipping industry. Her entry in trade on the lakes marked the first time that a large saltwater vessel had been converted for use by a U.S. Great Lakes fleet. She would also lay claim to several other honors. In short order, *Victory* was recognized as the fastest freighter on the lakes. Her 8,500 horsepower steam turbine engine pushed her along at speeds of more than twenty miles an hour, well in excess of that recorded by the less-streamlined ships built on the lakes. In 1957, twelve years after she was launched in Oregon and six years after joining the Cleveland-Cliffs fleet, *Victory* also became the Queen of the Lakes.

During the winter of 1956–57, *Victory* went into the AmShip yard at Chicago to be lengthened a second time. A section of new cargo hold 96 feet, 3 inches long was inserted into her deck between her forward cabins and the midship engine room. When the gates of the drydock were swung open and *Victory* steamed out to begin the 1957 shipping season, the

Cliffs Victory **became Queen of the Lakes in 1957, after her second lengthening. She was first lengthened in early 1951 during conversion from a saltwater cargo ship to a lake freighter. The former Victory-class freighter was one of the fastest ships on the Great Lakes, with a distinctive profile that made her a favorite with boatwatchers around the lakes. Sold to a Liberian shipping company in 1985, the colorful career of the** ***Victory*** **ended in 1987 when she was scrapped in Taiwan. (State Archives of Michigan)**

716-foot, 3-inch former salty edged out Hanna's *Joseph H. Thompson* for honors as the longest ship on the lakes. Again, the name *Cliffs Victory* found its way into the record books of the Great Lakes shipping industry.

The marine division of the Cleveland-Cliffs Iron Company, which had pioneered the shipment of ore on the lakes in 1867, prospered during the 1960s and 1970s. In 1972, the fleet beat out several competitors and won the giant Republic Steel contract, the largest ever awarded on the lakes. In 1978, Cliffs signed a major contract with Detroit Edison to move Western low-sulphur coal from Superior, Wisconsin, to Edison's power generating plants at Monroe and St. Clair, Michigan. As part of the agreement, Cliffs and Detroit Edison signed a letter of intent to jointly build a steam-powered, 1,000-foot-long freighter[3] for use in the coal trade.

The first thousand-footer, Bethlehem's *Stewart J. Cort*, had gone into service on the lakes in 1971, marking the beginning of a new era in Great Lakes shipping. The *Cort* and the thousand-footers that followed her were capable of carrying three times as much cargo as ships like the *Victory*. That translated into increased profits for the shipping companies that operated them and reduced costs for shippers. With the letter of intent in hand, officials from Cliffs arranged with American Ship Building to schedule construction of the new ship at their Lorain, Ohio, yard, which had a drydock specially designed for the construction of thousand-footers.

The massive black smokestack installed on ***Cliffs Victory*** **in 1950 bore the big orange "C" that indicated she was part of the Cleveland-Cliffs fleet, one of the oldest on the lakes. (Author's collection)**

Cleveland-Cliffs's fortunes took a turn for the worse shortly after entering into the agreement with Detroit Edison. As fleet engineering personnel enthusiastically set to work on designs for their planned thousand-footer, Republic Steel notified Cliffs of their intent to renegotiate their iron ore delivery contract. Republic was moving ahead with plans to build an ore transshipment terminal at the mouth of the Black River in Lorain, Ohio, just a few hundred yards downstream from the AmShip yard where Cliffs's thousand-footer was scheduled to be built. The transshipment terminal would allow Republic to have ore brought down the lakes on efficient 1,000-foot-long self-unloaders and offloaded at Lorain. The ore would then be loaded onto smaller self-unloaders that would carry it to nearby Cleveland and up the Cuyahoga River to Republic's mills. Even though the ore would have to be handled twice, Republic would realize significant economies by bringing it down the lakes in thousand-footers and moving it up the Cuyahoga in self-unloaders that would allow them to abandon their aging shoreside unloading equipment. Cliffs was at a disadvantage in the fierce bidding war that followed, for they didn't yet have a thousand-footer, and the only two self-unloaders in their fleet—the *Edward B. Greene* and *Walter A. Sterling*—were too long to negotiate the tight turns in the winding Cuyahoa. As a result, Cliffs lost the lucrative Republic contract, effective with the start of shipping in 1980.

To further compound Cliffs's problems, the Great Lakes shipping industry slipped into a recession in 1980 that reached depression-like proportions by 1982. From 220 million total tons in 1979, shipments fell off to only 128 million tons in 1982. Iron ore shipments, the mainstay for U.S. shipping companies on the lakes, dropped from a respectable 92 million tons in 1979—the second highest tonnage of ore ever shipped—to a mere 38 million tons in 1982. Cliffs, already crippled by loss of the Republic contract, struggled to stay alive. By 1982, they could find only enough cargo to operate the *Greene* and *Sterling*.

The *Victory* and the other ships in the once-proud Cleveland Cliffs fleet were laid-up at docks around the lakes, as were vessels from all of the other shipping companies. Over a thousand sailors were idled by the downturn in shipping. At Cliffs, and in the other fleets, only those at the top of the seniority list were able to hold jobs. On the *Greene* and *Sterling*, all of the mates who stood watches had previously commanded their own ships, all of the assistant engineers had previously been chief engineers. Most of the deckhands were in their fifties and sixties, sailors who had long ago achieved enough seniority to leave the deck for less strenuous positions as watchmen and wheelsmen. But they were the lucky ones. Hundreds of their peers would never work aboard ship again. Others somehow persevered during the recession and eventually returned to work on the boats after being unable to find a job on the lakes for three or four years.

In the fall of 1984, top fleet officials from the Cleveland office boarded both the *Greene* and *Sterling* to inform shocked crewmembers that Cleveland-Cliffs had made the difficult decision to abandon its shipping operations. The last two operating vessels in the fleet, the *Greene* and *Sterling*, had been sold to the Ford Motor Company. While the *Greene* and *Sterling* were being readied to begin the 1985 shipping season in Ford colors, Cleveland-Cliffs began to dispose of the remaining ships in the fleet, most of which had not operated since the end of the 1979 season. Most were destined for scrapping, but the diehard *Victory* was to be given yet another new lease on life.

In 1985, the former Victory ship was sold to a Liberian shipping company that announced plans to operate her in the coastal trade in the Pacific. After more than three decades on the freshwaters of the Great Lakes, the *Victory* would be returning to the venue where she first slipped into the water. *Victory*'s new owners transferred her registry to Panama and renamed her *Savic*. There was no significance to her new name. It was, rather, conveniently arrived at by having a crewmember paint out the CLIFF from CLIFFS and the TORY in VICTORY, then insert an *A* between her former two names. Voilà, the *Savic* is born!

The *Savic* took on a load of scrap iron and departed the lakes, wintering at Montreal before make the long voyage out the St. Lawrence Seaway to the ocean. Still sporting the distinctive black hull and pea-green cabins that had been associated with the Cleveland-Cliffs fleet for so many years, the distinctive ship left the friendly waters of the lakes for good. Little is known about her voyages on the oceans, but word filtered back to the lakes in 1987 that she was being scrapped in Taiwan.[4] When her registry was finally surrendered, she claimed yet another record: the *Savic*, née *Cliffs Victory*, née *Notre Dame Victory*, was the last of the famous World War II Victory ships to operate anywhere in the world.

While *Victory* may be best remembered for her peculiar appearance, she unalterably affected the history of shipping on the Great Lakes by forging a path for a long line of saltwater vessels that found their way onto the lakes. In the months and years after *Victory* first took her place in the U.S. fleet on the lakes, no less than thirteen converted saltwater ships and three new ships built at an East Coast shipyard followed in her wake.

Following the *Victory* to the lakes during the Korean War years were the converted C4 cargo ships, including Hanna's *Joseph H. Thompson*, Republic's *Tom M. Girdler*, *Troy H. Browning*, and *Charles M. White*, and Amersand's *McKee Sons*. During the same period, Huron Cement converted a C1 cargo ship and put it into the Great Lakes cement trade as the *Paul H. Townsend*. In addition to the converted ships, three new vessels were built for service on the lakes at Bethlehem Steel's shipyard at Sparrows Point, Maryland. They included Bethlehem's *Johnstown* and *Sparrows Point* and Interlake's *Elton Hoyt, 2d*. In 1956, the ships of the Korean War-era were joined by the *Aquarama*, a C4 that was converted into a passenger ship for operation between Detroit and Cleveland. It was owned by the McKee family, principals in Sand Products, who were also partners in ownership of the *McKee Sons*.

When tonnages shipped on the lakes began to increase in the early 1960s, six other former saltwater vessels were converted and brought in by way of the St. Lawrence Seaway, which had opened in 1959. All were former tankers operated by the Maritime Commission. They included Cleveland-Cliffs's

Walter A. Sterling, Columbia Transportation's *Middletown*, National Steel's *Paul H. Carnahan* and *Leon Falk, Jr.*, American Steamship's *H. Lee White*, and Huron Cement's *J. A. W. Iglehart*. American's *H. Lee White* was the last of the parade, entering service on the lakes in 1966.

The *Victory* and the thirteen ships that followed her on the long journey to the lakes played vital roles in the bulk shipping industry on the Great Lakes throughout their careers. Of the converted former Maritime Commission vessels, the *Thompson*, now operated as a tug-barge; *Sterling*, now the *Lee A. Tregurtha* of the Interlake fleet; Columbia's *Middletown*; and the *Iglehart* and *Townsend* of the Huron Cement fleet continue to operate yet today, as do the *Sparrows Point* and the *Hoyt*. It is also rumored that the *McKee Sons*, idle since the shipping recession of the 1980s, may be put back into service in the near future, possibly as a tug-barge. The contributions that all of the ships have made to their operating companies and to the Great Lakes shipping industry must to some degree be attributed to the leadership shown in 1950 by Cleveland-Cliffs and the incontrovertible fact that the way was paved for them by *Cliffs Victory*.

Notes

1. People in the Great Lakes shipping industry, particularly the sailors, are naysayers of world-class proportions. Historically, they have vocally and vehemently cast aspersions on almost any suggested deviation from the norm. They've unhesitatingly spoken out against longer ships, longer locks at the Soo, building ships with pilothouses at the stern, self-unloaders, the shift to diesel engines, cafeteria-style food service, and outfitting the ships for radio communications, among other changes. In an article entitled "The Captain Turned Red, the Air Turned Blue" in the March 1981 issue of *Telescope*, R. H. Davison recounts that, "Because they weren't served mashed potatoes for dinner, six firemen of the *Steamer Eastland* . . . went on strike just two hours out of South Haven [Michigan]. They not only wouldn't work, but they banked the fires." That's reflective of the intransigence that is common in the industry.
2. James Clary, *Ladies of the Lakes* (Lansing, MI: Michigan Natural Resources Magazine, 1981), 176.
3. The planned Cliffs-Detroit Edison vessel would have been the only thousand-footer on the lakes to be powered by a steam turbine engine. All of the other thousand-footers have diesel engines. Cliffs's officials felt that the higher initial construction cost of a steam plant would have been more than offset during the life of the vessel by reduced fuel and maintenance costs.
4. Ship Biography, Institute for Great Lakes Research, Bowling Green State University.

26

Columbia's Ill-Fated Queen

The freshwater of the Great Lakes drains into the saltwater of the Atlantic Ocean by way of the St. Lawrence River. The lakes lie at an elevation more than six hundred feet above that of the Atlantic, and as the lakewater flows unceasingly downhill to the sea it drops over the towering falls on the Niagara River and swirls through a series of turbulent rapids on the lower St. Lawrence. While a series of small locks and canals had been built around Niagara and the worst of the rapids on the St. Lawrence as early as 1829, it was impossible for large ships to travel between the lakes and the ocean until the opening of the St. Lawrence Seaway in 1959.[1] The Great Lakes were, for all intents and purposes, an inland waterway system.

Construction of a "seaway" connecting the Great Lakes with the Atlantic had been proposed by a Minnesota Congressman as early as 1892, during the presidency of Benjamin Harrison. The proposal generated immediate and strong opposition from a variety of powerful interests, including the railroads, utility companies, coal producers, Eastern and Gulf ports, the Lake Carriers' Association that represented bulk shipping interests on the lakes, and even Great Lakes ports like Cleveland, Chicago, and Buffalo. Over the next six decades, seaway proposals were regularly introduced in the U.S. Congress and the Canadian Parliament, and just as regularly they were defeated. It wasn't until 1954, under the presidency of Dwight D. Eisenhower, that U.S. and Canadian governments finally reached accord on a joint plan to build a route between the Great Lakes and the Atlantic.

Work on the monumental project began almost immediately. Over the next five years, scores of U.S. and Canadian construction firms worked virtually nonstop to create a waterway between Lake Erie and the upper St. Lawrence that could be navigated by large ships. In the process, they relocated the residents of all or parts of eight communities, moved 360 million tons of earth, raised bridges, and poured 6 million cubic yards of concrete. They built eight large locks on the Welland Canal around Niagara and seven on the lower St. Lawrence, constructed several massive power plants, and dredged the entire route to a depth of twenty-seven feet. The actual construction areas stretched for more than a hundred miles through some of the hardest rock on the North American continent. The cost exceeded $1 billion.

The St. Lawrence Seaway first opened to vessel traffic on April 25, 1959, and was officially dedicated by Queen Elizabeth II and U.S. Vice President Richard M. Nixon in late June of 1959 in ceremonies in both the U.S. and Canada. The natural barriers that lay between the Great Lakes and the Atlantic Ocean had finally been breached. For the first time, it was possible for large vessels to travel from the Atlantic Ocean more than 2,300 miles inland to Great Lakes ports such as Duluth, Minnesota, and Chicago, Illinois. Overnight, the inland ports of the Great Lakes became international ports, and North America's industrial and agricultural heartland was connected by a water route to ports around the world.[2]

For U.S. and Canadian bulk shipping companies on the lakes, opening the Seaway meant that the resource-rich regions of the upper lakes were linked for the first time with the heavily populated industrial regions of Canada concentrated along the shore of Lake Ontario and the lower St. Lawrence. At the same time, the way was also open for iron ore being mined in the Province of Labrador to be shipped by water to steel mills on the lakes. In the days prior to the actual opening of the Seaway, several U.S. and Canadian shipping companies moved to build new freighters to the maximum size that could be handled by the locks on the Welland and St. Lawrence.[3]

STR. EDMUND FITZGERALD

729'3"x75'1"x33'4"
Queen of the Lakes
June 7, 1958 to January 26, 1960

The first of the new "maximum Seaway-size" freighters was launched on June 7, 1958, at Great Lakes Engineering Works on the Rouge River at Detroit. While few people had been on hand in Chicago in 1957 when the lengthened *Cliffs Victory* emerged from the drydock at American Ship Building to claim honors as Queen of the Lakes, the 1958 launching of the *Edmund Fitzgerald* attracted a large and boisterous throng of onlookers and received much media coverage. In general terms, it was not a good year for Great Lakes shipping. The total tonnage carried on the lakes dropped from 196 million tons in 1957 to only 141 million tons in 1958. As workers at the Rouge River shipyard prepared the *Fitzgerald* for launching, only 104 of 205 U.S. freighters were in service.[4] For the industry, the launching of the new Queen of the Lake was a bright spot in an otherwise dismal season.

The "*Fitz*," as the massive new ship soon came to be called, had been built as an investment by Northwestern Mutual Life Insurance Company of Milwaukee, Wisconsin, and had been named for the firm's chairman of the board.[5] It was to be operated under a long-term charter arrangement by Oglebay Norton's Columbia Transportation Division.

The *Fitzgerald* was 729 feet long and just over 75 feet wide. She was a classic Great Lakes straight-decker, built along the lines of the *Sykes* and the AAA-class boats, but bigger. She was a splendidly outfitted ship, with passenger quarters that featured tiled baths, deep pile carpeting, and special furnishings purchased from the J. L. Hudson department store in Detroit.[6] But the *Fitz* was more than an aesthetically pleasing ship: the big freighter was a workhorse. She established many cargo records during her career, often breaking records she had set previously.

The *Fitz* was the first ship to carry more than 26,000 gross tons of iron ore and the first ship to carry more than 27,000 gross tons of ore.[7] In 1964 she set a new record by moving 1,159,805 tons through the Soo Locks during the season. During a period of exceptionally high water levels in 1968, *Fitz* again went into the record books as the first ship to carry more than 30,000 tons of iron ore through the Soo,[8] a record she broke during the 1969 season with a load that totalled 30,690 net tons.[9] That same year she set a new season record by carrying 1,230,553 net tons in forty-three trips down the lakes[10] and received a safety award for having completed eight years of operation without a lost-time accident.[11] While setting record after record, the *Fitz* also became a favorite with boatwatchers around the lakes. Her popularity was due in varying degrees to her size, her classic lines, the long string of records she amassed, and the antics of one of her captains.

Captain Peter Pulcer was in command of the *Fitzgerald* when many of the cargo records were set. He is best remembered, however, as the "dee jay captain" for his habit of piping music over the ship's intercom system to serenade people along the shore of the Detroit, St. Clair, and St. Marys rivers. His serenading wasn't limited to daytime hours: many tourists in campgrounds along the St. Marys River were aroused from their sleep by the sound of loud music blaring from the passing *Fitz*. The affable Pulcer would also frequently come out of the pilothouse when his ship was being raised or lowered in the Soo Locks and use a bullhorn to pass along information about the *Fitz* to the gathered throngs of delighted tourists.[12]

Although the *Fitzgerald*'s reign as Queen of the Lakes ended after less than a year, she remained exceptionally popular with boat buffs throughout her career. Even when the first of the thousand-footers came along in the early 1970s, the *Fitz* continued to be a favorite of boatwatchers. In all likelihood, however, she would eventually have suffered the fate of most other aging freighters, slipping gradually into obscurity, had it

The *Fitzgerald* was operated by Oglebay Norton's Columbia Transportation Division. The rust-red Columbia stack on the *Fitz* featured a fire engine red star with a white "C" on a band of gold. (Author's collection)

not been for a savage November storm in 1975 and a ballad by a Canadian songwriter that forever etched the memory of the *Fitz* into our minds.

In the early afternoon hours of November 9, 1975, having finished loading iron ore at the Burlington Northern Railroad dock in Superior, Wisconsin, the *Fitzgerald* steamed out onto Lake Superior and into the lore of shipwrecks on the lakes. Bound for an unloading dock at Detroit, Captain Ernest McSorley set a course along the north shore of Lake Superior, seeking shelter from a typical November storm passing across the lakes. Shortly after 10 a.m. on November 10, the *Fitzgerald* reached the eastern limits of the north shore, and a new course was set to carry the vessel southeast to the sheltered waters of Whitefish Bay at the headwaters of the St. Marys River. Gale warnings had been supplanted by storm warnings, and the steadily growing winds were whipping the lake into a frenzy. The seas had built until there were 12-16 foot waves. With just over 11 feet of freeboard, the *Fitz* was regularly shipping blackish-green water over her deck. In fact, the heavily-laden freighter was taking an awesome pounding in the furious seas.

At 3:30 in the afternoon, Captain McSorley made a radio call to the captain of the *Arthur M. Anderson*, a U.S. Steel freighter that was about seventeen miles behind the *Fitz* and also headed for the shelter of Whitefish Bay. McSorley told Captain Jesse Cooper of the *Anderson* that two vents on his ship had been damaged or lost and that it had taken on a list, even though he had his ballast pumps on. McSorley said that he was going to "check down," reduce speed, to close the distance between the two ships. Cooper told McSorley that he and his crew would keep an eye on the *Fitz*. Cooper and the two deck officers in the pilothouse with him at the time of the call from McSorley[13] later told Coast Guard investigators that none of them felt the *Fitzgerald*'s captain expressed any real concern for the safety of his ship during that conversation.[14]

Shortly after 4 p.m., the *Fitzgerald* made a second radio call to the *Anderson*, reporting that her two radars weren't working. With snow falling and darkness settling over the lake, and without radar to navigate by, the *Fitz* would have to rely on the *Anderson*'s crew to navigate for her. The radar set on the U.S. Steel freighter showed that the *Fitzgerald* was then about sixteen miles ahead of the *Anderson*, passing to the east of Caribou Island.

At 7:10 p.m., with winds of fifty to sixty miles an hour and seas as high as twenty-five feet, the *Anderson*'s first mate called the *Fitzgerald* to let them know there was a ship coming out of Whitefish Bay ahead of them. The *Fitz* was then about ten miles ahead of the *Anderson* and only fifteen miles from Whitefish Bay. The mate on the *Anderson* told the *Fitzgerald* that the ship leaving Whitefish Bay on its way up the lakes would pass west of them. "By the way, how are you making out with your problems?" asked the mate on the *Anderson*. "We are holding our own," came the reply from the *Fitzgerald*.[15]

Shortly after the radio conversation, the snow stopped and visibility improved considerably. In the darkened pilot-

The *Edmund Fitzgerald* was the first ship built to the maximum dimensions of the St. Lawrence Seaway, which was opened to vessel traffic in 1959. The "*Fitz*" was built by Northwestern Mutual Insurance Company of Milwaukee as an investment. The classic freighter was always immensely popular with boatwatchers around the lakes, due in part to the antics of one of the ship's captains. The *Fitzgerald* sank with all hands on November 10, 1975. (State Archives of Michigan)

house of the *Anderson*, the captain, mate, and wheelsman could see the running lights of three saltwater ships leaving Whitefish Bay and heading up the lake. The *Fitzgerald* should have been between the *Anderson* and the convoy of salties, but no one in the pilothouse could spot her lights. Captain Cooper thought the *Fitz* might have suffered a blackout, so he looked for her on his radar screen. He could clearly make out three targets on the green radar scope—the three salties—but nothing to indicate the location of the *Fitzgerald.* After trying unsuccessfully to call the Columbia freighter on the radio, Cooper contacted the U.S. pilot aboard one of the saltwater ships and asked him to look for the *Fitzgerald* on his radar. The pilot reported back that he could find no targets on his radar screen which could be the *Fitzgerald.* Cooper then called the Coast Guard.

At 8:32 p.m., radio operators at Coast Guard Group Sault Ste. Marie logged a call from the *Arthur M. Anderson* in which Captain Cooper told them: "I am very concerned with the welfare of the steamer *Edmund Fitzgerald.* He was right in front of us experiencing a little difficulty. He was taking on a small amount of water and none of the upbound ships have passed him. I can see no lights as before and don't have him on radar. I just hope he didn't take a nose dive." The radio operator in Sault Ste. Marie made several attempts to contact the *Fitzgerald* by radio before calling the Coast Guard Rescue Coordination Center in Cleveland at 8:40 to inform them that there was "an uncertainty" concerning the freighter.[16]

By the time the *Anderson* reached Whitefish Bay at about 9 p.m., Captain Cooper "was sure that the *Fitzgerald* was gone." At 9:03 p.m. he again called the Coast Guard station at Sault Ste. Marie. This time his message was more forceful: the *Fitzgerald* is missing! The call set in motion a major search and rescue effort involving Coast Guard surface units from Sault Ste. Marie and Duluth, Coast Guard helicopters and fixed-wing aircraft from the air station at Traverse City, Michigan, and the freighters *Anderson* and *William Clay Ford.* The Coast Guard also called six other freighters lying at anchor in Whitefish Bay and asked them to join in the search. Captains on five of the ships told the Coast Guard that venturing out of the sheltered waters of the bay would put their ships and crews in jeopardy. The sixth vessel, the *Hilda Marjanne*, a Canadian freighter operated by Upper Lakes Shipping, lifted anchor and got underway, but she had to turn back after only twenty or thirty minutes because conditions were too severe. The commanding officer of the Coast Guard Group Sault Ste. Marie also contacted pilots aboard the *Nanfri*, *Benfri*, and *Avafors*, the three saltwater ships that had headed up the lake earlier in the evening, and asked that they join in the search for the *Fitzgerald.*

The *Edmund Fitzgerald* sank with all hands during the evening hours of November 10, 1975, only sixteen miles from the sheltered waters of Whitefish Bay. After loading ore, the Columbia freighter had departed the American lakehead at Duluth on the morning of November 9 in the midst of a typical late season storm. Seeking shelter from the foul weather, the *Fitz* hugged the north shore of Lake Superior before changing course for the run down to Whitefish Bay and the headwaters of the St. Marys River. That leg of the voyage was never completed. (Author's collection)

All three answered that they did not believe they could safely turn their vessels around in the high seas.

The search continued throughout the night of November 10 and was expanded on November 11, 12, and 13, when additional U.S. and Canadian Coast Guard vessels and aircraft arrived in the area and a number of U.S. and Canadian freighters joined the effort. The *Anderson* found a piece of one of the *Fitzgerald*'s lifeboats on the morning of November 11, and a second lifeboat a few hours later. Two twenty-five-person inflatable life rafts from the *Fitzgerald* were found floating near the Canadian shore that same morning. Searchers also recovered twenty life preservers, or pieces of life preservers; eight oars or pieces of oars; one piece of a ballast tank sounding board, of the type used on the *Fitzgerald*; eight flotation tanks, identified as having come from the *Fitz*'s lifeboats; one large wooden fender block; two propane cylinders, similar to those used to fuel galley equipment on the *Fitzgerald*; thirteen life rings; two 2"x12" planks; one wooden stool; one heaving line; one-half of a lifeboat cover; one rudder from a lifeboat; one floodlight, like those that had been installed on the pilothouse and after deck of the *Fitzgerald*; one plastic spray bottle marked "pilothouse window"; one broken extension ladder; and assorted pieces of broken scrap wood. No survivors were found, nor were the bodies of any of the *Fitzgerald*'s twenty-nine crewmembers ever recovered. Captain Ernest McSorley and his crew disappeared with their ship.

A sonar search of the area was conducted by the Coast Guard Cutter *Woodrush* a few days later. Underwater wreckage, believed to be that of the *Fitzgerald*, was located in 530 feet of water, seventeen miles northwest of Whitefish Point. In May of 1976, the Coast Guard used an unmanned submersible borrowed from the Navy to confirm that the previously located wreckage was that of the missing Columbia freighter. The submersible was fitted with video and still-picture cameras, and over a period of twelve days more than 43,000 feet of videotape was shot of the sunken hull, along with 895 color slides. Early video confirmed that the wreckage was that of the *Fitzgerald*, her name clearly readable on her overturned stern. The freighter was found to be in two pieces. The bow section, 276 feet long, was resting upright on the bottom, while a 253-foot section of the overturned stern was found about 170 feet away. The bottom of the lake between the two intact sections was strewn with twisted metal and spilled iron ore pellets.[17]

After an eighteen-month study, a Coast Guard Board of Investigation concluded that the most probable cause of the sinking of the *Fitzgerald* was massive flooding of the cargo hold. Water had entered the cargo hold through "ineffective hatch closures," hatch covers which had not been properly maintained. Evidence suggested the possibility that not all of the clamps used to secure the covers to the hatch coamings had been in place at the time of the accident. As a result, waves breaking over the *Fitzgerald*'s deck throughout the day of November 10 had forced water into the ship's cargo hold. As water rose in the cargo hold, the vessel progressively lost buoyancy. With high seas swirling around the ship and no way to check the cargo hold for water, Captain McSorley and his crew might not have been aware that their ship was gradually sinking out from under them. Finally, one last deluge of water entered the cargo hold, the vessel lost its last measure of buoyancy, and the *Edmund Fitzgerald* dove like a rock to the bottom of the lake.[18]

The last moments would have been terrifying for the crew. As the bow dove below the turbulent waters of Lake Superior, the windows of the pilothouse would have exploded inward. A wall of water would have instantly filled the pilothouse, driving Captain McSorley, the first mate who was on watch, the wheelsman and anyone else in the *Fitzgerald*'s pilothouse at the time back against the aft bulkhead or sweeping them out the rear windows.

Elsewhere on the ship, most crewmembers would have been in their rooms, watching television, reading, or sleeping when their ship dove toward the bottom. As the ship tipped toward the bottom, they would have been thrown from their beds or chairs and sent crashing against the forward bulkheads

A Coast Guard drawing of the sunken bow section of the *Fitzgerald* as it lies in 530 feet of water. The drawing was constructed from videotape and still photos of the wreck taken by an unmanned Navy submersible. Much of the damage to the bow section resulted when the freighter impacted with the muddy bottom of the lake. Burrowed deeply into the mud, the *Fitzgerald* sits amid tons of taconite pellets that spilled from her hold when she hit bottom and tore in half. (Author's collection)

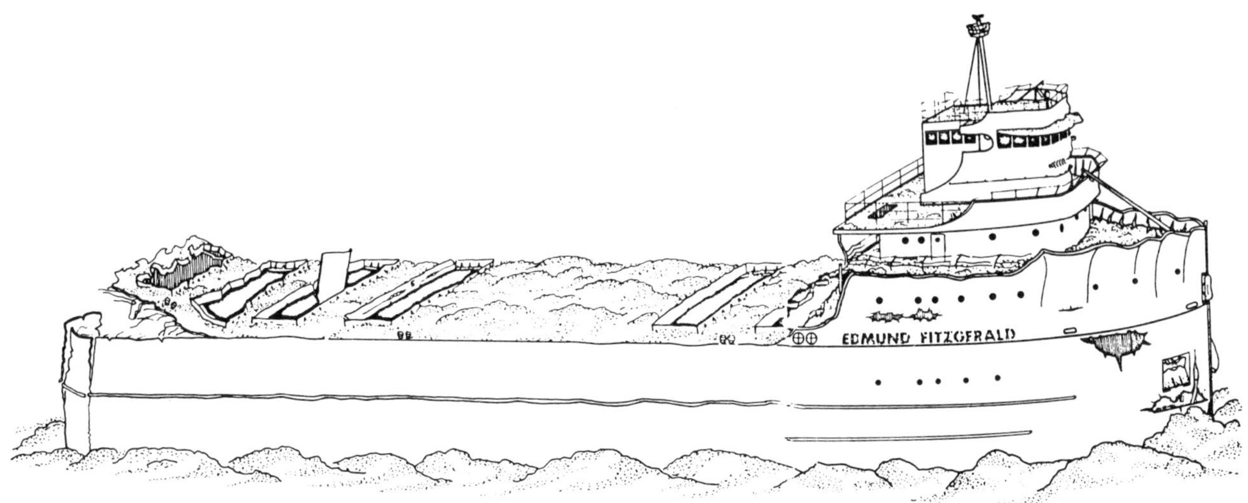

or furnishings in their rooms. Many would have been seriously injured. All would have been disoriented and probably unable to gain their footings. At least a few crewmembers would probably have been in the galley, always a popular gathering spot during the evening hours. They would have undoubtedly grabbed onto their stools or the messroom table, thinking that it was just another roll—a little worse than the ones they had been experiencing all day. But their ship would have continued to tip, and eventually they would have been thrown from their stools and into the forward bulkhead, showered by bottles of condiments, plates, silverware, drinking glasses, cookie jars, and boxes of cereal cluttering the messroom table. In the engine room, the engineer and oiler on watch would probably first have heard the ship's giant propeller overrev as it lifted clear of the water, something that had been happening intermittently throughout the day as big waves lifted the stern. As they moved to cut back on the throttle, they would have scrambled for footing as the stern continued to rise in the air and the ship plummeted toward the bottom of the lake.

Starting at the bow and proceeding toward the stern, portholes and deadlights would have exploded inward under the increasing pressure of the water. Rooms would have filled rapidly with frothing torrents of water. In minutes, the occupants of the rooms would have been dead. Once the *Fitzgerald* began her dive toward the bottom of Lake Superior there was nothing that anyone on the ship could have done to escape the fury of the angry seas. Nobody would have had time to don a lifejacket, much less get to the ship's lifeboats or life rafts. Virtually all would have died wherever they were when the ship lost buoyancy.

The story of the sinking of the big Columbia freighter was told in a popular song: "The Wreck of the *Edmund Fitzgerald*," by Canadian singer Gordon Lightfoot. For almost two decades now, the song's familiar lyrics and haunting melody have fixed in the minds of listeners the plight of *Fitz* and her crew.[19] It reminds us all of the massive freighters' fragility when pitted against the fury of nature on North America's inland seas. Even the biggest and strongest ship can be sent to a watery grave by the hurricane-strength winds and towering black waves of the Great Lakes—even the Queen of the Lakes.

Notes

1. Many Great Lakes cargo ships were put into operation on the oceans by the U.S. and Canadian governments during World War I and World War II, but they first had to be cut in half and towed out of the lakes in pieces. Similarly, cargo ships built in England and Scotland for the Canadian fleet had to be brought into the lakes in the same fashion.
2. Jacques LesStrang, *Seaway* (Vancouver: Superior Publishing, 1976).
3. The new locks on the Welland and St. Lawrence were 766 feet long, 80 feet wide, and had 30 feet of water over their sills. They were designed to handle ships of up to 730 feet in length and about 75 feet wide. The channels of the Welland and St. Lawrence were dredged to a minimum depth of 27 feet so ships drawing up to slightly more than 26 feet of water could pass through the system.
4. *1981 Annual Report* (Cleveland: Lake Carriers' Association, 1982), 21.
5. John O. Greenwood, *Namesakes of the Lakes* (Cleveland: Freshwater Press, 1970), 106.
6. James Clary, *Ladies of the Lakes* (Lansing, MI: Michigan Natural Resources Magazine, 1981), 157.
7. Greenwood, 106.
8. Dr. James A. Clark, "The Edmund Fitzgerald," *Telescope* 25, no. 1 (Jan.–Feb. 1976): 16.
9. Clary, 158.
10. *Telescope* 17, no. 8 (Nov.–Dec. 1968): 194.
11. Clary, 158.
12. Ibid.
13. The first mate was just in the process of relieving the second mate of the watch when the call was received. Normally, only one mate at a time is on watch in the pilothouse.
14. *Marine Casualty Report: SS Edmund Fitzgerald* (Washington: U.S. Coast Guard, 1977), 29.
15. Ibid., 29.
16. Ibid., 30.
17. Ibid., 34–55.
18. Ibid., 89–104.
19. There are, however, a number of factual errors in the song. The *Fitz* was not coming from a "mill" in Wisconsin, nor was it bound for Cleveland. It's also unlikely that the cook said it was too rough to feed the crew, and Captain McSorley never radioed that his ship was in peril. Despite those errors, it's a good song.

27

The 730s

Columbia's 729-foot *Edmund Fitzgerald* and the 715-foot *Menihek Lake* of Canada's Carryore fleet are generally considered the first maximum Seaway-size freighters in their respective U.S. and Canadian fleets. But even as those two ships were being put into service, U.S. and Canadian shipyards were building vessels that were slightly longer, at 730 feet. U.S. and Canadian Seaway officials had agreed to allow ships of up to that length to transit the locks on the Welland and St. Lawrence. That decision was the catalyst for a major overhauling of the Canadian bulk fleet as vessel owners north of the border placed orders for 730-foot ships.[1]

With trade between the upper lakes, Lake Ontario, and the St. Lawrence critical to the Canadian fleets, many of the ships they operated before 1959 were diminutive "canallers," less than 260 long, with maximum drafts of 14 feet. At the end of the 1958 season, 129 of 210 vessels in the Canadian fleet were canallers.[2] While those vessels' carrying capacities were severely limited, they could fit through the locks of the Welland and the Lachine Canal at Montreal. Once the Seaway opened, however, Canadian fleets moved rapidly to build or buy larger vessels. It was a relatively simple economic decision for Canadian owners: the combined carrying capacity of all 129 canallers could be replaced by only 14 of the 730s.[3]

Between 1959 and 1966, Canadian fleets built 42 new ships,[4] aided by forty percent construction subsidies enacted in 1961 by their government.[5] They also acquired 37 other ships from U.S. owners.[6] Most of the newly built vessels were 730s, while the ships bought from American owners were between 550 and about 600 feet in length, the largest being the 617-foot *Matthew Andrews* purchased by Misener Steamship in 1963.[7] Other well-known U.S. ships that took up operations under Canadian flag were the *J. Pierpont Morgan*, the first of the standard 600-footers, and the *George W. Perkins*, *Henry C. Frick*, and *William E. Corey*, 569-foot vessels built in 1905. All four of the ships had been Queens of the Lakes when they were launched. Although not built to the maximum dimensions of the Seaway locks, the vessels acquired from the U.S. were larger than the canallers and allowed their Canadian owners to increase the carrying capacities of their fleets.

The 730-foot length became the standard for the Canadian industry, however. Since 1959, some 70 Canadian freighters have been built to that length, compared to only 6 for the U.S. fleet.[8] After the opening of the Poe Lock at Sault Ste. Marie in 1971, U.S. shipowners began to build vessels that were 1,000 feet long and had several times the carrying capacity of the 730s. There are still no ships in the Canadian fleet, however, that are too large to operate in the vital Seaway trade.

The *Murray Bay*, preparing to depart a lock on the St. Lawrence Seaway. Prior to construction of the Seaway, most ships in the Canadian fleet were "canallers" less than 260 feet long, the maximum length that could be handled by the locks in the outdated Welland and Lachine canals. When the Seaway opened in 1959, Canadian shipowners rapidly replaced the diminutive canallers with 730-foot freighters like Canada Steamship's *Murray Bay*. (Institute for Great Lakes Research, Bowling Green State University)

STR. MURRAY BAY

730'x75'2"x34'3"
Queen of the Lakes
September 17, 1959 to December 7, 1962

The first 730 was launched at Collingwood Shipyard on September 17, 1959. Christened *Murray Bay*, the new Queen of the Lakes was owned by Canada Steamship Lines, the largest of the Canadian fleets. In 1963, CSL sold the landmark vessel to N. M. Paterson and Sons, another major Canadian bulk fleet. Under Paterson colors, the ship was rechristened *Comeaudoc*, the name under which it operates yet today.[9]

STR. ARTHUR B. HOMER

730'x75'1"x33'4"
Queen of the Lakes
November 7, 1959 to December 7, 1962

The *Murray Bay* was followed off the ways by the first of the 730s to join the U.S. fleet, the *Arthur B. Homer.* Launched on November 7, 1959, at Great Lakes Engineering Works on the Rouge River at Detroit, the *Homer* was owned by Bethlehem Steel and operated under their Great Lakes Steamship Division as the flagship of the fleet. The new freighter had been built to slightly modified versions of the plans used to construct the *Edmund Fitzgerald.* In 1975, the *Homer* was lengthened to 826 feet at Fraser Shipyard in Superior, Wisconsin. At that time she was the largest U.S. vessel to undergo lengthening.

In 1980, the *Homer* was laid-up at Erie, Pennsylvania, when the bottom dropped out of the Great Lakes shipping industry. When conditions on the lakes began to improve a few years later, the U.S. industry had undergone a dramatic and historic metamorphosis. The straight-deckers that had always been the backbone of the industry had been supplanted by the more efficient self-unloaders. No work could be found for the *Homer* and dozens of other U.S. ships without self-unloading capability. At the same time, U.S. fleet owners were still struggling, and few could justify the high cost of converting their straight-deckers to self-unloaders. In 1977, Bethlehem officials made the difficult decision to scrap the *Homer.* If the economic climate had been healthier on the lakes, it would probably have been rebuilt as a self-unloader and operated for another three or four decades. But the *Homer* could not escape the scrap heap. The beautiful ship was towed from its berth at Erie to Port Colborne, Ontario, and shipbreakers soon began the process of dismantling the former Queen of the Lakes.[10]

Between 1959 and late 1962, when a slightly larger Canadian ship was launched, the *Murray Bay* and the *Homer* were joined by thirteen other 730-foot freighters that shared honors with them as Queens of the Lakes. Five were U.S. vessels, while eight joined the growing Canadian fleet.

STR. EDWARD L. RYERSON

January 26, 1960 to December 7, 1962

The first of the five U.S. ships added to the 730-class was launched on January 26, 1960, at Manitowac Shipbuilding in Manitowac, Wisconsin, for the Inland Steel fleet. In ceremonies at the snow-covered shipyard, the new freighter was christened the *Edward L. Ryerson.* Ryerson was a former chairman of the board of Inland and its subsidiary, Joseph T. Ryerson and Son, the nation's largest steel service center. The scion of a wealthy family involved in the iron and steel industries since colonial days, Ryerson continued to be a major stockholder in Inland.[11]

The *Ryerson* was a slightly larger version of Inland's *Sykes,* which had been launched in 1949. As in the design and construction of the *Sykes,* much effort and expense had gone into making the big freighter as aesthetically attractive as possible. Compared to the basic, blocky laker, the *Ryerson* actually looks streamlined. Her bow and the top of her pilothouse have a graceful flare, and the massive smokestack on her stern is smoothly tapered and rounded. The effect is accentuated by the same striking painting scheme initially used on the *Sykes* and later adopted for use on all ships in the Inland fleet, including the infamous white stripe running just below the level of the deck for the entire length of the ship. Several generations of Inland fleet deckhands who have had to "polish the stripe" al-

Inland Steel's *Edward L. Ryerson* was one of the 730s that shared the Queen of the Lakes title between 1959 and 1962. Many feel that the *Ryerson* has an even more streamlined appearance than her sister ship, the *Wilfred Sykes.* Today, the striking *Ryerson* is the only straight-decker left in the U.S. fleet that primarily hauls iron ore. (Author's collection)

most every time the ship is in port have come to regard the innovative Inland paint scheme as an archenemy.

In her second season of operations on the lakes, the *Ryerson* set a cargo record for iron ore after loading 25,018 gross tons for delivery from Superior, Wisconsin, to the Inland mills at Indiana Harbor. That record stood until 1965. Today, the *Ryerson* is one of only four straight-deckers still operating in the U.S. fleet and the sole straight-decker committed to the iron ore trade.[12] A battery of bridge cranes unloads the ship when it arrives in the slip at the Inland mills. Whereas that process can often take twenty-four hours, a self-unloader of the same size could unload its cargo in four to six hours without having to rely on any shoreside equipment.

The other two ships in the Inland fleet are both self-unloaders. The *Sykes* was converted to a self-unloader in 1975, and the *Joseph L. Block* was launched as a self-unloader in 1976. Myth or reality, the story has circulated throughout the Great Lakes industry for many years that Inland fleet officials wanted to convert the *Ryerson* to a self-unloader at about the same time they had the *Sykes* rebuilt. That move was reportedly blocked by members of the Ryerson family, who still control a significant percentage of Inland's stock. The Ryersons allegedly did not want the striking appearance of the ship cluttered by the addition of a self-unloading boom and elevator casing.

STR. LEON FALK, JR.

1961 to December 7, 1962

The other four U.S. 730s were all former Maritime Commission T2 tankers that underwent conversion for use on the lakes. National Steel purchased two of the vessels—the *Leon Falk, Jr.*, and the *Atlantic Dealer*—to add to their fleet, which was managed by M. A. Hanna Company. The *Falk* had been built at Sun Ship Building in Chester, Pennsylvania, in 1945. The 526-foot tanker, christened as the *Winter Hill*, spent much of its life in the reserve fleet. After purchase by National Steel, the long-idle tanker was brought into the lakes by way of the St. Lawrence Seaway to be lengthened to 730 feet and converted to a Great Lakes bulk freighter at the Lorain yard of American Shipbuilding.

STR. PAUL H. CARNAHAN

1961 to December 7, 1962

National also bought the tanker *Atlantic Dealer* from Atlantic Refining Company of Philadelphia. The *Atlantic Dealer* had also been launched at the Sun shipyard in 1945 for the Maritime Commission. She was originally named the *Honey Hill*, but her name was changed when Atlantic Refining purchased her in 1946. The tanker operated in the coastal liquid bulk trade, but it had been laid up for several years before being purchased in 1960 for use on the lakes. National had the ship converted at AmShip's Lorain yard. As in the case of the *Falk*, the project included inserting a new section of midbody, just over 200 feet long. The midbody sections used on both the National ships had been built at the Schlieker-Werft shipyard in Hamburg, Germany, and towed across the Atlantic and down the St. Lawrence to Lorain.

The two T2 tankers converted by National were among five U.S. ships lengthened with foreign-built midbodies in the early 1960s.[13] Ship owners had found that while U.S. customs laws prohibited U.S. ships from being built overseas, there was nothing to preclude them from having midbody sections constructed at foreign yards. It did not take the government long to close that loophole, however, and the midbody sections subsequently used to lengthen ships on the lakes were all built at U.S. yards.[14]

After conversion, the 730-foot freighter was christened as the *Paul H. Carnahan*. It and the *Falk* were stalwarts in the Hanna-managed fleet until the early 1980s, when the lakes were hit by a shipping recession. After lying idle for several years with most of the other vessels in the Hanna fleet, the two ships were sent to the shipbreakers. The *Falk* was scrapped in Spain in 1985, and the *Carnahan* was broken up in Taiwan in 1987.[15]

STR. PIONEER CHALLENGER

1961 to December 7, 1962

The third T2 converted for use on the American side of the lakes in 1961 had been launched in the fall of 1942 at Bethlehem Steel's shipyard in Sparrows Point, Maryland. Christened as the *Neschanic* by the Maritime Commission, the 502-foot tanker was put into service with the Navy in 1943. It operated as an oiler, carrying oil and gasoline to fuel warships in the Pacific. In the three years that the *Neschanic* supported the war effort against the Japanese, she and her crew were awarded nine battle stars, more than were earned by many of the carriers, battleships, and cruisers operating in the war zones. Her combat record included service with the Pacific fleet at the battles of the Gilbert and Marshall islands, western New Guinea, Marianas, Guam, Iwo Jima, Okinawa, and the Third Fleet's operations against the Japanese homeland.

On June 18, 1944, *Neschanic* was attacked by a flight of Japanese bombers in the hours just before the battle of the Philippine Sea. The deck of the lightly armed tanker was struck by a bomb aft on the starboard side. The explosion blew three crewmembers over the side, and thirty-three of the 250 sailors aboard suffered serious burns. Damage control parties battled heroically to keep the ship's cargo from igniting and turning the vessel into a blazing inferno. At the same time, the *Neschanic*'s gunners exacted a toll on the Japanese bombers, downing two before the attack ended. Crewmembers aboard the tanker extinguished the fires, and hurried repairs were made to the ship's damaged fueling stations. That night, the indomitable tanker was once again at work fueling warships going out to meet the enemy.

In 1947, the tanker was purchased by Gulf Oil and renamed *Gulfoil*. The ship was part of the Gulf Oil fleet until 1958, when it collided with another tanker, the *S. E. Graham*, on August 7 at Newport, Rhode Island. The *Graham* was carrying a million gallons of gasoline at the time, and it blew up as a result of the collision. Fifteen crewmembers aboard the *Gulfoil* were killed by the explosion, and the ship was badly damaged. The crippled hull of the *Gulfoil* was purchased by Maryland Shipbuilding on speculation. They held title to the vessel from 1958 until 1960, when it was sold to Pioneer Steamship Company to be converted for service on the lakes. The ship underwent conversion at Maryland Shipbuilding, including lengthening with the addition of a new midbody built by Verholme United Shipyards in Rotterdam. On June 24, 1961, the vessel was christened as the *Pioneer Challenger* by her new owners before it departed on July 1 for its long voyage into the lakes. On July 16, the newly converted 730-foot freighter passed Detroit on its maiden voyage up the lakes.

On the lakes, the *Pioneer Challenger* was managed by Hutchinson and Company during the balance of the 1961 season. When Hutchinson folded early in 1962, the ship was sold to Oglebay Norton's Columbia Transportation, which rechristened the ship the *Middletown* in honor of the Middletown, Ohio, headquarters of Armco Steel, one of the fleet's major customers. In 1982, Columbia had the ship converted to a self-unloader at Bay Ship Building in Sturgeon Bay, Wisconsin.[16] While the *Falk* and *Carnahan* were long ago towed off to the shipbreakers, the *Middletown* is a familiar sight on the lakes yet today, still operating in Columbia's colors. Few who see her are aware of the former tanker's colorful past on both the Pacific and Atlantic oceans.

Among those who recall her earlier service are the U.S. Navy sailors who served aboard the tanker. They formed the USS Neschanic Veterans Association. They held annual reunions around the country at which they remembered the exploits of the gallant little tanker, which they thought had been scrapped. In 1988, Jon Palik, a *Neschanic* veteran living in a suburb of Cleveland, saw a newspaper story about Columbia Steamship's *Middletown*. The article said that the Columbia freighter was the former *Neschanic*. "My God," said Palik, "that's my old ship." After writing to officials at Columbia Steamship, Palik was afforded the opportunity to once again walk the decks of the ship he had served on during World War II. While the vessel's outward appearance had changed dramatically as a result of her conversion to a lake freighter, the machinery spaces that the former machinist's mate had grown so familiar with during the long war years were just as he had left them. "Except for the color of the paint on the bulkheads, it's all the same," he observed.[17]

STR. WALTER A. STERLING

1962 to December 7, 1962

The final converted T2 to join the U.S. fleet was the *Walter A. Sterling*, owned by Cleveland-Cliffs. Built in 1942 at Bethlehem's Sparrows Point, Maryland, shipyard, as the *Mobiloil*, the vessel had been renamed *Chiwawa* at its launching. Cliffs had the former tanker rebuilt and lengthened to 730 feet at the Lorain, Ohio, yard of American Ship Building.

In 1976, after the opening of the new Poe Lock at Sault Ste. Marie, Cliffs had the *Sterling* lengthened to 826 feet by adding a 96-foot section to the cargo hold. Two years later, the vessel went back into the shipyard to be converted to a self-unloader so that it could operate in the growing movement of western low sulphur coal on the lakes. Virtually all of the western coal was being shipped to power plants that did not have shoreside unloading equipment.

When the Cleveland-Cliffs fleet was sold to the Rouge Steel subsidiary of Ford Motor Company in the fall of 1984, the *Sterling* was renamed the *William Clay Ford*. It became the flagship of the Detroit-based fleet, replacing a scrapped AAA-class boat of the same name.[18] The former tanker changed hands again in 1989 when Ford decided to follow the lead of Hanna and Cleveland-Cliffs and get out of the shipping business. The ships in the Ford fleet were purchased by Interlake Steamship. As part of the purchase agreement, Interlake also received a large part of the contract to haul iron ore, coal, and stone to the mills at Rouge Steel. After the purchase, Interlake renamed the *William Clay Ford* the *Lee A. Tregurtha* in honor of the wife of one of Interlake's owners.

The former Ford ships are actually owned by Lakes Shipping, a subsidiary of Interlake set up solely to purchase the vessels. The decision to keep ownership of the Ford boats separate was based on a number of reasons. Primary was the fact that deck and engine officers on the Ford boats were non-union, while Interlake officers worked under a contract between the company and the Marine Engineers Beneficial Association (MEBA), the union representing most officers on the Great Lakes. As part of their contract to buy the boats, Interlake agreed to hire the former Ford officers. It was understood that the officers would then join MEBA, but no decision had been made as to whether the former Ford personnel would be somehow merged into the Interlake seniority lists. Such a merger would require approval by MEBA and Interlake's deck and engine officers, some of whom would drop down on their respective seniority lists if the Ford officers were added.

To expedite acquisition of the three Ford boats and forestall problems of merging the non-union officers into their fleet, Interlake officials set up Lakes Shipping to purchase the boats. If a plan allowing the Ford officers to merge into Interlake's MEBA seniority lists could not be agreed to, the company would have the option of operating the boats as a separate fleet. In that case, separate seniority lists would have been established for the former Ford officers, and they would have been covered under a separate contract between Lakes Shipping and MEBA. At the end of the 1980 season, however, Interlake officers and the former Ford officers agreed on a strategy that made it possible to merge their seniority lists. The ships acquired from Ford are technically still owned by Lakes Shipping, but in every other respect they function today as part of Interlake Steamship.

A similar situtation had occurred a decade earlier, when Oglebay Norton purchased the *William R. Roesch* and *Paul Thayer* from Kinsman Marine. Unlicensed crewmembers on the two Kinsman ships belonged to the Seafarers International Union (SIU), while personnel in Oglebay Norton's Columbia Transportation Division were members of Local 5000 of the Steelworkers. With no prospect of merging the members of the disparate unions, the two boats were assigned to another Oglebay Norton subsidiary, Pringle Transit, rather than to Columbia. They operate under the Pringle banner yet today, with SIU crews, even though they are managed by the same people who direct operations of ships in the Columbia Transportation fleet.

STR. RED WING

1960 to December 7, 1962

On the Canadian side of the lakes, the *Murray Bay* was joined in 1960 by the 730-foot *Red Wing* of Upper Lakes Shipping. Like the *Falk*, *Carnahan*, and *Middletown* of the U.S. fleet, the *Red Wing* had its genesis as a former T2 tanker. It had been launched for the Maritime Commission on February 12, 1943, at Sun Ship Building and named the *Boundbrook*. In 1947, the idle tanker was purchased from the reserve fleet by Imperial Oil of Canada. Her new owners renamed her the *Imperial Edmonton* and operated the tanker in the liquid bulk trade until 1958. At that time the vessel was purchased for $500,000 by St. Lawrence and Great Lakes Shipping for conversion to a dry bulk freighter. Only the stern section and engine machinery of the T2 were maintained during the conversion at Port Weller Dry Docks on the Welland Canal. Forward of the stern, the vessel was entirely rebuilt as a 730-foot laker.

After conversion, the ship was purchased by Upper Lakes Shipping and rechristened the *Red Wing*.[19] The Upper Lakes freighter is named in honor of the Detroit Red Wings hockey team. Mr. Bruce Norris, formerly the owner of the Red Wings, was also a major stockholder in Upper Lakes Shipping.[20] On her last trip of the 1961 season, the *Red Wing* set a Great Lakes cargo record when it loaded 25,004 tons of iron ore at Picton, Ontario, on December 1. That record was broken in 1962 by the *Ryerson*, which topped the record by a scant fourteen tons on August 28. Upper Lakes sold the *Red Wing* for scrap in 1986.

STR. WHITEFISH BAY

November 16, 1960 to December 7, 1962

Another 730 joined the Canadian fleet on November 16, 1960, when the steamer *Whitefish Bay* was launched at Davie Ship Building in Lauzon, Quebec. Built for Canada Steamship Lines, the freighter continues to operate for them today. During the winter of 1968-69, the freighter was converted to a self-unloader at Port Arthur Ship Building in Thunder Bay, Ontario. At the same time, her owners renamed her the *Quetico*, honoring a sprawling wilderness park located west of Thunder Bay. In 1972, title to the ship passed to Davie Ship Building, although CSL continued to operate the *Quetico*. Ownership changed again in 1973, when the vessel was purchased by Pipe Line Tankers, but it still operated as part of the CSL fleet. In 1983, the name of the ship was changed back to *Whitefish Bay*.

STR. LEECLIFFE HALL

September 10, 1961 to December 7, 1962

The fourth Canadian 730 made its debut on May 8, 1961, when the *Leecliffe Hall* was launched in ceremonies at Fairfield Ship Building in Govan, Scotland. Conceived as the new flagship of the Hall Corporation fleet (which operates on the lakes today as Halco), the big freighter was then the largest dry cargo ship ever built in the United Kingdom. After sailing the Atlantic, the *Leecliffe Hall* was feted at a second round of ceremonies held in Montreal in September. From there she departed on her maiden voyage on the lakes. On the downbound leg of that first trip, the vessel established a new record by carrying 1,030,979 bushels of mixed grains from the Canadian lakehead to the Bunge Elevator in Quebec City. During her career, the *Leecliffe Hall* set a number of other records.

The *Leecliffe Hall*'s final record was a tragic one. On September 5, 1964, she became the largest ship ever to sink in the Great Lakes and St. Lawrence system—a dubious mark that stands yet today. While upbound in the St. Lawrence River, sixty miles below Quebec City, the flagship of the Hall fleet collided with the Greek freighter *Apollonia* in heavy fog. The crew and passengers on the *Leecliffe Hall* managed to abandon ship safely, but one crewman chose to stay behind in an effort to save the badly damaged freighter.[21] Later, two other crewmembers returned to the ship to help their shipmate rig towing lines to the tug *Foundation* in an attempt to pull the vessel into shallow water where it could be beached. Sadly, the ship sank before it reached shallow water. The three crewmembers who had tried so valiantly to save their ship died in the effort. Resting in ninety feet of water, the tops of the *Leecliffe Hall*'s masts could clearly be seen rising out of the water at low tide.

After a number of salvage attempts that continued until 1966, her insurance underwriters declared the *Leecliffe Hall* a constructive total loss, and all efforts to raise the ship were abandoned. Because the sunken vessel represented a hazard to ships operating on the St. Lawrence, orders were soon issued to dynamite and remove the hull. In all, ten tons of dynamite were used to blast the sturdy ship into pieces that could be moved out of the navigational channel.[22]

In reviewing the sinking, the Canadian Admiralty blamed the casualty on the actions of officers aboard both ships. They concluded that neither ship's officers were using their radars wisely, even though they were depending on them for navigation in the fogbound St. Lawrence. Both vessels were also judged to have been going too fast for conditions, and the *Leecliffe Hall* was running too close to the center of the channel. The captain of the Hall freighter and pilots aboard both vessels had their licenses suspended until the start of the 1965 shipping season. The judge in the case said he would also have suspended the license of the Greek captain if it had been within his jurisdiction to do so.[23]

STR. MONTREALIS

1962 to December 7, 1962

The fifth Canadian 730 was the first Great Lakes ship built for the Papachristidis Company, which operated solely on the ocean before the opening of the St. Lawrence Seaway. The new freighter was christened the *Montrealis.* It was built at Montreal, Ontario . . . *and* at Lauzon, Quebec! The stern section of the vessel was built at Montreal by Canadian Vickers, which would actually own the ship. The bow was constructed at the George T. Davie shipyard at Lauzon. The two sections of the hull were both launched in September of 1961 and joined together at the Davie yard before going into service on the Great Lakes and St. Lawrence. In 1972, the ship was acquired by Jackes Shipping. Under Jackes ownership, the *Montrealis* was operated as part of the Upper Lakes Shipping fleet. ULS continued their management of the vessel when it was sold in 1975 to Leitch Transport. The following year, ULS purchased the ship, and they operate it yet today.[24]

STR. HAMILTONIAN

April 7, 1962 to December 7, 1962

A sixth Canadian 730, the *Hamiltonian*, was launched at St. Johns Ship Building in St. Johns, New Brunswick, on April 7, 1962. Financed and owned by Canadian General Electric, the *Hamiltonian* was managed by the Papachristidis Company fleet of Phrixos B. Papachristidis. In 1965, ownership of the vessel was transferred to Eastern Lake Carriers, but it continued to operate as part of the Papachristidis fleet. In 1967, the name of the ship was changed to the *Petite Hermine*, honoring one of the three small ships in the fleet that brought the explorer Jacques Cartier to Canada in 1535. Two other ships in the Papachristidis fleet were named the *Grande Hermine* and *Emerillon* after the other Cartier vessels. Interestingly, Cartier's *Petite Hermine* was a bad luck ship. Before Cartier's return to France in 1536, the vessel was abandoned after its crew was destroyed by scurvy.

Maybe use of the name *Petite Hermine* also brought bad luck to Phrixos Papachristidis, because his firm folded in 1972. At that time, the ten-year-old *Petite Hermine* was purchased by Jackes Shipping and came under the management of Upper Lakes Shipping as the *Canadian Hunter*. In 1975, ownership of the vessel shifted to Leitch Transport, and in 1976 it was purchased by Port Weller Dry Docks. Under both owners, the ship was managed by Upper Lakes, and they purchased the *Canadian Hunter* in 1979. It operates today as part of the ULS fleet.[25]

STR. LAKE WINNIPEG

1961 to December 7, 1962

The seventh 730 to join the Canadian fleet was another former T2 tanker. Launched at Portland, Oregon, on November 28, 1943, as the *Table Rock*, the ship had been operating since 1948 as the *Nivose*, owned by Compagnie Nationale De Navigation of Rouen, France. In 1961 it was acquired by Nipigon Transport, a Canadian shipping subsidiary of National Steel, and converted at Blythswood Ship Building in Glasgow, Scotland. Like the *Red Wing*, her entire hull forward of the stern cabins was scrapped and replaced during the conversion. Christened the *Lake Winnipeg* by her new owners, the ship crossed the Atlantic and arrived at Quebec City for formal dedication ceremonies on September 1, 1962. She went into service under management of Carryore, another Canadian subsidiary of National Steel. After she sat idle for several years during the early 1980s, the decision was made to scrap the ship. Again she crossed the Atlantic, this time under tow, en route to Lisbon, Spain, for scrapping. The *Lake Winnipeg* arrived there on May 19, 1985, and shipbreakers went to work on her shortly after that.[26]

STR. BLACK BAY

September 20, 1962 to December 7, 1962

On September 20, 1962, the eighth of the Canadian 730s was launched at Collingwood Shipyard. Christened the *Black Bay*, the new freighter was owned by Canadian General Electric and operated by Canada Steamship Lines. When she went into service on the lakes during the 1963 season, the *Black Bay* quickly set two new cargo records. The first was for carrying 24,457 gross tons of iron ore through the Seaway, the largest load ever to move through that system. She set the second cargo record by carrying 1,383,922 bushels of oats in a single load.[27] In 1976, ownership of the *Black Bay* was transferred from Canadian G.E. to Power Corporation of Canada, but CSL continued to operate the ship. The vessel's cabins were rebuilt in 1978 after they were destroyed by fire during the previous winter lay-up period. Damage was set at $1 million. While its cargo records have long since fallen to other, larger ships, the *Black Bay* is still one of the workhorses of the CSL fleet.[28]

STR. BAIE ST. PAUL

November 30, 1962 to December 7, 1962

The steamer *Baie St. Paul* was the ninth 730 to join the Canadian fleet and the last of the class to have any claim to honors as a Queen of the Lakes. It was launched at Davie Ship Building in Lauzon, Quebec, on November 30, 1962, for Canada Steamship Lines, which still operates the vessel today.[29] Before the *Baie St. Paul* went into service during the 1963 shipping season, however, the title as Queen of the Lakes had passed from that first batch of 730s to a slightly longer ship.

Notes

1. For the sake of brevity, the complete dimensions for the balance of the ships in the first group of 730s will not be given. Their overall lengths were 730 feet and their beams and depths were similar to those of the *Murray Bay* and *Homer*.
2. Gary Dewar, "Part II: Changes in the Post-War Fleet," Inland Seas 45, no. 3 (Fall 1989): 173.
3. Ibid., 173.
4. Ibid., 176.
5. Ibid., 173.
6. Ibid., 176.
7. The vessel was originally launched as the *Fred G. Hartwell* in 1923 for the Franklin Steamship Company of Duluth. It was a sister to the *Col. James M. Schoonmaker* and *William P. Snyder Jr.* that had been built in 1911 and 1912 for Shenango Furnace.
8. In sheer numbers, the 730s rival the standard 600-footers built earlier in the century. The combined carrying capacities of the 730s is about double that of the 600-footers, however.
9. Ship Biography, Institute for Great Lakes Research, Bowling Green State University.
10. Ibid.
11. John O. Greenwood, *Namesakes of the Lakes* (Cleveland: Freshwater Press, 1970), 205.

12. The other surviving U.S. straight-deckers are Interlake's *J. L. Mauthe* and Kinsman's *Kinsman Enterprise* and *Kinsman Independent*. They are devoted almost exclusively to carrying grain from elevators in Duluth and Superior to terminals at Buffalo, New York.
13. The others were Interlake's *Charles M. Schwab*, the *Walter A. Sterling* of the Cleveland-Cliffs fleet, and Columbia's *Middletown*. The *Schwab* has since been scrapped, but the other two vessels are still operating. The *Sterling*, a converted saltwater tanker, has changed ownership several times since being brought into the lakes in 1961. Today she operates as the *Lee A. Tregurtha* in the Interlake Steamship fleet.
14. Richard Wright, *Freshwater Whales* (Kent, OH: Kent State University Press, 1969), 246.
15. Ship Biography.
16. Howard W. Serig, "Navy Oiler Finds Second Life in the Great Lakes," *Inland Seas* 47, no. 1 (Spring 1991): 36–40, reprint from *Navy Times*.
17. Ship Biography.
18. The 1953-built *William Clay Ford* had the dubious distinction of being the first of the AAA-class boats to be scrapped. While newer than the *Sterling*, the Ford flagship was a straight-decker.
19. Ship Biography.
20. Greenwood, 405.
21. Hall Corporation President Frank Augsbury, Jr., and his wife and children were aboard the ship at the time and managed to reach safety. Ironically, the ship had been named for Hall's wife Lee.
22. Rev. Peter van der Linden, *Great Lakes Ships We Remember* (Cleveland: Freshwater Press, 1979), 250.
23. *Telescope* 14, no. 3 (March 1965), 67.
24. Ship Biography.
25. Ibid.
26. Ibid.
27. Greenwood, 50.
28. Ship Biography.
29. Ibid.

28

Queen by Inches

Before CSL's *Baie St. Paul* had a chance to go into service as one of the thirteen 730s that shared honors as Queen of the Lakes during the 1962 season,[1] the distinction of being the longest ship on the lakes shifted to a vessel launched at Lauzon just eight days after the *Baie St. Paul.* The *Frankcliffe Hall* is always referred to as a 730, but she is actually two inches longer than that. A trifling amount, to be sure, but enough for her to wrest the Queen of the Lakes title from the *Baie St. Paul* and the other pure 730s.

STR. FRANKCLIFFE HALL

730'2"x75'2"x35'7"
Queen of the Lakes
December 7, 1962 to April 14, 1965

Frankcliffe Hall was launched at the Davie shipyard on December 7, 1962, for the account of the Hall Corporation. Although marginally longer than the original batch of 730s, the ship set no new cargo records. Like most freighters on the Great Lakes, she has operated in relative obscurity throughout her career. The little notoriety the *Frankcliffe Hall* has received came as the result of several relatively minor casualties the vessel was involved in.

Two years after the *Leecliffe Hall* collided with a Greek freighter and sank in the St. Lawrence River, officials in the Hall fleet's offices received a start when they learned that the *Frankcliffe Hall* had also been involved in a collision near Montreal. The July 13, 1966, collision between the Hall freighter and the British-flag *Gloxinia* during a heavy rainstorm was minor, however, and neither ship was seriously damaged. A more serious casualty occurred on June 6, 1967, when the ship ran hard aground off Thunder Cape on Lake Superior while operating in heavy fog. Because she was heavily laden with 800,000 bushels of wheat at the time, it took salvors four days to pull the ship free. Fortunately, the *Frankcliffe Hall* suffered only relatively minor damage as a result of the grounding.

After operating as part of the Canadian straight-decker fleet for seventeen years, the ship was converted to a self-unloader and strengthened for ice operations at Port Arthur Ship Building during the winter of 1979-80.[2] When the new self-unloader returned to service at the start of the 1980 shipping season on the lakes, the *Frankcliffe Hall* joined a fleet that had changed markedly in the eighteen seasons that had passed since she was launched. In fact, the Hall freighter's conversion to a self-unloader reflected one of those changes.

By 1980, half of the ships in the U.S. fleet on the Great Lakes and one-quarter of the Canadian vessels were self-unloaders. Much larger percentages of the U.S. and Canadian ships actually in operation that year were self-unloaders. After reaching record levels during the 1979 season, tonnages shipped on the lakes fell off by over 33 million tons in 1980, as the industry plummeted into a severe and prolonged recession. The economic conditions that descended on the industry forced shipowners to put only their most efficient vessels into operation. For most fleets, that meant putting self-unloaders into service, while straight-deckers remained idle.

The stack of the *Frankcliffe Hall* is slightly taller than those on most U.S. freighters built during the same period. The black Halco stacks feature an inverted white chevron topped by a white "H." (Author's collection)

Although the U.S. and Canadian grain trade is still dominated by straight-deckers, by the time economic conditions on the lakes began to turn around in 1987, iron ore, coal, and stone were being hauled almost exclusively by self-unloaders. The shift to reliance on the efficient self-unloaders was most pronounced on the U.S. side of the industry. Since 1987, the

Halco's *Frankcliffe Hall* at National Steel's mill on Zug Island in the Detroit River, in 1987. The Hall freighter is two inches longer than the 730s that preceded her, possibly a result of her builders having used the metric system when designing the ship. During the winter of 1979–80, the *Frankcliffe Hall* was converted to a self-unloader and strengthened for ice operations. (Captain Sam Buchanan, J. W. Westcott Co.)

only U.S. straight-decker regularly engaged in carrying iron ore, coal, or stone is Inland's *Edward L. Ryerson.* The last straight-deckers added to the U.S. fleet were the *Carnahan, Falk, Sterling,* and *Middletown,* the four T2 tankers converted for use on the lakes in 1961. In 1978, the *Sterling* was converted to a self-unloader, followed in 1982 by the *Middletown.* Both survived the shipping recession of the 1980s. The *Carnahan* and *Falk,* on the other hand, remained as straight-deckers and were scrapped in the mid-1980s. The *Sterling* and *Middletown* were among seventeen U.S. ships converted from straight-deckers to self-unloaders during the 1970s and 1980s. Included were six of the eight AAA- class boats built during the Korean War. In addition, the twenty-seven new ships added by U.S. owners during the same period were all self-unloaders. On the U.S. side of the lakes today, the classic Great Lakes straight-decker is a vanishing breed.

In addition to shifting to self-unloaders, shipowners eager to increase the efficiency of their ships had also adopted several other design innovations. In 1961, Columbia's *J. R. Sensibar* and American Steamship's *J. F. Schoellkopf* were the first vessels on the lakes to be fitted with bow thrusters. The thruster is a propeller mounted transversely in a tunnel at the bow of the ship, below the waterline. In the same way that the ship's regular propeller drives it forward or backward, the thruster can be used to move the bow of the ship to the left or right.

The first record of attempts to develop thrusters dates to 1844. At that time, the *Storckton Collier,* a British vessel, was equipped with a thruster propeller mounted transversely in its stern skeg. Power to the rudimentary thruster was supplied by ten crewmen manning winches inside the hull of the ship. By cranking furiously at the winches, they were able to turn the ship around in four minutes and twenty-five seconds. While many patents had been issued for various types of thrusters over the years, the first modern thrusters weren't developed until the 1950s. By the early 1960s, the major manufacturers of thrusters had all targeted the Great Lakes as a prime market for their systems.

Since the earliest days of commerce on the lakes, vessel captains have had to maneuver their ships in and out of confined harbors and up and down narrow and winding rivers. Very often, they had to rely on assistance from tugs to help them negotiate the rivers and harbors. It was a common sight around the lakes to see tugs towing a freighter up or down the narrow confines of the Cuyahoga River at Cleveland, the Rouge River at Detroit, or the Calumet River outside Chicago. But "taking tugs" was expensive. Thruster manufacturers convinced fleets like Columbia and American that installing thrusters on their ships would actually save them money over the long term by greatly reducing their need to rely on assistance from tugs. The fleets decided to try the thrusters, despite outspoken opposition from most of their captains. The captains, who personally conned their ships when in maneuvering situations, preferred to follow the long-established practice of hiring tugs. In spite of the objections of the captains, Columbia and American pressed forward with their plans to try thrusters.

The first sea trials of a thruster-equipped ship were conducted aboard Columbia's *Sensibar* in 1961. The vessel was under the command of a young captain by the name of Ernest McSorley that season.[3] When the *Sensibar* left the American Ship Building yard in South Chicago after having the thruster installed, McSorley found that the new equipment greatly increased the ship's maneuverability at low speeds. The thruster was found to work best at speeds of less than three miles an hour. It was virtually ineffective if the vessel was moving at more than five miles an hour. Gradually, fleets on the lakes began to install thrusters on their ships. In 1965, thirty-six vessels had been equipped with bow thrusters, but by the end of the 1970s they were in almost universal usage. At the same time, tug business on the lakes declined in direct proportion to the number of ships equipped with thrusters.

Another design innovation that emerged on the lakes at about the same time the *Frankcliffe Hall* came out were the stern-enders, freighters with their pilothouses and all accommodations at their stern. Stern-enders became common in the ocean trades during the 1950s, rapidly replacing the three-island ships that had been used previously. People on the lakes weren't totally unfamiliar with stern-enders. A number of them had been built on the lakes over the years, but they had never caught on and were generally regarded as oddities.

There are a couple of possible explanations for why lakes sailors preferred to stick with the standard design that dated back to the *Hackett*: pilothouse and deck department accommodations forward, engine room and engine department accommodations aft.[4] The explanation heard most often is that having the pilothouse at the bow helped captains when they were docking or maneuvering their ships. If he were far forward on the ship, the captain had a better view of how far off a dock his ship was, and he could better gauge if the ship was closing at the appropriate speed.

An alternative explanation is that deck personnel simply didn't want to have to live with engine personnel! As a rule, people in the deck department don't have much use for people in the engine department, and vice versa. On traditional lakers, the two groups didn't come in contact with each other too often. In fact, they only had to mingle at mealtimes. During the rest of the day, people in the deck department stayed forward and engine room personnel stayed aft. It could easily be argued that the hostility that developed between the two departments is largely the result of their being segregated by the design of the ships they served on. Nevertheless, many sailors on the Great Lakes would not have looked favorably on a ship design that would force deck and engine personnel to share the same living spaces. And since many officials in the fleet offices were former sailors, it is reasonable to assume that they would have shared the same bias. Their feelings might not have been openly expressed, but they could easily have influenced decisions about ship designs.

Despite the arguments in favor of sticking with the traditional pilothouse forward design, Misener Shipping of Canada placed an order for a stern-ender in 1961. The decision may have been influenced by the fact that the new ship was built at the Verolme Shipyard in Cork, Ireland, a yard with extensive experience in building stern-enders for ocean trades. They would undoubtedly have discussed with Misener officials the economic savings that could be generated by putting the pilothouse and all accommodations aft over the engine room. That would eliminate the need to run miles of electrical cable and many hundreds of feet of piping for heating, water, and sewage between the two ends of the ship. With no forward cabin to impede it, the cargo hold could also be extended a little farther forward, increasing the ship's carrying capacity and profits.

The new Misener freighter first went into the water at Cork on November 23, 1962, and was christened the *Silver Isle* to commemorate the ship's Irish heritage. It crossed the Atlantic in the spring of the following year and arrived at Seven Island, Quebec, for formal commissioning ceremonies on May 8, 1963. Shortly after, the 730-foot ship departed on its first voyage into the lakes. While ships on their maiden voyages are generally accorded whistle salutes by passing freighters, the *Silver Isle* was often greeted only by cold stares from crewmembers aboard traditional lakers. As if to lend credence to the argument that stern-enders were not well-suited to conditions on the lakes, the *Silver Isle* was involved in a minor mishap on the return leg of that first voyage. On June 9, while running in a rain squall, the new freighter collided with the Dutch motorship *Prin Alexander* near Carleton Island in the St. Lawrence. Neither ship sustained serious damage, but the fact that both of the vessels were stern-enders did not go unnoticed by sailors on traditional lakers.[5]

Despite objections, the stern-enders gained a foothold on the lakes. In 1973, the first stern-ender on the U.S. side of the lakes was launched. Built at American Ship Building in Lorain, Ohio, the 630-foot *William R. Roesch* joined the Kinsman Marine fleet. The Kinsman fleet and American Ship Building were then both owned by George Steinbrenner, who also owned the New York Yankees baseball team. The *Roesch* and a sister ship, the *Paul Thayer*, were river-class freighters designed specifically to operate on the Cuyahoga River at Cleveland. The choice of the stern-ender design for the two ships was clearly one of economics, always a factor of paramount interest to the tight-fisted Steinbrenner.

The successes of the *Silver Isle*, *Roesch*, and *Thayer* paved the way for acceptance of the stern-ender design by shipowners on the Great Lakes. All of the ships launched after 1973 have their pilothouses and all accommodations on their sterns. After more than a century, the Great Lakes shipping industry scuttled the design pioneered in 1869 by Eli Peck and his *R. J. Hackett*. While many traditional lakers like the *Frankcliffe Hall* still operate on the lakes today, they are the last of a line. When they reach the ends of their useful lives and their owners send them off to the shipbreakers, the ships that replace them will be stern-enders.[6]

Notes

1. The *Leecliffe Hall*, one of the thirteen 730s that shared Queen of the Lakes honors, had sunk in 1964.
2. Ship Biography, Institute for Great Lakes Research, Bowling Green State University.
3. Later in his career, McSorley was captain of the *Edmund Fitzgerald* when it sank in 1975.
4. Additionally, sailors on the lakes are simply slow to accept change.
5. Ship Biography.
6. The *Frankcliffe Hall* was renamed the *Halifax* in 1988.

29

One Era Ends, Another Begins

In 1965, Hall Corporation officials gathered at the Davie shipyard in Lauzon, Quebec, for the launching of a 730-class freighter that was two inches longer than their *Frankcliffe Hall.* Christened the *Lawrencecliffe Hall,* the new $8 million ship was then the longest vessel on the Great Lakes. Its launching marked the most significant watershed in the long history of steel ships that have been Queen of the Lakes. First, the *Frankcliffe Hall* was diesel-powered; every previous Queen of the Lakes had been driven by steam engines. Second, while those gathered at Lauzon for the ceremonies could not have known, the new Hall freighter would also be the last straight-decker to claim the honor of being the Queen of the Lakes.

M/V LAWRENCECLIFFE HALL[1]

730'4"x75'x39'2"
Queen of the Lakes
April 14, 1965 to April 1, 1972

The "Lawrence" in the ship's name honored the St. Lawrence River, a waterway that was of immense importance to the Hall Corporation and the other Canadian fleets. The "cliffe" suffix in the vessel's first name followed a naming scheme established previously for bulk freighters in the Hall fleet. Use of the unusual suffix had originated with Albert Hutchinson, who had been president and chairman of the board of the shipping company in the 1940s and 1950s. Hutchinson was a native of Ayecliffe, in the craggy northeastern region of England. Many communities in that area had names ending in -cliffe, and Hutchinson decided to attach the suffix to the names of ships in the Hall fleet.[2]

The revelry surrounding the launching of the new ship provided a badly-needed break for Hall officials, who were still mired in the legal quagmire resulting from the loss the previous September of the *Leecliffe Hall.* They hoped that the launching of the *Lawrencecliffe Hall* would mark a turning point for them. Perhaps they would now be able to devote their efforts to the future of their fleet, instead of being mired in the past.

The positive atmosphere pervading the Hall Corporation offices in the days after the launching of the new freighter was rocked on November 16, 1965, when they received the shocking news that the *Lawrencecliffe Hall* had been seriously damaged in a collision in the St. Lawrence. Off the Ile de'Orléans, fourteen miles downstream from Quebec City, the freighter had collided with an approaching saltwater ship when both vessels had strayed into the middle of the narrow channel. The *Lawrencecliffe Hall* was struck on her starboard side by the bow of the *Sunek,* ripping a long gash from bow to midships below the waterline. Aware that their ship had received a fatal injury, the crew of the *Lawrencecliffe Hall* attempted to beach the big freighter. They managed to ground the ship in shallow water, but the rising tide lifted her, and she floated away from the shore and began to sink. Her crew abandoned ship and watched helplessly as the seven-month-old freighter settled to the bottom on its starboard side in thirty feet of water. The *Sunek*, with her bow crumbled and both anchors torn away, returned to Quebec under her own power.[3]

After a careful survey of the sunken hull, Hall executives decided to attempt to refloat the ship. The complex salvage effort involved divers putting a temporary patch on the long tear in the starboard side of the *Leecliffe Hall*. Because the ship was lying on its starboard side, the divers had to rig the patch from inside the hull. Working inside the hull of a sunken ship is always a dangerous undertaking, but salvage efforts on the Hall freighter were simplified by the fact that the ship was in relatively shallow water.

Once the patch was successfully rigged, twenty-seven electric submersible pumps were placed within the hull, and salvors began pumping water out of the sunken ship. After thousands of tons of water had been removed from the hull, the ship began to rise slowly out of the mud at the bottom of the St. Lawrence. A flotilla of tugs attached lines to the ship as it began to float clear of the bottom and managed to pull it into an upright position so that the deck of the *Lawrencecliffe Hall* was once again high and dry.

Stout hawsers were rigged from the wallowing hull to the

After unloading her cargo, the *Lawrencecliffe Hall* heads back up the lakes. As is the case with most ships in the Canadian fleet, the builders of the Hall freighter maximized her cubic capacity so that she could operate efficiently in the important grain trade between Lake Superior and elevators along the St. Lawrence Seaway. (Institute for Great Lakes Research, Bowling Green State University)

The sunken hull of the *Lawrencecliffe Hall* being raised from the bottom of the St. Lawrence River. Launched in April of 1965, the Hall freighter sank on November 16 of that same year after being holed in a collision with a saltwater ship near Quebec City. Crews worked furiously to raise the Queen of the Lakes before the worsening winter weather made salvage impossible. Towed to a shipyard at nearby Lauzon, Quebec, the *Lawrencecliffe Hall* underwent extensive repairs before returning to service the following August. (Author's collection)

six tugs which would tow it the fifteen miles to the shipyard at Lauzon. By the time the tugs were ready to take the *Lawrencecliffe Hall* in tow, night had desccended on the St. Lawrence. Many of those involved in the salvage effort argued that they should wait until daylight to begin the tricky operation of moving the crippled freighter. Weather conditions were deteriorating, however, and the risks associated with attempting to maneuver the wrecked ship to the safety of the shipyard at Lauzon in darkness were outweighed by fear that the temporary patch might not hold if the ship was caught in a storm. With a powerful Canadian icebreaker in the lead, the flotilla of tugs began to move toward Lauzon. In retrospect, the decision proved to be a sound one. By the time storm clouds swept over the St. Lawrence, the *Lawrencecliffe Hall* had been safely drydocked at the Davie shipyard. By August of the 1966 shipping season, the necessary repairs had been made. Engineers once again lit off the *Lawrencecliffe Hall*'s diesels, and the Queen of the Lakes returned to its rightful place in the Great Lakes fleet.[4]

While the *Lawrencecliffe Hall* was the first diesel-powered Queen of the Lakes, there were already a number of motor vessels in the U.S. and Canadian fleets when the Hall freighter first took to the water at Lauzon. The first diesel ship on the lakes was the *Toiler*, a 250-foot canaller built for James Playfair's fleet in 1910 at Newcastle, England, and brought into the lakes. While little is known about the *Toiler*'s rudimentary 400-horsepower engine, there is evidence to suggest that the experiment with diesel propulsion was not totally satisfactory. In 1914 the canaller's diesel was replaced with a more conventional steam plant.[5]

The first large ships on the lakes with diesel engines were the *Henry Ford II* and *Benson Ford*. The *Henry Ford II*, often referred to simply as the *Henry*, was the first freighter built for the Ford fleet, and its gala launching at the Lorain yard of American Ship Building in the summer of 1924 marked the giant automaker's entry into the Great Lakes shipping business. The first ship in the Ford fleet was powered by a 3,000-horsepower diesel engine, a reflection of Henry Ford's bias in favor of internal combustion engines. The second Ford freighter, the *Benson Ford*, was launched shortly after the *Henry* at Great Lakes Engineering Works on the Rouge River, within sight of the sprawling Ford steel mill and auto factory at Dearborn, Michigan. Both of the new ships were named for grandsons of Henry Ford, and the young boys played major roles in the launching festivities. There were only a handful of ships in the Great Lakes industry at that time larger than the 611-foot *Henry* and the 612-foot *Benson*. And by the standards of that era, their diesel engines were the most powerful propulsion systems in use. For example, the 625-foot *W. Grant Morden*, then the Queen of the Lakes, was driven by a more-conventional triple-expansion steam engine of only 2,000 horsepower. Even the most powerful steam engines in use in 1924 achieved a maximum of only about 2,600 horsepower. The landmark Ford motorships joined an industry that was at that time made up of 1,320 steamers and 75 sailing ships.[6]

Despite the success of the two Ford freighters, diesel engines didn't come into widespread use on the lakes until the 1960s. The shift from the use of steam turbines to diesel engines began north of the border with ships such as the *Lawrencecliffe Hall* that came out when the Canadian industry was retooling after the opening of the St. Lawrence Seaway. After the launching of the steamer *Edward L. Ryerson* in 1960, U.S. shipowners didn't build any new vessels until after the opening of the new Poe Lock at Sault Ste. Marie in 1971. All U.S. ships built since then, however, have been diesel-powered.

Not only was the *Lawrencecliffe Hall* the first Queen of the Lakes with a diesel engine. It also went into the record books as the last straight-decker to hold that title. All of the ships that have followed the Hall freighter as Queen of the Lakes have been self-unloaders. While the *Lawrencecliffe Hall* operates yet today as a classic straight-decker, it is part of an industry that relies almost totally on self-unloading ships in the iron ore, coal, and stone trades. Ships like the *Lawrencecliffe Hall* are now found almost solely in the grain trade, because most self-unloading systems are not well-suited to handling grain.

Iron ore, stone, and coal are the meat and potatoes of the U.S. shipping companies. Straight-deckers can no longer compete in those trades on the American side of the lakes. The need to operate and maintain shoreside unloading systems to service the straight-deckers proved to be too inefficient. Even more significantly, most of the ore, coal, and stone unloading ports at which today's ships call no longer have shoreside unloading systems. The Huletts and bridge cranes are either gone or have fallen into such disrepair that it would be too costly to put them back into service.

The situation is very different on the Canadian side of the lakes. The highly profitable grain trade is critical to most Canadian shipowners. While most U.S. grain is moved by railroads, or by barges operating on the Mississippi River, a relatively large percentage of Canadian grain is still shipped aboard lake freighters. From terminals in Duluth, Superior, and Thunder Bay, Canadian ships carry the grain to a score of elevators located along the St. Lawrence River in the provinces of Ontario and Quebec. The trade is made even more lucrative by the fact that many of the ships carrying grain out the Seaway return to the lakes with backhaul loads of iron ore mined in eastern Canada. While most Canadian coal and stone unloading docks are served by self-unloaders, shoreside unloading systems have been preserved at the largest of the Canadian steel mills,[7] which can still be served by straight-deckers.

Between 1972 and 1991, a total of thirty-two new ships were added to the Canadian fleet. Of those, fifteen were straight-deckers. That figure reflects the continuing importance of the grain trade to Canadian shipowners. At the same time, however, seventeen of the new ships, including the *Lawrencecliffe Hall*, were self-unloaders. Another five former straight-deckers were converted to self-unloaders during the same time frame. As the Canadian shipping industry sailed into the decade of the 1990s, a record forty-four percent of the fleet was made up of self-unloaders. In 1967, they had accounted for only seventeen percent.

It is obvious that under the influence of the compelling grain trade, straight-deckers will continue to play an important role in the Canadian fleet over the next several decades. At the same time, however, the tide is clearly turning. A growing number of Canadian self-unloaders are capable of carrying grain. Most of them are equipped with bucket-type elevator systems, as opposed to the more common loop belt elevators that cannot readily be used to unload grain. The biggest impediment to the use of self-unloaders in the grain trade today is the inability of most terminals to handle grain discharged by them. We can expect to see more Canadian grain-unloading ports installing the equipment necessary to handle self-unloaders, although such a trend is likely to generate strong opposition from the unions representing scoopers at the terminals who now unload the straight-deckers.

They will be battling some hard economic realities. A shift to the use of self-unloading ships in the grain trade will significantly increase the versatility of the Canadian fleets. When they're not hauling grain, the vessels will be more competitive in the ore, stone, and coal trades. At the same time, it is likely that using self-unloaders will produce significant savings for grain shippers by reducing vessel turnaround time at the unloading ports, eliminating the need to maintain shoreside unloading systems and cutting personnel costs.

The change will be a traumatic one for many of those who are employed by the elevators to unload grain from straight-deckers. Many of their well-paying jobs would be eliminated by a shift to the use of self-unloaders. It will also be a difficult time for fleets that are now operating a large number of straight-deckers in the grain trade. Some may go out of business because they lack the financial resources needed to convert their ships to self-unloaders. Those are the hard economic realities, probably unavoidable realities, of a switch to the use of self-unloaders in the grain trade. But the economies that would result from the reliance on self-unloaders in the grain trade can be expected to steadily push the industry in that direction. Even on the Canadian side of the lakes, the straight-decker seems to be facing eventual extinction.

Notes

1. The abbreviation M/V denotes "motor vessel," the terminology used to identify a diesel-powered ship. Throughout the world maritime community, the designation M/S, for "motor ship," is also used, though the industry on the Great Lakes has shown a preference for M/V.
2. Tankers in the Hall fleet followed a different naming scheme. All of the tankers have two names, the second of which is always "transport." The fleet included the *Bay Transport*, *Cape Transport*, and *Fuel Transport*, among others.
3. *Telescope* 14, no. 12 (December 1965): 281.
4. *Telescope* 15, no. 4 (April 1966): 94.
5. *Telescope* 13, no. 7 (July 1964): 12.
6. Ernest S. Clowes, *Shipways to the Seas* (Baltimore: Williams and Wilkins, 1929), 69.
7. The massive Stelco mill of the Steel Company of Canada, located in Hamilton, Ontario.

30

The Footers

In an article appearing in the May 5, 1898, edition of *Marine Review*, the author predicted what the Great Lakes shipping industry would be like in 1940: "What a change is here! Most of the fleet are 1,000-footers, some of them 100 feet wide and 50 feet deep."[1] Readers of the popular marine journal must have been astonished by the flamboyant prediction. At that time, the largest ship on the Great Lakes was the 450-foot-long by 50-foot wide *Superior City*, which had been launched less than a month before the article appeared. We can only speculate at how people in the industry would have reacted to the article, but it is safe to assume they might have questioned the author's sanity. They most certainly would have scoffed at his extravagant predictions. People in the Great Lakes shipping industry have generally not been regarded as a far-sighted lot. Most predictions they have made about the future of their industry have subsequently proven inaccurate.

Even by 1898, it was clear to most realists in the industry that historically there had been few real insights about the direction of shipping on the lakes. At the time, there were many so-called "experts" who claimed that the then-current generation of 450-foot ships would be the largest ever built on the lakes. And along comes some writer who prophesies an industry dominated by 1,000-foot leviathans!

By the time the 1940 shipping season rolled around, it's unlikely that many people remembered the article. If any did, they might have taken some satisfaction from pointing out that the largest ship on the lakes was then the 640-foot *Carl D. Bradley*. The prognosticator of 1898 had been way off base! In fact, if a similar prediction had been made in 1940—that there would be 1,000-foot freighters on the lakes in, say, 1980—that, too, would have been ridiculed. Few could envision that ships would ever reach the 1,000-foot mark. With the benefit of hindsight, however, we know that there was an uncanny accuracy to the predictions made by the writer in 1898. He got the outcome right, but erred on the time frame. He was off by about thirty years. The industry's first 1,000-foot ship wasn't launched until 1972. Today, they're a common sight on the lakes.

The debut of the first of the thousand-footers is rooted in the construction of a new lock on the St. Marys River at Sault Ste. Marie, Michigan. The first funds to study the possibility of building that lock were appropriated by Congress in 1958. At that time there were four locks at the Soo, the largest of which was the MacArthur. The MacArthur Lock had opened to vessel traffic early in World War II. It was 800 feet long, 80 feet wide, and had 30 feet of water over its sills. The Poe Lock of 1896 was 800 feet long and 100 feet wide, but it provided only 18 feet of water over its sills. Too shallow to accommodate most of the ships that were in operation on the lakes by the 1950s, the Poe was no longer being used. The other two locks, the Davis and Sabin, were twins. Opened to traffic in 1914 and 1919, respectively, they were both 1,350 feet long, 80 feet wide and had 24.5 feet of water over their sills. They were an improvement over the Poe Lock, to be sure, but many of the newest ships on the lakes had drafts exceeding the depth limits of the Davis and Sabin locks. Because of the shallowness of these passages, more than half of the ships then in operation could use only the MacArthur Lock.[2]

The growth in the size of ships on the lakes had already exceeded the design limits established when the MacArthur Lock had been built. It was originally intended to handle only ships of up to 660 feet in length. The longest ship in operation at the time the lock was designed was the 640-foot *Bradley*. By 1958, however, there were a number of ships longer than 660 feet. The new giant freighters would fit into the 800-foot lock, but not with the two safety booms in place.

The safety booms are designed to prevent a ship from crashing into and damaging the vital gates at each end of the locks. Before a ship enters the locks, a boom is lowered ahead of the forward lock gate so that if the ship cannot be stopped it will strike the boom and not the gate. Once the ship is stopped in the lock, a second boom is lowered behind it, so that the ship can't drift backward and hit the after gate.

To handle a ship of more than 660 feet in length, the vessel would be brought about halfway into the "Mac" under its own power with the safety booms up. The ship would then be stopped and secured by four steel mooring cables, two forward and two aft. Then the ship's mooring winches would be used to slowly inch the vessel ahead until the after lock gate could be closed. By following this procedure, ships of up to 730 feet long could be squeezed through the MacArthur Lock. By 1965, fifty-two ships exceeded the original 660-foot limits of the Mac and had to be locked through using the special procedure.[3]

By that time, work on a new, larger lock was already well-underway at the Soo. In 1960, the first contracts had been awarded for work on a new Poe Lock. The original plans were to build a lock that was 1,000 feet long, 100 feet wide, and with 32 feet of water over the sills. Work began on the lock in February of 1961—on the site of the 1896 Poe Lock—but the Corps of Engineers went back to the drawing boards the following year and made some changes to the previously adopted plans. At the urging of the Lake Carriers' Association, the Corps enlarged the new lock to 1,200 feet long and 110 feet wide.[4] Construction was completed in the summer of 1968, and after two months of testing, the 647-foot, AAA-class *Philip R. Clarke* made the first transit of the new lock in October.[5] By the time the new Poe Lock opened, construction had already begun at Erie, Pennsylvania, on a mammoth vessel that would revolutionize the shipping industry on the Great Lakes.

Construction of the new Poe Lock was only one of several factors that converged to set the stage for building the first of a new generation of super-carriers on the lakes. The shrinking of the U.S. fleet on the lakes, combined with steady increases in iron ore shipments, also played a role in the decision to build the big freighter. In 1950, there had been 266 U.S. ships that could operate in the iron ore trade, with a combined single-trip carrying capacity of 2.75 million gross tons. By 1965, the number had dropped to 160 vessels, with a carrying capacity of only 2.25 million gross tons.[6] No new ships had been added since the 1960 launching of the *Edward L. Ryerson* and the conversions of a number of former saltwater vessels brought into the lakes in 1962. The number of U.S. ships decreased a little each year, as aging freighters were disposed of by their owners.

At the same time, after dropping precipitously in the late 1950s, tonnages shipped on the lakes showed steady increases, beginning in 1961. Iron ore, representing the largest volume of cargo moved in the Great Lakes system, had shown dramatic rises. From a low of only 51 million tons during the 1959 season, shipments had increased to more than 78 million tons in 1965. A major portion of that expansion was attributable to steady growth in the shipments of pelletized iron ore, known as taconite.

Marble-sized taconite pellets had been developed in the early 1950s as a response to a widespread deterioration in the quality of iron ore being mined on the ranges in Michigan, Minnesota, and Wisconsin. In the pelletizing operation, low-grade ores are crushed, and iron is removed magnetically, or through a flotation process. The iron is then rolled into marble-sized balls and hardened by heating. The resulting pellets contain up to sixty-three percent iron. The first taconite pellets were shipped from the Davis Works of Reserve Mining at Silver Bay, Minnesota, on April 8, 1956, aboard the steamer *J. A. Campbell*.[7] Other pelletizing plants soon went into operation in Minnesota and Michigan. Steel mills around the lakes rapidly modified their operations to use the taconite pellets, which were far superior to the low-grade red ore they had grown used to. By 1965, about one-third of the iron ore moving down the lakes was taconite, and that percentage was expected to increase steadily in future years. Experts had predicted that total ore shipments would reach 97 million gross tons by 1990. That total was expected to be made up of 92 million tons of taconite pellets and only 5 million tons of natural ores.[8]

With predictions of steady increases in iron ore shipments, and the size of the U.S. fleet slowly declining, the time was ripe in 1965 to begin planning for the construction of a new generation of ships on the lakes. U.S. Steel was the first shipping company to seize the moment. In 1966, America's largest steelmaker contracted with Marine Consultants and Designers (MC&D) of Cleveland, Ohio, to design a new freighter to take advantage of the new Poe Lock then under construction at Sault Ste. Marie. Based on the recommendations of MC&D personnel, officials at U.S. Steel's Great Lakes Fleet accepted a plan to build a new self-unloader that would be 858 feet long and 105 feet wide, with a carrying capacity of 44,500 tons. The giant freighter was scheduled for launching at American Ship Building's Lorain yard in July of 1971. On June 24, 1971, a fire swept through the stern section of the vessel while it was still being fitted-out. Four shipyard workers died in the blaze, which also seriously damaged the vessel's engines and other machinery. Repairs delayed completion of the U.S. Steel freighter until June 13, 1972.[9] When the diesel-powered *Roger Blough* went into service, it was the largest ship totally built on the Great Lakes, but it was far from being the Queen of the Lakes.

M/V STEWART J. CORT

1,000'x105'x44'9"
Queen of the Lakes
April 1, 1972 to August 7, 1976

Shortly after U.S. Steel approached MC&D to begin design work for the *Blough*, the Cleveland-based firm was also contracted by Litton Industries to develop a ship design for them. Projections for dramatic increases in the amount of iron ore shipped on the lakes had not gone unnoticed by officials in Litton's Los Angeles headquarters. The multinational corporation, perhaps best known as the maker of microwave ovens, saw an opportunity to reap some significant profits by getting involved in the shipping industry on the Great Lakes. In 1966, the company purchased Wilson Marine Transit, an established fleet that operated ten bulk freighters.[10] Shortly after that, Litton announced plans to build a sophisticated automated ship assembly facility at Erie, Pennsylvania. That announcement was followed shortly by word of their decision to retain MC&D to design a ship for them. Litton was descending on the Great Lakes shipping industry in a storm.

The ship being designed by MC&D was not intended for Litton's Wilson fleet. Instead, Litton planned to convince another Great Lakes fleet to order the ship and have it built at their new shipyard in Erie. The staff at MC&D had been instructed to design the new freighter with the ultra-modern Litton yard in mind. They wanted the largest ship possible, within the constraints imposed by the new Poe Lock, the channels of the rivers and harbors the vessel would have to operate in, and the limitations of loading and unloading docks around the lakes.

The builders of the *Stewart J. Cort* abandoned the streamlined stacks that had become popular on the lakes and outfitted the first of the thousand-footers with an almost square stack that matches the boxiness of the ship's hull. The cream-colored stack is topped with a black cap and sports the stylized "I" of the Bethlehem Steel fleet. (Author's collection)

MC&D recommended to Litton the construction of a ship that would be 1,000 feet long, 105 feet wide, and with a depth of 46.5 feet. At maximum draft, the vessel would be capable of carrying 51,500 gross tons of iron ore. With a basic design in hand, Litton approached a number of Great Lakes shipping companies to determine their interest in the planned freighter. In April of 1968, officials at Bethlehem Steel's Great Lakes Steamship Division signed a contract with Litton to have a 1,000-foot vessel built at the Litton shipyard in Erie. At that juncture, MC&D personnel altered the design of the thousand-footer to meet Bethlehem's specific needs. Changes included deepening the hull to forty-nine feet so that the ship could operate at a draft of thirty feet, six inches if the harbors and channels on the Great Lakes were ever dredged to that depth. Actual construction of the ship began in 1968.[11]

Many things about the new Bethlehem freighter were unique, but none moreso than the way in which the vessel was built. The long midbody of the ship, containing the four cargo holds, was built at Litton's new facility at Erie. The bow and stern sections, however, were built several thousand miles away, at Ingalls Nuclear Shipbuilding in Pascagoula, Mississippi. When the bow and stern had been completed, the two ends of the ship were welded together for the long trip around the U.S. coast and down the St. Lawrence Seaway to the Litton shipyard. The odd-looking 184-foot vessel, officially named *Hull 1173*, but nicknamed "Stubby," made the trip under its own power. Because of the size restrictions of locks in the Seaway, the bow and stern sections could be only 75 feet wide, even though the finished ship would have a beam of 105 feet. The bow and stern sections arrived at Erie in June of 1970.[12]

Waiting at the Litton yard in Erie was the long midbody portion of the ship. It had been built on a virtual assembly line at the ultramodern shipyard. Steel fed into the system at one end moved along the assembly line where it was cut, shaped, and welded into panels and frames of specified dimensions by numerically controlled machines. The finished panels—each forty-eight feet long and ninety inches wide—and web frames were then moved to an assembly building to be welded together into subassemblies using state-of-the-art equipment. Each subassembly was made up of three of the panels, with necessary web frames welded into place. When it was finished, each subassembly was lowered onto a special building platen on the floor of the massive Litton drydock where the hull was being built. There the subassemblies were joined together and welded to form a hull module forty-eight feet long. To give welders access to all the seams in the hull plating, the hull modules were built standing on end. When each module had been completed, a hydraulically operated launch platen tipped the 1,000-ton module until it was in an upright position on the graving dock floor and ready to be welded to the growing midbody. Air winches and chain falls were used to move each module into position against the midbody. Proper alignment was accomplished by using a laser theodolite. In that way, all seventeen midbody modules were joined together. After each newly-completed module was attached, the drydock would be flooded and the hull moved forty-eight feet to made ready for attachment of the next module. From start to finish, it took two weeks to build each of the modules.[13]

When the entire midbody had been completed, it was floated out of the drydock. The still-joined bow and stern sections of the vessel were backed into the drydock, followed by the midbody. The bow and stern units were then cut apart,[14] and the bow section was rotated 180 degrees and attached to the end of the midbody. The bow and midbody were then floated out of the drydock, turned around, and floated back in so that the other end of the midbody was adjacent to the stern unit. The stern was then welded to the midbody, and sponsons were added to the bow and stern to bring them out to the full 105-foot width of the midbody.[15] After long months in the construction process, the Bethlehem freighter was finally in one piece. In January of 1971 it was floated out of the drydock, ready for sea trials.

Christened the *Stewart J. Cort* in honor of the former vice president and director of Bethlehem Steel who had died in 1958, the immense freighter looks much like a classic Great Lakes straight-decker—with a serious gland problem. It has its pilothouse and cabins forward, with a second set of cabins over the engine room at the stern and an unbroken expanse of deck in between. But in the case of the *Cort*, its looks are deceiving. All crew accommodations aboard the *Cort*, including the galley and dining rooms, are located in the forward cabin. It is the only ship on the lakes with such an arrangement. The large superstructure over the engine room at the stern does not contain cabins for crewmembers, as would be the case on a traditional laker. Instead, it encloses part of the ship's unique self-unloading system.

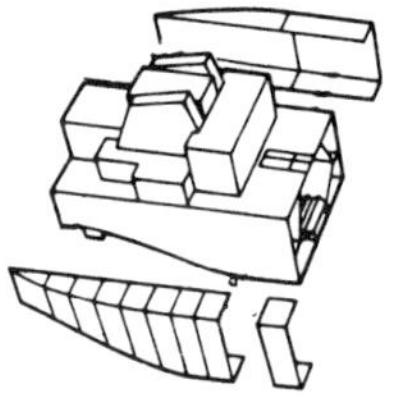
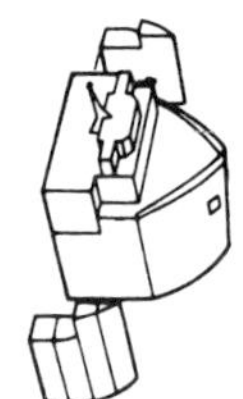

Because the bow and stern sections of the *Cort* were built at a shipyard on the Gulf of Mexico and had to be brought into the lakes by way of the St. Lawrence River, the sections were limited to a maximum beam of seventy-five feet. Sponsons were later added to the bow and stern to fair them out to the 105-foot width of the vessel's midbody. (Author's collection)

At first glance, the *Cort* appears to be a straight-decker. There is no telltale self-unloading boom on deck. Instead of a traditional skeleton-like boom on deck, the *Cort* has a smaller, ninety-nine-foot shuttle conveyor running the width of the hull just above the main deck. The boom can be extended out the side of the ship to a maximum distance of forty feet. It is designed to feed pellets into shoreside hoppers at ports served by the Bethlehem freighter. The enormous superstructure located over the engine room was needed to enclose the vessel's unique rotary elevator. Most self-unloaders on the lakes use bucket or loop belt elevators to raise cargo from the conveyor belt that runs under the cargo hold to the level of the unloading boom. On the *Cort*, however, the cargo is elevated by the rotary elevator, which looks much like a giant waterwheel. The conveyor belt carrying cargo from the ship's holds wraps around the wheel, and cargo is trapped between the belt and compartments around the outside of the wheel. As the rotary elevator turns at about five revolutions a minute, the cargo is carried up to the top of the wheel, where it falls into a hopper that feeds the shuttle boom. No other self-unloader has ever been built with an elevator like the one aboard the *Cort*.

Beneath the cargo hold, a steel-corded rubber conveyor belt ten feet wide carries cargo the length of the hold to the rotary elevator. Cargo flows out of the hold and onto the belt through 105 metered gates which are opened and closed by hydraulic cylinders operated from a central control station located atop the stern superstructure. On other Great Lakes self-unloaders, crewmen in the unloading tunnel below the cargo hold operate the gates during an unload. Until the conveyor belt is carrying the desired load, only a few gates are opened at a time. On the *Cort*, however, the entire operation is handled by a crewman in the central control station, and all 105 gates are opened simultaneously. Six scales spaced out along the length of the conveyor belt measure the amount of cargo falling onto the belt and automatically adjust the gate openings until the desired load is reached. The distinctive unloading system was designed by a subsidiary of Litton. It was intended to unload up to 20,000 tons of cargo per hour, double that of any other self-unloaders, but the system has never achieved that rate of discharge.[16]

In addition to its unique unloading system, the gigantic Bethlehem ship also has a propulsion system unlike that found on any other vessel on the lakes. The *Cort* has two engine rooms, separated by the massive rotary elevator. Each engine room houses two 3,500-horsepower diesel engines, one mounted on each side of a propeller shaft. Each shaft drives a controllable pitch propeller eighteen feet in diameter. The *Cort*'s twin screws can push the ship along at an average speed of about 16.5 miles an hour.[17]

The four main engines also supply power to electric motors that drive two 750-horsepower bow thrusters and two similar stern thrusters. The powerful thrusters are used to move the ship sideways when docking. Most ships on the Great Lakes have bow thrusters, and a few are also equipped with stern thrusters, but the *Cort* is the only vessel to have two of each. Designers of the *Cort* used two thrusters at each end of the ship so that the thruster tunnels could be made small enough to remain submerged when the vessel was not loaded. Use of a single thruster would have required a larger diameter thruster tunnel, which would not have been completely submerged when the ship was light.[18]

The hatches on the *Cort* are also different than those found on other lake freighters. The eighteen hatches down the center of its deck are only about 21 feet, 6 inches long and 11 feet, 6 inches wide. By comparison, most of the 647-foot AAA-class freighters were built with nineteen hatches, and they're each 46 feet long and 11 feet wide. The diminutive hatches on the *Cort* were possible because the ship was designed to load only at docks with conveyor belt loading shuttles that can extend out to the vessel's centerline. In order for the big ship to fit under the loading shuttles, its hatch coamings are only eight inches high, much shorter than on more conventional lakers.

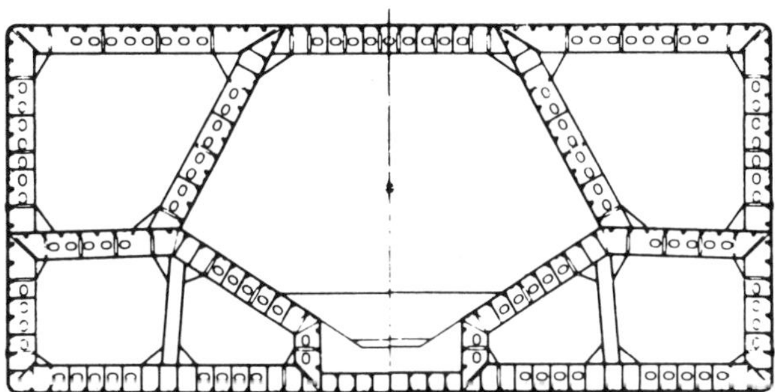

A cross section drawing of the *Stewart J. Cort* shows that the cargo hold takes up only about half of the midbody. Massive ballast tanks, capable of holding almost forty thousand tons of water, are located on each side of the cargo hold just beneath the level of the main deck. Beneath each ballast tank is a void area used primarily for storage and to move between the bow and stern sections of the *Cort*. Directly below the cargo hold is the tunnel housing the ship's self-unloading system. (Author's collection)

This drawing of the bow and stern sections of the *Stewart J. Cort* shows the significant degree to which the landmark freighter resembled the traditional Great Lakes bulk freighters dating back to the 1869 launch of the *R. J. Hackett*. The resemblance is deceiving, however, because the stern superstructure does not contain the galley and crew cabins that would normally be found on a laker. The imposing structure merely encloses the ship's one-of-a-kind, self-unloading system. All crewmembers aboard the *Cort* are housed in the large deckhouse at the bow. (Author's collection)

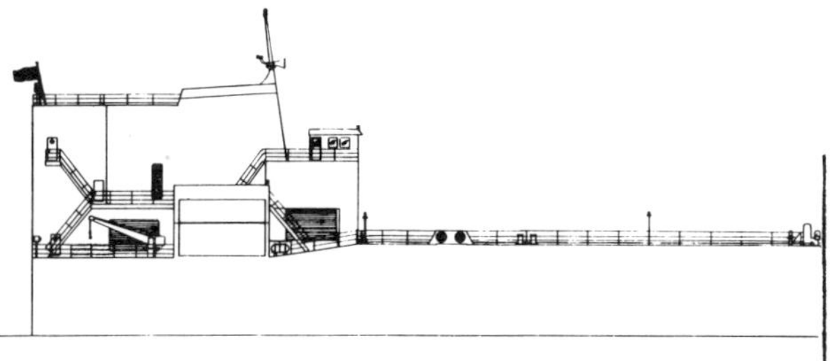

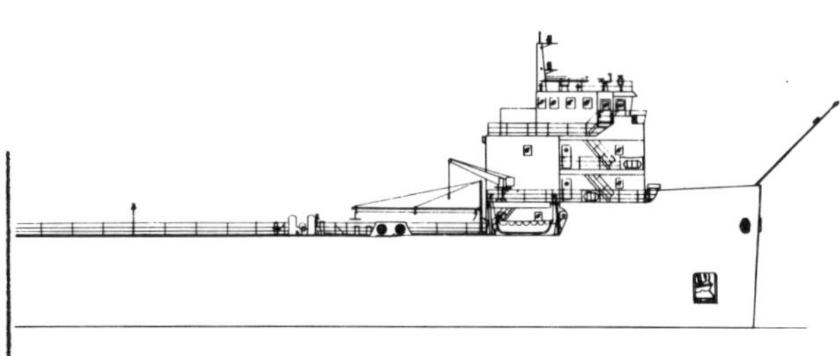

The *Stewart J. Cort* backing into Taconite Harbor, Minnesota, on her maiden voyage. Most of the ship's hydraulically controlled hatch covers have already been removed, but one hatch in the midship area is just in the process of being rotated back to the open position. Lining each side of the deck are the *Cort*'s thirty-six ballast pumps. On most other Great Lakes ships, the ballast pumps are located in the engine room or within the ballast tanks. (Institute for Great Lakes Research, Bowling Green State University)

Because of the arrangement of its hatches, the *Cort* cannot be loaded at a chute-type ore dock.

The *Cort*'s hatch covers are also different than those on other lakers. Virtually all of the other freighters have single piece steel hatch covers that are removed and replaced by a hatch crane. These hatch covers are secured to their coamings by scores of hatch clamps that must be taken off by crewmembers before the ship loads or unloads. The *Cort*, on the other hand, has single piece hatch covers that are hydraulically operated. The hatch covers are hinged along their forward edge: they can be tipped back out of the way by actuating the hydraulic units. Similarly, the hatch covers are secured in place by hydraulically operated pins, instead of by the more traditional hatch clamps. The system greatly reduces the amount of manual labor needed to remove or replace hatch covers, much to the delight of the deckhands who serve aboard the *Cort*.[19]

To get to their jobs, engine room personnel aboard the *Cort* must travel the full length of the ship's long deck. The author of the 1898 article predicting the use of thousand-footers on the lakes had foreseen such a problem. He had envisioned the use of a trolley to move personnel between the bow and stern sections of the ship. He wasn't far off. Crewmembers on the *Cort* travel from bow to stern, not on foot, but riding in electric golf carts!

No vessel in the long history of shipping on the Great Lakes has been built with as many innovative features as the *Cort*. In conceiving a ship twice as large as any previous vessel on the lakes, designers were confronted with innumerable problems. In virtually every instance, they formulated truly innovative solutions to those challenges. While they were guided by what had been done previously, they didn't feel bound by many of the conventions assiduously subscribed to by other Great Lakes boatbuilders. The creative staff at MC&D had to believe that they were taking the classic design of the Great Lakes ore freighter to a new level. In the *Cort*, the design that had been evolving for a century moved closer to perfection.

The *Cort* was Queen of the Lakes for just over four years. Beginning in 1976, a series of ships was built slightly larger than the Bethlehem freighter. These vessels looked nothing like the *Cort*, however. By then, ship owners on the lakes had adopted the saltwater design of stemwinders, or stern-enders, with pilothouses and all accommodations at their sterns. The *Cort* was the last Queen of the Lakes that looked like the classic lake freighters which had been evolving since the launching of Eli Peck's *R. J. Hackett* a century earlier.[20]

M/V PRESQUE ISLE

1000'x104'7"x46'6"
Queen of the Lakes
1973 to August 7, 1976

A little more than a year after the *Cort* went into service, Erie Marine launched a second thousand-footer that was even more unusual than the pioneering Bethlehem freighter. The *Presque Isle* was built as an integrated tug-barge (ITB), the first to operate on the lakes. Unlike the barge consorts that had previously been common in the industry, the barge portion of the *Presque Isle* was not intended to be towed by its tug. Instead, the tug unit is securely mated into a notch at the stern of the barge by hydraulic pins, and the two units are seldom separated. In fact, with the tug painted to match the barge, it's difficult to tell that the ITB is not a freighter with its pilothouse on the stern.

The process of building the *Presque Isle* was even more complicated than that of the *Cort*. The ITB was assembled in three different shipyards, two on the Great Lakes and one on the Mississippi River. As in the case of the Bethlehem freighter, the rectangular midbody of the *Presque Isle* was built at Litton's sophisticated yard at Erie. The rounded bow section was built at Defoe Ship Building in Bay City, Michigan, and towed to Erie to be joined to the midbody. The tug unit was a product of Halter Marine in New Orleans.

While the *Presque Isle* looks like most of the other thousand-footers on the lakes, it is actually an integrated tug-barge. Shown here waiting to enter the Poe Lock at Sault Ste. Marie, the unique freighter bears the familiar logo on its bow of the owners, Litton Corporation, better known as a manufacturer of microwave ovens. The scraped paint on the hull of the *Presque Isle* is the result of operating in early spring ice. (Author's collection)

Built as a self-unloader with a conventional unloading boom on deck, the *Presque Isle* was intended to operate as part of Litton's Wilson Transit fleet. In fact, the unloading boom for the ITB was built at Duluth, Minnesota, and brought down the lakes to Erie on the deck of Wilson's *A. T. Lawson*, which was bound for Ashtabula, Ohio, with a load of iron ore pellets. The 606-foot *Lawson* had been launched in 1909 as the *Shenango* and had reigned as Queen of the Lakes for several years. Before the *Presque Isle* was completed, however, Litton sold the ten-ship Wilson fleet to George Steinbrenner's American Ship Building. The vessels were intended to be operated as part of Steinbrenner's Kinsman Marine. The *Presque Isle* was not included in that transaction. When the ITB was ready to go into service, Litton formed Litton Great Lakes Corporation to operate the vessel in the iron ore trade under charter to U.S. Steel.

In designing the *Presque Isle*, Litton again dramatically deviated from long-established conventions for vessels on the lakes. The company obviously thought that the ITB represented the freighter of the future. As a tug-barge, the *Presque Isle* would come under the Coast Guard's crew standards for tugs, which were much more lenient than those for ships. That would allow Litton to operate the vessel with a much smaller crew than was required on conventional lakers. While most lake freighters carried about thirty crewmembers, the ITB might get by with as few as fifteen. The savings on salaries and fringe benefits would total in the neighborhood of $1 million a year for Litton and give them a competitive advantage in the ore trade.

To the obvious dismay of officials at Litton, when the Coast Guard inspected the *Presque Isle* they concluded that it did not qualify for the lenient crewing standards established for tugs. The tug portion of the *Presque Isle*, they argued, was not designed to operate independent of the barge unit. Separated from the barge, it wasn't even very seaworthy. With its stubby bow and the pilothouse and four accommodation decks towering above the spar deck, the tug unit was top heavy. In issuing the vessel's Certificate of Inspection, the Coast Guard inspectors set crewing standards virtually identical to those in place for conventional freighters. Litton's hopes for big savings in crew costs were dashed. If the ITB was the freighter of the future, it would have to prove that in head-to-head competition with other ships in the ore trade.

The launching of the *Presque Isle* did not prompt any

shift to the use of ITBs by shipowners on the Great Lakes. It was the only ITB on the lakes until the *Joseph H. Thompson* went into service during the 1991 shipping season. The *Thompson,* a converted C4 saltwater cargo ship, was brought into the lakes during the Korean War and operated as part of the M. A. Hanna fleet. The 714-foot freighter was then the longest ship in the industry and the Queen of the Lakes. When that long-established shipping company abandoned its marine operations during the shipping recession of the 1980s, the *Thompson* was purchased by Upper Great Lakes Shipping of Escanaba, Michigan, and converted to a self-unloading barge. It is pushed by the tug *Joseph H. Thompson, Jr.*, which was specially built for that role. Officials at Upper Great Lakes Shipping obviously learned from the experience their peers at Litton had with Coast Guard regulations. Unlike the *Presque Isle*, the *Thompson* is crewed as a tug.

Notes

1. Quoted without further reference in Harry Benford, Kent Thornton, and E. B. Williams, "Current Trends in the Design of Iron-Ore Ships," paper presented at the meeting of the Society of Naval Architects and Marine Engineers, June 21–22, 1962, 19.
2. John W. Larson, *Essayons: A History of the Detroit District, U.S. Army Corps of Engineers* (Detroit: U.S. Army Corps of Engineers, 1981), 151.
3. Ibid., 151.
4. Ibid., 152.
5. Ibid., 153.
6. C. E. Tripp and G. H. Plude, "One Thousand Foot Great Lakes Self-Unloader—Erie Marine Hull 101," paper presented to the Great Lakes and Great Rivers Section, Society of Naval Architects and Marine Engineers, January 21, 1971.
7. John O. Greenwood, "The Era of the Leviathans," paper presented at the 44th Annual International Joint Conference of the Dominion Marine Association and the Lake Carriers' Association, February 17, 1981.
8. Tripp and Plude, 1. The actual tonnages of iron ore shipped in 1990 fell far short of the prediction, but the projected ratio of taconite to natural ore was extremely accurate.
9. James Clary, *Ladies of the Lakes* (Lansing, MI: Michigan Natural Resources Magazine, 1981), 138–39.
10. Alexander C. Meakin, *Master of the Inland Seas* (Vermilion, OH: Great Lakes Historical Society, 1988), 297.
11. Tripp and Plude, 3.
12. Ibid., 37–39.
13. Ibid., 21–27.
14. To help workers at Erie, personnel at Pascagoula had painted a vertical line on the side of the hull where it was to be separated. Next to the line was the tongue-in-cheek instruction: "Cut here."
15. Tripp and Plude, 22.
16. Ibid., 59–62.
17. Ibid., 43.
18. Ibid., 14.
19. Ibid., 35–36.
20. If completion of the *Roger Blough* had not been delayed by fire, the *Cort* would have been the last double-ended freighter to go into service on the U.S. side of the lakes. All U.S. ships built since the *Blough* have been stern-enders.

31

Stern-Ender Queens

On November 19, 1973, officials of Pickands Mather rocked the Great Lakes shipping community with the announcement that they were entering into a contract with American Ship Building for construction of two 1,000-foot self-unloaders for their Interlake Steamship fleet. The $75 million price tag for the two ships made the contract the largest ever awarded in the long history of the industry on the lakes. The twin supercarriers were scheduled to be built in AmShip's massive drydock at Lorain, Ohio. They would be the first of the new generation of thousand-footers to be built totally on the Great Lakes. A few feet longer than Bethlehem's *Stewart J. Cort* or Litton's *Presque Isle*, the Interlake ships would also claim honors as Queens of the Lakes.

M/V JAMES R. BARKER

1,004'x105'x50'
Queen of the Lakes
August 7, 1976 to April 25, 1981

An artist's drawing released at the time of the announcement suggested that the two giant Interlake vessels would be modified versions of the trailblazing *Cort*. Like the *Cort*, they would follow the traditional Great Lakes practice of placing the pilothouse at the bow and the engine room at the stern. While all of the personnel aboard the *Cort* were housed in cabins located at the bow, the Interlake ships would follow the more traditional arrangement: housing deck personnel in cabins located below the pilothouse at the bow and engineering personnel in cabins over the engine room at the stern. The planned Interlake ships would also have cylindrical or rounded bows, instead of the more pointed bow used on the *Cort* and most other ships built on the lakes. The cylindrical bow had made its debut on the lakes in 1972 with the launching at Collingwood, Ontario, of Canada Steamship's 730-foot *J. W. McGiffin*. Tests had shown that rounded bows were stronger than pointed ones, especially when the vessel was operating in ice, and the design resulted in a slight increase in carrying capacity by reducing the length of the forepeak area. At the same time, the shift to a rounded bow was shown to have little effect on vessel speed. The artist's rendering of the planned Interlake freighters also showed that each would be built with a single smokestack (two stacks were necessary on the *Cort* because that vessel's two engine rooms were separated by its unique unloading system).

The planned thousand-footers would also have more conventional self-unloading systems than had been used on the *Cort*. While the *Cort* had only a short shuttle boom mounted transversely within its stern, the Interlake ships would have

Tugs help to maneuver the *James R. Barker* out of the Black River at Lorain, Ohio, on its maiden voyage. The giant Interlake Steamship freighter became the model for the ten thousand-footers that followed it into service on the lakes. Original plans called for the ship to be built in the century-old Great Lakes configuration, with pilothouse forward and engine room aft, but economic considerations subsequently led to a decision to locate the pilothouse and all accommodations over the engine room at the stern. (Institute for Great Lakes Research, Bowling Green State University)

longer, deck-mounted booms just forward of their engine rooms and aft cabins. Most self-unloaders on the Great Lakes at that time had booms at the forward end of their cargo holds, situated just aft of the forward cabins. The arrangement had been virtually standard on the lakes since the advent of the first self-unloaders during the early years of the twentieth century. The Interlake ships would not be the first self-unloaders with unloading booms at their sterns, however. In the months just prior to Interlake's announcement, five ships had come out with aft-mounted booms. They included Litton's tug-barge *Presque Isle*, Kinsman's *William R. Roesch* and *Paul Thayer*, and American's *Charles E. Wilson* and *Roger M. Kyes*. Unlike the planned Interlake vessels, all four of those self-unloaders had been built with their pilothouses and all crew accommodations located at the stern, atop their engine rooms, so their aft-mounted, self-unloading gear made abundant sense. The Interlake thousand-footers would be the first ships of the traditional fore-and-aft design to have their self-unloading booms located at their sterns.[1]

The first of the Interlake thousand-footers was completed at Lorain in August of 1976 and christened as the *James R. Barker*. The giant ship that emerged from the drydock at Lorain looked little like the artist's drawing unveiled almost three years earlier. During the process of actually developing prints to be followed in constructing the twin thousand-footers, officials from Interlake and AmShip had made dramatic changes in the design of the vessels.

After the construction in 1972–73 of Kinsman's *William R. Roesch*, the first modern ship built on the lakes that departed from the century-old fore-and-aft design pioneered in 1869 by the *R. J. Hackett*, Great Lakes shipbuilders never looked back. All of the ships that followed the *Roesch* off the ways, including the *Barker*, followed the more cost-efficient design of having their pilothouses and all crew accommodations on their sterns. After more than a hundred years, the separate evolution in ship design on the Great Lakes was finally merged with the evolutionary line that had previously emerged in ocean shipping. Almost overnight, the unique fore-and-aft design that had characterized ships on the Great Lakes was abandoned. Except for their self-unloading gear, vessels like the *Roesch* and *Barker* clearly belonged to the same family of ships as the saltwater freighters that were then being turned out at yards around the world. The *Barker*, not the *Cort*, became the prototype for the ten thousand-footers that were subsequently built on the lakes.

While the *Cort* was built with eighteen tiny hatches down the center of her deck, the *Barker* sports thirty-six hatches, each one 65 feet long and 11 feet wide. The *Cort* was designed to carry only iron ore pellets. As a result, the Bethlehem freighter's peculiar arrangement of hatches makes it impossible to fully fill her holds with cargoes like coal. The hatch arrangement on the *Barker* makes the Interlake vessel more versatile, and she has operated efficiently in both the taconite and coal trades.

Because of her stubby shuttle boom unloading system, the *Cort* can only unload at harbors that have dockside hoppers into which she can discharge her cargo into. The *Barker*, on the other hand, can unload at any dock on the lakes that is big enough to accommodate her. She can discharge cargo onto shoreside stockpiles or into a hopper.

The *Barker* features a conventional conveyor belt unloading system that feeds cargo to a loop belt elevator which carries the cargo up to the level of the deck-mounted unloading boom. While the *Cort* and most other self-unloaders use a single conveyor belt under their cargo holds, the *Barker* has three parallel belts. Use of three belts allowed builders to reduce the amount of slope built into the sides of the hold in order to get cargo to slide down to the belts. That resulted in an increase in the maximum carrying capacity of the ship. At the stern, cargo from the two outboard conveyor belts is carried to a center hopper by short crossover belts. The center hopper feeds the

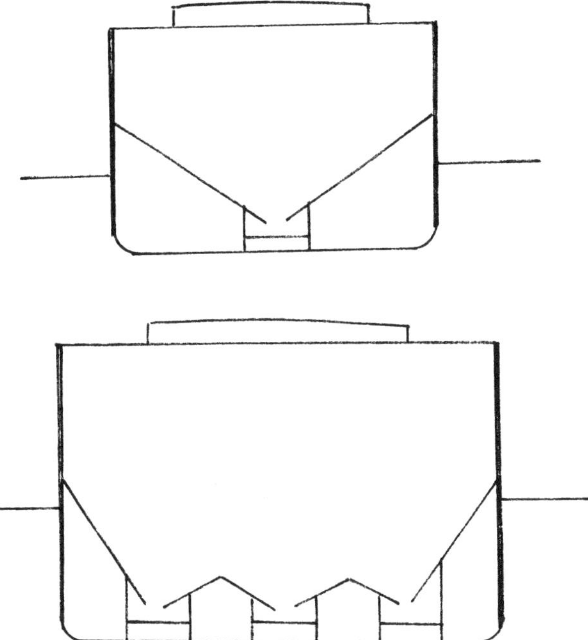

While most self-unloaders on the Great Lakes have a single conveyor belt running beneath their cargo holds, as at the top, the *Barker* features a three-belt system. The use of three belts allowed builders to maximize the size of the cargo hold, important when carrying cargoes with low weight-to-volume ratios, such as coal. At the after end of the *Barker*'s hold the three belts flow into a hopper feeding cargo to the loop belt elevator. (Author's collection)

loop belt elevator. Cargo is sandwiched between the two belts of the elevator and carried up to a hopper at the top of the elevator casing that feeds cargo to the 250-foot self-unloading boom.

While all crewmembers on the *Cort* are housed in the forward cabin structure, everyone aboard the *Barker* lives in the five-story aft cabin, located atop the engine room. The ship's galley, separate dining rooms for licensed and unlicensed personnel, and accommodations for the chief cook, second cook, and porter are located on the spar deck—or main deck—level. The next deck up is the poop deck, housing rooms mainly for unlicensed personnel from the deck, engine, and conveyor departments. Most of the unlicensed personnel live in two-person rooms—fairly cramped quarters, given the size of the *Barker*. Atop the poop deck is the accommodation deck, with private rooms for licensed deck and engine officers and a suite for the chief engineer that includes both an office and bedroom. The next deck up is referred to as the officers' deck, although the only officer with quarters there is the captain. Like the chief, he has a two-room suite. The officers' deck also includes passenger quarters, a bedroom with two twin beds that adjoins an observation lounge with a broad expanse of picture windows overlooking the deck of the ship. The pilothouse is located above the officers' deck.

Below the spar deck cabins are the four levels of the *Barker*'s massive engine room. The four powerful diesel generators that provide electricity for the ship are located on the main deck of the engine room, one deck below the spar deck. One deck down is the operating deck, where the ship's steering gear and state-of-the-art engine control room are located. The *Barker*'s two 8,000-horsepower diesel engines are located yet another deck down in segregated rooms above the bilge. The operating, main, spar, poop, accommodation, and officers' decks are served by an elevator that is very popular with most crewmembers.

The elevator, in fact, is probably the second most appreciated feature of the big ship: the most popular being the central air conditioning. The engine control room, galley, dining rooms, pilothouse, and all crew accommodations are air conditioned. Comfortable temperatures are maintained even on the hottest summer days, a dramatic departure from the situation on steamboats built only a generation earlier. Lacking air conditioning, and with roaring boilers generating heat that permeates the cabin areas above them, steamboats regularly have temperatures in the 100-degree range. In the engine rooms, cooled only by fans that draw air—often hot air—from outside the ship, temperatures often exceed the 100-degree mark, and engine personnel swelter in a stifling inferno. Little respite from the heat can be found in the galley or crew quarters located over the engine room. The deck in the galley has been known to get so hot that it melts the rubber soles on the shoes of galley personnel. There'll be no such horror stories told by crewmembers aboard the *Barker*, who found no trouble in adapting to the refreshingly cool temperatures.

One change that was less readily accepted by personnel aboard the *Barker* was the shift to cafeteria-style galley service. Until the 1970s, crewmembers aboard ships on the lakes were waited on by galley personnel. Generally, a porter waited on unlicensed crewmembers in the mess room, while the second cook waited on officers in the dining room. On the *Barker* and most of the ships built since, licensed and unlicensed crewmembers go through a serving line and place their own orders with the cook, then carry their own trays to the dining room or mess room. Although the story is disputed, some of those who were aboard the *Barker* in its initial season say that the captain refused to stand in line with deckhands and other unlicensed personnel. For three days he went in and sat down at his reserved seat in the dining room and waited to be served. For three days he was duly ignored by galley personnel. On the fourth day, the captain capitulated and stood in the serving line like everyone else on the ship. Since then, crewmembers have grown accustomed to the cafeteria-style service, and few complaints are heard anymore.

The changes made to the *Barker* between the artist's drawing of 1973 and her launch in 1976 pushed construction costs upward. Instead of costing $37.5 million, the final price tag for the big freighter topped $40 million. She quickly proved her worth, however. Shortly after going into service, the *Barker* established a new iron ore record when she loaded 58,293 tons, the first of numerous ore and coal records she would achieve. While she set a number of tonnage records, she'll claim no records for speed. It was expected that her two 8,000-horsepower diesels, driving two 17.5-foot diameter propellers would push the ship along at a speed of sixteen miles an hour when loaded. Actual performance fell far short of that mark, however, and the *Barker* can only do about fourteen miles an hour when loaded.

On a single trip from the loading ports on Lake Superior to the unloading ports on Lake Erie or Lake Michigan, the *Barker*'s powerful diesels will suck up about 70,000 gallons of blended fuel. On the same trip, a steamboat would burn about 50,000 gallons of heavier oil. An observer could easily conclude that the new thousand-footers are not fuel efficient, but fuel consumed is only part of the equation. On a single trip, a thousand-footer like the *Barker* will carry close to 60,000 tons. The 600-foot freighters that were replaced by the thousand-footers could carry only about 15,000 tons in a single trip, so it would take four of them to move as much tonnage as a ship like the *Barker*. Together, four 600-footers would burn 200,000 gallons of fuel to move as much cargo as one thousand-footer that burns only 70,000 gallons. In a season, the four steamboats would consume close to seven million gallons of heavy oil, compared to only about three million gallons for a ship like the *Barker*. Even though the blended fuel used by ships like the *Barker* is slightly more expensive then the heavier oil used by the steamboats, the vessel's fuel cost would still be only about half that of the four steamboats needed to move the same amount of cargo.[2] That is only one of the efficiencies that can be generated by a thousand-footer.

By replacing steamboats with thousand-footers, the shipping companies also dramatically reduced their crew costs. It takes about the same number of people to crew a thousand-footer as it did to crew the 600-foot steamboats they replaced. Since it would take four steamboats to carry as much cargo as can be moved by a single thousand-footer, the shift to use of a ship like the *Barker* allowed her owners to eliminate three full crews—about twenty-seven officers and fifty-four unlicensed crewmembers. At today's costs for wages and fringe benefits, the resulting savings amount to about $5 million per year. While construction of a thousand-footer represents a major outlay of capital for a shipping company, the efficiencies that result from replacing smaller vessels with a ship like the *Barker* make them a sound—almost mandatory—investment for fleets interested in competing in the iron ore and coal trades on the lakes. Other shipping companies rapidly followed the lead of Bethlehem, Litton, and Interlake and placed orders for thousand-footers.

M/V MESABI MINER

1,004'x105'x50'
Queen of the Lakes
February 14, 1977 to April 25, 1981

The second Interlake thousand-footer was launched at Lorain on February 14, 1977. Virtually identical to the *Barker*, the big freighter was christened at ceremonies held at the Port Terminal in Duluth, Minnesota, at 11:30 a.m. on Saturday, June 11, 1977. The traditional bottle of champagne was broken across the bow of the new ship by Muriel Humphrey, wife of Minnesota Senator Hubert H. Humphrey. As the bottle of champagne shattered against the rust-red hull of the newest thousand-footer, one hatch cover was lifted off, allowing thousands of red, white, and blue balloons to rise into the air. The big freighter was named *Mesabi Miner*, honoring the men and women of Minnesota's Mesabi iron range. Following remarks by Senator Humphrey, the *Miner* was open to the public that afternoon and the following morning, and thousands of people from the twin ports of Duluth and Superior toured the new Interlake vessel.[3] On Sunday afternoon, the ship shifted over to the Burlington Northern shuttle dock at Superior, which had opened just the week before, and took on its first load of taconite pellets.[4]

M/V GEORGE A. STINSON

1,004'x105'x50
Queen of the Lakes
July 15, 1978 to April 25, 1981

Two more thousand-footers were launched within days of each other in 1978. On July 15, 1978, the *George A. Stinson* was launched at Lorain for National Steel, to be operated as part of the Hanna fleet. It was followed on July 19, 1978, by the *Edwin H. Gott*, built at Bay Ship Building in Sturgeon Bay, Wisconsin,

M/V EDWIN H. GOTT

1,004'x105'x56'
Queen of the Lakes
July 19, 1978 to April 25, 1981

for the USS Great Lakes Fleet of U.S. Steel. After final fitting-out, the *Gott* went into service in February of 1979 as one of the ships participating in the winter navigation program. On her maiden voyage, the *Gott* damaged a side tank and lost one of her rudders while operating in the thick ice and had to go back to the shipyard for repairs. She came out of the shipyard two months later, but her luck hadn't improved much. On April 23 the giant ship lost her anchor and three hundred feet of stout anchor chain while attempting to take on supplies at Sault Ste. Marie. U.S. Steel added a second thousand-footer to its fleet on May 8, 1980, with the launching at Lorain of the *Edgar B. Speer*.[5]

M/V EDGAR B. SPEER

1,004'x105'x56'
Queen of the Lakes
May 8, 1980 to April 25, 1981

Like the *Cort*, the two U.S. Steel thousand-footers have shuttle-type self-unloading booms, instead of the more common deck booms like those used on the *Barker*, *Miner*, and *Stinson*. The shuttles on the *Gott* and *Speer* are located on the main deck, just forward of their cabins.

During the fall of 1986, officials in the Interlake Steamship offices in Cleveland were horrified when they received word that the *Barker*, the flagship of their fleet, was on fire on lower Lake Huron. The powerful diesel engines used in today's freighters vibrate constantly, and that vibrating had caused a fuel line to rupture in the *Barker*'s port engine room. Fuel pouring out of the ruptured line ignited, and by the time the personnel on watch discovered the fire it had spread throughout much of the engine room, filling the space with thick, black smoke. As engine room personnel prepared to battle the raging blaze, the captain ordered the balance of the crew to don their survival suits and prepare to abandon ship. Shipboard personnel managed to shut off the supply of fuel that was feeding the blaze, and the vessel's fire extinguishing system was activated to flood the engine room with carbon dioxide and snuff out the fire.

The fire destroyed much of the machinery in the *Barker*'s sophisticated engine room. Unable to operate under its own power, the giant ship was lashed alongside the *William J. DeLancey*, the newest thousand-footer in the Interlake fleet. The *DeLancey* took the damaged *Barker* in side-by-side tow for the long, slow trip up the lake to the shipyard at Sturgeon Bay, Wisconsin. It stands as perhaps the most unusual towing job in the history of the lakes. Through the winter months of 1986–87, workers at the shipyard completed the multimillion dollar repair job on the *Barker*, and it was able to return to service during the 1987 season. Many of the thousand-footers have been involved in casualties of one sort or another during their careers, but most of the resulting damage has been relatively minor. None has come as close to being lost as the *James R. Barker*.

A broken fuel line aboard the *James R. Barker* resulted in a massive fire that destroyed much of the ship's propulsion machinery and control systems in the fall of 1986 while the vessel was on lower Lake Huron. The crippled *Barker* was lashed alongside the *William J. DeLancey*, another Interlake thousand-footer, for the four-hundred-mile trip to a shipyard at Sturgeon Bay, Wisconsin. That voyage ranks as the most unusual towing job in the long history of shipping on the lakes. The *Barker* returned to service the following year. (Author's collection)

The *Barker*, *Mesabi Miner*, *Stinson*, *Gott*, and *Speer*, all 1,004 feet long, shared Queen of the Lakes honors until an even longer ship was launched in 1981. Today, they and the eight other thousand-footers form the backbone of the shipping industry on the lakes, representing almost half of the total carrying capacity of the U.S. fleet.

Notes

1. Russell Parkinson, "The American Ship Building Company Announces $95,000,000 in New Shipbuilding Contracts," *Telescope* 23 no. 1 (Jan.–Feb. 1974): 6.
2. Adapted from John O. Greenwood, "The Era of the Leviathans," paper presented at the 44th Annual International Joint Conference of the Dominion Marine Association and the Lake Carriers' Association, February 17, 1981, 4.
3. "Miner Launch Today," *Duluth News-Tribune*, June 11, 1977.
4. "Lakes Get New Giant," *Duluth News-Tribune*, June 12, 1977.
5. Ship Biographies, Institute for Great Lakes Research, Bowling Green State University.

32

Interlake's Fancy DeLancey

Many cultures celebrate spring as a time of rebirth and renewal. Nowhere is that more true than within the Great Lakes shipping industry. As mother nature gives up her icy grip on the shipping lanes, scores of merchant seamen begin to arrive at ports around the lakes where their ships have lain idle through the long winter months. Shutters are removed from the pilothouses, fires are started in the boilers, massive diesel engines are lit off, huge stores of groceries and supplies are brought aboard and stowed, and, in a matter of days, mooring lines are cast off and vessels steam out onto the lakes to begin another shipping season. The appearance of the first freighters on the lakes signals the beginning of spring just as regularly as the blooming of the first crocuses and tulips.

M/V WILLIAM J. DELANCEY

1,013'6"x105'x56'
Queen of the Lakes
April 25, 1981 to the Present

The spring of 1981 was a particularly joyous time for employees of Pickands Mather and the Interlake Steamship Company. On April 25, 1981, company officials who had been dispatched to ports around the lakes during the previous weeks to oversee fitout of the Interlake fleet gathered at American Ship Building in Lorain, Ohio, to participate in the launching and christening of a grand new vessel. Named the *William J. DeLancey* in honor of the president of LTV Steel—the nation's second largest steel manufacturer and the Cleveland-based fleet's most important customer—the mammoth new ship was the third thousand-footer to fly the Interlake house flag. It was more than just another "footer," however. Stretched to six inches over 1,013 feet in overall length by her designers and builders, the *DeLancey* was the longest ship on the lakes. With her official addition to commerce on the lakes, the majestic Interlake freighter displaced the *Barker*, the *Mesabi Miner*, and the other 1,004-foot ships as the newest Queen of the Lakes. As her throbbing 17,120-horsepower diesels moved the big ship past the lighthouse at the entrance to the harbor at Lorain and out onto Lake Erie, she fell heir to a title that had over the years been held by some of the finest ships ever to operate on the inland seas.

None of the thirteen thousand-footers that were in operation on the lakes by the end of the 1981 season could be considered "ordinary," but by any standards the *DeLancey* was an extraordinary vessel. While the economics of shipbuilding in the 1970s and 1980s dictated that most of the thousand-footers were strictly utilitarian, no-frills ships, Interlake had spared no

Interlake Steamship's *William J. DeLancey* in its fitting-out berth at American Ship Building in Lorain, Ohio, just prior to departing on its maiden voyage in 1981. Although the 1,013-foot freighter's name was changed to the *Paul R. Tregurtha* in 1990, the ship reigns yet today as the Queen of the Lakes. To the right of the *DeLancey* is an empty drydock. Along its bottom are the stout wooden blocks that ships rest on when in the drydock. (Author's collection)

expense on the *DeLancey*. Its splendid outfitting achieved a level of luxuriousness that had not been seen on the lakes since the early years of the twentieth century. The unique ship had been built to serve as the "passenger boat" for the Interlake fleet. Each season, the company's most important business customers would be wined and dined in the *DeLancey*'s elaborate passenger quarters as they enjoyed a trip on the lakes. Passenger quarters of some sort are found on most freighters, but none could compare with the elaborate accommodations on the new Interlake vessel. And the extraordinary luxuriousness of the accommodations on the *DeLancey* did not begin and end in the passenger quarters, either, which is commonly the case. The decor of the crew quarters, dining and mess rooms, and even the work spaces on the ship reflect a level of luxury that cannot be found aboard any other modern freighter. In fact, it is questionable whether any freighter on the lakes can tout accommodations as fine as those found aboard the *William J. DeLancey*. In short order, the new ship was nicknamed the "Fancy *DeLancey*" by the sailors who served aboard it.

The ship's elegance did not detract in any way from its primary mission, however. Above all else, the *DeLancey* was designed to haul iron ore, and in that respect it was the equal of any ship operating on the lakes. Built six feet deeper than the *Barker* or *Miner*, the *DeLancey* could carry 68,000 tons of iron ore at maximum midsummer draft. The ship was specifically designed to haul ore for LTV Steel from loading docks on Lake Superior to the LTV mill at Indiana Harbor, Indiana, or the company's transshipment terminal at Lorain, Ohio, just a few hundred feet downstream from where the Interlake freighter had been built. From Lorain, the ore was then shipped aboard smaller, river-class vessels to Cleveland and up the Cuyahoga River to LTV mills that could not be served by thousand-footers.

LTV was the successor to Republic Steel, formed by the merger of Republic and several other major steel producers. Interlake had been carrying ore for Republic and LTV for a decade, since wresting the contract from Cleveland-Cliffs. Several other shipping companies also shared in the LTV contract, including Columbia Transportation, which had just built their thousand-footer, the *Columbia Star*, to operate in the same service as the *DeLancey*. The naming of their grand new freighter after William J. DeLancey, the president of LTV, reflected the importance of the LTV contract to Interlake, and was a means by which the shipping company hoped to further solidify the relationship with their best customer.

The *DeLancey* joined a U.S. fleet that totalled 151 ships, with a combined single-trip carrying capacity of just over three million tons. While tonnages in that 1981 season lagged behind the record volumes moved in 1978 and 1979, almost 75 million tons of iron ore moved that season, along with more than 39 million tons of coal, 28 million tons of grain, and 24 million tons of stone, for total shipments of 175,811,959 tons.[1]

While the tonnages hauled by the *DeLancey* and the other freighters in the U.S. fleet were fairly respectable, demand had dropped off dramatically in the late fall, and most vessels went to their layup berths in December. The soft U.S. economy, combined with record imports of foreign steel, began to have an impact on the country's steel industry. The steel business was swiftly sliding into one of the worst recessions in its history, and it was dragging the Great Lakes shipping industry along with it.

After a reasonable season in 1981, tonnages plummeted in 1982. Iron ore shipments dropped from almost 75 million tons to only 38.5 million tons, while stone movements fell from 24.5 million tons to a mere 15 million tons. Total shipments on the lakes were down by almost thirty percent,[2] reaching their lowest level since the Great Depression of the 1930s. Fleets such as Interlake that were dependent on the ore and stone trades couldn't find enough cargoes to keep their vessels busy, and many ships spent all or part of the season lying idle at docks around the lakes. The *DeLancey* provided company officials with one of the few bright spots in the 1982 season: it established a new cargo record by loading 63,007 gross tons of iron ore at Escanaba, Michigan.[3]

While tonnages recovered modestly during the 1983 season, they remained far below normal levels. The recession in the steel and shipping industries continued throughout the remaining years of the 1980s. It would have a profound and permanent effect on the Great Lakes shipping industry. By 1990, the U.S. fleet on the lakes had shrunk to only sixty-nine vessels, less than half the number that had existed when the *DeLancey* came out in 1981. Most of the ships that had disappeared from the scene had been sent to the shipbreakers as fleets struggled to reduce their excess tonnage and adapt to the changed nature of shipping on the lakes. A number of fleets had not survived the lean years of the 1980s. Cleveland-Cliffs abandoned its marine operations during the 1984 season after operating for more than 125 years. M. A. Hanna Company, another firm that dated back to the early years of the shipping industry, followed suit in 1985.[4] In 1989, officials at Ford Motor Company decided to sell their Rouge Steel fleet, which had been operating on the lakes since 1924. The three Ford ships were purchased by Interlake, bringing the total size of that fleet to eleven vessels.[5] Interlake officials felt that the downsizing of the industry, combined with their projections that modest increases in tonnages could be expected, represented an opportunity for them to enlarge their fleet and increase their share of the Great Lakes market.

Interlake itself had undergone a change in management during the turbulent years of the 1980s. Since 1973, Interlake and its parent, Pickands Mather, had been owned by Moore McCormack, an ocean shipping company based on the East Coast. Moore McCormack was headed by James R. Barker, a native of Sault Ste. Marie, Michigan, and a former employee of Pickands Mather's marine department. Under Barker's leadership, the *James R. Barker*, *Mesabi Miner*, and *William J. DeLancey* had been added to the Interlake fleet. Moore McCormack was staggered by the shipping recession of the 1980s, which had affected fleets on the oceans as well as those on the Great Lakes. After experiencing financial losses that threatened the survival of the company, members of the firm's board of directors decided to abandon their shipping and mining interests on the Great Lakes. Pickands Mather, primarily involved in mining, was sold to Cleveland-Cliffs, uniting the two industry giants founded a century earlier by Samuel Mather. James R. Barker and a business partner, Paul R. Tregurtha, gained control of the Interlake fleet. Some say that Interlake was Barker's "golden parachute," a payoff for his years of service to

The massive twin stack casings on today's Queen of the Lakes are black with the familiar "Interlake orange" band. The actual exhaust stacks for the ship's two diesel engines are located within the casings. (Author's collection)

Moore McCormack. But Interlake was saddled with heavy debt incurred as a result of construction of their three thousand-footers and conversion of several of their other ships to self-unloaders. With shipping on the Great Lakes far from healthy, many questioned whether Interlake could survive.

Barker brought his years of business acumen in the maritime industry to bear on the ailing fleet. He moved rapidly to secure government assistance to insure that Interlake would not fail. At the same time, he secured contract concessions from the union representing unlicensed seamen in the fleet and began to renegotiate contracts with some of the companies that Interlake hauled for. Although Interlake was still on an unstable footing when Ford's three Rouge Steel ships were put up for sale in 1989, Barker and Tregurtha managed to put together a financial package that was acceptable to Ford management. With the three boats came a sizeable portion of the contract to carry iron ore, coal, and stone to Rouge Steel's mill on the Rouge River at Detroit. That tonnage would keep the former Ford ships and several of the smaller Interlake vessels busy throughout the term of the contract.

The transition in ownership of Interlake was underscored when several ships in the fleet were renamed. The former *William Clay Ford* and *Benson Ford* became the *Lee A. Tregurtha* and *Kaye E. Barker*, respectively, in honor of the wives of Interlake's two new owners. Jim Barker was already the namesake of Interlake's first thousand-footer, and in 1990 Paul Tregurtha was similarly honored when the *DeLancey* was renamed the *Paul R. Tregurtha*. That renaming also reflected a significant change in the relationship between Interlake and LTV.

When the bottom fell out of the U.S. steel industry in the early 1980s, LTV suffered massive financial losses. After accumulating a critical amount of debt, the company sought protection from its creditors by filing for Chapter 11 bankruptcy. Interlake was only one of a flotilla of LTV creditors left high and dry by the bankruptcy. LTV's actions made it unlikely that Interlake would collect more than pennies on the dollar for millions of dollars of shipments they had already hauled for LTV. The steelmaker further exacerbated the financial impact by abrogating the terms of their contract for iron ore shipments. LTV acted unilaterally to slash the contract rates for ore shipments virtually in half.

For fleets like Interlake that had built ships and incurred substantial amounts of debt based on their contracts with the steelmaker, the action by LTV represented a serious financial blow. In fact, the LTV bankruptcy and subsequent rate reductions were major factors in Moore McCormack's decision to rid themselves of Interlake. Under different circumstances, Interlake and the other affected fleets might have merely walked away from their contracts with LTV. But the fleets were already struggling financially, and they needed the income from those contracts—no matter how badly slashed—to make their own mortgage payments and retain their economic viability. All of the fleets have managed to survive, but their relationships with LTV are clearly strained yet today, although LTV remains an important customer. The renaming of the *William J. DeLancey* was at least in part a reflection of the change in the relationship between Interlake and LTV.

Today, the *Paul R. Tregurtha* seldom calls at LTV facilities around the lakes. Interlake has placed the giant ship in the coal trade, and it operates mainly between the Superior Midwest Energy Terminal in Superior, Wisconsin, and Detroit Edison power plants on the St. Clair River. The magnificent ship has now been Queen of the Lakes for more than a decade. Only the *Carl D. Bradley* held the title for a longer period of time. The long tenure of the Interlake freighter is due in part to the lack of new construction in the Great Lakes industry. On the U.S. side of the system, no new ships have been added since 1982, and none is presently on the drawing boards.

When growths in cargo tonnages force one of the U.S. fleets to build a new ship, it is likely that the vessel will be longer than the present Queen of the Lakes. The Poe Lock at Sault Ste. Marie was built to handle ships up to a maximum of 1,000 feet in length, but with special transitting procedures, vessels up to 1,100 feet long can now be locked through. A safe bet would be that the next ship built on the lakes will be 1,100 feet long, with the same beam and depth as vessels like the *Tregurtha*. Such a vessel would have a substantially greater carrying capacity than today's thousand-footers, and the prospect of the additional revenue it could generate would be necessary before any shipping company would incur the staggering cost of building a new freighter. While the *James R. Barker* and *Mesabi Miner* cost just over $40 million in the mid-1970s, costs had escalated to more than $60 million by the time the *DeLancey* was launched in 1981. It is estimated that it would cost about $130 million to build a similar ship today.[6] Today's economic conditions don't justify that sort of investment. Until cargo tonnages increase and the profitability of Great Lakes shipping companies improves, the *Paul R. Tregurtha* will continue its long reign as Queen of the Lakes.

Notes

1. *1981 Annual Report* (Cleveland: Lake Carriers' Association, 1982), 21.
2. *1982 Annual Report* (Cleveland: Lake Carriers' Association, 1983), 18.

3. Ibid., 34.
4. Hanna was forced to continue operating their thousand-footer, the *George A. Stinson*, when they were unable to find a buyer for the 1978-built freighter.
5. Two of the ships, the *Samuel Mather*—the former *Henry Ford II*—and the *John Sherwin*, were no longer viable freighters and have remained layed-up. Should tonnages under contract to Interlake increase, company officials have expressed their intention of converting the straight-decker *Sherwin* to a self-unloader and placing it back in service.
6. Jack Storey, "New Vessels Coming, But Not Tomorrow," *Evening News*, June 3, 1990.

Epilogue

As a result of the prolonged period of economic uncertainties, combined with such systemic limitations as the dimensions of the locks at Sault Ste. Marie and the depths of harbor and river channels, the size of ships on the Great Lakes has lagged far behind those found in ocean shipping. A 1977 study of vessel size on the Great Lakes noted that "in the the past twenty years the largest classes of ocean tankers have increased in deadweight[1] by a factor of about ten, while the largest classes of vessels on the lakes have increased by a factor of only two or three."[2] By the end of 1973, when the *Cort* and *Presque Isle* were the only thousand-footers operating on the lakes, there were 388 ships of 200,000 deadweight tons or more in service in ocean trades. Another 493 ships of that size were under construction, or on order, including 26 that were reported to be of more than 400,000 tons deadweight.[3] In 1974, the largest ship in the world was *Globtik London.* Built in Japan, the massive tanker was 1,220 feet long, 173 feet wide, and measured at 483,939 deadweight tons.[4] By comparison, thousand-footers like the *Cort*, *Presque Isle*, and *Tregurtha* are rated at less than 100,000 deadweight tons.

While most of the jumbo ocean freighters that began to appear in the early 1970s were tankers engaged in carrying crude oil from the Mideast to ports around the world, shipping companies hauling dry bulk cargoes were quick to follow suit. In 1986, a Norwegian shipping company took delivery of a bulk freighter of 365,000 deadweight tons built for them by a Korean shipyard owned by Hyandai Heavy Industries. Christened the *Berge Stahl*, the vessel was designed for service in the iron ore trade between the port of Ponta da Madeira, Brazil, and the port of Rotterdam, where the cargo would be offloaded for overland shipment to a steel mill in Germany. The immense freighter looks like a bloated version of Great Lakes thousand-footers like the *Tregurtha.* It is 1,346 feet long, with a beam of 250 feet and a depth of just over 118 feet. At maximum draft, it can carry more than four times as much iron ore as today's Queen of the Lakes. Interestingly, it does that with a crew of only fourteen, less than half as many as serve aboard the *Tregurtha.*[5]

It is unlikely that the Great Lakes will ever see ships as large as the *Berge Stahl* or the other very large cargo carriers that operate on the oceans. While the locks at Sault Ste. Marie could be enlarged to handle the length and beam of a ship the size of the Norwegian ore carrier, it would not be economically feasible to dredge the harbors and river channels to the depths necessary to handle their deep drafts. At maximum draft, the Berge Stahl draws over ninety-one feet of water. By comparison, ships on the lakes are forced to operate at drafts between only twenty-six and twenty-seven feet.

For a century, the bulk freighters plying the Great Lakes were among the largest ships of their type in the world. In fact, when the 714-foot *Joseph H. Thompson* went into service on the lakes in 1952, the former C-4 *was* the longest freight vessel in the world. Since then, the size of the ships launched on the Great Lakes has lagged far behind the awe-inspiring dimensions of the largest of the saltwater freighters. Gone, too, is the unique fore-and-aft design that was almost exclusively identified with cargo ships on the lakes for more than a hundred years after the unheralded launching of Captain Eli Peck's little *R. J. Hackett* at Cleveland in 1869. In terms of appearances, it's hard to tell the difference between the latest generation of lake freighters and vessels launched for saltwater service. The current Queen of the Lakes, Interlake's *Paul R. Tregurtha,* looks much the same as the Norwegian-owned *Berge Stahl,* except that it is a great deal smaller than the immense ocean freighter.

But in reality there's nothing *small* about the freighters presently operating on the lakes. The *Tregurtha* is longer than three football fields laid end to end. Even most of the smaller ships in the system—the *Joseph H. Thompson, Wilfred Sykes,* and the 730-class boats—are as long or longer than two football fields laid end to end. From its keel to the top of its pilothouse, the *Tregurtha* is more than 120 feet high, the equivalent of a twelve-story building. The amount of cargo the ships haul is almost beyond our comprehension. The record iron ore cargo for a thousand-footer now tops 70,000 tons, while normal loads are in the area of 60,000 tons. A mill will convert a single shipload of ore carried by a thousand-footer into enough steel to build 16,000 to 18,600 automobiles. In a nine-month shipping season, a single vessel like the *Tregurtha* will move more than 2.5 million tons of cargo down the lakes, enough to build 750,000 cars.

Making about forty-five round-trips during the season, a thousand-footer will travel 35–40,000 miles, equal to one-and-a-half times around the world. Its powerful diesel engines will burn more than three million gallons of fuel, enough to supply the needs of eight thousand private automobiles for the same period of time. Although the *Berge Stahl* can carry four times as much cargo per trip as a Great Lakes thousand-footer, it must spend the better part of a week dockside in Rotterdam while shoreside unloading equipment slowly scoops the ore out of its cavernous hold. By comparison, the *Tregurtha* and the other modern self-unloaders operating on the lakes can discharge their cargoes in only eight to twelve hours, without any assistance from shoreside equipment. The cargo handling efficiency of the self-unloading freighters on the Great Lakes is unmatched anywhere in the world maritime community.

At the same time, few saltwater captains would be bold enough to attempt to guide the *Paul R. Tregurtha* through the narrow river channels that are routinely traversed each day by ships operating on the Great Lakes system. They're used to running their ships on the wide expanses of the oceans. When their vessels approach a coastal port or the canals at Panama or Suez, the saltwater captains rely on assistance from local pilots and fleets of tugs to maneuver their ships in the confined waters. On the eight-hundred-mile trip from Lake Superior to the unloading ports on the lower lakes, the crew aboard a lake freighter will commonly maneuver the vessel into a lock at Sault Ste. Marie that is only a few feet bigger than their ship. They will carefully guide the freighter through several hundred miles of narrow, winding river channels where even a minor error in piloting could put their ship aground. Arriving off the unloading port, the captain will expertly spin his ship around, back it through the narrow opening in the piers, and maneuver the big freighter gently up against the dock—all without any assistance from tugs. The captains of the vessels in the Great Lakes fleet are simply the best shiphandlers in the world.

Taking a world view, ships on the Great Lakes may be surpassed in size and efficiency by many of the modern ocean freighters. When you take the inherent limitations of the Great Lakes system into consideration, however, the *Paul R. Tregurtha* and the other ships now sailing on the great freshwater seas of North America have achieved a level of operating efficiency that is unrivalled anywhere in the world. As today's Queen of the Lakes, the *Tregurtha* reigns as a model of unsurpassed maritime efficiency. It is heir to a long and glorious tradition of excellence. Each and every magnificent ship that has borne the title in the past has contributed in some part to the excellence embodied in the *Tregurtha.* In time, the *Tregurtha*'s title as Queen of the Lakes will pass to another monumental freighter that will carry the art and science of shipbuilding and operation to even higher heights.

Notes

1. "Deadweight tonnage" represents the number of long tons of cargo, stores, and fuel that a ship can carry at maximum draft. Because the weight of stores and fuel is included, deadweight tonnage is modestly higher than a ship's cargo carrying capacity.
2. Robert Scher, "Costs of Operating Alternative Sized Vessels," in Dennis Perkinson, ed., *Vessel Size: Its Implications for the Great Lakes-Seaway System,* proceedings of the Great Lakes Basin Commission conference, November 1-2, 1977.
3. Noel Mostert, *Supership* (New York: Crescent Books, 1975), 231.
4. Duncan Haws, *Ships and the Sea* (New York: Crescent Books, 1975), 231.
5. Hans Christian Oevstass, "Berge Stahl, World's Largest Bulk Carrier Commences Maiden Voyage," *Bulk Shipping* (Jan.–Mar. 1987): 76–77.

Bibliography

Anderson, Charles M. *Memo's of Betsie Bay.* Manistee, MI: J. B. Publications, 1988.

"Annual Compilation of Iron Ore Shipments by Companies in 1989." *Skillings Mining Review* 79, no. 26 (June 30, 1990): 4.

Archer, O. R., F. Giaquinto, and L. A. Dommin. "The American Ship Building Company Presents Basic Standard Great Lakes Self-Unloader, River Service Type." Paper presented to the Great Lakes and Great Rivers Section, Society of Naval Architects and Marine Engineers, January 1974.

Barcus, Frank. *Freshwater Fury.* Detroit: Wayne State University Press, 1960.

Barry, James P.. *The Fate of the Lakes.* Grand Rapids, MI: Baker Book House, 1972.

———. *Ships of the Great Lakes.* Berkeley: Howell- North Books, 1973.

———. *Wrecks and Rescues of the Great Lakes: A Photographic History.* San Diego: Howell-North Books, 1981.

Beasley, Norman. *Freighters of Fortune.* New York: Harper & Brothers, 1930.

Benford, Harry. "Sixty Years of Shipbuilding." Paper presented at the meeting of the Great Lakes Section of the Society of Naval Architects and Marine Engineers, October 1956.

———. "Tight Corners: The Innovative American Republic." *Seaway Review* (Autumn 1981): 33–46.

———. "Samuel Plimsoll: His Book and His Mark." *Seaway Review* (Jan.-Mar. 1986): 79.

———, Kent C. Thornton and E. B. Williams. "Current Trends in the Design of Iron Ore Ships." Paper presented at the meeting of the Society of Naval Architects and Marine Engineers, June 1962.

"Berge Stahl—World's Largest Bulk Carrier Commences Maiden Voyage." *Bulk Shipping* (Jan.-Mar. 1987): 76–79.

Beukema, Christian. "The Demonstration: U.S. Steel, Winter 1970–71." *Seaway Review* (Summer 1971): 11–15.

"Big Freighter Arrives." *Duluth Evening Herald* (July 8, 1909): 1.

"Big Ship Drops off at Ecorse." *Detroit Free Press* (January 28, 1912): 21.

Bowen, Dana Thomas. *Lore of the Lakes.* Daytona Beach: Dana Thomas Bowen, 1940.

———. *Memories of the Lakes.* Cleveland: Freshwater Press, 1969.

Boyer, Dwight. *Great Stories of the Great Lakes.* New York: Dodd, Mead, 1966.

———. *Ghost Ships of the Great Lakes.* New York: Dodd, Mead, 1968.

Bronson, L.D., Stephens-Adamson Company. Memo to author. August 12, 1987.

Brough, Lawrence A.. *Autos on the Water.* Columbus: Chatham Communicators, 1987.

Bugbee, Gordon P. "Iron Merchant Ships - Part Two." *Telescope* 11, no. 3 (March 1962): 46–51.

———. "The Life and Times of the Bessemer Fleet, Part 1." *Telescope* 27, no. 2 (Mar.-Apr. 1978): 35–44.

———. "The Life and Times of the Bessemer Fleet, Part 2." *Telescope* 27, no. 3 (May-June 1978): 70–80.

Cameron, Jeff. *The Wheelhouse* III, no. 1 (Aug.-Sep. 1990): 6–12.

"Centurion Launched." *Bay City Times-Press* (August 31, 1893): 3.
Channing, Edward and Marion F. Lansing. *The Story of the Great Lakes.* New York: Macmillan Company, 1909.
Characteristics and Index of Maritime Administration Ship Designs. Washington: U.S. Department of Transportation, 1987.
"Chemung Nearly Complete." *Marine Record* (February 16, 1888): 5.
"Christen Ship." *Duluth Evening Herald* (June 24, 1905): 9.
Clary, James. *Ladies of the Lakes.* Lansing, MI: Michigan Department of Natural Resources, 1981.
Clowes, Ernest S. *Shipways to the Sea.* Baltimore: Williams and Wilkins, 1929.
Conrad, Joseph. "Heart of Darkness." In *Tales of Land and Sea*, 33–104. Garden City, NY: Hanover House, 1953.
"Corey Launched." *Duluth Evening Herald* (June 24, 1905): 9.
Cowles, Walter C. "A Decade of Great Ships: 1948–1958." *Inland Seas* 45, no. 3 (Fall 1989): 193–211.
Croly, Herbert. *Marcus Alonzo Hanna.* New York: Macmillan Company, 1912.
Curwood, James Oliver. *The Great Lakes.* New York: G. P. Putnam's, 1909.
Cuthbertson, George A. *Freshwater.* New York: Macmillan, 1931.
Dean, Jewell R. "The Wilson Fleet, Freight Pioneers." *Inland Seas* (July, 1946): 159–64.
Deck and Engine Officers Supply and Demand, 1981-1990. Cleveland: Great Lakes Region Office, U.S. Maritime Administration, 1981.
Dewar, Gary. "Billboard Lettering on the Great Lakes." *Inland Seas* 44, no. 1 (Spring 1988): 21–31.
———. "A Forgotten Class." *Telescope* (Mar.-Apr. 1989): 31–39.
———. "Part II: Changes in the Post-War Fleet." *Inland Seas* 45, no. 3 (Fall 1989): 165–82.
———. "The Steamer William G. Mather and Her Contemporaries." *Inland Seas* 46, no. 2 (Summer 1990): 99–111.
"The Directions of Change." *Seaway Review* (Oct.-Dec. 1986): 9-104.
Dominion Marine Association Annual Report, 1986. Ottawa: Dominion Marine Association, 1986.
Doner, Mary Francis. *The Salvager: The Life of Captain Tom Reid on the Great Lakes.* Minneapolis: Ross and Haines, 1958.
Dorin, Patrick C. *The Lake Superior Iron Ore Railroads.* Seattle: Superior Publishing Company, 1969.
Dor-Ner, Zvi. *Columbus and the Age of Discovery.* New York: William Morrow, 1991.
Dowling, Rev. Edward J., S.J. *The Lakers of World War I.* Detroit: University of Detroit Press, 1967.
Driftmyer, G. E. "The Standard 600-Footer." *Telescope* 22, no. 4 (July-Aug. 1973): 95–103.
Duluth Evening Herald (December 3, 1892): 6.
——— (June 21, 1905): 12.
"Dynamite." *Detroit Free Press* (September 11, 1899): 1.
"Edenborn Launched." *Bay City Times-Press* (June 20, 1900): 1.
Ela, Jonathon. *The Faces of the Great Lakes.* San Francisco: Sierra Club Books, 1977.
Ellis, William Donohue. *The Cuyahoga.* New York: Holt, Rinehart and Winston, 1966.
Engle, Eloise and Arnold S. Lott. *America's Maritime Heritage.* Annapolis: Naval Institute Press, 1975.
Ericson, Bernard E. "The Evolution of Ships on the Great Lakes—Part I." Paper presented at the meeting of the Society of Naval Architects and Marine Engineers, October 1962.
———. "The Evolution of Ships on the Great Lakes—Part II." Paper presented at the January 24, 1968 meeting of the Society of Naval Architects and Marine Engineers, January 1968.
"Fairbairn Launched." *Detroit Free Press* (August 2, 1896): 2.
Farbrother, Robin, ed. *Ships.* London: Paul Hamlyn, 1963.
Feltner, Dr. Charles E. and Jeri Baron Feltner. *Great Lakes Maritime History: Bibliography and Sources of Information.* Dearborn, MI: Seajay Publications, 1982.
Final Survey Report on Navigation Season Extension for the Great Lakes and St. Lawrence Seaway. Fort Belvoir, VA: U.S. Army Corps of Engineers, 1981.
Final Survey Study for Great Lakes and St. Lawrence Seaway Navigation Extension. Detroit: U.S. Army Corps of Engineers, 1979.
Fisher, Douglas Alan. *United States Steel Corporation.* Pittsburgh: U.S. Steel Corporation, 1951.
"A 500-Footer Launched." *Detroit Free Press* (May 6, 1900): 6.
"Freighter Damaged." *Detroit Free Press* (April 7, 1898): 6.
Freuchen, Peter. *Peter Freuchen's Book of the Seven Seas.* New York: Julian Messner, 1957.
Gillham, Skip. "The Last of the Consorts." *Telescope* 25, no. 6 (Nov.–Dec. 1976): 155–61.
Glick, David T., ed. *Lake Log Chips* Perrysburg, OH: Institute for Great Lakes Research, Bowling Green State University, 1986–88.
Graham, R. D. "Benny and the Boom." *Telescope* (Nov.-Dec. 1980): 154–56.
The Great Lakes/Seaway: Setting a Course for the '80s. Ottawa: Ontario Provincial Great Lakes/Seaway Task Force, 1981.
Greenwood, John O. *Greenwood's Guide to Great Lakes Shipping.* Cleveland: Freshwater Press, 1967–85.
———. *Namesakes of the Lakes.* Cleveland: Freshwater Press, 1970.
———. *Namesakes II.* Cleveland: Freshwater Press, 1973.
———. *Namesakes, 1956–1980.* Cleveland: Freshwater Press, 1978.
———. *Namesakes, 1930–1955.* Cleveland: Freshwater Press, 1981.
———. "The Era of the Leviathans." Paper presented at the 44th Annual International Conference of the Dominion Marine Association and Lake Carriers' Association, February 1981.
———. *Namesakes, 1920–1929.* Cleveland: Freshwater Press, 1984.
———. *Namesakes, 1910–1919.* Cleveland: Freshwater Press, 1986.
———. *Namesakes, 1900–1909.* Cleveland: Freshwater Press, 1987.
Gross, Harriet Engle, Marie Van Gemert, and Christine Thomas. "A Distance Between Worlds." *Seaway Review* (Winter 1983): 83–87.
———. "The Ongoing Dilemma." *Seaway Review* (Spring 1984): 53–58.
———. "The Limitations They Cannot Ignore." *Seaway Review* (Summer 1984): 49–53.

Hardy, A. C. *The Book of the Ship.* New York: Macmillan Company, 1949.

Hassett, Chief Engineer Gerald P. Interview with author regarding the Shenango fleet. June 6, 1991.

Hatcher, Harlan. *The Great Lakes.* New York: Oxford University Press, 1944.

———. *Lake Erie.* New York: Bobbs-Merrill, 1945.

———. *A Century of Iron and Men.* New York: Bobbs-Merrill Company, 1950.

——— and Erich A. Walter. *A Pictorial History of the Great Lakes.* New York: Bonanza Books, 1963.

Havighurst, Walter. *The Long Ships Passing.* New York: Macmillan Company, 1942.

———. *Land of Promise.* New York: Macmillan Company, 1947.

———. *Vein of Iron.* New York: World Publishing, 1958.

———, ed. *The Great Lakes Reader.* New York: Macmillan Company, 1969.

Haws, Duncan. *Ships and the Sea.* New York: Crescent Books, 1975.

Heyl, Erik. *Early American Steamers, Vol. 3.* Buffalo: private publication, 1964.

Hilston, Christine Rohn. "A Queen in Limbo." *Telescope* 31, no. 5 (Sept.-Oct. 1982): 115–18.

"Holds World's Record." *Detroit Free Press* (July 1, 1911): 6.

"Houghton is Wreck." *Detroit Free Press* (September 6, 1899): 10.

Inches, H. C. *The Great Lakes Wooden Shipbuilding Era.* Cleveland: H. C. Inches, 1962.

"In the Water." *Duluth Evening Herald* (June 23, 1888): 4.

"The Isaac L. Ellwood." *Bay City Times-Press* (May 5, 1900): 1.

"Is Queen of Fresh Water." *Bay City Tribune* (August 27, 1905): 1.

Kelley, John. J. "An Historic Thirty-Six Hours of Superior Seamanship." *Inland Seas* (Summer 1984): 82–88.

Knight, David, ed. *Lake Log Chips.* Boyne City, MI: Harbor House Publishers, 1989–91.

Kuttruf, Karl, Robert E. Lee, and David T. Glick. *Ships of the Great Lakes: A Pictorial History.* Detroit: Wayne State University Press, 1976.

Lake Carriers' Association Annual Report. Cleveland: Lake Carriers' Association, 1905–1910, 1981–91.

"Lake Freights." *Bay City Times-Press* (June 19, 1900): 6.

"Lakes Get New Giant." *Duluth News-Tribune* (June 12, 1977): 1.

Landon, Fred. *Lake Huron.* New York: Bobbs-Merrill, 1944.

"The Largest Afloat." *Bay City Times* (April 30, 1893): 13.

"Largest Bulk Carrier on the Great Lakes Taking the Water at the Ecorse Shipyard." *Detroit Free Press* (May 2, 1909): 16.

"Largest Steamship Launched." *Marine Record* (September 9, 1886): 4.

"Largest Steel Bulk Freighter in the World is Successfully Dropped off at Ecorse Shipyard." *Detroit Free Press* (July 2, 1911): 12.

Larson, John W. *Essayons: A History of the Detroit District, U.S. Army Corps of Engineers.* Detroit: U.S. Army Corps of Engineers, 1981.

"Launching Tomorrow." *Duluth Evening Herald* (December 2, 1892): 2.

Lee, Robert E. "The Green Fleet." *Telescope* 10, no. 2 (July 1961): 123–26.

LesStrang, Jacques, ed. *The Great Lakes Ports of North America.* Ann Arbor: LesStrang Publishing Corporation, 1973.

———. *Seaway.* Seattle: Salisbury Press, 1976.

———, ed. *Seaway Review.* Boyne City, MI: Harbor House Publishers, 1979–88.

———. *Cargo Carriers of the Great Lakes.* New York: American Legacy Press, 1981.

———, ed. *The Great Lakes/St. Lawrence System.* Maple City, MI: Harbor House Publishers, 1984.

Mabee, Carleton. *The Seaway Story.* New York: Macmillan Company, 1961.

MacDonald, Robert J. "Captain Gridley and the German Gas Buoy." *Inland Seas* 15, no. 4 (Winter 1959): 288–90.

"A Mammoth Launch." *Detroit Free Press* (July 31, 1896): 2.

Manse, Thomas. *Know Your Ships.* Sault Ste. Marie, MI: Thomas Manse, 1985.

Mansfield, J. B., ed. *History of the Great Lakes.* Chicago: J. H. Beers and Co., 1899. Reprint. Cleveland: Freshwater Press, 1972.

Marine Casualty Report: SS Carl D. Bradley. Washington: U.S. Coast Guard, 1959.

Marine Casualty Report: SS Cedarville. Washington: U.S. Coast Guard, 1967.

Marine Casualty Report: SS Daniel J. Morrell. Washington: U.S. Coast Guard, 1968.

Marine Casualty Report: SS Edmund Fitzgerald. Washington: U.S. Coast Guard, 1977.

McCormick, Jay. *November Storm.* Garden City, NY: Doubleday, Doran and Company, 1943.

McKee, Russell. *Great Lakes Country.* New York: Thomas Y. Crowell Company, 1966.

Meakin, Alexander C. *G: The Story of The Great Lakes Towing Co..* Vermilion, OH: Great Lakes Historical Society, 1984.

———. *Master of the Inland Seas.* Vermilion, OH: Great Lakes Historical Society, 1988.

Medusa Challenger. Detroit: Medusa Cement Corp., 1967.

Meyer, Balthasar Henry, ed. *History of Transportation in the United States Before 1860.* Washington: Peter Smith, 1948.

Mills, James Cook. *Our Inland Seas.* Chicago: A. C. McClurg and Co., 1910. Reprint. Cleveland: Freshwater Press, 1976.

"Miner Launch Today." *Duluth News-Tribune* (June 11, 1977): 2A.

"Models of Great Lakes Vessels." *Telescope* 7, no. 1 (January 1958): 3–6.

Monson, Terry D. *The Role of Lakes Shipping in the Great Lakes Economy.* Houghton, MI: Michigan Technological University, 1980.

Mostert, Noel. *Supership.* New York: Alfred A. Knopf, 1974.

A Most Superior Land. Lansing: Two Peninsula Press, 1983.

M/V James R. Barker. Cleveland: Pickands Mather and Co., 1976.

Myers, Harry F. "Remembering the 504's." *Inland Seas* 44, no. 2 (Summer 1988): 76–93.

"Navigation Situation Appalling." *Detroit Free Press* (Septem ber 7, 1899): 1.

Newton, Stanley. *The Story of Sault Ste. Marie.* Sault Ste. Marie, MI: Sault News Printing Company, 1923. Reprint. Grand Rapids, MI: Black Letter Press, 1975.

"1927—Do You Remember?" *Michigan Limestone Screenings* (Winter 1958–59): 16–17.

Norrby, Ralph A. and Donald E. Ridley. "Notes on Thrusters for Ship Maneuvering and Dynamic Positioning." Paper presented at the Annual Meeting of the American Society of Naval Architects and Marine Engineers, November, 1980.

"Nothing to Carry." *Detroit Free Press* (July 30, 1896): 8.

"No Trace Found of 29 Crew in Lake Wreck." *Detroit Free Press* (August 22, 1920): 1.

Nute, Grace Lee. *Lake Superior.* New York: Bobbs-Merrill, 1944.

"The 101." *Duluth Evening Herald* (June 22, 1888): 1.

"107 Vessels Built in May." *Detroit Free Press* (June 3, 1907): 2.

"On Her Maiden Trip." *Detroit Free Press* (May 1, 1900): 6.

"Ore Cargo Record." *Marine Review* (April 21, 1898): 8.

"Owego Too Big." *Marine Record* (July 7, 1887): 1.

Palmer, Richard F. "First Steamboat on the Great Lakes." *Telescope* (Mar.–Apr. 1984): 37–38.

———. "The Age of Sail Ended on Ontario." *Inland Seas* 46, no. 1 (Spring 1990): 6–10.

Parker, Jack. *Shipwrecks of Lake Huron.* AuTrain, MI: Avery Color Studios, 1986.

Parkinson, Russell. "The American Ship Building Company Announces $95,000,000 in New Shipbuilding Contracts." *Telescope* 23, no. 1 (Jan.–Feb. 1974): 6–7.

"Perkins Goes In." *Duluth Evening Herald* (June 26, 1905): 10.

Plimsoll, Samuel. *Our Seamen, An Appeal.* London: Virtue and Co., 1873.

"Pumps Have Started." *Detroit Free Press* (September 8, 1899): 7.

Quaife, Milo M. *Lake Michigan.* New York: Bobbs-Merrill, 1944.

———. "Parade on the River." In Havighurst, Walter, ed. *The Great Lakes Reader.* New York: Macmillan, 1969.

Rabe, Jacqueline. "The Four Welland Canals." *Telescope* (Nov.–Dec. 1985): 147–51.

Radunz, Robert. "Marine Engineering." *Telescope* 5, no. 4, (April 1956): 7–15.

"Rapidly Laying Up." *Detroit Free Press* (July 22, 1896): 10.

Ratigan, William. *Great Lakes Shipwrecks & Survivals.* Grand Rapids, MI: Wm. B. Eerdmans, 1960.

Rondot, Peter T., ed. *Great Lakes Red Book.* St. Clair Shores, MI: Fourth Seacoast Publishing, 1971.

Rose, Robert N., "The Song of a Ship," In Herbert W. Warden, III, *In Praise of Sailors.* New York: Harry N. Abrams, 1978.

"Rush Last Night." *Detroit Free Press* (September 13, 1899): 3.

Ryan, George J. "Enhancing Weather Forecasting on the Great Lakes." *Seaway Review* (September 1984): 99.

———. "Great Lakes Shipping at Mid-Decade." *Seaway Review* (Jan.–Mar. 1986): 67–69.

———. "A Changing of the Guard." *Seaway Review* (Oct.–Dec. 1986): 71–72.

The St. Lawrence Seaway. Washington: U.S. Department of Transportation.

Scher, Robert. "Costs of Operating Alternative Sized Vessels." In Perkinson, Dennis, ed. *Vessel Size: Its Implications for the Great Lakes-Seaway System.* Proceedings of the Great Lakes Basin Commission Conference, November 1977.

Serig, Howard W. "Navy Oiler Finds Second Life in the Great Lakes." *Inland Seas* 47, no. 1 (Spring 1991): 36–40.

"She Did Not Slide." *Bay City Times* (June 31, 1898): 3.

Ship Biographies. Unpublished papers. Institute for Great Lakes Research, Bowling Green State University.

"A Short Historical Sketch of the Detroit Dry Dock Company." *Telescope* 14, no. 4 (April 1966): 76–91.

Skyker, Francis J. "Reinforced Wooden Vessels on the Great Lakes." *Telescope* 7, no. 4 (April 1958): 3–8.

———. "The Gothic Age on the Great Lakes." *Telescope* 8, no. 5 (May 1959): 8–12.

Smith, Suzanne. "History of Leathem D. Smith Shipbuilding Co." *Telescope* 5, no. 1 (January 1956): 9–16.

"S.S. Chas. C. West. *The Labor Saver* (October 1925): 3–8.

"Stmr. McKee Sons Cited for Outstanding Seamanship." *Bulletin of the Lake Carriers' Association* (Jul.–Sep. 1974) 3–6.

"Str. Selwyn Eddy Sunk in Collision." *Detroit Free Press* (June 2, 1907): 1.

Stonehouse, Frederick. *The Wreck of the Edmund Fitzgerald.* AuTrain, MI: Avery Color Studios, 1977.

———. *Keweenaw Shipwrecks.* AuTrain, MI: Avery Color Studios, 1988.

Storey, Jack. "New Vessels Coming, But Not Tomorrow." *Sault Evening News* (June 3, 1990): B-2.

Stories of the Great Lakes. New York: Century Co., 1893.

"Superior City." *Detroit Free Press* (April 14, 1898): 6.

"Taking Out the Ore." *Detroit Free Press* (September 9, 1899): 2.

"Talks Authoritatively." *Superior Daily Call* (May 2, 1892): 1.

Telescope. Detroit: Great Lakes Maritime Institute, 1952–90.

Thompson, Sheldon. "Models of Great Lakes Vessels." *Telescope* 7, no. 1 (January 1958): 3–6.

Tripp, C. E. and G. H. Plude. "One Thousand Foot Great Lakes Self-Unloader—Erie Marine Hull 101." Paper presented to Great Lakes and Great Rivers Section, Society of Naval Architects and Marine Engineers, January 1971.

True, Dwight. "Sixty Years of Shipbuilding." Paper presented to the Great Lakes Section of the Society of Naval Architects and Marine Engineers, October 1956.

Turpin, Edward A. and William A. MacEwen. *Merchant Marine Officers Handbook.* Cambridge, MD: Cornell Maritime Press, 1965.

"Two Hundred Vessels." *Detroit Free Press* (September 10, 1899): 9.

"Two Launchings Today." *Detroit Free Press* (June 1, 1907): 12.

"U.S.-Canadian Cargo Disparities." *Seaway Review* (Jan.-Mar. 1986): 59-61.

United States Coast Pilot, Volume 6 . Washington: U.S. Department of Commerce, 1988.

Van Der Linden, Rev. Peter, ed. *Great Lakes Ships We Remember.* Cleveland: Freshwater Press, 1979.

———, ed. *Great Lakes Ships We Remember II.* Cleveland: Freshwater Press, 1984.

Villiers, Capt. Alan. *Men, Ships and the Sea.* (Washington: National Geographic Society, 1962.

Walling, Regis M. and Rev. N. Daniel Rupp, eds. *The Diary of Bishop Frederic Baraga.* Detroit: Wayne State University Press, 1990.

Walton, Ivan H. "Developments on the Great Lakes, 1815-1943." *Michigan History Magazine* 27 (1943): 72-141.

Weborg, Captain Elmer. "Ice-bound." In Walter Havighurst, ed. *The Great Lakes Reader*, 335-37. New York: Macmillan Company, 1966. 335-37.

Whitlark, Frederick Louis. *Introduction to the Lakes.* New York: Greenwich Book Publishers, 1959.

Williams, E. B. "The American Shipbuilding Company." *Telescope* 7, no. 5 (May 1958): 3-10.

———, Kent C. Thornton, W. R. Douglas, and Paul Miedlich. "Design and Construction of Great Lakes Bulk Freighter Wilfred Sykes." Reprint. *Marine Engineering and Shipping Review.* June 1950.

Wilson, James A. "A Critical Look at our Marine Transportation." *Seaway Review* (September 1983): 11-13.

Wilson, Louden G. "How Now David Dows." *Telescope* 10, no. 6 (June 1961): 103-105.

Wilson Marine Transit Company. Cleveland: Wilson Marine Transit Company, 1966.

Wilterding, John H., Jr. *McDougall's Dream: The American Whaleback.* Duluth: Lakeside Printing, 1969.

Wolff, Julius F., Jr. "Grim November." In Havighurst, Walter, *The Great Lakes Reader*, 315-320. New York: Macmillan Company, 1966.

Woodford, Arthur M. *Charting the Inland Seas: A History of the U.S. Lake Survey.* Detroit: U.S. Army Corps of Engineers, Detroit District, 1991.

Wright, Richard. *Freshwater Whales.* Kent, OH: Kent State University Press, 1969.

Index

TITLES IN THE GREAT LAKES BOOKS SERIES

FRESHWATER FURY
Yarns and Reminiscences of the Greatest Storm in Inland Navigation
by Frank Barcus, 1986 (reprint)

CALL IT NORTH COUNTRY
The Story of Upper Michigan
by John Bartlow Martin, 1986 (reprint)

THE LAND OF THE CROOKED TREE
by U. P. Hedrick, 1986 (reprint)

MICHIGAN PLACE NAMES
by Walter Romig, 1986 (reprint)

LUKE KARAMAZOV
by Conrad Hilberry, 1987

THE LATE, GREAT LAKES
An Environmental History
by William Ashworth, 1987 (reprint)

GREAT PAGES OF MICHIGAN HISTORY FROM THE DETROIT FREE PRESS
1987

WAITING FOR THE MORNING TRAIN
An American Boyhood
by Bruce Catton, 1987 (reprint)

MICHIGAN VOICES
Our State's History in the Words of the People Who Lived It
compiled and edited by Joe Grimm, 1987

DANNY AND THE BOYS, BEING SOME LEGENDS OF HUNGRY HOLLOW
by Robert Traver, 1987 (reprint)

HANGING ON, OR HOW TO GET THROUGH A DEPRESSION AND ENJOY LIFE
by Edmund G. Love, 1987 (reprint)

THE SITUATION IN FLUSHING
by Edmund G. Love, 1987 (reprint)

A SMALL BEQUEST
by Edmund G. Love, 1987 (reprint)

THE SAGINAW PAUL BUNYAN
by James Stevens, 1987 (reprint)

THE AMBASSADOR BRIDGE
A Monument to Progress
by Philip P. Mason, 1988

LET THE DRUM BEAT
A History of the Detroit Light Guard
by Stanley D. Solvick, 1988

AN AFTERNOON IN WATERLOO PARK
by Gerald Dumas, 1988 (reprint)

CONTEMPORARY MICHIGAN POETRY
Poems from the Third Coast
edited by Michael Delp, Conrad Hilberry, and Herbert Scott, 1988

OVER THE GRAVES OF HORSES
by Michael Delp, 1988

WOLF IN SHEEP'S CLOTHING
The Search for a Child Killer
by Tommy McIntyre, 1988

COPPER-TOED BOOTS
by Marguerite de Angeli, 1989 (reprint)

DETROIT IMAGES
Photographs of the Renaissance City
edited by John J. Bukowczyk and Douglas Aikenhead, with Peter Slavcheff, 1989

HANGDOG REEF
Poems Sailing the Great Lakes
by Stephen Tudor, 1989

DETROIT
City of Race and Class Violence
revised edition, by B. J. Widick, 1989

DEEP WOODS FRONTIER
A History of Logging in Northern Michigan
by Theodore J. Karamanski, 1989

ORVIE, THE DICTATOR OF DEARBORN
by David L. Good, 1989

SEASONS OF GRACE
A History of the Catholic Archdiocese of Detroit
by Leslie Woodcock Tentler, 1990

THE POTTERY OF JOHN FOSTER
Form and Meaning
by Gordon and Elizabeth Orear, 1990

THE DIARY OF BISHOP FREDERIC BARAGA
First Bishop of Marquette, Michigan
edited by Regis M. Walling and Rev. N. Daniel Rupp, 1990

WALNUT PICKLES AND WATERMELON CAKE
A Century of Michigan Cooking
by Larry B. Massie and Priscilla Massie, 1990

THE MAKING OF MICHIGAN, 1820-1860
A Pioneer Anthology
edited by Justin L. Kestenbaum, 1990

AMERICA'S FAVORITE HOMES
A Guide to Popular Early Twentieth-Century Homes
by Robert Schweitzer and Michael W. R. Davis, 1990

BEYOND THE MODEL T
The Other Ventures of Henry Ford
by Ford R. Bryan, 1990

LIFE AFTER THE LINE
by Josie Kearns, 1990

MICHIGAN LUMBERTOWNS
Lumbermen and Laborers in Saginaw, Bay City, and Muskegon, 1870–1905
by Jeremy W. Kilar, 1990

DETROIT KIDS CATALOG
The Hometown Tourist
by Ellyce Field, 1990

WAITING FOR THE NEWS
by Leo Litwak, 1990 (reprint)

DETROIT PERSPECTIVES
edited by Wilma Wood Henrickson, 1991

LIFE ON THE GREAT LAKES
A Wheelsman's Story
by Fred W. Dutton, edited by William Donohue Ellis, 1991

COPPER COUNTRY JOURNAL
The Diary of Schoolmaster Henry Hobart, 1863–1864
by Henry Hobart, edited by Philip P. Mason, 1991

JOHN JACOB ASTOR
Business and Finance in the Early Republic
by John Denis Haeger, 1991

SURVIVAL AND REGENERATION
Detroit's American Indian Community
by Edmund J. Danziger, Jr., 1991

STEAMBOATS AND SAILORS OF THE GREAT LAKES
by Mark L. Thompson, 1991

COBB WOULD HAVE CAUGHT IT
The Golden Years of Baseball in Detroit
by Richard Bak, 1991

MICHIGAN IN LITERATURE
by Clarence Andrews, 1992

UNDER THE INFLUENCE OF WATER
Poems, Essays, and Stories
by Michael Delp, 1992

THE COUNTRY KITCHEN
by Della T. Lutes, 1992 (reprint)

THE MAKING OF A MINING DISTRICT
Keweenaw Native Copper 1500–1870
by David J. Krause, 1992

KIDS CATALOG OF MICHIGAN ADVENTURES
by Ellyce Field, 1993

HENRY'S LIEUTENANTS
by Ford R. Bryan, 1993

HISTORIC HIGHWAY BRIDGES OF MICHIGAN
by Charles K. Hyde, 1993

LAKE ERIE AND LAKE ST. CLAIR HANDBOOK
by Stanley J. Bolsenga and Charles E. Herndendorf, 1993

PONTIAC AND THE INDIAN UPRISING
by Howard H. Peckham, 1994 (reprint)

CHARTING THE INLAND SEAS
A History of the U.S. Lake Survey
by Arthur M. Woodford, 1994 (reprint)

IRON FLEET
The Great Lakes in World War II
by George J. Joachim, 1994

TURKEY STEARNES AND THE DETROIT STARS
The Negro Leagues in Detroit, 1919–1933
by Richard Bak, 1994

QUEEN OF THE LAKES
by Mark Thompson, 1994